JAN 16 1003		
	261-2500		Printed in USA

THE MEDIA AND
CRIMINAL JUSTICE POLICY

THE MEDIA AND CRIMINAL JUSTICE POLICY
Recent Research and Social Effects

Edited by

RAY SURETTE, PH.D.

School of Public Affairs and Services
Florida International University
North Miami, Florida

CHARLES C THOMAS • PUBLISHER
Springfield • Illinois • U.S.A.

Published and Distributed Throughout the World by

CHARLES C THOMAS • PUBLISHER
2600 South First Street
Springfield, Illinois 62794-9265

With THOMAS BOOKS *careful attention is given to all details of manufacturing
and design. It is the Publisher's desire to present books that are satisfactory as to their
physical qualities and artistic possibilities and appropriate for their particular use.*
THOMAS BOOKS *will be true to those laws of quality that assure a good name
and good will.*

Printed in the United States of America
SC-R-3

Library of Congress Cataloging-in-Publication Data

The Media and criminal justice policy : recent research and social
  effects / edited by Ray Surette.
    p. cm.
  Includes bibliographical references.
  ISBN 0-398-05687-0
  1. Mass media and criminal justice. 2. Criminal justice,
Administration of. 3. Mass media—Social aspects. I. Surette,
Ray.
P96.C74M4 1990
302.23—dc20
          90-10805
          CIP

CONTRIBUTORS

STEPHEN C. BROOKS, PH.D.
Political Science Department
University of Akron
Akron, Ohio

LUNDIE L. CARSTENSEN, M.S.
Department of Sociology
University of California at San Diego
La Jolla, California

STEVEN H. CHAFFEE, PH.D.
Department of Communication
McClatchy Hall
Sanford University
Sanford, California

EDWARD DONNERSTEIN, PH.D.
University of California at Santa Barbara
Communications Studies
Santa Barbara, California

JACK C. DOPPELT, J.D.
Medill School of Journalism and Research Faculty
Northwestern University
Evanston, Illinois

GEORGE GERBNER, PH.D.
The Annenberg School of Communications
University of Pennsylvania
Philadelphia, Pennsylvania

ALAN GRANT
Osgoode Hall Law School
York University
Toronto, Canada

DOROTHY J. IMRICH
Communication Studies
University of California at Santa Barbara,
Santa Barbara, California

C. RAY JEFFERY, PH.D.
School of Criminology
Florida State University
Tallahassee, Florida

JANE E. KIRTLEY, ESQ.
The Reporters Committee for Freedom of the Press
Washington, D.C.

PAUL J. LAVRAKAS, PH.D.
Medill School of Journalism
Northwestern University
Evanston, Illinois

DONNA R. LEFF, PH.D.
Northwestern University
633 Clark Street
Evanston, Illinois

DANIEL LINZ, PH.D.
Communication Studies
University of California at Santa Barbara,
Santa Barbara, California

WILLIAM LIQUORI
Altamonte Springs Police Department
Altomonte Springs, Florida

GUY LOMETTI, PH.D.
Capital Cities/American Broadcasting Company Inc.
77 W. 66th Street
New York, New York

ARTHUR J. LURIGIO, PH.D.
Department of Psychology
Center for Urban Affairs and Policy Research
Northwestern University
Evanston, Illinois

NEIL M. MALAMUTH, PH.D.
Communication Studies
University of California at Los Angeles
Los Angeles, California

PETER M. MANIKAS, M.A., J.D.
Director of the Criminal Justice Project of Cook County
Northwestern University
Evanston, Illinois

W. L. MARSHALL, PH.D.
Department of Psychology
Queen's University
Kingston, Ontario
Canada

DOUGLAS E. MOULD, PH.D.
Building 2200, Suite 202
3500 N. Rock Road
Witchita, Kansas

CHARLES MULLIN
Communication Studies
University of California at Santa Barbara,
Santa Barbara, California

BARBARA NIENSTEDT, DPA
Research and Information Specialist, Inc.
5839 North 46th. Street
Phoenix, Arizona

GARRETT J. O'KEEFE, PH.D.
Department of Agricultural Journalism
University of Wisconsin
Madison, Wisconsin

JAMES PERRY
Altamonte Springs Police Department
Altomonte Springs, Florida

CHESTER M. PIERCE, M.D.
Harvard Medical School
Department of Psychiatry
Cambridge, Massachusetts

DAVID P. PHILLIPS, PH.D.
Department of Sociology
University of California at San Diego
La Jolla, California

DAVID PRITCHARD, PH.D.
School of Journalism
Indiana University
Bloomington, Indiana

DAVID L. PROTESS, PH.D.
Northwestern University
633 Clark Street
Evanston, Illinois

KATHALEEN REID, PH.D.
Department of Language Arts
Lee College
Cleveland, Tennessee

DENNIS P. ROSENBAUM, PH.D.
Department of Criminal Justice
Center for Research in Law and Justice
University of Illinois-Chicago
Chicago, Illinois

ROBERT ROSENTHAL, PH.D.
Harvard University
Department of Psychology
33 Kirkland Street
Cambridge, Massachusetts

ELI A. RUBINSTEIN, PH.D.
University of North Carolina
Mass Communications
7007 Knotty Pine Drive
Chapel Hill, North Carolina

DALE K. SECHREST, D. CRIM.
Department of Criminal Justice
Florida International University
North Miami, Florida

ALBERTA E. SIEGEL, PH.D.
Sanford University
Department of Psychology
Sanford, California

JEROME L. SINGER
Department of Psychology
Yale University
New Haven, Connecticut

RAY SURETTE, PH.D.
School of Public Affairs and Services
Florida International University
North Miami, Florida

W. CLINTON TERRY, PH.D.
Department of Criminal Justice
Florida International University
North Miami, Florida

ALAN WURTZEL, PH.D.
Capital Cities/American Broadcasting Company Inc.
77 W. 66th Street
New York, New York

For Susan, Jennifer, and Paul

FOREWORD

This book offers a fascinating glimpse into some new uses of media and communications technology in criminal justice and reports recent research on some enduring questions. The book should be of interest to criminologists, communications researchers, those in the mass media, and criminal justice practitioners.

The articles offer strong support for the intertwining of the mass media and criminal justice. Yet there are few simple answers to the nature of this relationship. These articles directly confront the complexity of the questions. The reader seeking simple answers or monolithic, unidirectional impacts will be disappointed.

The first two sections of the book dealing with the effects of media on both individuals and the criminal justice system, offer a helpful review and some fresh insights. Relevant processes and models, gaps in knowledge, unresolved issues, and future research needs are identified. The third section goes beyond these traditional concerns to note how the criminal justice system itself is using communications technologies in new ways.

Looked at abstractly, the external and internal uses of the media which this book treats correspond to mass communication and mass surveillance. Modern technology has simultaneously increased the power of both.[1] The direct ties between central institutions and the public are intensified by the enhanced ability to watch and to send messages. Those controlling the communications levers can use them in a categorical, sponge-like fashion, or focus them with a laser-like specificity on particular subjects. This joining and versatility represents a powerful tool. It is vital to understand how these technologies are used and to note that they can enhance, as well as undermine democracy.

The new uses of the media in criminal justice—whether in the form of television crime simulations intended to help apprehend suspects, or cameras in the courtroom, or hidden in police stings, are part of broader changes wherein information gathering technology is more penetrating and prevalent. We are becoming a more transparent or porous society, in which information leakage and access to this previously confidential information is rampant. This, combined with dossiers, social engineering, suspiciousness, and self-monitoring are pushing us in the direction of becoming a "maximum security society".[2]

The issues these new uses and capabilities raise are complex and poorly understood, both conceptually and empirically. Even if we had better data whose meaning was clear, risks and trade-offs and disputes over how values should be balanced would remain.

On the positive side, the media bring visibility and thus enhance accountability. Openess in government is a fundamental American principle. As Justice Brandeis observed sunlight is the best disinfectant. The videotaping of police behavior in crowds or individual citizen contact situations, in booking rooms, and during interrogations can deter abuse or offer a documentary record. Without the incriminating tapes secretly recorded by President Richard Nixon, Watergate would have remained a case of breaking and entering; and without the back-up computer records in National Security Council files Oliver North thought he erased, we would know far less about the Iran-Contra affair. Yet visibility may have negative consequences.

It can conflict with privacy and diplomacy. It can lead to unwarranted stigmatization and a hesitancy to take risks and to experiment. Making a permanent record of interaction can also destroy spontaneity and mediated interaction across a video terminal may have a dehumanizing or depersonalizing effect.

The freedom to communicate is central to our notion of liberty. It is not by chance that the drafters of the Constitution put the Amendment protecting freedom of speech *first*. Yet as some of the evidence reported here suggests, there may be instances in which this freedom encourages victimization and interferes with the right to a fair trial. The rights of the media to discover, and the public to know, can conflict with due process and privacy. While cooperation between the mass media and the criminal justice system can further the public interest, it can also undermine the media's importance as an independent watchdog.

The new uses of the media also raise important issues about truth. When offered as evidence they can easily lead to a misplaced confidence in the validity of what is seen or heard. Seeing should not always lead to believing, particularly when the replay occurs in an environment far removed in space, time, culture and social setting from the original. There is a danger of decontextualizing the interaction. Video technology, for example, can beguile us into confusing image with reality, because the video record is believed to more fully approximate real experience than witnesses who merely tell what they remember. Video can distort in a number of ways from high-tech editing in which things are added or deleted, to unrepresentative sampling, to naive subjects who are manipulated in performing before a camera or audio recorder they are unaware of. It is important to always ask what went on before the machine was turned on.

In its documentation of new developments this book stimulates one to ask where are we headed? What forms and policy impacts would a book such as this consider a decade or two from now? It is easy to imagine: perhaps visual subliminal messages that crime doesn't pay in cinemas, video and computer screens and equivalent audio messages in omnipresent music; the careful production and pretesting of mass communications to insure that they have socially constructive effects (perhaps a social impact statement would have to be filed before any general communication could be offered); or a less sweeping rating of communications materials and the granting of access only to those whose characteristics suggest they would not be influenced in an antisocial fashion; the widespread availability of highly differentiated anonymous hotlines (e.g., there might be one specifically targeted at families and friends to encourage parents, spouses, children, and colleagues to report violations of those they are closest to); the use of video scanning devices (e.g., on busy streets or transportation centers) to search for wanted individuals; voice and speech recognition systems that are able to identify individuals of interest and key words by remote monitoring of communications; biometric measuring devices that must be worn at all times by violent offenders (should the measuring device suggest heightened emotions, the probation officer would be notified at once, or a remote shock might even be administered); a requirement that uniformed police and those on probation (and perhaps those juridically determined to be habitual criminals) wear unobtrusive video and audio recording devices at all times; and computer displayed pin-point visual location monitoring of all persons and valuable property via satellite. Of course, the above sounds implausible, but in 1970 some of the things discussed in Part III of this book would also have sounded implausible.

Technology and media cheerleaders argue that tools and mediums are neutral. It is true that any technique can be used for good or ill, although observers with different values may well differ on just what constitutes these, on how competing rights and wrongs ought to be weighed and as several articles here indicate, on how evidence should be interpreted.

But there is an important sense in which technology and mass media are not neutral. Both develop out of a social context for particular purposes. In the United States the major creators of new technologies are the military and industry; the major utilizers of the mass media are government and corporations, not environmental, consumer, or civil liberties groups, the elderly, farm laborers or the least privileged segments of society. From this perspective neither the technology nor the media is hardly neutral, nor do all groups have equivalent access. It is thus vital that claims about social usefulness be empirically documented.

We live in a democracy, not a technocracy. Just because a communications technology is able to do something, it does not mean that it should be done. A police leader's belief that "it is not only our duty, but also our responsibility to utilize available state-of-the-art technology" must be tempered by asking additional questions.

In thinking about the policy issues the media raises for the criminal justice system, it is important to go beyond the conventional questions of "is it legal?" and "does it work?", to additional questions such as: is this a wise policy? what are the costs of a particular policy relative to other policies, or the cost of doing nothing? what are the risks and likely consequences if the policy fails? is there solid ground for believing that the technology will only be used for its intended purpose? will the system become unduly mechanical and impersonal? will there still be room for the professional exercise of vigilance and discretion? can the technology be used in a focused fashion so that only those there is some reason to suspect are subject to it? will information collected be treated confidentially and destroyed when it is no longer needed? what symbolic meaning does the policy communicate? will the sanctity of institutions such as the courts be undermined by communications technology? what precedents does the policy establish and where might this lead? As Justice Potter Stewart observed in a First Amendment case in which police searched a news office, just because there is a legal right to do something does not mean that it's the right thing to do. The magnifying glass of contemporary mass media and communications technology can clarify, but it can also burn. The careful analysis and reflection of the essays in this book are fortunately conducive to the former.

1. For example see the discussions in E. Shils, (1975) *Center and Periphery,* (Chicago: Univ. of Chicago) M. Foucault, (1977) *Discipline and Punish* (New York: Pantheon) and J. Rule, (1984) "1984—The Ingredients of Totalitarianism" in *1984: Totalitarianism in Our Century,* (ed.) I. Howe, (New York: Harper and Row).
2. G. Marx (1988), *Undercover: Police Surveillance in America,* (Berkeley: University of California Press).

GARY T. MARX
Massachusetts Institute of Technology
Department of Urban Studies and Planning
Cambridge, Massachusetts

CONTENTS

THE MEDIA AND
CRIMINAL JUSTICE POLICY

Chapter 1
INTRODUCTION

CRIMINAL JUSTICE POLICY AND THE MEDIA
RAY SURETTE

*People today live in two worlds: a real world and a media world. The first is
limited by direct experience. The second spans the world bounded only by the
decisions of editors and produces* (Zucker, 1978:239).

Five years ago I wrote that the knowledge base necessary for sweeping
policy recommendations regarding the mass media and justice is not
available (Surette, 1984:331). This lack of knowledge has not prevented
sweeping mass media policy effects from being instituted in the interven-
ing years, however. In that policy effects are forwarded as the most
important possible media effects due to their basic and pervasive impact
on society, its use of resources and its attempts to solve problems, this
volume will present a focused exploration of the mass media's influence
on criminal justice policy. In this exploration, it will specifically review
new research and knowledge that has been developed in the last five
years.

The study of the mass media and criminal justice policy involves the
examination of two large contemporary organizational systems. Both
systems have been independently studied extensively and both have
been found to have profound far-reaching influences in our society.
However, the interaction of these systems has not received extensive
study and, in particular, the influence of the mass media on criminal
justice policy has not been closely explored. This is particularly unfortu-
nate because of the increasing number of activities and developments in
the mass media that have profound effects upon activities and developments in the criminal justice system. This influence is nowhere more
important than in terms of the criminal justice policies which society
creates and implements, for these policies determine what behaviors we
criminalize, what crimes we tolerate, how we treat criminals, and how we
fight crime and, in doing so, reflect our most basic values and beliefs. A
premise of this effort is that there exists reasonable evidence from prior

3

research and literature to believe that a media effect on criminal justice policy is in operation.

Similar to pornography, the concept of "public policy" is one that appears to be easy to recognize but difficult to define, although a number of definitions of public policy are available.[1] A basic definition is that policymaking involves government decision making. More important than defining public policy however is inquiring about the causes or determinants of public policy. In this work the primary factor to be examined is the mass media, an external factor forwarded as crucial for comprehending public policy (cf. Dye, 1985).[2] Mass media has been cited as a significant factor in the general public policy process and suggested as especially important for criminal justice policy. An examination of the research literature reveals that three research areas bear direct support for the operative premise of this volume: violent media and viewer aggression research, public opinion research, and media agenda-setting research. The first area provides suggestive evidence of individual behavioral and attitudinal media effects that on the one hand create behavioral problems that society must develop policies to deal with and on the other hand affects the perceptions of and tolerance for these behaviors. Public opinion research explores the origins of the public's perceptions and programs aimed at specifically using the media to influence the public. Third, agenda setting involves research which indicates that the media has an influence on the list of issues that are rated as urgent social problems and which therefore receive policy attention.

Violent Media and Viewer Aggression. In reviewing the evidence concerning possible mass media effects on aggressive behavior, it should be remembered that the mass media was not created to have either positive or negative effects on the behavior of individuals but was created simply to entertain or inform. However, whether intended or not, the mass

---

1. To sample a few (Dye, 1985:2)
    1. is whatever governments choose to do or not to do.
    2. the authoritative allocation of values for the whole society
    3. a projected program of goals, values, and practices

2. As defined in this work, mass media involves media which is easily, inexpensively, and simultaneously accessible to the majority of a population. Thus, mass production and mass distribution information systems are necessary before a society can have a mass media. These pre-conditions were reached in the United States in the late 1800s and during the first half of this century with the development of films, radio networks, and large-circulation corporate newspapers. Once established, the mass media became and has remained a dominate element in American life.

media has been long accused of having negative behavioral effects, and possible negative media effects have been a concern for a longer time span than any other related mass media related topic.[3] The available research in this area has been soundly critiqued.[4] However, irrespective of all the doubts and criticisms expressed, most reviewers agree with Cook and his colleagues' final assessment (Cook et al., 1983:191–192):

> ... no effects emerge that are so large as to hit one between the eyes, but early measures of viewing violence add to the predictability of later aggression over and above the predictability afforded by earlier measures of aggression. These lagged effects are consistently positive, but not large and they are rarely statistically significant, although no reliable lagged negative effects have been reported. The evidence indicates that a small association can regularly be found between viewing violence and later aggression when individual differences in aggression are controlled at one time. But is the association causal? If we were forced to render a judgment, probably yes. ... There is strong evidence of causation in the wrong setting (the laboratory) with the right population (normal children) and in the right setting (outside of the lab) with the wrong population (abnormal adults). However, trivial proportions of variance in aggression are accounted for and there exists an exaggerated sense of confidence in the research supporting an important causal connection. ... But the effects may aggregate when large numbers of children each are affected slightly, or a small number suffer much larger consequences.

There is consensus that, at least in the laboratory, television or screen violence can elicit aggressive behavior in some viewers (cf. Phillips, 1982:388). Although not without contradiction, the convergence of find-

---

3. As early as 1908 journal and newspaper articles appeared expressing the worry that the media (then newspapers) was creating a tolerance atmosphere for criminality and causing delinquency. W. I. Thomas, 1908 (cited by Fenton, 1910:491): "The condition of morality, as well as of mental life, in a community depends on the prevailing copies of the newspaper. A people is profoundly influenced by whatever is persistently brought to its attention. In the same way, advertising crime, vice, and vulgarity on a scale unheard of before in the annals of history has the same effect—it increases crime, vice, and vulgarity enormously."

4. For example, Cook and his colleagues critique the nature of the evidence gathered, stating that lab experiments contain a positive bias which exaggerates any link between media and aggression. This is due, they argue, to aggression being a relatively rare event so experiments are designed to (a) minimize internal inhibitions against aggression, (b) minimize external cues sanctioning aggression, [to limit possible causes to media effects only] and (c) maximize the clarity and intensity of experimental treatments. The end result is a lack of realistic settings and little ability to generalize to home settings (Cook et al., 1983:180). They feel that a positive bias is also likely in cross-sectional surveys. Lastly they state that field experiments produce little consistent evidence of effects, and in the instances where an effect is claimed, the populations involved seem to be initially more aggressive (Cook et al., 1983:181–182). See also Milavsky et al., 1982; Freedman, 1984.

ings indicate that a causal relationship does exist between viewing violent media and aggressive behavior. We are left with the idea that in magnitude, media violence is as strongly correlated and as causally related with aggressive behavior as any other social behavioral variable that has been studied. There is additional evidence of a normative socialization process in which exposure to mass media portrayals of violence over a long period of time socializes audiences to norms, attitudes, and values supportive of violence. That is, the more a person watches, the more accepting is his attitude toward aggressive behavior (Huesmann, 1982:132; Bandura, 1968; Drabman and Thomas, 1974). In that aggressive behavior is not necessarily criminal, this body of research does not establish a criminalizing media effect on individuals, at a minimum it does support its possibility.

Public Opinion. There has been a long tradition in mass communication research to link the media with public opinion formation (see Stroman and Seltzer, 1985:340). In this process, it is felt that over time the redundant themes and content of the mass media homogenizes the viewpoints and perspectives of the public. People come to think like the media, and subsequently, it is argued, to think alike. In understanding this process, a beginning point is the work of George Gerbner and his associates (Gerbner, G. et al., 1978, 1979, 1980). Gerbner investigated the association between watching large quantities of television and audience perceptions about the world with the idea that the media creates a social reality for its audience. The process is one of "cultivation" of a world view and is felt to be directly related to the number of hours of television viewed (Carlson, 1985:7). However, due to critics pointing out that the correlations between television viewing and expected media-influenced opinions were small and were often reduced substantially when simultaneous controls for social background characteristics were applied (see Hughes, 1980), the concept of cultivation was subsequently altered to "mainstreaming." In mainstreaming it is hypothesized that the media's influence will be greatest on those viewers whose views are outside of the middle conservative "mainstream" of American opinion. That is, by sending pervasive, uniform messages concerning the structure and operation of society, the mass media streamlines and standardizes toward the middle the perceptions held by its more dedicated viewers (Gerbner, 1976:176). Eventually, the media due to its pervasiveness influences even isolated groups to more reflect the views of Middle America (Gerbner and Gross, 1980:156).

Recent research suggests a significant media effect on general public opinions and policy preferences. For example, Page and his colleagues (1987) examine news broadcast, and policy questions are able to explain nearly half of the variation in opinion changes on the basis of newscasts' variables. They report evidence which suggests that both short-and medium-term opinion changes are tied to television news content. A journalist's comment in favor of some policy is associated with an average opinion shift of more than 4 percent in the same direction.[5] Although a causal linkage is not established and the shifts may be due to journalists relaying the consensus of elite opinion, the correlation was interpreted as part of a causal chain that results in changes in public support for policies favored in the media (Page et al., 1987:31; see also Hallin, 1984; McClosky and Zaller, 1984; Noelle-Neumann, 1974, 1980).

Criminality and the criminal justice system would, of course, not be immune to the effect of a media culture and both have been forwarded as similarly affected. In terms of the criminal justice system, the media has been credited with a number of public policy effects such as increasing acquittals, making witnesses more argumentative and thereby slowing trials, affecting police recruitment, influencing investigation procedures to match media-induced public expectations, and decreasing the support for civil liberties (see Stack, 1987:258–259, 267). To what extent these processes actually operate and how relevant they are to issues of crime and justice has been the subject of some argument, however.

On the side of a significant media effect, it has been stated that the vast majority of our exposure to crime and violence is obtained though the media (Dominick, 1978:106; Greenberg, 1969). Since the majority of people have little direct experience with crime, it is argued that the media will be a significant source in forming public attitudes and perceptions concerning crime and justice (Barber, 1987; Stroman and Seltzer, 1985:340). Furthermore, since 95 percent of the population cite the mass media as their primary source of crime information, particularly details about specific crimes, and crime is a well-covered media topic,[6] there

---

5. Of further note is their finding that news reports of actual events in the world seemed to have no effect upon changes in public opinion (Page et al., 1987:38).

6. Crime-related topics are among those most frequently mentioned in media presentations. Crime news, in relation to other news, is prominently displayed (Graber, 1980; Cohen, 1975).

has existed a long-standing concern regarding the potential of the media to direct public opinion in this area.[7]

In examining the evidence of a relationship between exposure to the mass media and one's beliefs about crime (i.e., one's crime facts or what one believes to be true about crime), the best-known works supporting a relationship are those of George Gerbner and his associates discussed earlier. Their research finds an association between television viewing and a "mean world view" characterized by mistrust, cynicism, alienation, and perceptions of higher than average levels of threat and crime in society. This translates into attitudes regarding who can employ violence against whom, who are appropriate victims of crime, and who are likely to be criminals. Subsequent research has mostly substantiated the association between television viewing and these mean world views for specific audience sub-sets and has shown that, at least concerning television, heavy consumers do share beliefs about high societal crime and victimization levels (see, for example, Barrile, 1985; Carlson, 1985; Marks, 1987; Surette, 1985; and Tyler, 1980; see also Bennack, 1983; and Robinson, 1976).[8] From the perspective of the criminal justice system official, the media influence can operate in both a reactive and anticipatory sense. That is, the press can influence policy because officials react to what they see and hear in the media or because they act on the basis of anticipated media attention. Thus, even if the media ultimately pay no attention, an official may still act on the idea that attention might be forthcoming. Therefore, it is argued that even if the media try to eschew any policymaking role in the criminal justice system, that would be impossible (Drechsel, 1983:14).[9]

Other research has revealed, however, that the extent of this influence on beliefs is not absolute, and severe limitations to the media's effects have been forwarded (Cook et al., 1983b; Hirsch, 1980; Hughes, 1980;

---

7. For example, a national survey for Hearst Newspapers concluded that the media is a much more important source of information about the courts than are lawyers, the public's own personal experience, schools, or libraries. In fact, TV drama shows by themselves rank ahead of these sources (see Table 22 of Bennack, F. (1983) *The American Public, the Media and the Judicial System: A National Survey on Public Awareness and Personal experience.* The Hearst Corporation.

8. Robinson (1976) using both experimental and survey results showed that reliance on TV news was associated with anti-establishment attitudes that included social distrust, political cynicism, and powerlessness. He termed these set of attitudes as videomalaise. A general ability of television to effect the beliefs of its audience through a single specially designed program is reported by Ball-Rokeach et al. (1984).

9. The John Hinckley Jr. case is an additional example of the media influencing public policy by reporting on an ongoing case. Following Hinckley's acquittal by reason of insanity, the demand for a revamping of the insanity plea is credited to the inflammatory manner in which the verdict for Hinckley was reported (see Snow, 1984).

Sacco, 1982). Carlson (1985) reports that mainstreaming effects are haphazard and in certain groups appear to run opposite predicted directions while other groups appear to be especially susceptible (Carlson, 1985:135, 191). He also reports that television crime shows contribute nothing to levels of knowledge about the criminal justice system (Carlson, 1985:116).[10] Concerning crime beliefs, Sacco (1982:475) reports no significant relationship between patterns of newspaper and television consumption and their respondent's views on crime. In another more extensive study, Doob and MacDonald (1980) examined television viewing and fear of crime while controlling for crime rates in four communities. They discovered that the association between television viewing and a "mean world" view tends to diminish when actual neighborhood crime levels are taken into account. In essence, if one's world is truly mean, television has a reduced importance on one's view of the world. This finding is consistent with the general proposition that media effects are most powerful on subjects that are outside of people's personal experiences. If one has direct experience with crime, the media is less important and the more people trust their own knowledge (cf. Lichter, 1988:38).

In a related study, Heath (1984) reports that newspaper crime news has differing effects on readers' fear of crime depending upon how the crime news is reported. Specifically, if a high proportion of local crime news is covered and is portrayed as predominantly sensational or random crime, higher levels of fear of crime are reported by those papers' readers. Therefore, random crime is frightening when close because it denotes loss of personal control, but reassuring when distant because it denotes that conditions in other places are worse and one has less to fear in one's own immediate environment. Additionally, Sheley and Ashkins (1981), in a comparison of television news, newspapers, and public opinion, found television's impact to be relatively minor on the public's view of crime and less important than that of newspapers. Other relevant works include Trevan and Hartnagel (1976) who found only weak relationships between viewing television violence (as measured by a preference for violent shows) and perceptions of societal violence or in displays of defensive reactions to crime among adolescents. Smith (1984) concludes that the media reporting of crime might create and define a broad public awareness of crime, but that many other factors, such as social and

---

10. In that he also found that most people in general also are characterized by low levels of knowledge of the criminal justice system, television reinforces the mainstream (Carlson, 1985:118).

physical environmental conditions, are more responsible for shaping related public beliefs.

In sum, the media has been forwarded as significantly related to particular beliefs about crime but not in a straightforward or universal manner. When beliefs are affected, they tend to be steered toward perceptions of increased crime and victimization. Unexplored issues are whether these media-induced public beliefs translate into support for specific policies regarding crime and the possible mechanisms and pathways for their effects.[11] In addition to the work of Doob and MacDonald cited earlier, other past studies also report a linkage between mass media consumption and support for particular public policies regarding crime. These include Barrile (1980) who reports an association between television viewing and punitive attitudes toward criminals. Barrile's work has methodological deficiencies, but the reported results do show an association between viewing and a "retributive justice perspective" (a punishment orientation toward the individual criminal and support for authority). Barrile concludes that television viewing is related to a distorted view of crime, but more importantly, he states that the influence of viewing television appears to carry over into support for punitive policies such as harsher punishments and the death penalty. He also reports weaker but still significant relationships between media use and support for the police and tolerance for the use of force by police. Marks (1987) reports evidence of both direct and indirect effects of television exposure on adopting protective anti-crime behaviors. The media directly influences people to adopt protective behaviors and indirectly influences them through increasing their fear of crime and perceived vulnerability, which in turn encourages protective behavior.

Surette (1985) examined the relationship between television viewing and criminal justice policy support by investigating the capability of quantity and quality of television viewing to discriminate between viewers

---

11. Unfortunately, in many of the studies in which a media effect upon criminal justice policy is discussed, it is only alluded to as a "potential" result of media consumption and actual relationships left unmeasured and unanalyzed. For example, Pandiani (1978:455) states the expected relationship as follows: "television viewing elicits irrational policy support, heavily tilted toward a law and order punitive orientation." He does not, however, offer any empirical evidence for accepting this proposition. Gerbner (1976) and Culver and Knight (1979) also forward the supposition that increased public support for the acceptance of police violence could result from heavy television viewing. And Culver and Knight (1979), and Estep and MacDonald (1984) state that television viewers could have their expectations of police and the criminal justice system unrealistically raised by media portrayals due to the incredible success rate of television crime fighters. They feel that such expectations could result in support for pro-law and order policies. Again, all of these statements are unfortunately not supported by data.

who support punitive criminal justice policies and those who do not. The results of his analysis indicate that the quality of television (a preference for crime shows) is more important for supporting punitive policies than the quantity of television (total time spent viewing), but that viewer demographic characteristics such as sex and race remain the most important factors.[12] Carlson (1985) using survey data from 619 sixth to twelfth graders identified groups holding views outside of the mainstream and then examined whether television crime show viewing moved these groups toward mainstream views. He reports that adolescents who are heavy viewers of crime shows measure lower on knowledge of criminal justice processes, are disposed to support the legal system, more highly value norm compliance, and hold a crime control as opposed to a due process point of view concerning law enforcement (Carlson, 1985:189). Pre-adults are therefore cultivated into a media-influenced view of the world. For those already in the mainstream heavy crime show viewing promotes conventionality and social control (cf. Carlson, 1985:189), and for certain groups the effects on support for criminal justice related policies appear to be quite strong. Thus, even students who achieve high grades, are heavy readers, and are aware that television content is "unreal" learn to not support civil liberties (Carlson, 1985:150).

The implications of all of this research is reflected in a current perception of a moderate media influence and support for a contemporary public opinion model in which multiple paths exist between the media, social networks, and the public, through which media influence and information flow (cf. Page et al., 1987). Only in the case of socially isolated people is it felt that the media has a primary influence on information, attitudes and opinions (see Lazarsfeld, 1948; Robinson, 1976). Paradoxically, it is also generally accepted that the media's influence can affect even those that do not watch, read or listen (Zucker, 1978:226). The mass media is recognized as a possible source of strong influence in specific situations. Its effects are thought to be complex, intermixed with other factors, and difficult to discern. Media influence thus nearly never works in isolation of other social variables, but its influence is pervasive enough to reach via social networks even individuals who totally ignore the media.

---

12. The implication is that further causal analysis studies could show that television programmers can influence public policy when they increase the number of crime shows offered and when they place popular stars in these programs, thereby increasing the viewing of and preference for crime shows.

Agenda Setting. A third manner by which the media could potentially influence policy is by demonstrating the ability to affect the public agenda. As opposed to public opinion formation, here the media is seen to influence the lists of issues that are considered important and significant by the public—what the public thinks about, rather than what the public thinks. In this perspective it is felt that people tend to judge a topic to be significant to the extent that it is emphasized in the media. In time, the media agenda becomes the public agenda (see McLeod et al., 1974). For example, Hofferbert (1974) argues that media stories do far more than tell us what is important; they tell us who is important, where important things happen, when to expect important things, and why to think about these things. The mere fact of coverage conveys an important message (Hofferbert, 1974:45). The existence of such wide-ranging cognitive effects assumes that the media can influence our orientation to the social environment in quite subtle ways, without directly conveying specific information or promoting specific opinions or attitudes.

Despite much interest in this question, however, the research is still inconsistent regarding the media's ability to affect the content or order of the public agenda. Some authors have reported that the media does not have a significant effect on the public agenda (Cumberbatch and Beardsworth, 1976; Sacco, 1982; Stroman and Seltzer, 1985) and at best the relationship appears to be secondary to other factors such as the age, sex, or income of the individual persons (see Shaw and McCombs, 1977) and mediated through multi-step flows and social networks (Page et al., 1987 citing Katz and Lazarsfeld, 1965). Confounding the question a number of studies report only minimal media effects (see Chaffee, 1975; Klapper, 1960; Kraus and Davis, 1976; and McGuire, 1985). Most have concluded, however, that the media is having an effect, but the exact nature of the effect is not clear (cf. Leff, Protess and Brooks, Chapter 11; Protess et al., 1985; Zucker, 1978). Protess and his colleagues (1985:30), for example, report that the strongest media agenda setting effect they found in a Chicago area study was a cyclical effect back onto the media, while, in other studies, effects were found but only for television (Leff et al., 1986; Cook et al., 1983b; see also Cook et al., 1983; Funkhauser, 1973; Iyengar et al., 1982; McCombs and Shaw, 1972; MacKuen, 1981, 1984).

Regarding criminality, the media emphasis on crime has been credited with raising the fear of victimization to disproportionate levels and in giving crime an inappropriate high ranking on the public agenda (Gordon and Heath, 1981:228–229; see also Swank, Jacob, and Moran, 1982). The ultimate effect of this disproportionate ranking in the public agenda is argued to be media-directed "moral crusades" against specific crime issues, raised public anxiety about crime, and, conversely, removal or blockage of other serious social problems (for example, hunger) from reaching the public agenda (Cohen and Young, 1981). The gist of the research indicates that media effects on the public agenda are variable, appear to increase with exposure (those who watch or read more, match the media agenda more), diminish over time, are more significant the less direct experience people have with an issue, are more significant for newer issues, and are highly interactive with other social and individual processes and therefore difficult to control or predict. It appears that for some individuals the media can raise crime's significance as a social problem, and some individuals appear to largely obtain their personal agenda of social concerns from what the media tells them to be concerned about. Not surprisingly, those who are exposed the most to the mass media are more likely to show this association.

Conclusion. As a group, the findings of the violent media and viewer aggression, public opinion, and agenda setting research indicates support for the contention that the media does influence in various degrees, but not in direct or simple ways, crime-related policies. The balance of this book will explore the current levels of knowledge regarding this hypothesis. The material presented is divided into three sections which reflect what are felt to be the three primary points of potential media effects on criminal justice policies: individual behavior, policy formation, and the impact of technology.[13]

The first section, "Individual Effects—Suicide, Copycats and Pornography," is composed of articles that explore the evidence of media effects at the individual offender level. The basic question this section addresses is what is the state of the evidence that suggests that the mass media influences anti-social behaviors in offenders. These individual level behaviors are those that society wishes to curtail and which result in increased crime and violence. Effects here are felt to result in an increase in behaviors that the criminal justice system is expected to deal with and thus directly affect resource utilization, enforcement and punishment policies. As the chapters in this section reveal, despite long-term interest and concerted research efforts there is still a heated debate concerning

---

13. These sections represent aids for the organization of the material and should not be perceived as a theoretical typology or mutually exclusive.

the significance of the media in the area of individual level behavioral effects, especially in the areas of violent media and pornography. Suicide is offered as the area where the research has progressed the farthest in establishing a significant media-behavior link; copycat crime and pornography as the areas where there exists the strongest current policy concerns.

Section II is titled "System Effects—Policy Formation, Implementation and Agenda Setting." As the title suggests, it presents articles and arguments that review the media's ability to influence the formation and implementation of criminal justice policy in our society and the rank of various policies on the public agenda. In a way, the effects discussed within this section are also individual effects; herein however the individuals are system policymakers and personnel, the decision makers of the system—the prosecutors, legislators, administrators and news reporters.

Section III, "System Applications of Media Technology," extends the concept of policy to explore the extent to which the technology of mass media and access to a mass media system has been utilized by the criminal justice system in crime control and administrative purposes. This process of technology diffusion is essentially a policy effect by default, in that the media through its devices and communication system is changing the manner in which the criminal justice system pursues its goals and fulfills its functions in society.

Each section has a brief preface in which its individual chapters are introduced and a capstone chapter which provides an overview, reviews the research literature, and summarizes the current state of knowledge and its relevance for criminal justice policy in each realm. The other chapters are examples of specific media-based research methodologies, debates, and findings. The three sections provide a survey of the current knowledge of the mass media's total relationship with and influence upon criminal justice policy. The final chapter will bring the three areas together and attempt to review and summarize the most important points of this survey of the mass media and criminal justice policy.

REFERENCES

Ball-Rokeach, S. et al. (1984). *The Great American Values Test: Influencing Behavior and Belief through Television.* Free Press.

Bandura, A. (1968). "What tv violence can do to your child" in *Violence and the Mass Media.* (ed) O. M. Larson. Harper and Row.

Barber, S. (1987). *News Cameras in the Courtroom.* Ablex Pub.

Barrile, L. (1980). *Television and Attitudes about Crime.* Ph.D. Diss., Sociology, Boston College.

Bennack, F. (1983). *The American Public, the Media and the Judicial System: A National Survey on Public Awareness and Personal experience.* The Hearst Corporation.

Carlson, J. (1985). *Prime Time Law Enforcement.* Praeger Press.

Chaffee, S. (1975). *Political Communication: Enduring Issues for Research.* Sage.

Cohen, S. (1975). "A comparison of crime coverage in Detroit and Atlanta Newspapers: *J.Q.* 52:726–730.

Cohen, S. and Young, J. (1981). *The Manufacture of News.* Sage.

Cook, T. et al. (1983a). "The implicit assumptions of television research: An analysis of the 1982 NIMH report on television and behavior." *Public Opinion Quarterly.* 47:161–201.

Cook, T. et al. (1983b). "Media and agenda-setting: effects on the public, interest group leaders, policy makers, and policy" *Public Opinion Quarterly.* 47:16–35.

Culver, J. and Knight, K. (1979). "Evaluating TV Impressions of Law-enforcement roles" in *Evaluating Alternative Law enforcement Policies.* (eds) R. Baker and F. Mayer, Lexington Books.

Cumberbatch, G. and Beardsworth, A. (1976). "Criminals, victims, and mass communications, in *Victims and Society.* E.C. Viano (ed) Visage Press.

Dominick, J. (1978). "Crime and Law Enforcement in the Mass Media" pps. 105–128 in *Deviance and Mass Media.* Sage.

Doob, A. and Macdonald, G. (1979). "Television viewing and fear of victimization: Is the relationship causal? *J. of Person. and Soc. Psych.* 37:170–179.

Drabman, R. S. and Thomas, M. J. (1974). "Does media violence increase children's toleration of real-life aggression? *Devel. Psych.* 10:418–421.

Drechsel, R. (1983). *News Making in the Trial Courts.* Longman.

Dye, T. R. (1985). *Understanding Public Policy.* (5th ed.) Chapter 1, 13. Prentice-Hall.

Estep, R. and Macdonald, P. (1984). "How prime-time crime evolved on TV, 1976 to 1983" in R. Surette *Justice and the Media.* Charles C Thomas.

Faunkhouser, G.R. (1973). "The issues of the sixties: An exploratory study in the dynamics of public opinion" *Public Opinion Q.* 3763–75.

Fenton, F. (1910). "The influence of newspaper presentations upon the growth of crime and other anti-social activity" *Am. J. of Soc.* 7:342–371,538–564.

Freedman, J. (1984). "Effect of television violence on aggressiveness" *Psychological Bulletin,* 96:227–246.

Gerbner, G. and Gross, L. (1980). "The violent face of television and its lessons" in *Children and the Faces of Television.* E. Palmer and A. Dorr. (eds) Academic Press.

Gerbner, G. et al. (1978). "Cultural indicators: Violence profile no. 9" *J. of Communication,* 29: 176–207.

Gerbner, G. et al. (1979). "The demonstration of power: Violence profile no. 10" *J. of Communication* 29:177–196.

Gerbner, G. et al. (1980). "The mainstreaming of America: Violence profile no. 11" *J. of Communication,* 30:10–29.

Gordon, M. and Heath, L. (1981). "The news business, crime and fear" in *Reaction to Crime*. D. Lewis, (ed) Sage.

Graber, D. (1980). *Crime News and the Public.* Praeger.

Greenberg, B. (1969). "The content and context of violence in the media" pps. 423–449 in Baker, R. and Ball, S. (eds) *Violence and The Media.* Govt. Printing Office, Wash. D.C.

Hallin, D. (1984). "The media, the war in Vietnam, and political Support" *J. of Politics,* 46:2–24.

Heath, L. (1984). "Impact of newspaper crime reports on fear of crime: Multi-methodological investigation" *J. of Personality and Social Psych.* 47:263–276.

Hirsch, P. (1980). "The 'scary world' of the nonviewer and other anomalies" *Comm. Research.* 7:403–456.

Huesmann, L. (1982). "Television violence and aggressive behavior" in *Television and Behavior,* vol. 2: U.S. Dept. of Health and Human Services, Wash. D.C.

Hughes, M. (1980). "The fruits of cultivation analysis: A reexamination of some effects of television watching" *Public Opinion Q.* 44:287–302.

Iyengar, S. et al. (1982). "Experimental demonstrations of the "not-so-minimal" consequences of television news programs" *Am. Pol. Sci. Re.* 76:848–858.

Katz, E. and Lazarsfeld, P. (1965). *Personal Influence: The Part Played by People in the Flow of Communications.* Free Press.

Klapper, J. (1960). *The Effects of Mass Communications.* Free Press.

Kraus, S. and Davis, D. (1976). *The Effects of Mass Communication on Political Behavior.* Penn. State Univ. Press.

Lazarsfeld, P. et al. (1948). *The People's Choice.* N.Y. Columbia Univ. Press.

Lichter, S. (1988). "Media power: The influence of media on politics and business" *Florida Policy Review,* 4:35–41.

MacKuen, M. (1981). "Social communications and mass policy agenda" in *More than news: Media power in public affairs.* (eds) M. Mackuen and S. Combs, Sage.

MacKuen, M. (1984). "Exposure to information, belief integration, and individual responsiveness to agenda change" *Am. Pol. Sci. Re.* 78:372–392.

Marks, A. (1987). *Television Exposure, Fear of Crime and Concern about Serious Illness.* Unpub. Dissert, Northwestern Univ.

McClosky, H and Zaller, J. (1984). *The American ethos: Public Attitudes toward Capitalism and Democracy.* Harvard Univ. Press.

McCombs, M. and Shaw, D. (1972). "The agenda-setting function of the mass media" *Public Opinion Q.* 36:1760187.

McGuire, W. (1985). "The myth of mass media effectiveness: Savagings and salvagings" in *Public Communication and Behavior,* (ed) G. Comstock, Sage.

McLeod, J., Becker, L., and Byrnes, J. (1974). "Another look at the agenda-setting function of the press" *Communication Research.* 1:137–144.

MacKuen, M. (1981). "Social communications and mass policy agenda" in *More than news: Media power in public affairs.* (eds) M. Mackuen and S. Combs, Sage.

MacKuen, M. (1984). "Exposure to information, belief integration, and individual responsiveness to agenda change" *Am. Pol. Sci. Re.* 78:372–392.

Milavsky, J. et al. (1982). Television and Aggression: Results of a panel study" in

Television and Behavior vol. 2 U.S. Dept. of Health and Human Services: Wash. D.C.

Noelle-Neumann, E. (1974) "The spiral of silence" *The J. of Comm.,* 24:3–51.

Noelle-Neumann, E. (1980). "Mass media and social change in developed societies" in Mass Communication Review Yearbook. Vol. 1, (ed) Wilhoit and de Bock, Sage.

Pandiani, J. (1978). "Crime Time TV: If all we knew is what we saw. . . . " *Contemporary Crises,* 2: 437–458.

Phillips, D. (1982). "The behavioral impact of violence in the mass media: A review of the evidence from laboratory and non-laboratory investigations," *Soc. and Soc. Research.* 66:387–398.

Protess, D. et al. (1985). "Uncovering rape: The watchdog press and the limits of agenda setting" *Pub. Opin. Q.* 49:19–37.

Robinson, J. (1976). "Interpersonal influence in election campaigns: Two step-flow hypotheses" *Public Opinion Q.* 40:304–319.

Sacco, V. (1982). "The effects of mass media on perceptions of crime" *Pacific Soc. Re.* 25:475–493.

Shaw, D. and McCombs, M. (1977). *The Emergence of American Political Issues: The Agenda-Setting Function of the Press.* West.

Sheley, J. and Ashkins, C. (1981). "Crime, Crime News, and Crime Views" *Public Opinion Quart.* 45; 492–506.

Smith, S. (1984). "Crime in the news" *Brit. J. of Crim.* 24:289–295.

Stroman, C. and Seltzer, R. (1985). "Media use and perceptions of crime" *Journalism Quarterly.* 62:340–345.

Surette, R. (1985). "Television viewing and support of punitive criminal justice policy" *Journ. Quart.* 62:373–377,450.

Swank, D., Jacob, H., and Moran, J. (1982). "Newspaper attentiveness to crime" in *Governmental Responses to Crime.* (eds) H. Jacob and R. Lineberry, National Institute of Justice, Wash. D.C.

Thomas, W. I. (1908). "The psychology of yellow journalism" *American Magazine,* March.

Treevan, J. and Hartnagel, P. (1976). "The effect of television violence on the perceptions of crime by adolescents" *Soc. and Soc. Res.* 60:337–348.

Tyler, T. (1980). "Impact of directly and indirectly experienced event: The origin of crime related judgments and behavior" *Journal of Personality and Social Psychology,* 39:13–28.

Zucker, H. (1978). "The variable nature of news media influence" *Communication Yearbook.* (ed.) B. Ruben, Transaction Books.

Section I

INDIVIDUAL EFFECTS— SUICIDE, COPYCATS AND PORNOGRAPHY

The premise that the media can influence individual social behavior is the foundation of our enormous advertising and marketing industries. The most worrisome media behavioral effect is the possibility of the media inducing violence, aggression, and criminal behavior in individuals. The articles presented in the first section focus on research of the media's behavioral effects that increase levels of crime and victimization. Despite a significant amount of research into this issue there still exists strident disagreement regarding the media's actual effects. Chapters 2 and 3 reflect this debate and its tone. Chapter 2 presents an exchange of views regarding the impact of media (in this case television) on violence in society. Chapter 3 presents the second debate which involves the effect of pornography on individuals. Both debates are marked by polarized positions, attempts to discredits large bodies of research, and imputations regarding the motives and standards of other researchers. They clearly show that discussions regarding the media, its effects, and crime can have nearly ideological overtones and delve into emotionally sensitive areas. One's media is not to be lightly attacked or defended.

The heat generated is related to the policy issues associated with these questions. If the media clearly and conclusively induces criminal or anti-social behaviors, then strong public intervention, beyond the media industry self-imposed limitations now in place, regarding its content and distribution are mandated. In addition, the media could be held liable for resultant injury of victims if a clear link is established between a media style or content and subsequent crimes (a few unsuccessful court cases have been attempted). Both prospects are not attractive to the media industry. In their reviews of the research, media proponents

19

argue that pernicious effects have not been consistently demonstrated, are limited to a small and unique set of people, and are insignificant when compared to other factors. In essence, they argue that an effect has not been proven, and even if one is eventually established and substantiated it will not be of a magnitude to warrant policy attention.

It is this last point in Chapter 4 that Rosenthal addresses. His chapter empirically estimates the potential effects of media violence on social behaviors. Utilizing the available correlational studies he finds those effects to be quite significant despite the small correlations reported in the research. If the prior research on which his estimates are based are sound (and as the opening articles reveal, not all feel the research is), society needs to be concerned about the media and its influence. On the positive side, he also concludes that interventions are also likely to have significant effects despite the low associated correlations.

The remaining chapters, 5 through 8, deal respectively with suicide, copycat crime and pornography. Phillips and Carstensen in Chapter 5 offer recent research into the relationship between viewer suicide and the mass media. Media-induced suicide is important because the most extensive and suggestive empirical work has been done regarding this individual level behavioral response to the content of the media. A common extrapolation of this research is that if the media can induce an individual to kill him- or herself, then it certainly seems possible and likely for it to be able to induce other less personally drastic criminal and violent behaviors. Termed the Werther effect, the ability of the media to induce suicides is found to be especially important for teenagers and to have small but not negligible effects on most other segments of society. Marshall follows in Chapter 6 with an example of research examining the use of pornography by sexual offenders. He reports associations between use of pornography and sexual offenses for a group of 89 offenders in a clinical treatment program. Marshall's chapter points out the difficulty of pinning down causal relationships in the area of media and criminal behavior. He must contend with the limitations of retrospective data from the offenders, nonequivalent comparison groups, and the realization that the associations discovered may simply reflect the deviant sexual appetites of his subjects, and, therefore, exposure to sexual pornography may not be a causal factor in their deviance but another manifestation of their basic deviant orientations. However, due to the nature of the behavior under study, experimental research that could more clearly establish causal relationships cannot be easily conducted.

The section concludes with two literature overviews and theoretical discussions. The first, Chapter 7 by Surette, draws from the media, suicide, mass communication, and social imitation research and literature to extract an initial understanding of the phenomenon of copycat crime. Relevant empirical research is limited and much of what is known about copycat crime is based upon a small but steadily increasing number of anecdotal cases. Surette presents a reiterative multi-factor copycat crime model in an attempt to develop the conceptualization of copycat crime beyond simple imitation and to guide future quantitative research efforts. In Chapter 8, Imrich, Mullin and Linz discuss the relationship between sexually violent media and crime. The authors review the recent research regarding exposure to pornography and attitudes concerning rape and rape victims and attempts to link pornography consumption with criminal behavior. They conclude that violent pornography seems to result in anti-social attitudes about rape and rape victims. Furthermore, the generated attitudes may be predictive of self-reported sexually coercive behavior. However, they find no evidence of a direct link between exposure to violent pornography and sexually coercive behavior, self-reported or otherwise. Most interesting from a policy standpoint, the research suggests that R- or X-rated depictions that emphasize female promiscuity or overt violence against women or when sex is linked with aggression can affect attitudes, but that sexually graphic depictions of mutually consenting sex does not appear to have such effects. Sexually violent material more than sexually explicit material is indicted as the main source at anti-social effects that arise from sexual materials. Lastly, similar to the multi-factor model forwarded for copycat crime, the research in this area suggests that a complex interaction of media, individual and social/cultural variables determine and mediate individual level effects of violent pornography. This makes these effects no less important but more difficult to predict or to formulate policy regarding.

Chapter 2

THE TELEVISION VIOLENCE—
VIEWER AGGRESSION DEBATE[1]

ALAN WURTZEL AND GUY LOMETTI

Researching Television Violence. Recently, the National Institute of Mental Health (NIMH) released a report entitled *Television and Behavior: Ten Years of Scientific Progress and Implications for the Eighties.* Among many of its findings was the conclusion that a causal relationship exists between television violence and aggressive behavior. However, a careful examination of the research which was used to support the NIMH position indicates that the evidence does not warrant such a conclusion. ABC feels, therefore, a responsibility to place the NIMH report—and other research regarding television's effects—into perspective.

Background of the NIMH Report

The 1982 NIMH report, *Television and Behavior,* is a follow-up to the 1972 *Surgeon General's Report on Television and Violence,* a study which was initiated after a series of congressional hearings on the impact of television violence on behavior.

- NIMH conclusion no: 1: the research findings support the conclusion of a causal relationship between television violence and aggressive behavior.
  ABC response: the research does not support the conclusion of a causal relationship.
- NIMH conclusion no. 2: there is a clear concensus among most researchers that television violence leads to aggressive behavior.
  ABC response: there exists a significant debate within the research community over the relationship between television violence and aggressive behavior.

---

1. Reprinted by permission from the American Broadcasting Companies, *A Research Perspective on Television and Violence,* and Transaction Publishers, from *Society,* vol. 21, No. 6. Copyright © 1984 by Transaction Publishers.

- NIMH conclusion no. 3: despite slight variations over the past decade, the amount of violence on television has remained at consistently high levels.

  ABC response: there has been a decrease in the overall amount of violence in recent years.

- NIMH conclusion no. 4: television has been shown to cultivate television-influenced attitudes among viewers. Heavy viewers are more likely to be more fearful and less trusting of other people than are light viewers as a result of their exposure to television.

  ABC response: the research does not support the conclusion that television significantly cultivates viewer attitudes and perception of social reality.

The NIMH report concludes that a cause-effect relationship between television viewing and aggressive behavior has been clearly established. This assumption is based on a variety of studies which utilize "correlational" techniques. Few research techniques create as much confusion and are subject to as much misinterpretation as correlation. The problem with a correlation is that while it can tell us the degree to which two things are related, it cannot tell us which came first nor whether one caused the other. Thus, when we talk about correlation between television viewing and aggressive behavior, all we are really saying is that there seems to be some relationship between the two. And when a causal relationship does exist (determined by other methods), a correlation does not necessarily indicate which of the two variables is the cause and which is the effect.

A correlation between viewing television violence and aggressive behavior could be produced by any of the following: (1) viewing violence leads to aggression; (2) aggressive tendencies lead to viewing violence; (3) both viewing violence and aggressive behavior are the products of a third condition or set of conditions such as age, sex, income, or family socioeconomic level. In those correlational field studies which do control for these third factors, the extremely small levels of association between television and behavior virtually disappear. This indicates that the "relationship" between television viewing and subsequent behavior is more likely the result of a variety of external conditions which have absolutely nothing to do with television itself. Some of these third variables include the level of aggressiveness among peers, parental behavior (aggressiveness, anger, etc.), parent-child interaction (ways children are punished, nurtured, etc.), demographic factors, and intelligence.

The NIMH report acknowledges that no single study conclusively links viewing television with violent behavior. However, the advisory panel insists that because there is a "convergence" of scientific evidence their conclusion is justified. The problem, however, is that the use of convergence can perpetuate unintended biases, flaws, or illogical assumptions which may exist within even a large body of research literature. It was the application of the convergence approach which led to the widespread belief among the scientific community of the time that the world was flat and that the sun revolved around the earth. By relying on a similar approach and by refusing to challenge basic assumptions, a variety of scientists made the same mistake despite the fact that convergence theory would suggest that they were all correct.

In sum, a review of the studies and their findings strongly indicates that the NIMH Advisory Panel's conclusion of a causal relationship between television and violence is ill-founded and unsupported by any of the research data which is currently available. The NIMH panel arrives at this conclusion based upon two points: first, that a majority of academic researchers believe that a causal relationship exists between television and aggressive behavior; and second, that the sheer number of scientific studies in the literature supports the contention as opposed to the number of studies which do not.

In fact, there is no consensus among researchers regarding the relationship between television and aggression, and a spirited debate continues within the scientific community. In a recent study by Bybee, 486 academic researchers were asked their professional opinion of the influence of television on aggressive behavior. Only 1 percent reported that television was "the cause" of aggressive behavior. Further, the majority did not feel that television was an important contributory cause of aggressive behavior. Clearly, this is not a consensus.

The research literature on television and violence has been reviewed and evaluated by other academic scientists than those who participated in the NIMH study. Although many have concluded that the research evidence does not support the conclusion that television violence causes aggressive behavior, their work was ignored by the NIMH panel. A number of independent researchers have been strongly critical of the cultivation hypothesis and of the research that supports it. The cultivation hypothesis states that television viewing causes distorted social attitudes and perceptions. What is especially significant is that television's minuscule relationship to social perceptions decreases even further when we consider such important external conditions as the individual's age, sex, race, and place of residence. Once these variables are taken into account, the cultivation effect of television on social attitudes and behaviors is virtually nonexistent.

One of the major criticisms of the cultivation theory involves the various procedures that are used to investigate the hypothesis. A number of researchers have attempted to replicate the findings of Gerbner and his colleagues and were unable to find the effects which were predicted by the cultivation theory.

Other researchers have been highly critical of specific methods. For example, a number of studies used a sliding baseline in segmenting individuals into the crucial "heavy" and "light" viewing categories which, according to the theory, determines how they will perceive the world. Instead of establishing a strict definition of "heavy" and "light" viewers, these categories are frequently determined by the idiosyncrasies of each sample. Further, although the categories are not consistent from study to study, findings are compared as though they were identical.

Another point of criticism is that cultivation researchers group together viewers who fall into differing categories. When these groups are analyzed separately, the findings do not support the cultivation theory. For example, cultivation researchers group "nonviewers" who do not watch television with "light" viewers who watch less than average. When nonviewers are analyzed independently of light viewers, their fear and mistrust scores are actually *higher* than light viewers. Similarly, "extremely heavy viewers" are grouped with "heavy viewers." When extremely heavy viewers—who view eight or more hours of television daily—are analyzed independently, they are found to be *less* fearful and mistrusting than heavy viewers. In both of these instances, when unlike groups were analyzed separately, the findings were in direct opposition to what the cultivation theory predicts.

Overall, when the cultivation theory is examined closely, it is found to be far less compelling than the NIMH report indicates. Consequently, there is no justification for the strong conclusions which the advisory panel reached.

Response.[2] Steven H. Chaffee, George Gerbner, Chester M. Pierce, Eli A. Rubinstein, Alberta E. Siegel, and Jerome L. Singer

The ABC statement purports to be a rigorous and objective reputation of the NIMH report; however, it is neither rigorous nor objective. It is a shallow attempt, ostensibly for public consumption, to focus on only one portion of the NIMH review, rehash industry attacks on independent research of the past ten years, ignore or distort both the evidence presented in the NIMH report and the consensus of the field, and present conclusions that obscure the issue and deceive the readers.

A telling indictment of the ABC position is inherent in findings on the effects of television that are ignored in their statement. Research has long since gone beyond the issue of violence. The summary (Volume 1) of the NIMH report devotes only 9 out of 91 pages to that topic. Similarly, only 72 out of 362 pages of technical reports in Volume 2 deal with violence and aggression. Some other topics include: health-promoting possibilities; effects on cognitive and emotional functioning; effects on imagination, creativity, and prosocial behavior; and effects on education and learning. These are all parts of a related body of data that only confirms the obvious conclusion: Television is an influential teacher of children and adults. Ironically, the networks have pursued and used the concept of positive programming in defense of some of their children's productions. The research on positive effects is no better or worse than that on violence and aggression, yet the industry, by some convenient logic, accepts the former and disputes the latter.

Wurtzel and Lometti develop something called "convergence theory" to argue that scientists can be led to accept any "widespread belief" on which many different studies seem to converge. If there is any substance to that curious criticism, it must be in the basic assumption behind the operation of the television industry itself. Ten billion dollars annually are expended on the "widespread belief" that advertising induces people to buy products. There is no more definitive causal relationship between advertising on television and subsequent buying behavior than there is between televised violence and later aggressive behavior.

ABC has not refuted the NIMH conclusion of a causal relationship

2. The National Institute of Mental Health (NIMH) project for which we were senior scientific advisers resulted in the publication of *Television and Behavior: Ten Years of Scientific Progress and Implications for the Eighties.* The two-volume report was prepared as an update to a 1972 report to the surgeon general. The new NIMH report has recently come under public attack. The substance of that criticism, which we believe to be unfounded, calls for an informed response.

between television violence and aggression and has misstated both the convergence and weight of evidence bearing on the issue. ABC found one (unpublished) study, by Bybee et al., that it could construe as suggesting there is no consensus among academic researchers, ABC misrepresented that study. The sample polled was not all "academic researchers" as ABC states but members of professional societies in speech and journalism, an unknown proportion of which are researchers. More importantly, researchers in the field of television include many social scientists who were absent from the sample.

Even more deceptive is ABC's interpretation of the results of that survey. The issue is not whether television is *the* cause of aggression. No responsible researcher makes that claim. All complex behavior has many causes. What the research results showed is that television is a significant contributor to such behavior. On that point, the Bybee study cited by ABC actually showed a clear consensus. About two-thirds of those polled agreed that television increased children's aggressive behavior. Had more scientists from other fields been included, that consensus would probably have been even higher. The authors of the Bybee study are themselves distressed at ABC's misrepresentation of their findings.

ABC cites seven references to claim than many academic scientists have concluded that the research evidence does not support the causal linkage. That list of seven all but exhausts that list of "many." ABC has not refuted the NIMH conclusion that there is a clear consensus among research scientists on this issue.

ABC challenges the extensive body of research findings on television's cultivation of viewer attitudes and perceptions of reality. The ABC statement claims that although the NIMH report accepted many of the findings of the cultivation analysis, "the authors of the technical report chapter reach a different conclusion." Those authors state, "The evidence concerning the causal direction of television's impact on social reality is not sufficient for strong conclusions." The technical report chapter by Hawkins and Pingree supports the cultivation theory which holds that the pervasive and repetitive patterns of television cultivate, rather than only create, attitudes and perceptions. After the passage cited by ABC, Hawkins and Pingree observe that "the relationship between viewing and social reality may be reciprocal."

Another example of the criticisms cited by ABC is the assertion that cultivation researchers group nonviewers with light viewers. When nonviewers are analyzed independently, ABC states "their fear and mistrust scores are actually *higher* than light viewers." Similarly, it is said that extremely heavy viewers are grouped with heavy viewers, but when extremely heavy viewers are analyzed independently, "they are found to be *less* fearful and mistrusting than heavy viewers." The facts were reported in an article in the same journal from which ABC selected its information, but they were omitted from the ABC statement. Nonviewers and "extremely heavy viewers" are very small and atypical groups (about 5 percent of the population each). Their deviant responses are trivial in size and not significant statistically. The inclusion of these deviant groups means that the NIMH conclusions about cultivation are underestimated; when they are excluded, the resulting patterns are even stronger for the remaining 90 percent of the population.

A series of additional repetitions of criticisms already dealt with in the research literature and reviewed in the NIMH report further strains the credibility of the ABC "critique." Clearly, its authors are aware of the scholarly exchanges that have taken place; they seem not to have missed a single negative comment, no matter how farfetched. Yet they seem to be oblivious to the more numerous extensions and confirmations of findings by independent scholars in the United States and abroad.

The ABC statement deceives the reader not familiar with the research literature. It is thus the ABC statement and not the NIMH report that distorts, in its general design as well as its details, the evidence on television and violence that it purports to place in perspective.

Rebuttal. Alan Wurtzel and Guy Lometti

Our review of the NIMH Advisory Panel's critique of our preceding statement indicates that its conclusion is without merit. Not only is it unsuccessful in challenging our fundamental criticisms regarding the NIMH report, but it fails to address many of the most salient issues included in our statement regarding the research on television and its relationship to subsequent violent behavior.

The ABC statement was not prepared as a response to the entire NIMH report. Its stated intention was to address the issue of television and violence since this had received the greatest amount of press coverage and comment. We addressed not only the NIMH report regarding its evaluation of the research on violence since this had received the greatest amount of press coverage and comment but a substantial amount of material regarding the research techniques that have been used to study the question of television violence and its possible impact on behavior and attitudes. The material was ignored by the NIMH critique.

We have demonstrated that the NIMH report on violence was not a "comprehensive and integrative review of existing research. A number of significant studies that did not support the NIMH panel's conclusion were ignored. Other studies were cited but never considered in the overall evaluation of the research. We did not suggest that old research is necessarily "stale" or loses validity. We suggested that research that is significantly flawed in methodology or analysis, regardless of how old or new, is simply bad research. That it has appeared in the literature for a long period of time does not necessarily guarantee its validity.

The NIMH critique accuses ABC of ignoring television's potential as a "teacher." They contend that a massive body of research points to the fact that television entertainment is a teacher. They ask, how do we contend that violence has no effect? Our response revolves around three points.

First, the research literature examining television's ability to teach does not report large and consistent effects. Second, television has the capability to present viewers with ideas and behavioral models, but this is a very complex capability which depends upon a multitude of variables regarding the characteristics of the individual, the way in which the information is presented, and the reinforcement (or lack of reinforcement) in the "real world." Aggressive behavior in which a child may engage is likely to be discouraged by parents and teachers. Third, the analogy raised between the impact of television commercials on consumer behavior is completely invalid. In the case of violence, network guidelines prohibit the glorification of violence or its depictions in any way to suggest that it is an activity that should be emulated or copied. Violence is not socially sanctioned, and television does not operate within a social vacuum.

The fundamental point is that violence and the way it is depicted on a network television bears no resemblance to the way in which prosocial, positive, and socially sanctioned activities are presented. The attempt to link the two is a comparison that cannot be made logically.

The critique misquotes references to the Belson study. We did not dismiss that study as merely correlational. We noted that the primary criticism of Belson is that the findings run counter to the NIMH conclusions. Belson found that light viewers and heavy viewers were less likely to engage in aggressive behavior; moderate viewers were more likely. Thus, the Belson study does not support the NIMH claim of a linear, causal relationship between television viewing and subsequent aggression.

The NIMH contends that the Belson study is a notable instance in which research has explored the connection between televised violence and real "violent behavior." When assessing the validity of this study we must realize that no observations of violent behavior were employed. The researchers relied upon self-reports. Involvement in violent behavior was measured by asking the boys in the study if they had committed any of the fifty-three violent acts in the last six months. The validity of these reports is limited by the veracity of the boys' statements and their ability to accurately recall their past behavior. Many people would have trouble believing the self-reports of juvenile delinquents.

The NIMH critique suggests that we "invented" the notion of convergence. In the summary volume of their report, the NIMH states: "the convergence of findings supports the conclusion of a causal relationship." Regarding the issue of convergence, consistency in prior research findings does not eliminate the possibility of drawing erroneous conclusions. In order to appropriately apply the convergence approach to research conclusions, one must assume that different studies do not have any systematic biases that operate in the same direction and that no invalid measurement techniques are employed. Our review of the NIMH research indicates that many studies share a number of significant flaws that are simply perpetuated from one study to the next. The NIMH critique misses this point and instead suggests that we are engaging in a "head count" of individual studies. This was not done at all. The point is made that every research study must be individually evaluated for its strengths and weaknesses before determining how much credibility to place in its results and conclusions. Using the convergence approach eliminates this crucial evaluative element and leads to distorted conclusions.

The statement about 95 articles supporting the cause-effect conclusion is not true. There are only 14 studies that lead the NIMH technical chapter author to the conclusion: "the evidence seems overwhelming that television violence viewing and aggression are positively correlated to children." The remaining studies, which are referred to as the "95 studies," deal with other issues such as catharsis, attitude change, and observational learning.

The purpose in citing the Bybee study was not to provide a definitive poll of the scientific community but to put forth the only empirical evidence which was available at the time regarding the issue of consensus in the research community. Rather than making a statement without substantiation regarding consensus, as the NIMH report does, we felt that it would be useful to indicate the degree to which there is a continuing debate among researchers. Regarding Bybee's methodology, we find another instance in which the critique offers a misleading statement. According to the critique, the sample consists of many irrelevant individuals with expertise outside the mass communication field. According to Bybee's own paper, the sample was a poll of "mass media scholars" who are members of the mass media communication division of the theory and methodology division of two nationally recognized professional organizations. They are actively involved in these research issues.

The Bybee study shows tremendous variability among researchers' agreement with the cause-effect conclusion posited by the NIMH. Less than 1 percent believed television was "the cause" of aggressive behavior, another 21 percent believed it was an "important cause," and another 44 percent considered television a "somewhat important cause." Twenty-four percent said television had "no relationship" and 11 percent "didn't know." In spite of this, we find fully one-third of all researchers questioned do not report a relationship at all, and only one-fifth—at most—concur with the NIMH claim of a strong and direct causal relationship. This is not a consensus.

Seven literature reviews originally cited by us conclude that television and violent behavior are not causally related. These are not seven individual studies but a compilation of many independent studies with conclusions that run counter to those of the NIMH. We never suggested that the ABC statement was designed to be an exhaustive review of the literature. It was the NIMH, not ABC, that claimed to conduct a "comprehensive" and "integrative" review of the relevant literature. Yet this comprehensive review failed to cite or to mention over forty published articles, dissertations, and papers with conclusions running counter to the cause-effect relationship claimed by the NIMH report. These studies and literature reviews are not simply dismissed by the NIMH, they are completely ignored.

The NIMH critique refuses to address the issues we raised. They refer to ABC's argument as "claims by network publicists." The statement was written by social scientists and it makes reference to sources from the social science literature to substantiate its arguments.

The notion of cultivation does indicate that a causal relationship exists between exposure and impact, with Gerbner stating that one's perceptions of reality are distorted in direct proportion to the amount of exposure to television. Thus, causal direction is the issue involved, and on this the NIMH report states: "the evidence is not sufficient for strong conclusions."

The advisory panel employs a quote by Hawkins and Pingree to establish the validity of a relationship between viewing television and perceptions of social reality. The quote, taken from the NIMH report, omits the paragraph that follows immediately after: "there does seem to be a relationship then, but is it real or is it an artifact of some third variable? The research does not easily answer this question."

Our review of the arguments put forth by the NIMH critique demonstrates that they are without merit. Significantly, the critique ignored a number of additional points made in our statement that are crucial to the central issues.

In many social sciences, statistical results of this magnitude would lead to a conclusion of "no significant relationship." In the NIMH studies the same small correlations are interpreted as signifying very important behavioral and attitudinal relationships. Social science depends heavily on the interpretation of data in order to reach conclusions and to determine implications. That the behavior observed in these research studies does not constitute real violence and the statistical correlations are extremely low suggests that conclusions and inferences are being drawn that go far beyond what the empirical data warrant. In ABC's view, the research is being interpreted and used in a way that is not consistent with the rigor and objectivity of the scientific method.

Chapter 3

THE PORNOGRAPHY—SEXUAL CRIME DEBATE

Douglas E. Mould

A Critical Analysis of Recent Research on Violent Erotica. Scientific evidence used as a rationale for formulating social policy must stand above other research not only in its clarity and definitiveness but also in the cogency with which it can be generalized beyond experimental constraints (Krathwhol, 1985). It is my contention that a critical evaluation of this literature, of which these two studies stand out as major contributions, demonstrates methodological, analytical, and conceptual flaws rendering suspect all but the most tentative conclusions. The authors frequently imply stronger relationships among variables than are warranted, language is frequently used which leads the reader to conclude that the experimental effects are greater than they really are, and data are misinterpreted, often as a function of inadequate or inappropriate statistics. Most important, there is a conspicuous *lack* of validation for pivotal constructs, as well as implausible extrapolation from the experimental data to real-world phenomena.

Malamuth and Check (1980) are primarily concerned with the relationships among men's sexual arousal to erotica depicting violence against a female victim, the propensity or "proclivity" to rape, and differential responses to realistic rape depictions. Donnerstein and Berkowitz (1981) are focused on the effects of violent erotica on subsequent aggressive behavior by angered individuals.

Sexual Arousal, Rape Proclivity, and the Content of Sexually Explicit Materials. Malamuth and Check (1980) attempted to replicate and to extend previous research by examining the physiological and self-report responses of male subjects to erotic stimuli varied as to the content of sexual violence. Malamuth and Check (1980) attempted to demonstrate

Reprinted by permission from *Journal of Sex Research*, 25:267–288 (1988).

that sexually explicit rape depictions portraying the victim experiencing sexual arousal have an antisocial effect by changing the perception of
an actual rape experience to one in which the victim is seen as being
minimally damaged, as well as helping maintain the rape myth that
women secretly desire to be raped. It was also anticipated that a rape-
arousal depiction would be more sexually stimulating than a depiction
in which the victim consistently responds negatively.

The low degree of association between the measures of arousal, in
combination with the failure to find significant results for both measures
in the ANOVAs, limits the construct validity, which in turn dictates
cautious interpretation. Instead, the authors conclude "the results *very
clearly* extend the earlier findings . . . subjects were *considerably more*
sexually aroused" (p. 543, emphasis added) to the rape-arousal tape than
the rape-abhorrence tape.

In a similar misstatement, the authors state that those exposed to the rape-
arousal tape "perceived *little* victim trauma in the rape-criterion depiction
relative to those earlier exposed to the rape-abhorrence or the mutually-
desired depiction" (p. 544, emphasis added). In fact, the mean level of
victim trauma indicated for this group was the midpoint of the scale (3.00
versus 3.96 and 3.83, on a 1 to 5 scale). Thus, the difference is between char-
acterizing the victim as "traumatized" rather than "moderately traumatized."

In short, there is very little evidence in these data suggesting the
pre-exposure tape had more than marginal impact on the subjects' subsequent perception of the rape-criterion tape. These results replicate the
failure to find differences among the pre-exposure groups by Malamuth,
Haber, and Feshbach (1980), where virtually all significant effects were a
result of sex of the experimenter.

As used by Malamuth, rape proclivity is defined by "the *relative*
likelihood for men to rape" (Malamuth, 1981, p. 139, emphasis added).
In essence, rape proclivity is used here as a personality or character trait.
The construct as used by Abel et al. and the construct as used by
Malamuth are then linked by the similarity between those who have
aggressed against women and those who have a propensity for doing so.
The validity of Malamuth's rape-proclivity construct depends upon the
extent of convergent evidence bridging the gap between an actual behavior and the theorized tendency to exhibit that behavior. There are, of
course, several ways in which this can be done. The most powerful
manner would be to show that men who score high on Malamuth's
measure of rape proclivity commit rapes at a higher rate than men who

score low on rape proclivity. A less powerful, but still clearly related manner would be to demonstrate that men who score higher commit more acts of violence against women than those scoring low. A still less powerful manner in which validity can be demonstrated is by demonstrating congruency on theoretical relevant variables between those known to have raped and those who score high on the measure of rape proclivity (or LR for likelihood of raping).

This conceptualization of rape proclivity bears careful consideration as it presents an ambiguity easily overlooked. In the first part, Malamuth is asking if those high in rape proclivity are more like rapists than those low in rape proclivity. There is a corollary question which I believe to be of even greater importance: Are those high in rape proclivity *more* like rapists *than* they are like those low in rape proclivity? This may at first seem like picking nits. Thus, the issue vis-a-vis rape proclivity is whether those scoring high are more like rapists than they are like those scoring low.

Intimately connected to this is the second part of Malamuth's definition/ question: Does high rape proclivity "predict responses known to be associated with rapists?" More specifically, are the responses on the relevant variables of those high in Malamuth's measure similar to rapists? To be answered affirmatively, the similarity must be demonstrated; that is, *if convicted rapists demonstrate a callous attitude toward the rape victim, those high in rape proclivity must also demonstrate a similar attitude.* Failure to do so renders the construct invalid. Rape proclivity as Malamuth uses it implies a probability of sexually violent behavior; at the very least there must be a congruency of attitudes, if not behavior, between those high in rape proclivity and those who rape.

Malamuth and Check (1980) provide no data indicating there were significant mean differences between those scoring high and low in rape proclivity on the relevant variables. Thus, the authors' claim that the self-report of the subjects in this study are "associated with a generally callous attitude about rape that is similar to the reported attitudes of many convicted rapists" (p. 540) has no supporting data. The results indicate a conclusion contrary to the authors': There is virtually no evidence that self-reported rape proclivity is associated with arousal to sexual violence.

A final issue is the use of a 1-item scale for measuring a continuous variable such as rape proclivity. According to Sax (1980), "Highly *unreliable* information will come from a single item, and any decision based on very short tests is likely to lead to many wrong decisions" (p. 271).

Furthermore, the validity of a measure is limited by its reliability (Cronbach, 1984). Inasmuch as this measure of rape proclivity is likely to be highly unreliable, the validity of any inferences are likewise limited. As discussed above, it is possible that the limitation of inference is an artifact of the inherent low reliability of a 1-item scale. That is, the low reliability of a 1-item scale limits the possibility of finding high validity coefficients.

Nowhere in these data are there any internally consistent or externally convergent results. To suggest that the construct of rape proclivity, as Malamuth employs it, is linked to the construct as Abel et al. (1977) employ it via a commonality of callous attitudes toward rape is simply not borne out by the data. Further, in a recent study of college males, rape proclivity was not found to be correlated with self-reported sexual aggression (Greendlinger & Byrne, 1987).

Anger, Aggression, and Victim Behavior in Erotic Films. In two experiments, Donnerstein and Berkowitz (1981) investigated (a) whether the behavior exhibited by the women characters in erotic films differentially affects subsequent aggression against male or female targets by angered subjects and (b) what sorts of differential effects could be elicited by varying anger, as well as film content, in subjects' aggression against female targets.

The authors made three predictions. First, they predicted that the non-aggressive erotic movie would elicit a stronger attack on the male target than on the female target. Second, they predicted (a) that the aggressive erotic film with a positive ending and a female target would elicit more aggression than the nonaggressive erotic film with a female target and (b) that the aggressive erotic film with a positive ending and a female target would draw more aggression than the same film condition with a male target. Third, they predicted that (a) with female targets, the aggressive erotic film with the positive ending would elicit greater aggression than the aggressive erotic film with the negative ending, and (b) the aggressive erotic film with the negative ending and a female target would elicit more aggression than the same film with a male target.

In the first case the authors' rationale was that even though the subjects were energized by the facilitating effect of the sexual arousal on their anger, socialized sanctions inhibiting aggression by men against women would lead to stronger attacks against the male target. The second set of predictions was based on the beliefs that the aggressive erotic, positive outcome film would disinhibit male subjects as a consequence of its positive outcome, elicit strong aggressive reactions because of its angry content, and also serve as a sex-linked cue to the female target. The third prediction stemmed from the belief that the pain cues associated with the negative-outcome film would stimulate aggression, but some inhibition would remain because the assault was not justified and that, via their association, aggression would transfer from the female victim to the female target.

The authors' rationale for predicting higher aggression against the female target in the positive-ending, aggressive condition than either the female target in the erotic condition or a male target in the positive-ending, aggressive condition was that "(a) the aggressive content of the sex film would evoke strong aggressive reactions from the angry viewers, (b) the positive outcome would lower their inhibitions against attacking women, and (c) the female target's sex-linked association with the victim of the assault on the screen would facilitate attacks on her" (p. 712). Of these, the last two are sex specific, whereas the first is sex neutral. Furthermore, since the subjects were angry, they were "disposed" or "predisposed" toward aggression (Donnerstein & Berkowitz, 1981, pp. 712, 713). Consequently, it would also be expected for those in the positive ending, aggressive condition with a male target to evidence greater aggression than in either of the erotic or neutral conditions with a male target. In fact, this group showed the *lowest* level of aggression of all conditions having a male target. Whether this difference is significant or not is not reported. In sum, there is (a) little clarity as to the factors producing the experimental effects, and (b) there are no significant effects for the rewarding behavior of the subjects, constituting a failure at convergent validation.

In their second experiment, Donnerstein and Berkowitz hypothesized that the pain cues inherent in the aggressive erotic films were the primary mediators of the increased aggression found in the first experiment. They proposed that the "anger arousal presumable converted the movie victim's suffering into an aggression-eliciting cue for them (the experimental subjects)" (p. 717). From this, six predictions were made: First, angry subjects exposed to the negative-ending aggressive erotic film would aggress more than nonangry subjects viewing the negative-ending aggressive erotic film; second, nonangry subjects seeing the positive-ending aggressive erotic film would aggress more than nonangry subjects seeing the neutral film; third, nonangry subjects seeing the positive-ending aggressive film would aggress more than nonangry subjects seeing the nonaggressive erotic film; fourth, angered subjects exposed to the positive-ending aggressive erotic film would aggress more than angered subjects seeing the neutral film; fifth, angered subjects exposed to the positive-ending aggressive erotic film would aggress more than angered subjects seeing the nonaggressive erotic film; and sixth, angered subjects viewing the positive-ending aggressive erotic film would aggress more than nonangered subjects viewing the aggressive erotic film. The experimental procedure differed in two respects: All targets were female and an anger/no anger condition was employed. Significant results were found for the first five predictions, whereas for the sixth the difference was not significant.

From these results the authors argue that the increased aggression, rather than being derived from either a transfer of arousal or a misattribution of arousal, resulted instead from a combination of (a) disinhibition, (b) the apparent "inherent" ability of observed aggression to stimulate aggression, and (c) an S–R bond between the female victim in the film and the female target, mediated by the similarity in sex.

One would expect a conclusion of this certitude to have both compelling theoretical underpinnings and empirical support. As they replace the previous theoretical foundations with new ones (e.g., the authors set aside the arousal transfer hypothesis, an hypothesis purportedly validated by the senior author in prior research).

However, although there was an apparent differential effect for the films and conditions, other effects consistent with the theoretical contentions did not emerge. Thus, there is little consistency and congruency among effects and theoretical explanations. It follows that only the most speculative of conclusions may be drawn from the experimental findings.

The importance of this research hinges on the singular issue of the extent to which the findings can be extended beyond the laboratory. Donnerstein and Berkowitz's research has relevance only in circumstances in which an already angry individual views a sexually violent depiction and subsequently has access to, and circumstances that permit, aggression against the anger-instigating individual. Thus, its application is severely restricted in the scope of circumstances that might lead to aggression.

Within this restricted range, there is also an interpersonal variable limiting even further extrapolations. The primary vehicle through which attempts are made to demonstrate increased aggressiveness is the application of electric shock. The shock was administered to a target in another room where the only means of communication was through a microphone. The subjects neither saw the target nor received any feedback concerning the effects of delivering the shocks. As Milgram (1974) demonstrated, the demand characteristics of an experiment of this nature lead "normal" subjects to deliver punishments in spite of questioning whether they are doing the right thing; more importantly, the willingness of a subject to deliver shocks, even when directed to by someone in authority, is limited by the proximity of the target to the subject. Thus, when it was necessary for Milgram's subjects to touch the target physically in order to deliver the shock, far fewer subjects were willing to continue the experiment. In these experiments, we are asked to extrapolate from an experimental situation in which mild electric shocks are delivered, without feedback, by a subject who is mildly/moderately angry at the target, to a situation in which a violent sexual attack is made on another. This seems to be an inference involving a quantum leap from the laboratory to the real world.

Conclusion. The threat of sexual violence is a subliminal companion of most women and a harsh reality for many. This fact alone demands assessment of factors contributing to sexual violence as well as implementation of effective intervention. On one level, it seems so intuitively obvious that violent erotica must contribute to sexual violence. Erotica, and especially erotica depicting violence, are easy targets for those wishing to find simplistic answers to the complex question of why sexual violence occurs. A close examination of research directly concerned with violence embedded in erotica indicates serious flaws in the design, validity, and generalizability of virtually every aspect considered.

Valid inferences stand upon properly interpreted data grounded in validly measured constructs. At each of these levels, the research examined fails. Without doubt, the ambiguity of the area itself renders good research difficult. It follows from the difficulty itself that all results and conclusions should be viewed tentatively and circumspectly, the singular violation of which encompasses the papers reviewed.

"VIOLENT EROTICA": A REPLY

NEIL M. MALAMUTH[1]

I will discuss the three areas Mould tries to discredit: sexual arousal, perceptions of rape, and self-reported likelihood of raping.

Sexual Arousal. The criticisms center on the following: (a) He questions our assertion that a mean arousal level of about 48% can be labeled "highly aroused"; (b) he asserts that there was a low relationship between the two measures of sexual arousal, thereby questioning the convergent validity of the measures; and (c) he asserts that our conclusion that exposure to a rape-abhorrence tape resulted in inhibited sexual arousal to a subsequent rape depiction is "incompatible with the authors' main hypothesis" (p. 329). I will briefly address each of these three points. First, even a cursory survey of literature on sexual arousal will show that an *average* self-reported sexual arousal of close to 50% in response to a brief story, particularly a rape story, is a very high level indeed. Second, Mould also shows little awareness of the literature when he argues that the lack of high correlations between physiological and self-report measures of sexual arousal indicates a lack of validity in these measures. There has been considerable discussion regarding the conditions under which such measures yield high or low correlations (e.g., Earls & Marshall, 1983). It has been suggested that sexual arousal is not a unitary construct and that self-report and physiological measures may be assessing differing dimensions of a multidimensional construct (Blader & Marshall, 1984). Additionally, it is noteworthy that very frequently, researchers have relied only on self-report (e.g., Mosher & Anderson, 1986) or physiological measures (e.g., Freund, Scher, Racansky, Campbell, & Heasman, 1986) of sexual arousal. We have typically used both, and, consistent with other studies using similar conditions, we have found significant, albeit not very high, correlations between them. We continue to believe that the use of both measures enhances our research by providing useful information regarding a multidimensional construct.

Mould's third criticism is completely incorrect. The fact that exposure to a rape decpiction emphasizing the victim's abhorrence resulted in inhibited sexual arousal to a subsequent rape depiction is compatible with our hypotheses and is consistent with "debriefing effects" (Check & Malamuth, 1984; Malamuth & Check, 1984).

---

1. Malamuth has published recently two more articles in the *Journal of Sex Research* which support his positions as described herein.

Perceptions. Here Mould claims that we made a "misstatement" by indicating that significant differences occurred between conditions that actually did not differ significantly. His accusation is totally false. After finding a significant ANOVA effect, we very appropriately stated that although there were different *means* in three conditions, statistical analyses revealed significant differences only between two of these groups.

In explaining why he doubts whether effects actually occurred in Malamuth and Check (1980), Mould indicated that only a couple of items on a questionnaire consisting of 16 items showed significant effects. However, he fails to note that a multivariate effect was significant, thereby justifying the single-item comparisons. He also fails to consider that the item set showing the clearest effect is the one that theoretically would be expected to do so. It may be useful to add that any effects found in this area are likely to be relatively subtle and temporary. Rather severe ethical restrictions exist concerning the type and amount of exposure, as well as the age and background characteristics of subjects, that can be used within experimental studies in this area.

Rape Proclivity. Here Mould discusses our data regarding men's self-reported likelihood of raping (LR). Although here he no longer fully limits himself to the data reported in Malamuth and Check (1980), he takes into account only a small portion of the other relevant data (see Malamuth, 1981, 1984, in press-a; Smith, 1984). From the very first article where we assessed LR reports we stated that "It would seem highly inappropriate to argue that those subjects who indicated a possibility of engaging in rape, particularly under the hypothetical circumstances of being assured of not being caught, are actually likely to rape" (Malamuth et al., 1980, p. 134). We further noted that only in an "exaggerated form" and in combination with other factors might such a tendency be predictive of actual aggressive behavior (Malamuth et al., p. 134). Yet, he discusses the construct of LR as if it were intended to be a measure directly predictive of sexually assaultive behavior rather than a measure of inclinations or motivation.

Mould appears to recognize, to some degree at least, that the research shows that men who reported higher LR ratings are more similar to convicted rapists on relevant dimensions than those with lower LR ratings. However, he argues that a more important questions is, "are those high in rape proclivity *more* like rapists *than* they are like those low in rape proclivity?" He does not explain why this is a more important question. Although I strongly disagree with Mould regarding the priority of questions, I think that an appropriate review of the literature would show that those scoring very high on LR ratings (i.e., 4 or 5 on the 5-point scale) are more similar to convicted rapists on relevant dimensions than they are to those scoring very low on LR (i.e., a 1 on the 5-point scale).

As Mould notes, a disadvantage of single-item measures is that they are likely to be less reliable that multi-item measures and therefore to show weaker relationships with other variables. It is, therefore, quite impressive that across a rather substantial number of studies conducted throughout North America there have been consistent relationships obtained between LR ratings and a variety of attitudinal, arousal and behavioral measured *despite the fact that a single-item measure was used to assess LR* (for reviews, see Malamuth, 1981, 1984, in press-a; Rapaport, 1984; Smith 1984).

In closing it is important to examine whether the conclusions reached by Malamuth and Check (1980) have been successfully replicated in other research. Indeed, each of the major conclusions has been successfully replicated in several studies. The first conclusion that subjects are more sexually aroused by a rape depiction in which the victim shows involuntary sexual arousal than when she continuously abhorred the assault has been replicated by Malamuth and Check (1983), Quinsey and Chaplin (1984), and Rapaport (1984). The second finding, that exposure to "favorable" depictions of rape does not alter subsequent sexual responsiveness to similar depictions, has been replicated in several studies (e.g., Ceniti & Malamuth, 1984). Changes in perceptions and attitudes as a function of exposure to sexually violent depictions have been found by others (e.g., Demare, 1985; Linz, 1985; Malamuth & Check, 1981, 1985), supporting the third finding.

Finally, LR rating has been consistently found to relate to perceptions and attitudes pertaining to violence against women (e.g., Greendlinger & Byrne, 1986; Malamuth & Check, 1985; Rapaport, 1984; Tieger, 1981), to sexual arousal to violence (e.g., Malamuth & Check, 1983; Smith, 1984) and to aggressive behavior both in the laboratory (Malamuth & Ceniti, 1986) and in naturalistic settings (e.g., Malamuth, in press-a; Murphy et al., 1986; Rapaport, 1984). Therefore, contrary to the erroneous impression created by Mould's article, the conclusions reported by Malamuth and Check (1980) were fully justified by their data and have proven to be highly reliable in subsequent research.

Violent Erotica: A Reply

EDWARD DONNERSTEIN AND DANIEL LINZ

After reading Mould's paper one is left with the impression that the Malamuth and Check (1980) and Donnerstein and Berkowitz (1981) papers are the definitive statements on the effects of violent pornography. They are not.

Many of the issues raised by Mould have been raised by these authors themselves and responded to in subsequent research and writing. We would suggest that Mould consult a more up-to-date overview and critique of this area. Much has been accomplished since 1981, and the critical reader in the field needs to be acquainted with the most recent research (see, for example: Donnerstein & Linz, 1986a).

Mould also makes the assumption that "the works and opinions of these authors are being used in the formation of social policy" (p. 326). What opinions are being referred to here? Where in the Donnerstein and Berkowitz article are opinions offered "which may affect civil rights" as the author suggests? More recently we have been quite active in writing about the use (and misuse) of our research in the justification for certain social policies (e.g., Donnerstein, 1986; Donnerstein & Linz, 1986a, 1986b; Donnerstein et al., 1987; Linz, Donnerstein, & Penrod, 1987a, 1987b; Linz, Penrod, & Donnerstein, 1986, 1987). In each of these discussions we have eschewed policy solutions to the problem of pornography that infringe on civil rights (e.g., stricter obscenity laws). Instead, we have advocated sex education as a solution to the problem.

Mould leaves the reader with the impression that we design our research on the effects of exposure to pornography with specific policies in mind. Our research interests have been and continue to be, primarily theoretical (although we are currently involved in projects designed to test the effectiveness of educational interventions concerning sexual violence). The studies to which Mould refers were conducted before the recent political debates in this area surfaced. Although Mould is correct in noting that certain individuals have made use of this research for their own purposes, this was not our intent in the initial design of this research. Most of the research we conduct has been funded by grants from National Science Foundation and the National Institute of Mental Health. As such, it is evaluated on its scientific merit, not its political implications of "opinions" of its authors.

Attacking laboratory experimentation for its lack of a one-to-one physical resemblance to the world outside the laboratory (people do not normally deliver electric shocks, so we cannot generalize to the real world from an experiment which uses electric shock) reveals a misunderstanding of why experiments are carried out.

Turning now to the first experiment conducted by Donnerstein and Berkowitz, Mould partially describes the hypotheses and design. He is correct in noting that the major dependent variable in this study was aggression (i.e., shock intensity), but he fails to note that other measures, particularly those dealing with the film victim's suffering, enjoyment, and responsibility, were also measured in both this study and the second study. These are important data and should not be neglected as they support the findings of the Malamuth and Check (1980) study criticized by Mould for indicating that male subjects who view a rape victim "enjoying" her assault tend to have different perceptions of the victim's plight. Given the fact that these studies have different perceptions of the victim's plight and given the fact that these studies had different methodologies, subjects and stimuli, the relative similarity in outcome between the two should not be overlooked.

Further, it should be remembered that our interest is in aggression toward women. Why spend time on this finding when the major focus of the study is with men's exposure to aggressive pornography and subsequent violence against women?

Mould maintains that although Donnerstein and Berkowitz (1981) found an increase in aggression against females after exposure to aggressive pornography, the reader should not be "enthusiastic" about the conclusions. As support for this assertion he again discusses why they did or did not find effects for *male* targets despite the fact that they are talking about effects for female targets. Once again, this does not seem at all relevant to the findings that exposure to aggressive pornography increased aggression towards females. In the article the authors are quite clear as to why they expected certain findings for females and different findings for males. It seems that Mould's major objection to the findings in Study 1 is that they should have found an increase in aggression toward males as well as females. Nowhere does he refute the finding that there is more aggression against a female after exposure to aggressive pornography in comparison to nonaggressive pornography. We feel that to discuss the results for male targets, while omitting discussion of the female target findings, is to set up a "straw man."

Nowhere does Mould suggest a methodological or statistical problem with the study. Rather he is concerned with how the authors *explain* their results. Even if we accept his explanation, the results do not go away — exposure to aggressive pornography increases aggression against a female.

Mould ends his critique by suggesting that the Donnerstein and Berkowitz (1981) results are weak mainly on theoretical grounds and because of the inability to generalize beyond the laboratory. Much has changed since this study was conducted, and if Mould had based his paper on the *current* literature, we are sure that he would have found that many of his concerns are no longer relevant. The Mould critique might have facilitated a better understanding some years ago. Today, however, it is out of date and it is time to move forward armed with more current knowledge.

A REPLY TO MALAMUTH AND DONNERSTEIN AND LINZ

Douglas E. Mould

I believe Malamuth's response to my criticism demonstrates and validates many of the objections I have raised. Considering the issue of sexual arousal, Malamuth sidesteps the first issue. That an average self-reported sexual arousal of 50% is high *compared to other studies* in the literature is beside the point. Being 50% aroused does not justify labeling the level as "highly aroused." To do so misrepresents the actual level and implies an effect greater than really found. Most important, Malamuth completely avoids the main issue I have raised here. Malamuth and Check (1980) attempted to account for the failure to find a predicted effect by attributing it to one group having "very high" arousal when in fact that group was no more than moderately aroused.

Where perceptions of rape are concerned, Malamuth's first rebuttal to my critique demonstrates a fundamental misunderstanding of his statistics. Malamuth seems to misunderstand that a significant ANOVA indicates only that a statistically significant difference exists among means; it is the function of the post-hoc tests to detect where that difference lies. He clearly states that subjects in the rape-arousal condition "believed that a greater percentage of men . . . would rape than subjects who had first listened to the rape-abhorrence story" (p. 540) even though the post-hoc analysis was nonsignificant. The fact that later in the paragraph he reports the results of the post-hoc tests does not negate the fact that the initial assertion is a misstatement.

Malamuth states that he believes it unnecessary to defend the magnitudes of the correlations found between LR and attitudes supportive of violence because there is a consistency of such findings across studies. He is correct that consistently finding low correlations among relevant variables provides an element of construct validation (Cronbach & Meehl, 1955). However, accounting for variance *is the essence* of construct validation. It is the strength of the relationship between a measure and relevant variables that tell us how closely tied the measure is to what it purports to measure. Consistently, finding low-order correlations merely demonstrates a consistency in finding weak relationships between variables. Malamuth suggests that if other measures of assessing the importance of statistical relationships were used to assess his findings, different results would emerge.

In responding to Donnerstein and Linz (1988), I will begin with a disclaimer. It was neither my purpose nor my intent to imply or give the impression that Donnerstein and his associates design their research to support specific policies or political ends. Rather, my endeavor has been to evaluate the scientific merits of the studies considered. However, the fact remains that much of this body of research has been used to pursue right-wing political agendas, and that at least some of this is a consequence of careless speculation that has been light-years away from the data. Admittedly, many of these statements were made prior to the current furor over pornography, and perhaps it is a lesson for us all to label clearly possibilities and speculations as hypotheses to be tested.

Where "external validity" and "surface realism" are concerned, I believe Donnerstein and Linz have sidestepped the issue. My "attack" here has less to do with the "lack of one-to-one physical resemblance to the world outside the laboratory" (p. 305) and more to do with plausibility. Speculating, as Donnerstein and Berkowitz do, that aggressive pornography may cause men with weak inhibition to assault available women seems to me to greatly exceed the bounds of plausible inference.

In several places Donnerstein and Linz indicate that the failure to find significant results for males is irrelevant and that my raising this issue is a straw man. They also note that my major issue concerning their second experiment is "with how the authors *explain* their results" (p. 351). The importance of this cannot be underestimated. Donnerstein and Berkowitz propose a set of predictions based upon a set of propositions, that is, a theory which entails a set of interlocking ideas, or what Cronbach and Meehl (1955) call a "nomological network." If statements of causation are made such as "exposure to aggressive pornography increases aggression against a female" (Donnerstein & Linz, 1988, p. 351), there should be, at the very least, a general agreement between theory and data. If, as part of their theory, they make assertions about effects that are sex neutral, then a failure to find effects for males as well as females indicates a flaw in the theory. If they are going to use withholding of reward as a measure of aggression and they fail to find results, this indicates a flaw in the theory, a lack of convergent validation. Undoubtedly, I am concerned with the manner in which the authors explain their results. That is because there is a marked lack of agreement between their theory and their data.

The issue of pornography *is* enormously ladened with emotionality; research on the determinants of sexual violence *is* exceedingly difficult. But, let us not make the mistake of the drunk looking for his keys under the streetlamp because "that is where the light is." I, for one, remain skeptical that research with college males is going to reveal much at all about rapists and sexual aggression. Malamuth, Donnerstein, and Linz all assert that recent research has corrected the flaws and oversights of the early research. Let us hope so. However, if it, too, fails to withstand careful scrutiny and critical analysis, as I believe the early research fails in this respect, little has been gained and much time and many resources have been squandered.

REFERENCES

Abel, G. G., Barlow, D. H., Blanchard, E., & Guild, D. (1977). The components of rapists' sexual arousal. *Archives of General Psychiatry*, 34, 895–903.

Blader, J.C., & Marshall, W.L. (1984). The relationship between cognitive and erectile measures of sexual arousal in nonrapist males as a function of depicted aggression. *Behavior Research and Therapy*, 22, 623–630.

Ceniti, J., & Malamuth, N. (1984). Effects of repeated exposure to sexually violent or non-violent stimuli on sexual arousal to rape and nonrape depictions. *Behavior Research and Therapy*, 22, 535–548.

Check, J.V.P., & Malamuth, N.M. (1984). Can there be positive effects of participation in pornography experiments? *Journal of Sex Research*, 20, 14–31.

Cronbach, L.J., & Meehl, P.E. (1955). Construct validity in psychological tests. *Psychological Bulletin*, 52, 281–302.

Cronbach, L.J. (1984). Essentials of psychological testing. New York: Harper & Row.

Demare, D., & Brier, J., (in press). Violent pornography and self-reported likelihood of sexual aggression. *Journal of Research in Personality*.

Donnerstein, E. (1986). The Pornography Commission report: Do findings fit conclusions? *Sexual Coercion and Assault*, 1, 185–188.

Donnerstein, E., & Berkowitz, L. (1981). Victim reactions in aggressive erotic films as a factor in violence against women. *Journal of Personality and Social Psychology,* 41, 710–724.

Donnerstein, E., & Linz, D. (1986a). Mass media sexual violence and male viewers: Current theory and research. *American Behavioral Scientist,* 29, 601–618.

Donnerstein, E., & Linz, D. (1986b, December). The question of pornography. *Psychology Today,* pp. 56–59.

Donnerstein, E., & Linz, D. (1988). A critical analysis of recent research on violent erotica. *The Journal of Sex Research,* 24, 348–352.

Earls, C.M., & Marshall, W.L. (1983). The current state of technology in the laboratory assessment of sexual arousal patterns. In J.G. Greer (Eds.), *The sexual aggressor: Current perspectives on treatment* (pp. 336–362). New York: Van Nostrand Reinhold.

Freund, K., Scher, H., Racansky, I.G., Campbell, K., & Heasman, G. (1986). Males disposed to commit rape. *Archives of Sexual Behavior,* 15, 23–35.

Greendlinger, V., & Byrne, D. (1987). Coercive sexual fantasies of college men as predictors of self-reported likelihood to rape and overt sexual aggression. *The Journal of Sex Research,* 23, 1–11.

Krathwohl, D. (1985). *Social behavioral science research.* San Francisco: Jossey-Bass.

Linz, D. (1985). *Sexual violence in the media: Effects on male viewers and implication for society.* Unpublished doctoral dissertation, University of Wisconsin, Madison.

Linz, D., Donnerstein, E., & Penrod, S. (1987a). The findings and recommendations of the Attorney General's Commission on Pornography: Do the psychological facts fit the political fury? *American Psychologist,* 42(10), 946–953.

Linz, D., Donnerstein, E., & Penrod, S. (1987b). Sexual violence in the mass media: Social psychological implications. In P. Shaver & C. Hendrick (Eds.). *Review of personality and social psychology* (Vol. 7, pp. 135–175). Newbury Park, CA: Sage.

Linz, D., Penrod, S. & Donnerstein, E. (1986). Issues bearing on the legal regulation of violent and sexually violent media. *Journal of Social Issues,* 42(3), 171–193.

Linz, D., Penrod, S. & Donnerstein, E. (1987). The Attorney General's Commission on Pornography: The gap between "findings" and facts. *The American Bar Foundation Research Journal,* 1987(4), 301–324.

Malamuth, N.M. (1981). Rape proclivity among males. *Journal of Social Issues,* 37(4), 138–157.

Malamuth, N.M. (1984). Aggression against women: Cultural and individual causes. In N.M. Malamuth & E. Donnerstein (Eds.), *Pornography and sexual aggression* (pp. 19–52). Orlando, FL: Academic Press.

Malamuth, N.M. (in press). A multidimensional approach to sexual aggression: Combining measures of past behavior and present likelihood. In R.A. Prentky & V.L. Quinsey (Eds.), *Sexual Aggression: Current perspectives. Annals of the New York Academy of Sciences.*

Malamuth, N.M. and Ceniti, J. (1986). Repeated exposure to violent and nonviolent pornography: Likelihood of raping ratings and laboratory aggression against women. *Aggressive Behavior,* 12, 129–137.

Malamuth, N.M., & Check, J.V.P. (1980). Penile tumescence and perceptual responses to rape as a function of victim's perceived reactions. *Journal of Applied Social Psychology*, 10, 528–547.

Malamuth, N.M., & Check, J.V.P. (1983). Sexual arousal to rape depictions: Individual differences. *Journal of Abnormal Psychology*, 92, 55–67.

Malamuth, N.M., & Check, J.V.P. (1984). Debriefing effectiveness following exposure to pornographic rape depictions. *Journal of Sex Research*, 20, 1–13.

Malamuth, N.M., & Check, J.V.P. (1985). The effects of aggressive pornography on beliefs of rape myths: Individual differences. *Journal of Research in Personality*, 19, 299–320.

Malamuth, N., Haber, & Feshbach, S. (1980). Testing hypotheses regarding rape: Exposure to sexual violence, sex differences, and the "normality" of rapists. *Journal of Research in Personality*, 14, 121–137.

Milgram, S. (1974). *Obedience to authority*. New York: Harper & Row.

Mosher, D.L., & Anderson, R.D. (1986). Macho personality, sexual aggression, and reactions to guided imagery of realistic rape. *Journal of Research in Personality*, 20, 77–94.

Murphy, W.D., Coleman, E.M., & Haynes, M.R. (1986). Factors related to coercive sexual behavior in a nonclinical sample of males. *Violence and victims*, 1, 255–278.

Quinsey, V.L., & Chaplin, T.C. (1984). Stimulus control of rapists' and non-sex offenders' sexual arousal. *Behavioral Assessment*, 6, 169–176.

Rapaport, K. (1984). *Sexually aggressive males: Characterological features and sexual responsiveness to rape depictions*. Unpublished doctoral dissertation. Auburn University, Auburn, Alabama.

Sax, G. (1980). Principles of educational and psychological measurement and evaluation (2nd ed.). Belmont, CA: Wadsworth.

Smith, R.E.S. (1984). *Discriminating likelihood of rape ratings: Attitudinal, perceptual, sexual arousal and aggression discriminators*. Unpublished master's thesis, University of Manitoba, Winnipeg, Canada.

Tieger, T. (1981). Self-reported likelihood of raping and the social perception of rape. *Journal of Research in Personality*, 15, 147–158.

Chapter 4

MEDIA VIOLENCE, ANTISOCIAL BEHAVIOR, AND THE SOCIAL CONSEQUENCES OF SMALL EFFECTS

ROBERT ROSENTHAL

Few topics of social research have so engaged the interest and excited the imagination of social scientists, private citizens, and the makers of societal policy as the effects of media violence on social behavior. The reasons for this are not obscure. Few areas of social research are so rich in theoretical and practical implications. While the theoretical implications may be obvious only to social scientists, the practical implications are obvious to private citizens and policymakers alike.

Whether vs. How Much. When the social science community agrees that there is a significant relationship between media violence and antisocial behavior, it can only be said that the relationship between these variables is seen not to be zero. It says nothing about the magnitude of the relationship. Significance testing, in short, tells only whether nonzero relationships are likely. If we want to know more accurately how much of a relationship between our two variables is likely we must compute an effect size estimate.

It has been traditional in social science research to index the magnitude of effect by r^2. Over the years dissatisfaction with this index of effect size has grown, as workers realized that r^2 or "the proportion of variance accounted for" is not a very informative index of the practical importance of relationships found in the social or biomedical sciences (Abelson, 1985; Cohen, 1977; D'Andrade & Dart, 1983; Levy, 1967; Ozer, 1985; Rosenthal, 1984; Rosenthal & Rubin, 1979, 1982).

The purpose of the present paper is to show in practical quantitative yet intuitive terms just what the social consequences are likely to be of the "small effects" typically found in research on media violence and

Reprinted by permission from the Society for the Psychological Study of Social Issues, *Journal of Social Issues*, vol. 42, no. 3 (1986).

antisocial behavior. Four specific questions to be addressed are as follows:

1. In practical terms, how well can we predict adult antisocial behavior from childhood antisocial behavior?
2. In practical terms, how well can be predict current antisocial behavior from current exposure to media violence?
3. In practical terms, how well can we predict later antisocial behavior from earlier exposure to media violence, adjusting for earlier levels of antisocial behavior?
4. In practical terms, how much can we decrease antisocial behavioral means of special intervention designed to decrease the negative effect of high levels of exposure to media violence?

The Binomial Effect Size Display. Rosenthal and Rubin (1979, 1982) introduced a quantitative yet intuitive general purpose effect size display whose interpretation is straightforward: *the binomial effect size display* (BESD). They have not claimed to have resolved the controversies surrounding the use of various effect size estimators, but their display is useful because it is (a) easily understood by scientists, students, lay persons, and policymakers; (b) applicable in a wide range of situations; and (c) readily computed.

The basic question addressed by the BESD is, What is the effect on the success rate (e.g., survival rate, cure rate, improvement rate, selection rate, etc.) of the institution of a new treatment procedure? It therefore displays the change in success rate (e.g., survival rate, cure rate, improvement rate, selection rate, etc.) attributable to the new treatment procedure.

It is absurd to label as "modest indeed" an effect size equivalent to increasing the success rate from 34 to 66% (e.g., reducing a death rate from 66 to 34%). Even so small an r as .20 accounting for "only 4% of the variance" is associated with an increase in success rate from 40 to 60%, e.g., a decrease in death rate from 60 to 40%, hardly, a trivial effect. It might be thought that the BESD can be employed only for dichotomous outcomes (e.g., scores on a continuous scale of degree of antisocial behavior). Fortunately, however, the BESD) works well for *both* types of outcomes under a wide variety of conditions (Rosenthal & Rubin, 1982). On the independent variable side, when we are faced with a continuous rather than a dichotomous variable, the BESD requires that we can make a sensible medium split, as in above- vs. below-average (a) test scores, (b) exposure to media violence, or (c) amount of violent behavior. This is almost always a reasonable conceptual step.

Media Violence, Antisocial Behavior, and Social Consequences

The Stability of Aggression. One of the remarkable results obtained in the general area of research on media violence and antisocial behavior is the relationship between peer-nominated aggressive behavior at age eight and criminality in adulthood (Huesmann, Eron, Lefkowitz, & Walder, 1984). Table 2 provides a representative demonstration of the stability of aggression over a 22-year follow-up period; the data are from Table 2 of Huesmann et al. (1984).

The three columns represent three levels of childhood aggression: low, medium, and high. The rows give the number of subjects not convicted (*A*) and convicted (*B*) of crimes before age 30, the total number of subjects (*A* + *B*), the proportion of all subjects that were convicted (*P*), the variance of the proportion (*S²*p) and the weights (A) for the contrast testing the hypothesis that the higher the level of aggression at age 8, the higher the proportion of subjects convicted of a crime by age 30. Date are given separately for males and females.

Table 1

Subjects Convicted or Not Convicted for a Crime Before Age 30 at
Each of Three Levels of Aggression at Age 8

	Peer-nominated aggression at age 8		
	Low	Medium	High
Males			
(A) not convicted	81	138	63
(B) convicted	9	25	19
(A + B) total	90	163	82
$P = B/(A + B)$	.1000	.1534	.2317
$S_p^2 = [P(1 - P)]/(A + B)$	.0010	.0008	.0022
λ (contrast weights)	−1	0	+1
Females			
(A) not convicted	49	108	45
(B) convicted	0	2	3
(A + B) total	49	110	48
$P = B/(A + B)$	.0000	.0182	.0625
$S_p^2 = [P(1 - P)]/(A + B)$	.0000	.0002	.0012
λ (contrast weights)	−1	0	+1

For males: $\quad r = \sqrt{\dfrac{Z^2}{N}} = \sqrt{\dfrac{(2.33)^2}{335}} = .1273$

The same computations carried out for the female subjects yields a Z of 1.80, p = 0.36, one tailed, and an associated effect size r of .1251, a value remarkably similar to that obtained from male subjects. When male and female subjects are together, so that all six proportions (P) are examined simultaneously, the resulting test of significance yields a Z of 2,93.**p** = .0017, one tailed, and an associated effect size r of .1258.

An alternative procedure for computing an effect size r between the variables of childhood levels of aggression (e.g., as -1.0 and $+1$, respectively). Then the directly computed effect size rs are found as .1287, .1390, and .1183 for males, females, and total of all subjects respectively. In short, for these 542 subjects, the correlation between early aggression and later conviction for a crime is about .12 for either sex, no matter how computed. This effect size of .12 might be said to account for only about 1½% of the variance in the criminal conviction score (0.1), from a knowledge of childhood aggression scores ($-1,0$, $+1$). However, Table 2 shows that there is a very substantial difference in adult criminality rate between those who were assessed as dichtomously above or below the typical level of childhood aggression. For every 100 children below average in childhood aggression, only 44 will be above the median in adult criminality compared to the 56 we would find among the 100 children above average in childhood aggression. That difference of 12 per 100 can translate into enormous social, economic, and human differences.

Table 2

Childhood Aggression as Predictor of Adult Criminality: BESD for an r of .12

Childhood aggression	Adult criminality		
	Above median	Below median	Σ
Above median	56	44	100
Below median	44	56	100
Σ	100	100	200

The investigator studying Table 1 might feel a clearer picture of the relationship between childhood aggressive and adult criminal convictions might be obtained if the data from the medium aggressive children were omitted from the analysis. Such an analysis would yield effect size estimates of r = .178 for male subjects and r = .180 for female subjects, respectively. There is nothing intrinsically wrong with these estimates, but they are based on only the extreme 51 and 47% of the distribution of childhood aggression for males and females, respectively. Dropping the middle scores tends to inflate the obtained offer size over what a median split of the full sample would yield, though the test of significance is not necessarily affected. The loss of N "compensates" to some degree for the inflated effect size: since tests of significance are a joint function of effect size and sample size, results of significance tests can remain fairly stable when a change in effect size is offset by a change in sample size.

Media Violence and Synchronous Aggressive Behavior. The basic result that there is a positive relationship between television violence viewing and peer-nominated aggression measured at about the same time is well established (Huesmann & Eron, 1983; Milavsky, Kessler, Stipp & Rubens, 1982). Table 3 presents a stem-and-leaf plot of these correlations for 32 samples of females (16) in grades 1–5 from four countries (United States, Finland, Poland, and Australia), with a mean sample size of 47.[1]

---

1. Tukey (1977) developed the stem-and-leaf plot as a special form of frequency distribution to facilitate the inspection of a batch of data. Each number in the data batch is made up of one stem and one leaf, but each stem may serve several leaves. Thus the sixth stem, a .1 followed by two leaves of three and four, representing the *rs* of .13 and .14. The first digit is the stem, the next digit is the leaf. The eye takes in a stem-and-leaf plot as it does any other frequency distribution, but the original data are preserved with greater precision in a stem-and-leaf plot than would be the case with ordinary frequency distributions (Rosenthal, 1984; Rosenthal & Rosnow, 1975).

Table 3

Stem-and-Leaf Plot and Statistical Summary of
Correlations Between Media Violence and Aggressive Behavior
(Mean *N* per Correlation = 47)

Stem	Leaf	Summary statistics (based on *r*, not on Z_r)	
.3	8	Maximum	.38
.3	0	Quartile 3 (Q_3)	.24
.2	6 6 7 8 9	Median (Q_2)	.19
.2	0 0 0 0 1 4 4 4	Quartile 1 (Q_1)	.08
.1	6 6 7 7 8 9 9	Minimum	−.16
.1	3 4	$Q_3 - Q_1$	.16
.0	6 7	$\sigma[.75(Q_3 - Q_1)]$	.12
.0	2 3 4 4	S	.11
−.0		Mean	.16
−.0	8	Mode	.20
−.1		N	32
−.1	6	P (proportion with positive sign)	.94
		p of P > .5	.000001

Media Violence and Subsequent Aggressive Behavior. When we want to draw casual inferences about the "effects" of exposure to media violence on subsequent aggressive behavior it is necessary to adjust for the "effects" of aggressive behavior assessed at about the same time as the exposure to media violence. Such adjusting may be done in the context of multiple regression. For the consistent use of the effect size r from the t test of the significance of the regression coefficient for the relation between earlier exposure to media violence and later aggressive behavior, partialing out the earlier aggressive behavior (and other variables as well, if desired).

Based on the multiple regression analyses described by Huesmann and Eron (1983), these partial rs or effect sizes were estimated to be approximately .14 for girls and .09 for boys, when later aggression (third year) was predicted from earlier exposure to media violence (first year) controlling for initial aggression (first year). Table 5 shows the BESD for both these correlations. Thus these two results suggest that the difference between above vs. below-medium levels of exposure to media violence is followed by differences of 9–14% in degree of above- vs. below-median aggression, even after adjusting for initial levels of aggression. The adjustment for initial level of aggression makes far more plausible the

---

Table 3 shows a wide range of rs, but the bulk (66%) of the distribution falling between rs of .16 and .30. Table 4 shows the BESD displays for both values. Thus, the bulk of the correlations suggest that we can increase the accuracy of selection of high- vs. low-aggressive children from a knowledge of high vs. low exposure to media violence, most of the time from 16 to 30%. These are dramatic improvements of accuracy of classification even though the proportions of variance accounted for by rs of .16 and .30 are only .026 and .090, respectively.

Table 4

Viewing of Media Violence as Predictor of Childhood Aggression: BESDs for rs of .16 and .30

Exposure to media violence	Childhood aggression					
	$r = .16$			$r = .30$		
	Above median	Below median	Σ	Above median	Below median	Σ
Above median	58	42	100	65	35	100
Below median	42	58	100	35	65	100
Σ	100	100	200	100	100	200

Table 5

Viewing of Media Violence as Predictor of Subsequent Aggression, Adjusting for Earlier Level of Aggression: BESDs for *rs* of .14 and .09

| Exposure to media violence | Subsequent aggression adjusted for earlier level of aggression | | | | | |
| | Girls (*r* = .14) | | | Boys (*r* = .09) | | |
	Above median	Below median	Σ	Above median	Below median	Σ
Above median	57	43	100	54.5	45.5	100.0
Below median	43	57	100	45.5	54.5	100.0
Σ	100	100	200	100.0	100.0	200.0

drawing of causal inferences about the effect of media violence on subsequent aggressive behavior.

An Experimental Intervention to Decrease Antisocial Behavior. In an attempt to mitigate the effects of media violence, an experimental treatment condition was designed to convince children who were high in exposure to television violence that such violence was unrealistic and should not be imitated (Huesmann & Eron, 1983). Several months later, the children randomly assigned to this treatment condition showed significantly less aggression than did the children of the control group ($F(,112 = 6.40, p = .013, r = .232$). Table 6 shows this result as a BESD (with *r* rounded to .24). This treatment, therefore, showed dramatic effects, lowering the proportion of children showing above average aggression from .62 to .38. This dramatic effect occurred despite the fact that the factor of experimental condition accounted for less than 6% of the variance.

Conclusion. In this paper the attempt is made to provide estimates in

Table 6

Experimental Treatment to Lower Levels of Aggressive Behavior: BESD for *r* of .24

| Condition | Subsequent aggression | | |
	Above median	Below median	Σ
Placebo	62	38	100
Treatment	38	62	100
Σ	100	100	200

very practical terms of how well we can predict (a) adult antisocial behavior from childhood and social behavior; (b) current antisocial behavior from current exposure to media violence; (c) subsequent antisocial behavior from earlier exposure to media violence, adjusting for earlier levels of antisocial behavior; and (d) how much we can decrease antisocial behavior by means of special intervention.

The quantitative answers to these questions are intended to be illustrative other than definitive. More definitive answers will depend upon the results of more meta-analytic summaries of large numbers of studies such as those of Andison (1977) and Hearold (1985). Nevertheless, on the basis of the displays presented in this paper, it seems clear that our ability to predict and control antisocial behavior is not all trivial in practical terms, despite the apparently small r^2s obtained in most studies. For example, there is nothing trivial about being able to reduce rates of aggressive behavior from about 62 to about 38% by means of an experimental intervention, even though the proportion of variance accounted for is less than 6%.

Social scientists often feel discouraged because research so often yields only "small" effect sizes such as those found in the area of predicting antisocial behavior. We are inclined to envy our colleagues in the physical sciences. Perhaps we could feel less discouraged if we kept in mind that in the younger physical sciences, those that also involve complete variable arrays, the same order of magnitude of prediction is obtained as in the social sciences. Meteorologists can inform us that the prediction of stormy weather is no more (and often no less) successful than the prediction of stormy human behavior (Kerr, 1985).

REFERENCES

Abelson, R. P. (1985). A variance explanation paradox. When a little is a lot. *Psychological Bulletin*, 97, 129–133.

Andison, F.S. (1977). TV violence and viewer aggression. A cumulation of study results, 1956–1976. *Opinion Quarterly*, 41, 314–331.

Cohen, J. (1977). *Statistical power analysis for the behavioral sciences* (rev. ed.). New York: Academic Press.

D'Andrade, R. G., & Dart, J. (1983). *The interpretation of r versus r²*. Unpublished manuscript, University of California, San Diego.

Hearold S. (1986). A synthesis of 1043 effects of television on social behavior. *Public Communication and Behavior*, 1, 65–133.

Huesman, L.R. & Eron, L.D. (1983) Factors influencing the effect of television violence on children. in M.J.A. Howe (Ed.) *Learning from Television: Psychological and Educational Research* (pp. 153–177). New York: Academic Press.

Huesmann, L. R., Eron, L. D., Lefkowitz, M. M., & Walder, L. O. (1984). Stability of aggression over time and generations. *Developmental Psychology, 20,* 1120–1134.

Kerr, R. A. (1985). Pity the poor weatherman. *Science, 214,* 704–706.

Levy, P. (1967), Substantive significance of significant differences between two groups. *Psychological Bulletin, 67,* 37–40.

Milavsky, J. R., Kessler, R. C., Stipp, H. H., & Rubens, W. S. (1982). *Television and aggression: A panel study.* New York: Academic Press.

Ozer, D. J. (1985). Correlation and the coefficient of determination. *Psychological Bulletin, 97,* 307–315.

Rosenthal, R. (1984). *Meta-analytic procedures for social research.* Beverly Hills, CA: Sage.

Rosenthal, R., & Rosnow, R. L. (1975). *The volunteer subject.* New York: John Wiley.

Rosenthal, R., & Rosnow, R. L. (1984). *Essentials of behavioral research: Methods and data analysis.* New York: McGraw-Hill.

Rosenthal, R., & Rubin, D. B. (1979). A note on percent variance explained as a measure of the importance of effects. *Journal of Applied Social Psychology, 9,* 395–396.

Rosenthal, R., & Rubin, D. B. (1982). A simple general purpose display of magnitude of experimental effect. *Journal of Educational Psychology, 74,* 166–169.

Tukey, J. W. (1977). *Exploratory data analysis.* Reading, MA: Addison-Wesley.

Chapter 5

THE EFFECT OF SUICIDE STORIES ON VARIOUS DEMOGRAPHIC GROUPS 1968–1985

DAVID P. PHILLIPS AND LUNDIE L. CARSTENSEN

In 1774 Johannn Wolfgang von Goethe published a romantic novel, *The Sorrows of Young Werther*, in which the hero committed suicide. The book was widely read throughout Europe, and its hero's behavior was apparently imitated. Some people committed suicide while dressed as Werther was; others killed themselves in the same manner as Werther, with a copy of the novel opened to the page describing his suicide. Alarmed by the apparent effect of the book, authorities banned the novel in parts of Italy, Denmark, and Germany (Gray, 1967; Rose, 1929). Seventy years later, William Farr, the British Registrar General of Births, Deaths, and Marriages, noted, "No fact is better established in science than that suicide (and murder may perhaps be added) is often committed from imitation" (cited by Phelps, 1911; Pell & Watters, 1982).

In 1897 Durkheim acknowledged that imitation may affect suicide, but only in the sense that it precipitates a few suicides that would have occurred very soon anyway, even in the absence of imitation (Durkheim, 1897/1962). He also maintained that while suicide may precipitate a few deaths, it cannot do so in sufficient numbers to affect the social suicide rate. For 75 years after Durkheim's influential book, there was no large-scale study of imitative suicide. The few small-scale studies that were undertaken were inconclusive (Motto 1967), contradictory (Crawford & Willis, 1966; Seiden, 1968), or susceptible to various explanations other than imitation (Kreitman, Smith, & Tan, 1969; Weiss, 1958).

It was not until 1974 that the first large-scale study of imitative suicide appeared (Phillips, 1974). Phillips examined the fluctuation of U.S.

Reprinted by permission from Guilford Press, from *Suicide and Life-Threatening Behavior*, vol. 18, no. 1 (1988).

monthly suicides before and after the appearance of heavily publicized suicide stories. Correcting for the effects of seasons and secular trends, he found that U.S. suicides had a statistically significant tendency to increase after suicide stories, by about 58 suicides per story. The more publicity given to the story, the greater the increase in suicides thereafter. The increase in suicides occurred mainly in the geographic areas where the suicide story was publicized. In honor of Goethe's hero, Phillips named the post-story increase in suicides the "Werther effect."

Suicide stories do not appear merely to precipitate suicides that would have occurred anyway. If the "precipitation explanation" were correct, the post-story rise in suicides should be followed by an equally large drop in suicides below the normal level, caused by people "moving up" their death dates. No such drop has been found, and this suggests that Durkheim was incorrect. Suicide stories seem to trigger some deaths that would not have occurred otherwise. Phillips assessed four additional alternative explanations for his findings, including the possibility that they were due to misclassification or to prior events that triggered both the publicized suicide and the rise in suicides thereafter. He concluded that the best available explanation for his findings was that suicide stories elicit some imitative behavior; the precise nature of these imitative processes was not then (and is not now) understood.

In a study of U.S. monthly suicides, Wasserman (1984) concluded that suicide stories trigger imitation only if the story concerns a celebrity suicide. However, Stack (1984) noted that Wasserman had inadvertently omitted some publicized stories from his analysis; when these stories were included, Stack found no significant difference between the effect of celebrity and noncelebrity suicide stories (after correction for the amount of publicity devoted to each story). We (Phillips, Paight, & Carstensen, in press) uncovered similar findings with a different data.

The studies reviewed above were typically concerned with the impact of *newspaper* stories on *monthly* suicides. We (Phillips & Carstensen, 1986) also examined the impact of television network news suicide stories on daily U.S. suicides from 1973 to 1979. Examination of daily figures yielded a more detailed picture of the timing and duration of the suicide peak just after suicide stories. The Werther effect seemed to persist for 0–7 days after the television story. The peak in suicides remained statistically significant after corrections for day of the week, seasons, trends, and holidays.

In the present study, we sought to broaden the work on television news stories (Phillips & Carstensen, 1986) in two ways. First, we nearly tripled the time period under analysis (from 1973–1979 to 1968–1985). Second, and more important, we analyzed the differential effect of suicide stories on a wide variety of demographic groups. It is important to determine whether the effect of suicide stories pervades all segments of society or is concentrated in a few groups. Information of this sort can deepen our understanding of imitative processes and enhance our ability to reduce their harmful consequences; knowing which groups are most affected by suicide stories can help us to target efforts to help them.[1]

Sources and Characteristics of Data under Analysis

The current investigation examined the impact of suicide stories that appeared on network television news programs from 1968 to 1985. The study period began with 1968, because this was the first year covered by the Vanderbilt Television News Index; 1985 was the last year under examination because computerized California mortality data were not yet available for later years. Our earlier findings (Phillips & Carstensen, 1986, Table 1) indicated that suicides increased only after suicide stories that were carried on several television programs. The difference between the effect of single-program and multiprogram stories was statistically significant ($t = 3.42$, $p = .0015$). Because of this evidence, the present study examined the impact of multiprogram suicide stories.

These stories were chosen in the following fashion: Multiprogram stories for 1973–1979 were precisely those used earlier (Phillips & Carstensen, 1986). Stories for the remaining years under study (1968–1972, 1980–1985) were chosen from the same television news indexes (CBS News Index, Vanderbilt TV News Index) and according to the same selection criteria used earlier (Phillips & Carstensen, 1986). In addition, we added stories about the "right to die," because stories on this topic have begun to appear under the index heading of suicide in recent years (1980–1985). Stories of this type are likely to become increasingly frequent and we felt it would be important not to exclude them from this and from future analyses.[2]

1This review has been restricted to the impact of nonfictional suicide stories; this has been the primary focus of the literature on imitative suicide. Very recently, researchers have begun to examine the impact of fictional stories as well (see Gould & Shaffer, 1986, Phillips & Paight, 1987; Platt, 1987; Schmidtke & Hafner, 1986).

2. Unfortunately, there were only two "right to die" stories listed under the index heading "suicide," so that it is not meaningful to provide a separate analysis of their effects.

Method of Analyses

We used the same time series regression model employed in an earlier work (e.g., Bollen & Phillips, 1982; Phillips & Carstensen, 1986). As in our 1986 study, we sought the effect of a suicide story in the period 0–7 days after its appearance by creating a chummy variable that took the value "1" in this period and "0" elsewhere. In order to correct for the effects of day of the week, month, and year, we created dummy variables for Monday through Saturday, January through November, and 1986 through 1984. In addition, a dummy variable was constructed for each holiday and for each of the days immediately surrounding that holiday. This procedure helped to correct for the impact of holidays on suicide. In addition, we made doubly sure that holiday effects and story effects were not confounded, by omitting a suicide story if the observation period following that story (i.e., 0–7 days after the story) overlapped with a holiday period.

Results

We note first that male and female suicides increased significantly 0–7 days after a publicized suicide story. The coefficient 0.381 indicates that male suicides increased by 0.381 per day in this 8-day observation period, for a total increase of 3.048 male suicides (8 × 0.381) per story. Similarly, female suicides increased by a total of 1.592 (8 × 0.190) per story. Thus, for both sexes combined, California suicides increased by 4.64 (3.048 + 1.592) for each multiprogram suicide story broadcast on network television news programs. Since a total of 43 television news stories were examined, this implies a total increase of 199.52 California suicides after suicide stories. California accounts for about 10% of the U.S. population; if its imitative processes are representative of the United States as a whole, then U.S. suicides increased by a little less than 2,000 after the suicide stories under discussion.

Perhaps the most important finding is that the effect of suicide stories was relatively stable over time: The Werther effect remained statistically significant when our original study period (1973–1979) was nearly tripled in size (to 1968–1985).

The remainder of the findings reveal patterns similar to those noted elsewhere in the literature. For example, both males and females displayed a significant peak in suicides on Monday. Neither sex showed a very strong seasonal pattern in suicide, but there was some tendency for the level of suicides to be a little higher in spring and early summer. For both sexes, there was a tendency for suicide levels to decline on and immediately before most holidays. There was also a tendency for suicide levels to increase after some holidays, most notably New Year's Day and Labor Day.

In examining Table 1, we turn to the central questions of this chapter. Does the Werther effect pervade all segments of society? Is it concentrated in some groups and not in others? Column 1 of Table 1 displays the total rise in suicides (correcting for the effect of other variables) in the observation period after the suicide story. It is evident that nearly all demographic groups displayed a rise in suicides after publicized suicide stories. Only persons aged 30–39 displayed a statistically insignificant drop in suicides after these stories. However, although the Werther effect was pervasive, it was quite small for nearly all groups, with the notable exception of teenagers. For this group, the daily rise in suicides during the observation period was approximately 22%. (This figure was calculated in the following fashion: Column 1 gives the total increase in suicides above normal during the 8-day observation period following the suicide story; the *daily* increase in suicides was one-eighth of this figure. When this daily increase was divided by the normal daily number of suicides (Column 2), we obtained an estimate of the size of the story effect.) It is interesting to note that teenagers behaved very differently from the next highest age group; this suggests that future studies of "youth" suicide should not lump together teens and young adults, as has frequently been the case to date.

One might expect the Werther effect to be stronger for groups that are already strongly predisposed to suicide. By this logic, a suicide story is most likely to trigger suicides in those who are already "close to the edge." However, the findings shown in Table 1 do not seem to support this expectation:

1. The male suicide rate was much higher than the female rate, but the Werther effect seemed to be no stronger for males than for females.
2. The white suicide rate was higher than that for blacks, but the Werther effect was not bigger for whites than for blacks.
3. The nonmarried suicide rate was higher than the rate for married people, but the Werther effect was not larger for unmarried people.

Table 1
Size of Story Effect for Various Demographic Groups, California, 1968–1985

Demographic group	Total rise in suicides 0–7 days after the suicide story	Average no. of daily suicides during the year	t	Rank of story effect vs. effect of other variables	Percentage increase per day 0–7 days after the suicide story
Male	3.048	6.25	2.66	2	6.09
Female	1.593	2.92	2.02	5	6.82
Teenagers	0.985	0.56	2.87	1	22.08
Age 20–29	1.159	2.07	1.74	2	6.99
Age 30–39	−0.059	1.57	−0.10	56	−0.47
Age 40–49	0.774	1.41	1.46	3	6.87
Age 50–64	1.267	1.98	1.98	2	8.01
Retired	0.547	1.59	0.94	9	4.30
Married	2.258	3.79	2.54	4	7.44
Nonmarried	3.043	4.87	3.05	4	7.82
White	3.985	8.52	2.99	2	5.84
Nonwhite	0.660	0.65	1.79	3	12.73
Suicide at home[a]	4.103	8.46	3.09	2	6.06
Suicide not at home	0.532	0.71	1.37	2	9.32

[a]The term "suicide at home" signifies a death for which the county of residence was the same as the county of death. The term "suicide not at home" signifies a death for which the county of death was not the county of residence.

4. Those of retirement age typically have the highest suicide rates of all age groups, but the Werther effect for those who were retired seemed to be small, not large.

Only persons dying away from home provided some tentative support for the notion that unintegrated people are most prone to imitative suicide. The Werther effect was slightly stronger for persons dying outside their county of residence than it was for persons dying at home. However, this evidence must be considered to have ambiguous implications, since it is by no means certain that persons who kill themselves away from home are on the average less socially integrated than persons who kill themselves at home.

Thus far, we have been discussing the size of the story effect in terms of a percentage increase above the normal level of suicides. It is interesting to consider the size of the story effect in a different fashion, by comparing the story effect with the effects of other variables known to influence suicide. Column 4 of Table 1 summarizes a great many comparisons of this sort. For example, the figure '1' in this column associated with teenagers indicates that the effect of a suicide story in the 8-day observation period was larger than the effect of any of the other 88 variables analyzed in the regression equating: day of week, month, holidays, and so on. Similarly, the figure "2" for persons aged 20–29 indicates that for this group the suicide story had the second largest effect of all the variables considered.[3]

Discussion

It is evident from Table 1 that for nearly all demographic groups, suicide stories have an unusually large effect, in comparison with the effect of other temporal variables. This conclusion needs to be qualified in various ways. First, although the effect of the average suicide story is far greater than the effect of (say) the average Wednesday, the cumulative effect of Wednesdays is far greater than the cumulative effect of suicide stories, because there are so many more Wednesdays than suicide stories. Second, although the effect of a suicide story is large when compared with the effect of temporal variables (e.g., day of the week, month, etc.), it

---

3. One may wish to recast this analysis by comparing the story effect with the total effect of each holiday: HOL $(-4 + $ HOL $(-3), \ldots, +$ HOL $(+4)$. Even when this is done, however, the effect of the story remains pre-eminent.

is not large when compared with the effect of demographic variables (e.g., age, race, and sex). Thus, it may be wisest to consider that for most segments of society, the suicide story exerts an effect that is not so small as to be negligible nor so large as to preclude consideration of all other etiological factors.

A somewhat different conclusion seems appropriate for teenagers, for whom the suicide story does seem to exert a very important effect. For this group, it seems appropriate to consider ways of reducing the harmful effect of suicide stories.

It is worth noting that, in comparison with all the other temporal and demographic variables under discussion, the suicide story seems most amenable to social control. One cannot plausibly abolish Mondays, even though they are associated with a significant rise in suicides. Nor can one transform white into nonwhites so as to reduce their predisposition to suicide. But it is possible to reduce the publicity accorded to suicide stories and to change the manner in which the suicide story is reported.

One way to address this issue is to consider the suicide story as a type of "natural advertisement." Studies of advertising suggest that the effect of an advertisement is reduced if it is treated in the following way:

1. If the advertisement is not repeated. Thus, suicide stories (or advertisements) appearing on a single program seem to have a smaller effect than multiprogram stories of advertisements.
2. If the advertisement is placed in an obscure location. Cover-page advertisements in magazines are more expensive because they are thought to be more effective. Similarly, Phillips (unpublished research) found that front-page suicide stories had a detectable effect whereas inside-page stories did not. This suggests that some suicide stories might be moved to inside sections of the newspapers.
3. If the characters in the advertisement are presented in a neutral or unsympathetic light. People are probably less likely to imitate a character in the advertisement (or suicide story) if it is difficult to identify with him or her.
4. If the negative consequences of the advertised behavior are mentioned in the advertisement. Thus the inclusion of the Surgeon General's warning is designed to reduce the impact of cigarette commercials. It is noteworthy that suicide stories typically fail to mention negative consequences (e.g., pain and disfigurement) that often accompany a suicide. It is possible that if these things were

mentioned in a realistic description of the suicide story, this would reduce the level of imitation.

5. If the advertisement mentions alternatives to the advertised product. Commercial advertisements never mention competing products (unless with the intent of disparaging them). Thus a McDonald's commercial does not mention Burger King or Kentucky Fried Chicken. It is interesting to note that the "natural advertisement" of a suicide story often has the same monolithic character: The story focuses on one response to psychological anguish-suicide-without indicating that there are many other possible responses as well. It is possible that mention of these alternatives (hotlines, counselling, self-help groups, etc.) in the suicide story would reduce the tendency to imitative suicide.

Nearly 150 years ago, the British Registrar General of Births, Deaths, and Marriages asked rather plaintively in his annual report, "Why should cases of suicide be recorded at length in public papers any more than cases of fever?" (General Register Office of Great Britain, 1841). The imitative behavior that prompted this question still exists today, and we need to remain concerned about the impact of publicized suicide stories. Our solution to the problem need not be Draconian, however. It seems likely that the effects of these stories can be greatly reduced by changing the manner in which they are reported, rather than by omitting them entirely from the news.

REFERENCES

Bolen, K. A., & Phillips, D. P. Imitative suicides: A national study of the effects of television news stories. *American Sociological Review,* 1982, 47 802–809.

Crawford, J. P., & Willis, J. H. Double suicide in psychiatric hospital patients. *British Journal of Psychiatry,* 1966, 112, 1231–1235.

Durkheim, E. *Suicide.* Glencoe, Ill.: Free Press, 1951, (Originally published, 1897.)

General Register Office of Great Britain. *The Registrar General's annual report on births, deaths, and marriages,* 1841. London: Her Majesty's Stationery Office, 1841.

Gould, M. S., & Shaffer, D. The impact of suicide in television movies: Evidence of imitation. *New England Journal of Medicine,* 1986, 315, 690–694.

Gray, R. *Goethe: A critical introduction.* Cambridge, England: Cambridge University Press, 1967.

Kreitman, N., Smith, P. & Tan, E. Attempted suicide in social networks. *British Journal of Preventive and Social Medicine,* 1969, 23, 116–123.

Motto, J. A. Suicide and suggestibility. *American Journal of Psychiatry,* 1967, 124, 252–256.

Pell, B., & Watters, D. Newspaper policies on suicide stories. *Canada's Mental Health,* 1982, 30, 8–9.

Phelps, E. Neurotic books and newspapers as factors in the mortality of suicide and crime. *Journal of Social Medicine,* 1911, 12, 264–306.

Phillips, D. P. The influence of suggestion on suicide: Substantive and theoretical implications of the Werther effect. *American Sociological Review,* 1974, 39, 340–354.

Phillips, D. P., & Carstensen, L. L. Clustering of teenage suicides after television news stories about suicide. *New England Journal of Medicine,* 1986, 315, 685–689.

Phillips, D. P., & Paight, D. J. The impact of television movies about suicide: A replicative study. *New England Journal of Medicine,* 1987, 317, 809–811.

Phillips, D. P., Paight, D. J., & Carstensen, L. L. Effects of mass media stories on suicides, with new evidence on the role of story content. In C. Pfeffer (Ed.), *New biopsychosocial perspectives on youth suicide.* NY: American Psychiatric Press, forthcoming.

Platt, S. The aftermath of Angie's overdose: Is soap (opera) dangerous to your health? *British Medical Journal,* 1987, 294, 954–957.

Rose, W. Introduction. In J. W. von Goethe, *The sorrows of young Werther.* London: Scholastic Press, 1929.

Schmidtke, A., & Hafner, H. Die vermittlung von selbatmordmotivation und selbstmordhandlung durch fiktive modelle. Nervenarzt, 1986, 57, 502–610.

Seiden, R. H. Suicide behavior contagion on a college campus. In N. L. Farberow (Ed.) *Proceedings of the Fourth International Conference on Suicide Prevention.* Los Angeles: Delmaro, 1968.

Stack, S. Celebrities and suicide: A taxonomy and analysis. *American Sociological Review,* 1987, 52, 401–412.

Wasserman, I. Imitation and suicide: A reexamination of the Werther effect. *American Sociological Review,* 1984, 49, 427–436.

Weiss, E. The clinical significance of the anniversary reaction. *General Practitioner,* 1958, 17, 117–119.

Chapter 6

EXPOSURE TO AND INCITEFUL USE OF HARD CORE PORNOGRAPHY BY SEX OFFENDERS

W. L. MARSHALL

Legislation regulating the availability of pornography continues to be a controversial issue in most Western societies. With the publication of the report from the United States Commission on Obscenity and Pornography (1970), many writers and officials concluded that eliminating legal constraints on pornography would exert little or no negative influence on society's citizens. Considering, in particular, Kutchinsky's (1971) report to the Commission, it has been suggested that abolishing restrictions might even have beneficial effects (Ward & Woods, 1972).

Subsequent reviews of the commissions' findings, as well as further analyses of the effects of loosening legal constraints on pornography, have revealed several facets of the issue which do not encourage the same optimistic views of the benefits of pornography (Cline, 1974; Court, 1976; Eysenck & Nias, 1978); however, these reviews have themselves been criticized and found wanting in several respects (Cochrane, 1978). What has become clear is that the term *pornography* has been applied to a wide variety of materials without much concern for the actual content of these materials or their use by particular classes of individuals.

Those men whose experiences have shaped their perceptions in the ways described should be particularly receptive to information that they take to confirm their beliefs. These beliefs include the notion that women enjoy being raped and that masculinity is reflected in coercing someone to have sex and in humiliating and degrading that person. These are just the types of views presented in those examples of pornography that depict a man forcing a woman to have sex with him. For some of these men, the thought of struggling to overpower a woman is too threatening,

Reprinted by permission of *Journal of Sex Research*, Vol. 25, No. 2 (1988).

so they look to other sources of power and prestige in a sexual context. These men are ready to believe that children want to have sex with adults; child pornography clearly suggests this and also clearly demonstrates that the man in the scenario is in control of the sexual interaction.

Previous research with sex offenders has failed to clarify either the degree of exposure to sexually explicit materials by these men or the effects this exposure had upon them. However, the report by Goldstein et al. (1973) is valuable since it suggests an unusual response to such exposure by sex offenders (despite their finding, which confirmed the observation of others, that sex offenders have less exposure to pornography than others). Rapists were more likely to masturbate to the pornography they had seen, and, most importantly, they were more likely to emulate what they had seen than were other men. Perhaps, this is an illustration of vulnerability to the influence of pornography amongst sex offenders, which we have proposed elsewhere (Marshall & Barbaree, 1984).

In the present study, I attempted to obtain information, by way of retrospective recall, from rapists and child molesters attending a treatment clinic, and from nonoffenders recruited from the local community regarding their exposure to media depictions of sex.

Given our earlier claim (Marshall & Barbaree, 1984) that sex offenders are particularly vulnerable (in a negative way) by exposure to specific types of pornography, the most appropriate comparison group to answer the question of the precise influence of pornography would be a group of similarly vulnerable men who did not develop into sex offenders. Of course, it would be very difficult to find such a group; and if we were able to identify these men, this very fact would undermine our general argument that rape results from the confluence of a variety of factors. Exposure to pornography, we have suggested, is but one of these factors and it may account for only a limited amount of the variance. Given the problems in securing a perfect control group, I chose, in this initial study, men selected from volunteers referred by local employment agencies, who approximately matched the offenders on socioeconomic status, age, and intelligence.

Methods

Subjects. Over a 6-year period, all patients voluntarily attending the Kingston Sexual Offenders' Clinic who admitted to having engaged in other forceful acts with adult females or sex with children and who came to at least five evaluation sessions (including an assessment of their sexual preferences) were interviewed about their use of sexually explicit materials. A total of 89 patients, all of whom had sexually molested either children or adults. Those men who molested children were subclassified according to whether their victims were their own children (15 incest offenders) or those of others (51 child molesters). The incest offenders had all molested only their female children. The child molesters were further subcategorized depending on whether the victims were male (18 homosexual child molesters) or female (33 heterosexual child molesters). The 23 men who molested adults had all either raped, attempted to rape, or had sexually assaulted at least one adult female. These men were all Caucasian; 40 were married, 20 divorced or separated, and 29 had never been married.

Twenty-four Caucasian males with no history of sexual offending were recruited from volunteers for four other research projects concerned with the sexual preferences of nonoffending males for consenting sex, forced sex, and sex with male and female children. From amongst these volunteers, I selected men whose ages, intelligence, and socioeconomic class approximately matched those of the child molesters rather than the rapists, who were clearly different from the rest of the offenders and who constituted the smaller sample compared with those men who had offended against children. All of the nonoffenders reported themselves to be exclusively heterosexual and to have never engaged in any type of sexual offense.

Each patient's sexual preferences were assessed using mercury-in-rubber strain gauge plethysmography (Earls & Marshall, 1983). This permits the description of erectile responses to various categories of sexually explicit stimuli. In this way each man's gender preferences, age preferences, and preference for forced versus consenting sex are discerned.

For each of the offender groups, the deviant index reflects their relative preference for the deviant acts that define their group categorization. The sexual responses to female children of the incest offenders and heterosexual child molesters were indexed as a proportion of their responses to adult women; for the homosexual child molesters their responses to male children were indexed as proportional to their responses to adult partners (when these men displayed a preference for adult men over adult women at assessment, their responses to boys were compared to their responses to men; otherwise, their responses to boys were compared to their responses to women; the response to forced versus consenting sex was indexed for the rapists; whereas for the nonoffenders indices were derived for all these categories.

Given that the deviant quotients for each of the patient groups were derived in different ways, we cannot compare across all groups. Therefore, the homosexual child molesters were compared with the nonoffenders on responses to boys relative to responses to adults and these differences were significant $F(,40) = 27.56$, $p < .001$. Rapists, on the other hand, were compared with nonoffenders in terms of their relative responses to forced versus consenting sex and here the differences were not significant, $F(1,45) = 3.05$, $p = .09$. This latter observation is consistent with our recent findings involving a large sample of incarcerated rapists (Baxter, Marshall, Barbaree, Davidson, & Malcolm, 1984) who we found did not differ from a large sample of nonoffender men. The heterosexual child molesters, the incest offenders, and the nonoffenders were compared with one another on their responses to female children relative to their responses to adult women, and there was an overall significant difference between groups, $F(2,69) = 7.06$, $p < .01$. The heterosexual child molesters had higher deviant quotients than both the incest offenders $F(1,69) = 11.57$, p, $< .001$, and the nonoffenders $F(1,69 = 7.41$, $p < .01$, whereas the nonoffenders and the incest offenders and the incest offenders did not differ from one another $(F < 1)$.

Procedure. After the fifth session of attendance at the clinic (including the assessment sessions) or later, if satisfactory rapport had not developed (only 11 of the offenders required more than five sessions to attain satisfactory rapport, and then all but two seemed ready after one extra session), each of the patients was interviewed in depth concerning his use of particular types of sexual stimuli. This procedural tactic may be important, in that all of the earlier studies of the use of pornography by sex offenders appear to have been based on either a single interview or on the completion of a questionnaire.

The sexual preferences of the nonoffenders' subjects were assessed in two sessions (approximately 1½ hours each), and then in a third session they were questioned about their exposure to and use of sexually explicit materials. This, of course, does not match the number of contacts (prior to questioning) that was set for the offenders. The different tactics have made the nonoffenders somewhat more circumspect about revealing their exposure to these materials, although the impression was that they were relaxed and forthright.

Although an explicit interview structure was not used, each subject was asked about access to and use of particular types of sexually explicit materials at pubescence (defined for each subject as the period bounded by approximately 2 years before and after his first ejaculatory release). They were also asked about their current use. For the patients, the questions concerning these issues were asked within the context of a general investigation of their sexual history and current practices, and it typically took two to three sessions to complete this data collection. This procedure was meant to diminish the central relevance of the issue so that the patients might see it as simply part of the overall evaluation of their problem, although they were informed that some of the information gathered from interviews would be used in research reports. They were, of course, guaranteed anonymity, as were the nonoffender subjects. The nonoffenders were told that this single interview (their third contact with us) was aimed at discerning their experience with these materials and that they were part of a research project, although they were not told that their reports would be compared with sex offenders.

Inquiries were made about the content of the materials the patients used. All subjects were told that I was not interested in their use of "soft-core" pornography, which I defined as openly displayed magazines typically available at corner stores, news vendors, etc. As examples of such materials I showed them copies of *Penthouse, Playboy, Hustler,* and *Swank.* What I was interested in, so they were told, was their use of "hard-core" materials, which were defined as those available only in specialized stores (or from illegal sources) and depicting explicit sexual acts with nothing left to the imagination. Again, I provided examples from our stock of materials, which we use in assessment and treatment. Indeed, I defined each category (i.e., forced sex, sex with children, consenting sex between adults) both connotatively and denotatively. For example, I described forced sex as sexual relations between an adult man and an adult woman where the woman displayed a clear unwillingness to participate by both her verbal refusals and her physical attempts to prevent the attack, and the man in the depiction was said to recognize their refusal but ignored it by forcefully enacting his sexual wishes. I described consenting sex between adults as involving a man and a woman engaged in mutually enjoyable sexual relations. Sex with children was described as sex between an adult man and a person under age 14 years. I then provided both magazines' depictions and videotaped scenarios that illustrated unequivocal examples of these three categories of sexual behaviors.

I also investigated the use of these materials, by the patients, in the processes that initiated sexual offenses. In this circumstance, patients were asked whether or not they had used such stimuli, either deliberately or without planning, in the period immediately prior to a sexual offense. All subjects were asked about the occurrence of deviant fantasies (thoughts of rape or of sex with children either during or independent of masturbation), as well as the frequency of their masturbatory activities. Independent occurrence of deviant fantasies was said to occur if the man was prompted to fantasize rape or sex with children when walking about the streets, when watching television, while at the beach, or during daydreams when the man was not being physically stimulated. I omitted from consideration here uses of deviant fantasies while having consenting sex with an adult, although numerous offenders have told us they engage in such practices in order to maintain an appearance of normality by participating in adult heterosexual relations.

Results

The results concerning the use of these materials are described in Table 1. These data summarize the more detailed information collected that illustrated the frequency (*rarely, occasional, frequent*) of use of the materials and the type (consenting vs. force, adult vs. child) of stimuli used at the three different stages. However, this degree of detail has been collapsed. Oddly enough, however, neither access at puberty nor current use reflect a clear preference for content that matches the group categorization of subjects. For instance, child molesters do not have remarkedly higher access to "kiddie porn" than do other subjects, nor do rapists show particularly greater use of forced sex materials than do other subjects.

Access during pubescence was usually a result of seeing the collection of the patient's father or father-surrogate or that belonging to the father of a friend. Although most of these men came across sexually explicit materials as children in a fortuitous manner, at least 11 of them (8 heterosexual child molesters, 1 homosexual child molester, and 2 rapists) actively sought it out. None of the nonoffenders reported seeking out these materials as children.

The percentage data in Table 1 were then subjected to nonparametric analyses appropriate to proportional data (Siegel, 1956). Chi-square analyses revealed significant differences between groups in terms of exposure

Table 1
Use of Any type of "Hard Core" Sexual Stimuli

	Pubescence	Currently	As an Instigator
Heterosexual child molesters	11 (33%)	22 (67%)	12 (36%)
Homosexual child molesters	7 (39%)	12 (67%)	7 (38%)
Incest offenders	0 (0%)	8 (53%)	2 (13%)
Rapists	8 (33%)	19 (83%)	8 (35%)
Non-offenders	5 (21%)	7 (29%)	

during pubescence. $X^2(4,N = 25 = 40.63, p < .001$. There can be no doubt that the absence of any reported exposure by the incest offenders accounts for most of the variance between groups, and indeed, with this group removed from the analyses, the chi-square is no longer significant $X^2(3,N = 25) = 5.37$. In terms of current use, again the analyses revealed significant differences between groups, $X^2(4,N = 68) = 27.37, p < .10$, s001, with the nonoffenders having less current exposure. Dropping the nonoffender group from the analysis resulted in a chi-square that approached significance, $X^2(3,N = 61 = 6.83, p < .10$, suggesting that the incest offenders currently use these materials less than do the other three groups.

Finally, there were significant differences among the four patient groups in whether or not the materials served as an instigator for their crimes, $X^2(4,N = 29) = 13.53, p < .01$. Again, it is the incest subjects who made less use of these materials. On this point, it appears from their descriptions that when the stimuli in question did incite incest offenders, this was accidental in that neither of the two who were occasionally incited to commit incest by looking at sexually explicit materials had looked at the depictions with this in mind. On the other hand, 53% of the child molesters and 33% of the rapists who were so incited, intentionally viewed these materials as part of their deliberate preoffense preparation. On this issue, an unexpected finding, and one that was not explicitly sought after, occurred about one third of the way through the data collection with the patient groups. One of the rapists reported that he characteristically used consenting-sex depictions to incite rape images in the process of preparing himself to attack a woman. Subsequent questioning (which could not entirely avoid having a leading nature to it) revealed a further five rapists who made similar claims and 10 of the 19 rapists who currently used consenting sex depictions for enjoyment (not necessarily preparatory to offending) also said they used it to incite rape fantasies.

It is possible that rates of masturbatory activity differ between offenders and nonoffenders, and this may be related to the distribution of differences in exposure to pornography. Analyses of these data reported in Table 2 indicated an overall significant difference between groups, $X^2(12,N113) = 68.5$, $p <.001$, in the distribution of frequencies of masturbatory activities. Further analyses revealed significant differences within three of four frequency categories (> 1/day: $X^2(4,N = 15) = 24.32$, $p <.001$; $1-2$/wk:$X^2(4,N = 44) = 18.50$, $p <.01$; < 1/wk: $X^2(4,N = 23) = 18.89$, $p < .01$); in the category where masturbation occurred $3-6$/week, there were no significant differences, $X^2(4,N = 31) = 6.80$.

Inspection of Table 2 reveals that the incest group had a frequency distribution across categories that approximated that of the nonoffenders, with the modal frequency occurring in the $1-2$/wk category. The child molesters and the rapists differed from the nonoffenders and the incest offenders by having more subjects who engaged in high rate (> 1/day) masturbatory activity, and the heterosexual child molesters also had more subjects who practiced masturbation at very low rates (< 1/wk).

The data in Table 2 concerning the use of deviant fantasies during masturbation were collapsed into three groups (Always plus Usually; Occasionally plus Rarely; and Never) in order to simplify the analyses. Analyses of these data revealed significant differences between groups, $x^2(8, N = 113) = 227.11$, $p < .001$. These differences occur most profoundly in the highest frequency category, $x^2(4, N = 38) = 115.76$, $p < .001$, and in the totally absent category, $x^2(4,N = 25) = 94.40$, $p < .001$. Although the distribution of differences in the "Occasionally plus Rarely" category was also significant, $X^2(4, N = 50) = 16.95$, $p < .01$, it was not so pronounced as in the other two categories. The distribution of the proportions of rapists and heterosexual child molesters across categories is quite similar with each group having proportionally more men who use deviant fantasies quite commonly during masturbation. Very few of the rapists and none of the heterosexual child molesters fell into the category of never having deviant thoughts when masturbating. Similarly, none of the homosexual child molesters fell into this category, although slightly more of them were occasional or rare users rather than frequent users of deviant masturbatory fantasies. On the other hand, none of the incest subjects and none of the nonoffenders made frequent use of deviant fantasies when masturbating, and each of these groups had

Table 2
Masturbation and Deviant Fantasies*

| | Rate of Masturbation | | | |
	>1/day	3-6/week	1-2/week	<1/week
Heterosexual child molesters	21	21	24	33
Homosexual child molesters	11	27	39	22
Incest offenders	0	20	60	20
Rapists	17	35	35	13
Non-offenders	8	33	50	8

Use of Deviant fantasies

| | During masturbation | | | | |
	Always	Usually	Occasionally	Rarely	Never
Heterosexual child molesters	30	12	21	36	0
Homosexual child molesters	39	27	17	11	6
Incest offenders	0	0	20	33	47
Rapists	22	30	13	17	18
Non-offenders	0	0	17	29	54

| | Independent of masturbation | | |
	Frequently	Occasionally	Never
Heterosexual child molesters	24	36	40
Homosexual child molesters	44	22	34
Incest offenders	0	13	87
Rapists	22	48	30
Non-offenders	0	8	92

*Data are presented as percentages of each group.

approximately the same proportion of subjects who occasionally or rarely used such fantasies, as they had subjects who never engaged in such practices. The deviant masturbatory fantasies of the nonoffenders, when they did occur, were always of rape. The deviant fantasies of the incest offenders were typically of sex with their own children, but two of these men said they also had fantasies of raping women. Similarly, three of the heterosexual child molesters occasionally fantasized rape, and three of the rapists had on occasion imagined having sex with a young girl.

The analyses of the data concerning the occurrence of masturbatory-independent deviant fantasies revealed a significant difference among groups in their proportional distributions across the frequency categories, $X^2(8,N = 113) = 184.27$, $p < .001$. The distribution reveals very clear differences between the nonoffenders and incest offenders, on the one hand (who almost exactly match each other) and the other three patient groups. Incest offenders and non-offenders rarely have deviant sexual thoughts during daydreams.

In an attempt to understand the relationship between the use of the sexually explicit materials described in this study and other features of the patients, I examined usage in relation to IQ (above or below IQ = 90), deviant sexual quotients (above or below DQ = 0.6), and number of victims (more or less than three victims, this being the approximate average of the three offender groups who made significant use of pornography). The incest offenders and nonoffenders were excluded from this analysis. In none of the groups did the IQ criterion reveal differences in use, whereas the deviant quotient cutoff did discriminate users but only amongst the heterosexual child molesters. Heterosexual child molesters with deviant quotients above 0.6 were more likely than those with deviant quotients below this to use these materials as instigators for their crimes, x^2, N = 33) = 89.64, $p < .001$. However, since deviant quotients and number of victims assaulted are highly related in the heterosexual child molesters, it appears likely from the following data that the more important factor is the number of victims. For these men, $X^2(5,N = 33) = 200.20$, p .001, and for the homosexual child molesters, $X^2(5, N = 18) = 117.59$, $p < .001$, those who had more than three victims each were far more likely to use these sexual stimuli as instigators, and amongst the heterosexual child molesters (but not the homosexuals), offenders with the most victims were also more likely to currently use these materials. There were no differences between the high and low victimization rates in terms of exposure at pubescence. No relationship between use of these materials across any of the categories and the other features (IQ, deviant quotient, and number of victims) of the offenders was apparent amongst the rapists. Perhaps this is because although the rapists had much the same mean number of victims, the variance in these data was far more restricted.

Finally, I looked at the relationship between the use of pornography and the frequency of masturbation. Here I will only report the relationship, with respect to current use and use as an instigator, amongst the heterosexual child molesters since they were the only group where this relationship was apparent. High-frequency masturbations (those who reported rates of either > 1/day or 3–6/week, i.e., 42% of the group) were far more likely to be current users, $X^2(,N = 33) = 103.85$, $p < .001$, and were far more likely to use the materials as an instigator in their crimes, $X^2(5,N = 33) = 54,02$ $p < .001$, than were those who masturbated less frequently (those who reported rates of 1–2/wk or less; i.e., 57% of the group).

Discussion

It is important to recall that the sexually explicit materials of interest in this study refer to what is often called "hard-core" pornography; that is, depictions that are very explicit, showing genital contact, etc. and which leave nothing to the imagination. Also the content of these explicit materials was restricted to either depictions of sex with children or sex between adult men and women that was either mutually consenting or forced by the man upon the woman. Therefore, the present findings cannot be construed as relevant to any broader issues concerning pornography in general.

Child molesters (heterosexual and homosexual) and rapists were more frequently exposed to these sexual stimuli during pubescence (±2 years from first ejaculatory release) than were incest offenders. However, the nonoffenders were also exposed to these very explicit materials during pubescence. As adults, the child molesters and rapists made more use of these materials than did either the nonoffenders or the incest offenders. Similarly, the child molesters and rapists were more likely to entertain fantasies during masturbatory activities, and during nonmasturbatory daydreams, than were the incest offenders or the nonoffenders. On this point, it is interesting to note that the rates of masturbatory activities of the nonoffender men and the men who had molested their own children matched that reported in earlier studies of male college students (Arafat & Cotton, 1974). On the other hand, the frequency of masturbatory activities of the child molesters and the rapists revealed that a larger proportion of them engaged in either very high rates of masturbation or very low rates; the heterosexual child molesters were particularly characteristic in this regard.

One very important set of observations of the present study concerns the use of sexually explicit materials by sex offenders as an incitor to commit their illegal behaviors. Slightly more than one third of the child molesters and rapists claim to have at least occasionally been incited to commit an offense by exposure to one or the other type of the sexual materials specified in this study. For some of them, the role of sexual depiction as an instigator to offend was accidental, or at least the stimuli were not deliberately sought out to excite them to offend. However, amongst these child molesters who were incited, 53% of them deliberately used the stimuli in their typical planned preparation for offending, as did 33% of the rapists who were incited to offend by these materials. The demonstration of relationships between the use of sexual stimuli as instigators to offend, the strength of deviant sexual interest (as measured by deviant quotients), and the rates of masturbatory activities, strengthens the conviction that child molesters (in particular) are preoccupied with deviant thoughts that unfortunately appear to mediate a high rate of sexual offending.

A serendipitous finding concerns the observed use of consenting sexual stimuli by the rapists. Although the data set are not complete on this issue, six of the eight rapists who were incited to offend by sexual materials had at least occasionally used "consenting" stimuli to elicit rape fantasies which in turn led to the commission of a rape (or an attempt to committing a rape). Similarly, 10 of the 19 rapists who reported currently using "consenting" materials (not necessarily incitefully) did so in order to evoke rape fantasies.

The present data are, therefore, consistent with our earlier hypotheses regarding the use of sexually explicit materials by sex offenders and point to the need to consider these issues in both the treatment of offenders and in programs aimed at preventing sexual crimes. Of course, it is possible that the use of these stimuli by sex offenders reflects the generally deviant sexual appetites of these men. According to this view, rather than exposure to sexual materials contributing to their deviance, the fact that these offenders seek it out is simply another manifestation of their basic deviant interests.

Clearly, a proportion of rapists and child molesters use sexually explicit stimuli to incite both deviant sexual fantasies and deviant sexual acts. However, given that even the sight of women or children on the street prompts these men to entertain deviant sexual fantasies (i.e., they have masturbatory-independent deviant thoughts), it is clear that their tendency to engage in such thoughts is of importance for treatment. Nevertheless, any treatment program for these men must include consideration, not just of the rate and intensity of deviant thoughts, but also of the possible functional relationship between exposure to sexually explicit materials and these deviant thoughts. Similarly, treatment programs should attend to the possible link between exposure to such stimuli and the actual offensive acts of these men. Furthermore, one must also consider the way in which sexually explicit depictions may encourage, or at least support, negative attitudes toward women and children particularly in sexual matters. Finally, it is important to note for treatment considerations that the role of these depictions as sexually offensive behavior is not as apparent amongst incest offenders as it is in the other groups studied herein.

REFERENCES

Arafat, I. S., & Cotton, W. L. (1974). Masturbation practices of males and females. *Journal of Sex Research, 10,* 293–307.

Baxter, D. J., Marshall, W. I., Barbaree, H. E., Davidson, P. R., & Malcolm, P. B. (1984). Differentiating sex offenders by criminal and personal history, psychometric measures, and sexual responses. *Criminal Justice and Behavior, 11,* 477–501.

Cline, V. (1974). *Where do you draw the line?* Provo, UT: Brigham Young University Press.

Cochrane, P. (1978). Sex crimes and pornography revisited. *International Journal of Criminology and Penology, 6,* 307–317.

Commission on Obscenity and Pornography. (1970). *The technical report of the Commission on Obscenity and Pornography.* Washington, DC: U.S. Government Printing Office.

Court, J. H. (1976). Pornography and sex crimes: A re-evaluation in the light of recent trends around the world. *International Journal of Criminology and Penology, 5,* 129–157.

Earls, C. M., & Marshall, W. L. (1983). The current state of technology in the laboratory assessment of sexual arousal patterns. In J. G. Greer & I. R. Stuart (Eds.). *The sexual aggressor: Current perspectives on treatment* (pp. 336–362). New York: Van Nostrand Reinhold.

Eysenck, H. J., & Nias, D. K. B. (1976). *Sex, violence and the media.* London: Maurice Temple Smith.

Goldstein, M. J., Kant, H. S., & Harman, J. J. (1973). *Pornography and sexual deviance.* Berkeley, CA: University of California Press.

Kutchinsky, B. (1971). Towards an explanation of the decrease in registered sex crimes in Copenhagen. In *Technical report of the Commission on Obscenity and Pornography* (Vol. 7, pp. 263–310). Washington, DC: U.S. Printing Office.

Marshall, W. L., & Barbaree, H. E. (1984). A behavioral view of rape. *International Journal of Law and Psychiatry, 7,* 51–77.

Siegel, S. (1956). *Nonparametric statistics for the behavioral sciences.* New York: McGraw-Hill.

Ward, P., & Woods, G. (1972). *Law and order in Australia.* Sydney: Angus & Robertson.

Chapter 7

ESTIMATING THE MAGNITUDE AND MECHANISMS OF COPYCAT CRIME

RAY SURETTE

Introduction: Media and the Imitation of Crime. It is generally perceived by the police, news media, and the public that certain individuals copy crimes that are publicized by the news and entertainment media. Historically, references to possible copycat effects emerge simultaneously with the birth of the mass media in the early 1800s.[1] And although the term "copycat crime" has appeared in the literature for a number of years (see Eysenck and Nias, 1978; Toplin, 1975; Berkowitz et al., 1978; Siegel, 1974), there are only a few empirical studies that touch upon this phenomenon. Researchers have relied on anecdotal evidence to argue the existence of a copycat phenomenon. Aside from this collection of anecdotal evidence, little is known about the extent of copycat crime or the copycat criminal. Not surprisingly, there is a dearth of explanatory, descriptive, or predictive models and a number of basic questions have not been answered. Is copycat crime a persistent social phenomena? How common a phenomenon is copycat crime and what, if any, is the prevalent form or mechanism of copycat crime? Does the media predominantly provide criminal motivations and values, and/or specific crime techniques to copycat criminals? What kind of individuals are most likely to be copycat criminals? Is the media more relevant to established career criminals or to novice first offenders, to violent or to property offenders? Is there a discernible pattern or constant relationship between publicity and the appearance of copycat crimes? What societal factors are important and are there cultural or ethnic differences

---

1. Police court reporting was thusly described in 1828, "[it is] of little benefit to the cause of morals thus to familiarize the community, and especially the younger parts of it, to the details of misdemeanor and crime. . . . besides, it suggests to the novice in vice all the means of becoming expert in its devices" (Bleyer, 1927:157 quoting New York Evening Post., June 6, 1828).

in the genesis of copycat crime? What policies might be effective and acceptable in reducing copycat crime?

A major reason why so many issues remain unaddressed is that there are inherent difficulties in researching copycat crime. For a crime to be defined as a copycat crime there must be a generating impetus from an earlier publicized crime—a media-linked pair of crimes must exist. The perpetrators of copycat crimes must have been exposed to the publicity of an original initial crime and have incorporated major elements into their crimes. The nature, choice of victim, motivation, or technique of a copycat crime must be lifted from an earlier media-portrayed crime. Research is further complicated because the size of the "at-risk" pool of individuals who are likely to be criminally influenced by the media is unknown, but is postulated to be small and therefore difficult to isolate, and, regardless, has not been characterized or identified well enough to initiate experimental research. Due to these limitations, the simple identification of copycat cases is problematic, in that two independent but similar crimes may be erroneously labeled as a copycat pair or a true copycat crime may go unrecognized and unidentified. Lastly, the possible ways that the media can induce crime can be either qualitatively or quantitatively,[2] making the specification of a general "copycat" process difficult. Subsequently nearly all of the evidence and information regarding copycat crime consists of anecdotal reports rather than empirical data. That being the case, what is the evidence that copycat crime is a persistent significant occurrence as opposed to being just a rare ephemeral social aberration not worthy of policy attention?

The Persistence of Copycat Crime. The compiled anecdotal reports provide a slowly growing file of case studies of imitative crime which indicates that criminal events which are rare in real life have sometimes been committed soon after they were shown as part of a dramatic fictional show or a news account (Cook et al., 1983). Collectively, this file provides significant and growing evidence of the persistent reality of a copycat crime phenomena. Examples include a Canadian boy who attempted to extort $50,000 from a local mayor after watching an episode of "Starsky and Hutch" (Nettler, 1982) and a case in which a nine-year-

---

2. Wilson and Herrnstein (1983) suggest five ways that do not include specific copying: (1) by raising our desire for certain things, (2) by suggesting that things we desire are more accessible than we had thought and increase our awareness of opportunities to acquire them illegally, (3) by increasing the envy of persons who own things, (4) by increasing the excitement and satisfaction derived from crime, and (5) by encouraging instant gratification and impulsiveness.

old girl was raped by several girls on a California beach a few days after a television movie containing a similar rape scene was shown. In Boston, a woman was doused with gasoline and set afire following a movie on television in which teenage boys roam Boston burning tramps. The same evening that a television movie of a battered wife who pours gasoline on her sleeping husband was shown, a man poured gasoline on his sleeping wife and set her afire. An eleven-year-old boy copied an adventure show by murdering a postman. Another eleven-year-old boy, who became fascinated by strangulation scenes on television, strangled a four-year-old girl (Toplin, 1975). Murders and delinquent gangs in England developed based on the movie *A Clockwork Orange*. A number of extortion calls to airlines relating a pressurized bomb threat followed the plot of a television movie *Doomsday Flight*.

In an extensive review of the relationship between terrorism and the media, Schmid and De Graaf (1982) conclude that while extra-media factors are probably at least equally important, media coverage is sufficient to lead to acts of imitative terrorism. The effects of this coverage on copycat crime is twofold. First, anecdotal evidence exists which indicates that the coverage encourages false threats and bluffs in pseudo copycat reactions. For example, a May 1981 bombing in New York City's Kennedy Airport was followed by over 600 bomb threats the next week (Mazur, 1982:407). Secondly, real copycat events follow in significant numbers in a process termed "contagion" in the terrorism literature. Again, much anecdotal evidence is available that events such as corpse stealing for ransom, hostage bank robberies, kidnappings, hijackings, parachute hijackings (27 from 1971 to 1977), and airline altitude bomb plantings occur in clusters (Livingstone, 1982:71 see also Schmid and De Graaf, 1982: 128–136). These effects appear to be especially strong following a successful terrorist act using a novel approach (Bassiouni, 1979:19). Although their number waxes and wanes, the historical pattern of these cases suggests that copycat crime has been and remains a persistent element of the total crime picture.

Further support for copycat crime's reality and significance is established by the reported association between levels of media coverage of an event and the number of subsequent similar events. Aggregate empirical evidence of such a relationship is supplied by Phillips (1974, 1979, 1980, 1982b, 1983, Chapter 5) and others in reports that the likelihood and number of suicides increases significantly with the level of coverage of a suicide in the media.[3] The most disturbing finding is that media portrayals of suicide, whether in the news (Phillips and Carstensen, 1986) or when placed within anti-suicide programming (Gould and Shaffer, 1986), appear to trigger imitative suicides, particularly among teenagers. This set of research indicates that fictional and non-fictional stories that are widely publicized by the mass media appear to produce fatal imitative acts. Although not without contradiction, in total, the anecdotal cases when combined with the media suicide research supports the conclusion that copycat crime is persistent.[4] However, how much it is affecting crime, its prevalence, is not clear.

The Prevalence of Copycat Crime. The anecdotal cases broadly suggest that copycat crime can affect societal crime in two ways. In the first scenario, the media both trigger the occurrence of crime and shape its form, creating crime that otherwise would not exist and criminalizing prior law-abiding individuals. The result is an immediate increase in the quantity of crime in society. In the second scenario, the media shapes the ongoing criminal behavior of established criminals in society, molding the quality of crime without actually triggering it through the sophistication or brutalization of criminals. The Ronny Samora murder case in which a youth stomps an elderly female neighbor to death and claims "television intoxication" as a defense is a well-known anecdotal example of the first model. Terrorist airline hijackings exemplify the second model. However, due to the research and identification difficulties detailed previously there are no direct measures of copycat crime's actual prevalence within either scenario. But an estimate of the prevalence of copycat crime can be made by referring to the literature concerning the relationship between media and aggregate crime rates. For if aggregate crime rates are media influenced, then the number of people being criminogenically influenced can be hypothesized to be large and the pool of potential copycat criminal's significant.

In the best study of aggregate crime and the media, Hennigan and her

---

3. Phillips (1974) calculated that within two months after the suicide of Marilyn Monroe in 1962, for example, there were three hundred more suicides in this country than would have occurred in the absence of her death (see also Stack, 1987; Bollen and Phillips, 1981; Phillips and Hensley, 1984).

4. A 1973 study by Milgram and Shotland (1973) addressed the issue of a media portrayal of crime directly causing individual adults to commit a similar crime. They found no evidence of an immediate effect of a single portrayal of a crime followed by an opportunity to commit a similar crime a week later. The difficulty with this study is that an effect would have to be incredibly strong for a single show to affect a random sample of noncriminal adults to steal or not (cf. Comstock, 1983:252). The suicide studies are felt to measure the influence of the media upon pre-disposed individuals rather than a random population.

colleagues (1982) examined aggregate crime rates in the U.S. prior to and following the introduction of television in the 1950s. Using state-wide and city-wide data, they report that the introduction of commercial television is not associated with increases in the rates of violent crime but is associated with increases in the rates of selective property crimes. The criminogenic effect of television is attributed to exposure to high levels of material consumption and the hypothesized development of feelings of relative deprivation and frustration by viewers, rather than to the social learning or imitation (Hennigan et al., 1982:461), regarding an aggregate effect of newspapers, although some research reports effects (Berkowitz and Macaulay, 1971; Payne and Payne, 1970). Overall, consistent evidence of a general criminal effect between newspapers and crime has not been discovered (cf. Dominick, 1978; Payne, 1974).

In sum, this research leads to greater concerns regarding the electronic than the print media while indicating that there is a large pool of individuals that can be criminally influenced in some degree by the media. How many "at-risk" or potential copycat criminals exist? For terrorism, one estimate that has circulated is as follows.

> Typical reporting of a terrorist event might reach an audience of conservatively 40,000,000 people. If we were to consider that just 1/10 of one percent of the audience were borderline psychopaths, that would be 40,000 potential maniacs. If we took on 1/1000 of one percent we're still got 400. If we took 1/100,000 of one percent, we would still have the four that are necessary to carry out a typical terrorist episode (McEwen quoted by Alexander, 1978:105).

In addition to such hypothetical estimates, there do exist a limited number of studies and reports which directly attempt to assess the proportion of copycat criminals in the offender population. In one study, Heller and Polsky (1976) interviewed 100 young male offenders and found that 22% report trying criminal techniques seen on television, with only 3 of the 22 reporting failure or arrest. An additional 22% further relate that they have contemplated committing crimes seen on television. In another interesting report compiled by an incarcerated life term offender, Hendrick (1977) surveyed 208 of 688 inmates at Michigan's Marquette Prison regarding television as a source of crime techniques. He reports that many prisoners take notes while watching crime shows and that 9 out of 10 inmates state that they had learned new tricks and had increased their criminal expertise by watching crime programs. In addition, 4 out of 10 report that they have attempted specific crimes seen on television. Lastly, in an unpublished 1984 pilot study, 71 randomly selected adult male inmates incarcerated at The Federal Correctional Institution at Butner, North Carolina were surveyed concerning their perceptions of the media, crime, and the prevalence and form of copycat crime (Pease and Love, 1984a). In the study about one-fifth (21%) of the inmates report that they have attempted crimes seen in the media.

The above results are interesting and suggestive but are inconclusive due to the limited samples and methodologies and the fact that all three efforts examine only offender populations. Whether the results generalize to a wider population of offenders or non-offenders is unknown. In addition, none examined for differences between the self-reported copycat criminal and non-copycat criminals. With these limitations in mind, the anecdotal events combined with the restricted offender research indicates that the current best supposition is that copycat crimes are largely limited to and significant among the pre-existing offender population (influencing somewhere between 20 and 40 percent), are rare but not nonexistent among the general non-criminal population. In the anecdotal case histories, most of the individuals who mimic media crimes have pre-existing criminal records or histories of violence, supporting the contention that the effect of the media is more qualitative (affecting criminal behavior) rather than quantitative (affecting the number of criminals).[5] Limited empirical support for this position is also provided by the offender studies. Heller and Polsky state (1976: 151–152):

> A significant number of our subjects, already embarked on a criminal career, consciously recall and relate having imitated techniques of crimes... for such men, detailed portrayals of criminal techniques must be viewed as a learning process. None of our subjects ascribed any causative role to television viewing... they would, in all probability, have engaged in the same pursuits, but their style was influenced to some degree by previously having watched skillful experts perform similar tasks on television.

Hendricks (1977) and Pease and Love (1982a) also report that the media is seldom cited by offenders as a motivating source. Pease and Love (1982a) report that only about 12% of the inmates in their study cite the media as a cause in their criminality, ranking it second to last behind all other possible factors except for "too much junk food." As a source of information about crime techniques, however, 21% of the inmates endorse

---

5. See Comstock, 1980; Dominick, 1978; Lewis, 1984; Greene and Bynum, 1982; Huesmann, 1982:132; NCCPV, 1969:376–378).

the media as a source for crime techniques, with books and magazines followed closely by movies about crime as the most often cited media components. In sum, the media ranks fourth as a crime information source behind "developing techniques by myself," "friends," and "fellow inmates."[6] Pease and Love (1984b) also conclude that except for isolated cases of mentally ill individuals, copycat offenders possess a criminal intent to commit a particular crime before they copy a publicized technique. Holding true for terrorist acts, few reports suggest a copycat crime occurs because an otherwise law-abiding person was influenced by the media to do so (cf. Schmid and de Graff, 1982). The scenario of the media triggering copycat crimes is not found to be pervasive or significant. But the shaping of ongoing crime by pre-existing criminals is forwarded as substantively important and as a hypothesized source of significantly increased crime in society. For copycat crime, the media appears to be a rudder more than a trigger.

The Mechanisms of Copycat Crime. By what mechanism does the media input its copycat effects? Here, again, direct research is limited. In that the concept implies the imitation of an initial crime, the most obvious starting point to discuss copycat crime mechanisms is with imitation, and copycat crime has been credited to a simple and direct imitative process (Livingstone, 1982; Bassiouni, 1981; Schmid and de Graaf, 1982). Gabriel Tarde in the beginning decades of this century is the first to offer a theoretical discussion of copycat crime. Focusing on violent crime and observing that sensational violent crime appears to prompt similar incidents, he coined the term "suggesto-imitative assaults" to describe the phenomena. In a pithy summation, he concluded (1912) that: "Epidemics of crime follow the line of the telegraph." However, Tarde's line of research was largely ignored until the 1970s when a surge of copycat crimes and media interest in them resulted in renewed attention to the role of imitation in the generation of crime. However, imitation has been critiqued as too simplistic a process to fully understand copycat crime. Hence, Pease and Love (1984b) fault imitation theory as an adequate explanation of copycat crime because it fails to explain why most children imitate aggression within socially acceptable limits and only a few imitate aggression with a real gun. They also note that

---

6. These categories are similar to the general information sources influencing attitudes. Personal experiences, family and friends, and peer groups rank before the media as general influence sources.

imitation theory focuses on the copycat criminal and tends to downplay other contextual social factors.

As when estimating the prevalence of copycat crime, it is necessary to examine research from other areas to derive a comprehensive conception of a copycat crime mechanism. Looking first at mechanisms for copying aggressive behaviors, the 1982 National Institute of Health report *Television and Behavior* (NIMH, 1982:38–39) forwards two mechanisms by which violent media appear to encourage viewer aggressive behaviors: "observational learning" and "supportive attitude changes." In observational learning, children learn aggression in the same way they learn cognitive and social skills: from watching parents, siblings, peers, teachers, and the media. Demonstrated in many laboratory studies, children imitate aggressive behavior immediately after they have seen it on film or television, and field studies provide support for this process occurring in natural settings. In addition, the more television children watch, the more accepting are their attitudes toward aggressive behavior. Looking at violent scenes for even a very brief time makes young children more willing to accept the aggressive behavior of other children. This acceptance of aggression also makes it likely that the children will themselves be more aggressive.[7]

The majority of reviewers of this research agree that there is significant evidence of a causal effect of media violence on subsequent viewer aggression.[8] The research also reveals, however, that violent media does not affect all viewers in a similar fashion and has indicated a number of specific factors as significant in the determination of a media effect.[9] In sum, it is obvious that while there are positive correlations between watching media violence and aggressive behavior, people do not become aggressive or violent solely from watching television or

---

7. Two other mechanisms are mentioned but are currently lacking supportive evidence (see Pearl, 1984): "Psychological Arousal Processes"—physiological arousal is thought to have three possible consequences: (1) desensitization, (2) general arousal increase that will boost aggressiveness, or (3) desensitized persons who may act aggressively to raise their levels of arousal. All these arousal theories need empirical verification. "Justification"—people who are already aggressive like to look at violent tv so they can then justify their own behavior. Watching violence is a result, rather than a cause.

8. See Murray, 1980, Lewis, 1984; Andison; 1977; The National Institute of Mental Health, 1982; Phillips, 1982a, 1982b; Comstock, 1975; Comstock and Fisher, 1975; Comstock and Lindsey, 1975; Comstock et al., 1978; Garofalo, 1978).

9. Following his review of the relevant literature Comstock (1980:250–251) cites 12 factors as interactive or important in determining the effect a particular piece of violent media has on a particular viewer. Most of the factors relate to characteristics of the media, not of the viewers, a focus that reveals a deficiency in the approach of the general research in this area.

violent movies (Signorielli and Gerbner, 1988:xxi). In a similar manner, the media does not appear to create criminals but instead influences those we have. Furthermore, although the process of imitation is most often described as simple observation followed by learning, it is apparent that observational learning is not the only media influence to produce imitation (cf. Berkowitz, 1984; see also Bandura, 1965, 1971, 1973). It is better to consider imitation as a necessary but not sufficient factor in the production of copycat crime. Imitation's primary flaw is that it generally implies that the reproduced action be physically similar to the portrayed behavior and therefore falls short in explaining any generalized effects or innovative applications (Berkowitz, 1984:414). Note that Hennigan et al. (1982) earlier dismiss imitation as an explanation for the aggregated criminal effects they discover, and the offender studies found more linkages to property crime than violent crime (cf. Hendricks, 1977; Heller and Polsky, 1976). The media and aggression research indicates that a three-prong interactive model operates concerning the media and its effects on individual aggressive behavior (cf. Berkowitz, 1984). Characteristics of the content of the media, the setting in which it is viewed, and the viewer all interact to determine what effects, if any, a particular exposure to media will have on the subsequent behavior of each viewer.[10] This gives the media significant aggregated effects but individual level effects which are difficult to predict.[11]

In addition to a multi-factor imitation based process, Berkowitz (1984) has forwarded an additional mechanism more general than imitation by which the media can activate observed behavior. Termed a "priming" effect, the media-portrayed behaviors are felt to activate a network of associated ideas and concepts within the viewer and increase the likelihood that similar but not necessarily identical behaviors will occur (Berkowitz, 1984:414).[12] Berkowitz feels that priming offers a conceptual explanation of both prosocial and anti-social media effects, as well as the

---

10. Comstock (1983:255–256) for example concludes: "contrary results [should not be viewed] in the role of disconfirmation but in that of qualification. They simply demonstrate that in some circumstances a relationship does not occur, either because of attributes of the subjects, the particular portrayals involved, or the circumstances of exposure or subsequent behavior.

11. The 1982 NIMH report (1982:89–90) concedes "A distinction must be made, however, between groups and individuals. All the studies that support the causal relationships demonstrate group differences. None supports the case for particular individuals. . . . This distinction does not, of course, minimize the significance of the findings, even though it delimits their applicability."

12. This concept is analogous to the "cognitive maps" Graber (1980) forwards to explain the effects of crime news on viewers.

effects reported in the suicide, and aggregate crime effect studies discussed earlier. He concludes that priming occurs within a multi-factor model incorporating media content, viewer interpretation, viewer characteristics, and viewing settings. The media can thus encourage and instruct criminal behavior through priming processes, desensitization to violence, and attitude changes, as well as the direct imitation of behavior. For the pre-disposed individual, especially those who rely heavily on the media for worldly information and escape and have a tenuous grasp of reality, the influence can be significant. The evidence which is available concerning copycat crime supports the contention of pre-disposed "at-risk" individuals, who are primed by media crime characterizations, being the primary agents of copycat crime (Comstock, 1980:131).

Copycat Crime: A Model. The above proposition leads to a copycat crime model similar to the multi-factor media-aggression model. Copycat crime is the result of the interaction of factors from four areas: the initial crime, media coverage, societal contextual factors, and copycat criminal characteristics as shown in Figure 1.

FIGURE 1.
A REITERATIVE COPY CAT
CRIME MODEL

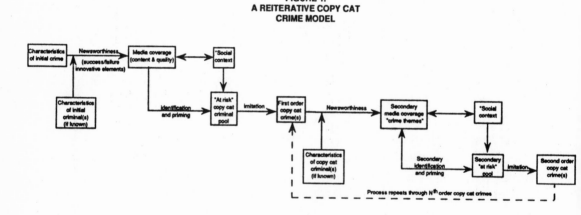

* Includes: Social norms regarding crime and news reporting, opportunities to copy, social tensions, (racism, economic strife, etc.) organization of mass media (state, private, profit, non-profit, accessibility, regulation, audience size and credibility).

The above model denotes a process in which select, usually highly newsworthy and successful initial crimes and criminals (after interacting with media coverage) emerge as candidates to be copied. The first media effects are felt to be identification with the initial crime or criminal and general priming effects on a pool of potential "at-risk" copycat criminals. The size of this potential pool is affected by both the media coverage and other social context factors such as norms regarding deviance and violence, the existence of social conflicts, the number of opportunities available to employ a copycat crime technique (there are more sites to employ a copycat car theft than a copycat bank robbery), the nature and pervasiveness of the mass media (private, competitive, ratings sensitive) and the size of the pre-existing criminalized population. Media coverage and content and the social context are felt to mutually influence each other (cf. Meyrowitz, 1985). Then via a process of imitation bounded by opportunity copycat crimes result. Should these first-order copycat crimes receive further media attention and particularly if they should become incorporated into a news media crime theme, the likelihood of additional order copycat crime increases (cf. Fishman, 1978). This theoretical model is offered as a first step in developing an empirically based theory of copycat crime by directing data collection efforts toward testing and measuring its posited relationships. The specification of the characteristics of the model's components and the measurement of the magnitude and nature of the paths between the components (or its empirical rejection) will hopefully result in an understanding of copycat crime great enough to aid in associated policy development.

Conclusion. Of the set of questions posed at the beginning of this chapter, which ones can responses be forwarded to? The materials available suggest the following. Copycat crime appears to be a persistent social phenomena, common enough to influence the total crime picture mostly by influencing crime techniques rather than criminal motivations. A copycat criminal is more likely a career criminal involved in property offenses rather than a first offender of violent offenses (although a violent copycat episode will receive an immense amount of media coverage when identified). The specific relationship between coverage and the generation of copycat crime remains unknown as do the social context factors that are most important. The best candidate mechanism of copycat crime is through a process of identification and priming leading to some degree of generalized imitation. Lastly, regarding the question of inducing non-criminals to commit crimes, there is no empirical evidence of a significant criminalizing media effect (Comstock, 1980:131; cf. Milgram and Shotland, 1973). The current perspective is that the media has the ability to influence how people commit crimes to a far greater extent than whether they actually commit crime.[13]

Regarding policies, the basic copycat crime policy problem is deciding when to publicize information about sensational crimes. The proper
decision in such cases as the Tylenol poisonings[14] is clear, in that there
is an obvious need to warn consumers of a poisoned, over-the-counter
drug, but in non-product tampering crimes such as bombings the issue is
unresolved. The news media argues that the decision to publish is
correct in nearly every case, while law enforcement and other public
officials argue for restrictions.[15] More proactive policies focus on the
initial coverage given crimes and the suggested reforms include delaying
coverage, avoiding live coverage, using screen crawl lines rather than
program interruptions, downplaying staged events and the celebritizing
and heroizing of criminals, avoiding crime "educational" coverage, and,
finally, providing fuller reporting and follow-up stories that deal with
prosecution and punishment noting that most identified copycat crimes
are usually unsuccessful. The best policy course at this time may be in
the defining of the characteristics of the "at risk" copycat population
with subsequent attempts to limit the size of that population via deterrence efforts. It should be recognized in the final analysis, however, that
some level of copycat crime may be an unavoidable negative aspect
which accompanies the benefits of a free private mass media.

---

13. There is a large body of detailed material on how to commit specific crime readily available through
publishers such as Paladin Press. For example, the following basic crime instruction manuals are listed in
their 1986 catalog: *Gunrunning for Fun and Profit, Expedient Hand Grenades, Improvised Explosives: How to
Make Your Own; New I.D. in America; The Complete Book of International Terrorism; How to Kill* (6 volumes);
The Perfect Crime and How to Commit It. These texts are complete with diagrams and directions to commit
robberies, murder, and numerous acts of terrorism. Historically, such "how to" manuals can be traced to
the writings of Johann Most, *Revolutionary War Science* ((1885) who published instructions on making
nitroglycerin and dynamite, inflammable liquids and poisons and advocated their use in radical bombings
and attacks. The 1886 Chicago Haymarket Square bombing is thought to be a result (Papke, 1987:171–172).

14. The initial murders occurred after the victims had purchased Extra-Strength Tylenol that had been
laced with cyanide. After the story broke, it received intense national coverage and within a short time
copycat poisonings and product tamperings were reported around the nation.

15. The confusion surrounding the best policy course in regards to copycat crime is exemplified by one
commentator, "There seems to be only one way to end the copycat tamperings. I think it will be short
lived . . . before long, copycat tamperings will become so common that they will no longer provide thrill
seekers with the excitement that they crave" (quoted by Church, 1982:27). This non-sequitur that copycat
crime will disappear by becoming common is interpreted that they will be less newsworthy, receive less
coverage, and therefore become less likely to occur. A plausible but unproven proposition.

REFERENCES

Bandura, A. (1965). Influence of models' reinforcement contingencies on the acquisition of imitative responses. *J. of Person. and Soc Psych.*, 1:589–595.

Bandura, A. (1971). *Social Learning Theory.* N.Y., General Learning Press.

Bandura, A. (1973). *Aggression: A Social Learning Analysis.* Prentice-Hall.

Bandura, A., Ross, D. and Ross, S. (1963). Imitation of film-mediated aggressive models. *J. of Ab. and Soc. Psych.*, 66:3–11.

Bassiouni, M. (1979). Prolegomenon to terror violence, 12 *Creighton L. Rev.:*745–752.

Bassiouni, M. (1981). Terrorism, law enforcement, and the mass media: Perspectives, problems, proposals. *J. of Crim. Law & Criminology.* 72: 1–51.

Berkowitz, L. (1984). Some effects of thoughts on anti- and prosocial influences of media events: A cognitive-neoassociation analysis. *Psych. Bulletin,* 95:410–417.

Berkowitz, L., and Macaulay, J. (1971). The contagion of criminal violence. *Sociometry.* 34:238–260.

Berkowitz, L. et al. (1978). Experiments on the reactions of juvenile delinquents to filmed violence. In L.A. Hersov and M. Berger (eds.) *Aggression and Antisocial Behavior in Childhood Adolescence.* Oxford: Pergamon Press.

Bleyer, W. (1927). *Main Currents in the History of American Journalism.* Houghton Mifflin.

Bollen, K. A. and Phillips, D. (1981). Suicidal motor vehicle fatalities in Detroit: A replication, *Am. J. of Soc.* 87:404–412.

Church, G. (1982). "Copy cats are on the prowl" *Time.* Nov.:27.

Comstock, G. (1975). *Television and Human Behavior: The Key Studies.* Santa Monica, Rand Corp.

Comstock, G. (1980). *Television in America.* Sage.

Comstock, G. et al. (1978). *Television and Human Behavior.* Columbia Univ. Press.

Comstock, G. and Fisher, M. (1975). *Television and Human Behavior: A Guide to Pertinent Scientific Literature.* Rand Corp.

Comstock, G. and Lindsey, G. (1975). *TV and Human Behavior: The Research Horizon, Future and Present.* Rand Corp.

Cook, T. et al. (1983). "The implicit assumptions of television research: An analysis of the 1982 NIMH report on television and behavior." *Public Opinion Quarterly,* 47:161–201.

Dominick, J. (1978). "Crime and Law Enforcement in the Mass media" in *Deviance and Mass Media.* pgs. 105–128, Sage.

Eysenck, H. and Nias, D. (1978). *Sex, Violence and the Media.* New York: Harper and Row.

Fishman, M. (1978). "Crime waves as ideology" *Soc. Prob.* 25: 531–543.

Garofalo, J. (1982). "Crime and the mass media: A selected review of research," *J. of Res. in Crime and Delin.* 18:319–350.

Gould, M. and Shaffer, D. (1986). "The impact of suicide in television movies" *The New England Journal of Medicine.* 315:690–694.

Graber, D. (1980). *Crime News and the Public.* Praeger.

Greene, J. and Bynum, T. (1982). "T.V. crooks: Implications of latent role models for theories of delinquency" *J. of C.J.* 10: 177–190.

Hans, V. and Slater, D. (1983). "John Hinckley, Jr. and the Insanity Defense: The Public's Verdict" *Public Opinion Quarterly.* 47:202–212.

Heller, M. and Polsky, S. (1976). *Studies in Violence and Television.* American Broadcasting Co.

Hendrick, G. (1977). "When TV is a School for Criminals" *TV Guide,* January, 29.

Hennigan, K. et al. (1982). "Impact of the introduction of television on crime in the United States: Empirical findings and theoretical implications" *J. of Personality and Social Psych.* 42:461–477.

Huesmann, L. R. (1982). "Television violence and aggressive behavior" In *Television and Behavior* vol. 2 U.S. Dept. of Health and Human Services, Wash, D.C. U.S. Govt. Printing Office.

Lewis, R. (1984). "The media" Violence and criminal behavior" in R. Surette pgs. 51–69 *Justice and The Media.* Charles C Thomas, Publisher.

Livingstone, N. (1982). *The War Against Terrorism.* D.C. Heath Pub.

Mazur, A. (1982). "Bomb threats and the mass media: evidence for a theory of suggestion," *A.S.R.* 47:407–411.

Meyrowitz, M. (1985). *No Sense of Place.* Oxford Univ. Press.

Milgram, S. and Shotland, R. (1973). *Television and Antisocial Behavior: Field Experiments.* N.Y. Academic Press.

Murray, J. (1980). *Television and Youth: 25 Years of Research.* Boys Town Center for the Study of Youth Development, Stanford, Wash.

NIMH [National Institute of Mental Health]. (1982). *Television and Behavior: Ten years of scientific progress and implications for the Eighties.* Vol. 1, Summary Report. Rockville, Med. Nat. Inst. of Mental Health.

NCCPV [National Commission on the Causes and Prevention of Violence]. (1969). *Mass Media and Violence.* Vol. 9 and 9a, U.S. Govt. Printing Office.

Nettler, G. (1982). *Killing One Another.* Cincinnati, Oh. Anderson.

Papke, D. (1987). *Framing the Criminal.* Archon Books.

Parke, R. D. et al. (1977). "Some effects of violent and non-violent movies on the behavior of juvenile delinquents" in L. Berkowitz (ed) *Advances in Experimental Social Psychology* (vol. 19) Academic Press.

Payne, D. (1974). "Newspapers and Crime: What happens during strike periods" *Jour. Q.* 51:607–612.

Payne, D. and Payne, K. (1970). "Newspapers and crime in Detroit" *Jour. Q.* 47:233–238.

Pearl, D. (1984). "Violence and Aggression" *Society,* 21:17–20.

Pease, S. and Love, C. (1984a). "The prisoner's perspective of copy cat crime." Paper presented at the Annual Meeting of the American Society of Criminology, Cincinnati, Ohio, November, 1984.

Pease, S. and Love, C. (1984b). "The copy cat crime phenomenon" in R. Surette (ed.) *Justice and the Media.* pg. 199–212, Charles C Thomas.

Phillips, D. (1974). "The influence of suggestion on suicide: Substantive and theoretical implications of the Werther effect." *Am. Soc. Re.,* 39:340–354.

Phillips, D. (1979). "Suicide, motor vehicle fatalities, and the mass media: Evidence toward a theory of suggestion," *Am. J. of Soc.* 84: 1150–1174.

Phillips, D. (1980). "Airplane accidents, murder, and the mass media: Toward a theory of imitation," *Social Forces,* 58:1001–1024.

Phillips, D. (1982a). "The behavioral impact of violence in the mass media: A review of the evidence from laboratory and non-laboratory investigations," *Soc. and Soc. Research,* 66:387–398.

Phillips, D. (1982b). "The impact of fictional television stories on U.S. adult fatalities: New evidence on the effect of mass media on violence," *Am. J. of Soc.*

Phillips, D. (1983). "The impact of mass media violence on U.S. homicides" *Am. Soc. Re.* 48:560–568.

Phillips, D. and Carstensen, L. (1986). "Clustering of teenage suicides after television news stories about suicide" *The New England Journal of Medicine,* 315:685–689.

Phillips, D. and Hensley, J. (1984). "When violence is rewarded or punished: The impact of mass media stories on homicide" *J. of Communication,* Summer:101–116.

Schmid, A. and de Graaf, J. (1982). *Violence as Communication.* Sage.

Siegel, A. "The effects of media violence on social learning" in V.B.Cline (ed.) *Where Do You Draw the Line? An Exploration Into Media Violence, Pornography, and Censorship.* Brigham Young Univ. Press.

Signorielli, N. and Gerbner, G. (1988). *Violence and Terror in the Mass Media.* Westport, Conn. Greenwood Press.

Snow, R. (1984). "Crime and Justice in Prime-time news; The John Hinckley Jr. Case" in Surette (ed.) *Justice and The Media.* pg. 212–232, Charles C Thomas.

Stack, S. (1987). "Celebrities and Suicide: A Taxonomy and Analysis 1948–1983" *Am. Soc. Res.* 52

Tarde, G. (1912). *Penal Philosophy.* Boston little, Brown.

Toplin, R. (1975). *Unchallenged Violence: An American Ordeal.* Westport, Conn., Greenwood.

Trafford, A. et al. (1982). "Lessons that emerge from Tylenol Disaster" *U.S. News and World Report.* Oct, 18:67–68.

USDHHS [U.S. Dept. of Health and Human Services]. (1982). *Television and Behavior.* Volumes 1–2, U.S. Govt. Printing Office.

Wilson, J. Q. and R. Hennerstein. (1986). *Crime and Human Behavior.* Simon and Schuster.

Chapter 8

SEXUALLY VIOLENT MEDIA AND CRIMINAL JUSTICE POLICY

DOROTHY J. IMRICH, CHARLES MULLIN, AND DANIEL LINZ

In this chapter we discuss recent research on the relationship between exposure to pornography and attitudes about rape and rape victims. We then discuss the implications of this research for understanding self-reports of sexual coercion and assault. We then focus upon studies that have attempted to link pornography consumption with criminal behavior including rape and assault. Our review suggests that certain forms of pornography (i.e., violent pornography) may engender antisocial attitudes about rape and rape victims. These same attitudes may, in turn, be predictive of self-reports of sexually coercive behavior. However, there is no definitive evidence of a direct link between exposure to violent pornography and self-reports of sexually coercive behavior. Finally, we explore several promising avenues for future research and criminal justice policy.

Pornography and Attitudes about Crime

Much experimental research in the laboratory and the field since the time of the 1970 Presidential Commission on Obscenity and Pornography has addressed the following question: Are there negative effects on people's attitudes and perceptions about rape and rape victims following exposure to nonviolent or violent sexual materials? Although many of the nonviolent messages used in these studies fit neither contemporary definitions of "hard-core" pornography nor the legal definition of obscenity in most states (Penrod & Linz, 1984), many of these are the studies considered by the Attorney General's Commission on Pornography (1986), which concluded that exposure to certain forms of nonviolent pornography results in antisocial effects.

103

In these experiments, subjects have been asked to watch film clips or listen to messages that last anywhere from a few minutes in a single session to over 15 hours across several weeks. The research is divided into two categories for purposes of discussion: "short-term" and "long-term" exposure. Short-term exposure is defined as subjects viewing, reading or listening to the communication for periods of less than one hour. Long-term exposure is anything beyond an hour. The cutoff at one hour is arbitrary, but the theoretical rational behind separating the studies according to length of stimulus presentation is not. Zillmann and Bryant (1984), as well as others (Berkowitz, 1984), have maintained that *continued* exposure to explicit depictions of women engaged in sexual activity may activate thoughts about female promiscuity in viewers that would not occur with shorter exposure. Presumably, the availability of these thoughts in memory (Tversky & Kahneman, 1973) may lead to inflated estimates of women's tendency to desire and engage in unusual and abnormal sexual activities, including rape.

Short-Term Exposure to Nonviolent vs. Violent Pornography

The effects for the short-term exposure studies are summarized in Table 1. Many studies have included a neutral or no-exposure control group with which to compare subjects exposed to either violent or nonviolent sexually explicit materials. Malamuth, Reisin, and Spinner (1979) had male and female subjects look at issues of *Playboy* and *Penthouse* that contained either nonaggressive scenes or portrayals of sadomasochism and rape. A third group was given neutral materials. Subjects then watched a videotaped interview with an actual rape victim and answered a questionnaire assessing their perception of the victim, attitudes toward the rape act, and beliefs about their own behavior in such situations. Two weeks later subjects were presented copies of newspaper articles on several topics, including one on rape. Results showed no effects for either violent or nonviolent materials relative to the control on perceptions of the rape victim or for attitudes about rape assessed later.

In a study by Intons-Peterson, Roskos-Ewoldsen, Thomas, Shirley, and Blut (1989), subjects were exposed to a 15-minute film segment depicting sexual violence (from the R-rated slasher film *Toolbox Murders*), nonviolent sexuality (from the X-rated film *Pretty Girl*), or neutral activities. Results revealed that exposure to sexual violence produced greater acceptance of rape myths than exposure to either nonviolent sexual or nonviolent nonsexual. Also, in their evaluations of a victim from an

Table 1

Summary of Short-Term Exposure to Pornography and Attitudes Towards Women and Rape

Study	Stimuli	Subjects	Dependent Measures	Results
Malamuth, Haber, & Feshbach (1980)	S's divided into two groups: 1. Approximately 400-word essay describing sado-masochistic heterosexual encounter. 2. Same essay without sadomasochism.	91 male and female college students	1. S's read 500-word depiction of male student raping a resisting female student. 2. S's recommended prison sentence for perpe-trator and indicated willingness to grant parole. Measures of perceptions of assailant: 1. personal identification with the perpetrator 2. ratings of intelligence and attractiveness 3. the justification for and dangerousness of the assault 4. the percentage of men who would behave in the same manner as the perpetrator if assured of not being caught. Measures of perceptions of victim: 1. victim's experience of pain and trauma 2. victim responsibility and level of resistance 3. the percentage of women who would have enjoyed such an experience Females asked about fearfulness of being raped; males asked how likely it was that they would behave like the rapist if assured of not being caught.	*No main effects* for exposure to either the sexually violent or nonviolent sexually explicit communication on any of the per-ception or attitude variables. Several interactions: 1. Males in the violent condition more punitive to the perpetrator. 2. Females in the violent condition were less punitive to the perpetrator. 3. Low aggression-anxious males in violent condition perceived less victim pain than low-anxious S's in the non-violent sexually explicit condition.
Malamuth & Check (1980)	Males heard 1 of 3 audiotapes: 1. Rape story in which the rapist perceives that the victim becomes sexually aroused. 2. Rape in which the victim continually abhors the assault. 3. Mutually desired inter-course story.	109 male college students	All S's listened to "rape criterion" story and rated: 1. the victim's experience 2. the normality of rape 3. the criminal aspect of rape 4. the victim 5. the rapist	1. Significant effect for type of communi-cation on the victim's experience factor. 2. Significant effect for the individual item assessing perceptions of the women's trauma only. 3. Rape-arousal S's rated woman as experiencing less trauma than rape-abhorrence or mutually desired S's. 4. Rape arousal S's indicated greater per-centage of men would rape than rape-abhorrence or mutually desired S's.

Table 1 (continued)

Study	Stimuli	Subjects	Dependent Measures	Results
Linz, Donnerstein, & Penrod (1988)	Males viewed one of three types of films: R-rated violent, R-rated nonviolent (teenage sex), or X-rated nonviolent; or participated as no-exposure control S's.	156 male college students	S's seated in courtroom, with controls recruited only for this phase, and completed pretrial questionnaire. Included in latter was Rape Empathy scale and modified version of Rape Myth Acceptance scale. In addition, three new scales were constructed: 1) Belief in conservative sex roles 2) Endorsement of force in sexual relations 3) Tendency to view women as sexual objects. S's viewed one of two versions of reenactment of rape trial: acquaintance or non-acquaintance. Then S's completed scales measuring: (1) victim sympathy; (2) victim injury; (3) the degree to which victim resisted her assailant; (4) defendant responsibility for assault; (5) victim responsibility for for her own assult; (6) probability of guilt (1 to 9 scale); (7) verdict (guilty; not guilty); and (8) sentence assigned to defendant if guilty (in months and years).	1) "R-rated violent" S's scored lower on the sympathy than other S's. 2) High "R-rated violence" S's had lower scores on rape empathy compared to all other subjects. There were no effects for other dependent variables.
Krafka (1985)	Women exposed to one film per day for 4 days from one of the following categories: 1) sexually explicit but nonviolent stimuli, 2) sexually explicit and sexually violent stimuli, or 3) graphically violent stimuli ("Slasher films").	121 female college students	(1) short form of the Personal Attributes Questionnaire; (2) short form of the Texas Social Behavior Inventory (TSBI) measuring general self-esteem; (3) the Body Esteem Scale (BES); (4) a questionnaire measuring perceived risk of falling victim to 4 types of crime: (a) nonviolent sexual crimes, (b) violent sexual crimes, (c) nonviolent nonsexual crime, and (d) violent nonsexual crime; (5) scales assessing likelihood of subject reporting sexual coercion and assault; (6) Acceptance of Interpersonal Violence scale (AIV); (7) short form of RMA.	"Slasher film" S's differed from controls only with respect to indicators of victimized thinking. Direction of findings showed "Slasher film" subjects claiming a *decreased* sense of vulnerability over the possibility of their being affected by crime, less at risk to nonviolent sexual crime, less at risk to nonviolent nonsexual crime and less at risk to violent nonsexual crime. "Slasher film" S's were also more likely than control subjects to indicate that injury in violent nonsexual

Study	Stimuli	Subjects	Dependant Measures	Results
Donnerstein, Berkowitz, & Linz (1986)	S's angered or treated in neutral manner by female, then S's viewed one of three four-minute films. Nonaggressive pornography depicted young couple in various stages of sexual intercourse, aggressive pornographic condition depicted woman who is tied up, stripped, slapped and raped by a man at gunpoint. Third film not sexually explicit but aggressive in content — same events as aggressive pornographic — but no nudity or simulated sexual activity.	72 male college students	Immediately after viewing films, S's completed dependent measure questionnaires: (1) selected items from Rape Myth Acceptance scale (RMA), (2) males' self-reported willingness to use force to have sex with a woman, and (3) males' self-reported likelihood that they would commit a rape if assured of not being caught or punished.	Both aggressive pornographic and aggressive nonpornographic films produced significantly higher scores on Rape Myth Acceptance scale, and willingness to use force and willingness to rape questions compared to nonagressive pornographic film. Effects occurred regardless of whether or not subjects had been angered by female.
Intons-Peterson, Roskos-Ewoldsen, Thomas, Shirley, & Blut (1987)	S's watched a 15-minute segment from a commercially released film depicting (1) sexual violence, (2) nonviolent sexuality, or (3) neutral content. Then retested on RMA.	105 male college students	S's pretested on RMA scale. S's watched videotaped reenactment of a rape trial and completed battery of questions about victim and defendant.	S's exposed to sexual violence showed greater increase in Rape Myth Acceptance than did groups that saw either nonviolent sexual or nonviolent nonsexual material. Exposure to sexual violence produced greater acceptance of rape myths than exposure to either nonviolent sexual or nonviolent nonsexual material.

Study	Stimuli	Subjects	Dependent Measures	Results
Weaver (1987)	S's exposed to one of five short films (neutral, consensual sex, female-instigated sex, male-coerced sex, and eroticized violence).	60 male and 60 female college students	1) S's given exemplars of man and woman "submissive" or "promiscuous." Then S's rate target on list of 24 adjectives before and after film viewing. 2) Person perception task involved showing S's 16 slides of male and female "peers" and "nonpeers" in nonsexual settings. S's rated each person in the slide on 24 adjectives. 3) Legal judgement task. S's given: a) one-page story about conviction of a man charged with physical abuse of a female cohabitant and b) story about the rape of a female stranger. After reading these stories, subjects indicated: a) the number of years the assailant should be incarcerated for each crime, b) the amount of money the victim should be awarded for damages.	1) "Eroticized violence" and "male-coerced sex" S's rated nonpermissive female peer as less "pleasant" and "innocent" compared to neutral S's. 2) "Female-instigated sex" males rated nonpermissive female more "innocent" than "erotic violence" males. Opposite effect was found among female subjects. 3) "Consensual sex" and "female-instigated sex" males perceived nonpermissive peers as more "permissive" than neutral males. 4) Female-instigated sex males rated nonpermissive peers as less "assertive." 5) Compared to neutral S's, all other S's perceived females as more similar to sexually promiscuous and sexually submissive exemplars. 6) Of four dependant measures, only sentencing for rapist significant: "Female-instigated" S's compared to "consenting sex" or "neutral" S's recommended lower sentence. Nearly identical effect for "male coerced" and "eroticized violence" S's.

enacted rape trial, viewers of the sexually violent slasher film were less favorably disposed toward the victim than the viewers of nonviolent pornography or neutral films.

Weaver (1987) compared two types of nonviolent sexual depictions and two violent forms with a neutral control. In this study it was consistently found that the consenting sex depiction group did not differ from the neutral exposure control group on any measure for males or females. Both the male-coerced sex (men physically and verbally abusing women in order to have sex with them) and erotic violence condition (graphic violence occurring in a sexual context; i.e., "slasher film") *did* differ significantly from the neutral film clip control group. Both of these groups recommended lower sentences than the neutral fare control group after reading a description of a rapist.

There also appears to be evidence that short-term exposure to a certain type of sexually oriented communication may produce other antisocial effects (albeit somewhat less harmful than a diminished concern for a rape victim). Two studies (Mohr & Zanna, in press; Weaver, 1987) indicate that material that depicts the acts of prostitutes, or portrayals of women as indiscriminate in their choice of sexual partners, may prime ideas about female promiscuity in general or produce a cognitive set whereby men attend more to the physical characteristics of a woman in a situation immediately following exposure than would otherwise be the case. A critical consideration, however, is the level of sexual explicitness in the materials used by the investigators in both of these studies—and whether ideas about promiscuity need to be presented in a sexually explicit context in order to produce antisocial effects. Weaver (1987) reports using "R-rated" materials, depictions that would undoubtedly not be adjudicated obscene. Mohr and Zanna report exposing subjects to materials that were classified as "X-rated" and thus were probably much more sexually explicit than those used by Weaver. It would appear, then, that the idea or "theme" of promiscuity regardless of whether or not it appears in a sexually explicit context accounts for the effects. This would imply that many sexually graphic depictions—in particular, depictions of couples engaged in mutually consenting sex— that do not emphasize notions of promiscuity may not have the same effect.

The studies that have compared subjects exposed to sexually aggressive communications with subjects exposed to nonaggressive sexually explicit communications clearly indicate that nonviolent material results in fewer antisocial attitudes and beliefs than violent material.

The reader should note, however, that virtually none of the communication effects in these studies are main effects. Most of the studies have revealed interactions between the violent/sexual communication variable and some individual disposition. For example, Malamuth and Check (1985) found that differences between groups exposed to stories about consenting versus nonconsenting sex, on a dependent variable relating to the percentage of women they know would enjoy being raped, was evident only among those subjects who were classified as "high likelihood of raping." Similarly, an earlier study (Malamuth, Haber & Feshbach, 1980) found effects only for subjects low in aggression anxiety.

Finally, as Table 1 indicates, many dependent measures have been taken, but significant changes resulting from exposure to sexually explicit communications are observed on only a few of these. Most consistently, effects have been found for perceptions, judgments and attitudes about rape, or female victims portrayed in other contexts. Perceptions, judgments and attitudes about males in general, and male perpetrators of sexual violence, have either been unaffected or the results have been contradictory. An example of the latter is the finding by Malamuth, Haber and Feshbach (1980) that males who read a sexually violent passage were *more* punitive towards a rapist described later than those exposed to a consenting sex passage, while Weaver (1987) reports that subjects exposed to male coerced and eroticized violence were *less* punitive towards a fictional rapist.

Long-Term Exposure to Non-Violent vs. Violent Pornography

Table 2 presents the results of studies conducted after the 1970 commission in which subjects have been exposed to sexually explicit or suggestive communications for one hour or longer.

The studies that have examined the effects of long-term exposure to nonviolent pornography and attitudes towards women and rape have yielded mixed results. Zillmann and Bryant (1982) report that exposure to nonviolent pornography that is "degrading" to women may result in more leniency toward an assailant in a rape case described in a newspaper account and may also result in increased sexual callousness. Padgett and Brislin-Slutz (1987), however, found no differences between subjects exposed to nonviolent pornographic movies (over the course of a week) and a control group, on a variety of measures designed to test lessened sensitivity towards women, including rape myth acceptance.

Malamuth and Ceniti (1986), in a study which examined the effects of

Table 2

Summary of Long-Term Exposure to Pornography and Attitudes Towards Women and Rape

Study	Stimuli	Subjects	Dependent Measures	Results
Zillman & Bryant (1982)	S's viewed films of heterosexual activities over several weeks. Four conditions: (1) massive exposure (4 hours/48 minutes); (2) intermediate exposure (2 hours/24 minutes); (3) neutral exposure (36 nonerotic films); and (4) no-treatment controls.	80 male and 80 female college students	Estimation of percentage of American adults that perform common and uncommon sexual acts; recommendation of a prison sentence for rapist described in newspaper account; level of support for the women's liberation movement (a one-item scale); and the Sexual Callousness Toward Women scale.	Male *and* female subjects in intermediate and massive exposure condition: (1) estimated higher percentages of persons involved in fellatio-cunnilingus, anal intercourse, group sex sadomasochism and bestiality, (2) less supportive of sexual equality, (3) more lenient in assigning punishment to rapist in the newspaper account. Males' sexual callousness toward women was significantly increased.
Check (1985)	S's assigned to one of four conditions: (1) "sexually violent"; (2) "nonviolent dehumanizing pornography; (3) "nonviolent erotica"; and (4) no-exposure controls.	436 adult and college age males	Rape Myth Acceptance Scale, Adversarial Sex Beliefs scale, and five items from the Acceptance of Interpersonal Violence scale. S's asked "how likely they would be to commit rape if they could be assured that no one would know and that they could in no way be punished," and how likely they would be "to force a female to do something sexual she really didn't want to do." S's also completed Sexual Callousness scale.	No main effects, simple effects analysis showed: 1) higher scores on liklihood to rape item for violent pornography S's than no-exposure control S's. Similar results for use of force item. 2) Comparisons of nonviolent dehumanizing pornography and the no-exposure S's yielded same effects. 3) Three-way interaction between exposure to pornography, type of subject and psychoticism. High psychoticism S's in violent or dehumanizing condition show greater likelihood of rape and forced sex acts.
Donnerstein (1984)	S's viewed five films over five days, three experimental film conditions: 1) X-rated nonviolent 2) X-rated violent 3) "Slasher" film No exposure controls.	52 male college students	Immediately after fifth film, S's watched videotaped reenactment of rape trial with control subjects who had not viewed any films. After trial, S's indicated verdict and defendant's intentions, sympathy for the victim, victim's resistance, responsibility, attractiveness, level of injury and worthiness.	No effects for verdict or judgements about assailant. No significant differences between subjects in any film condition and no-exposure control group on attractiveness, responsibility, resistance or sympathy variables. S's in all three exposure conditions rated the victim of sexual assault as less "injured" and less "worthy" than the no-exposure controls.

Table 2 (continued)

Study	Stimuli	Subjects	Dependent Measures	Results
Malamuth & Check (1985)	Six audiotaped 1000-word stories in a fully crossed factorial design: (woman's consent vs. nonconsent) × pain (woman's pain vs. no pain) × outcome (woman's arousal vs. disgust).	145 male college students	S's heard story portraying a rape or mutually consenting intercourse. Perceptions of stories included: 1. the degree to which the woman was traumatized 2. her willingness to engage in sex 3. the extent of her pleasure and her pain. S's given questionnaire that asked percentage of women who would enjoy various acts. It included items asking subjects about their beliefs in rape myths, specifically the percentage of women, if any, who would derive some pleasure from being forced into sexual acts and the percentage of women who would derive pleasure from being raped.	Nonconsenting woman's arousal S's differed from nonconsenting woman's disgust S's in that the former: 1. perceived more victim pleasure in the rape criterion story. 2. thought a higher percentage of women would enjoy being raped and enjoy doing something sexual that they did not want to do (this effect only significant for S's "high" in self-reported likelihood of raping). Nonconsenting woman's arousal S's thought women enjoy rape and forced sex more than consenting woman's arousal S's.
Malamuth, Reisin, & Spinner (1979)	1. One group of S's looked at issues of *Playboy* and *Penthouse* that contained scenes of sadomasochism and rape. 2. Another group looked through issues of the same magazines that contained only nonagressive images. 3. A third group was given neutral materials (*National Geographic Magazine*).	42 male and 38 female college students	After 10 minutes, all S's watched videotaped interview with rape victim, answered questionnaire assessing: 1. perception of the victim (e.g., her pain, trauma, etc.) 2. attitudes toward the rape act (e.g., responsibility, possible justification, punishment merited, sexual vs. violent motive) 3. subjects' beliefs about their own behavior in such situations (e.g., the possibility of engaging in sexual assault). Two weeks later, S's answered another questionnaire that ostensibly assessed public attitudes about a variety of contemporary issues. S's indicated views on newspaper articles, including one on rape.	Sexual stimuli subjects (violent or nonviolent) were *less* likely to perceive pornography as a cause of rape compared to the neutral-fare control S's.

Study	Stimuli	Subjects	Dependent Measures	Results
			After viewing rape trial, S's were provided with copy of state statute governing sexual assault and were then asked to complete a final questionnaire. They provided individual verdicts in case and completed multi-item Likert scales assessing victim responsibility, defendant responsibility, severity of victim's injury, victim resistance, and victim credibility.	attacks could be avoided. "Slasher film" S's were significantly less sensitive to the victim of a sexual assault than were either the sexually explicit violent and sexually explicit nonviolent S's. No effect on either dependent variables.
Malamuth & Ceniti (1986)	S's randomly assigned to the "sexually violent," "sexually nonviolent" or to a no-exposure control condition. Subjects in the sexually violent condition were exposed to six "soft-core," feature-length films—two per week for three consecutive weeks.	42 male college students	Males' likelihood of raping if he was assured of not being caught and punished (LR). S's participated in an "ESP" experiment where a female confederate could be punished with an aversive blast of noise.	No significant results.
Padgett & Brislin-Slütz (1987)	S's assigned to view one hour of "erotic" or "non-erotic" film every day for five days or were assigned to neutral fare film exposure group.	43 female and 32 male college students	S's completed 30-item questionnaire which measured attitudes toward variety of women's issues from "Attitudes Towards Women scale," "Sex Role Stereotyping," "Adversarial Sexual Beliefs," "Rape Myth Acceptance," "Acceptance of Interpersonal Violence" and "Sexual Conservatism."	No differences between experimental and control group on post-exposure questionnaire.

exposure to violent and nonviolent pornography on self-reported likelihood of raping (LR) if assured of not being caught or punished, also
failed to find negative effects for exposure to non-violent pornography.
In this study, subjects were pretested to assess their LR, then randomly
assigned to conditions which were exposed to either "sexually violent"
or "sexually nonviolent" materials over a four-week period, or they were
assigned to a no-exposure control group. Following the exposure period,
subjects participated in what they thought was a different experiment,
where their attitudes and aggressive behaviors toward a female confederate were measured as well as their LR. An analysis of variance with LR
(measured before an after viewing the films) as a dependent variable,
and pornography exposure as an independent variable, revealed no
significant main effects for pornography exposure, nor any interaction
between an LR administration. A multivariate analysis of variance, with
pre-LR and pornography exposure as the independent variables, and
four dependent variables (e.g., anger towards and desire to hurt the
confederate) also revealed no significant effects.

An experiment by Check (1985) was intended as a step toward disen-
tangling the effects of prolonged exposure to sexually explicit images
that were non-degrading from the effects of exposure to sexual portrayals
that are dehumanizing or degrading. The results indicated that for some
men (students with relatively high scores on a measure of psychoticism)
exposure to both sexually degrading but nonviolent and sexually violent pornography resulted in a tendency to say they would rape if
assured of not being caught.

However, there are problems with the Check study. First, subjects in
this experiment were told that the evaluations of pornography they
would be giving in the study would be used by the Parliament of Canada
to help decide policy on the issue of pornography. In fact, subjects were
told: "This is one of the rare opportunities which you will have to say
something *DIRECTLY* to the government of Canada" (emphasis in the
original). With instructions like these, it is quite possible that the effects
observed in the experiment were due to the desire to give the most
socially desirable responses. Thus, if subjects believed that their responses
were going directly to the government they might rate violent and
degrading forms of pornography as less arousing, more degrading and
more obscene. Also, in his analysis, Check undertakes 1 degree of freedom tests of each film exposure group versus the control group on

several dependent variables, despite the fact that there were not statistically significant omnibus F tests for any variable.

Donnerstein (1984) also reported findings which suggested that long-term exposure to nonviolent pornography could result in reductions in perceptions of injury and worthiness of a victim portrayed in a videotaped reenactment of a rape trial. However, a subsequent investigation by Linz, Donnerstein and Penrod (1988) with male subjects, and Krafka (1985), with females, failed to substantiate this initial finding. In these later studies, exposure to sexually explicit, nonviolent materials resulted in no attitudinal changes following exposure. In both studies, only the slasher-film conditions showed negative effects (i.e., tendencies toward less empathy for rape victims overall, and a tendency to evaluate a victim of rape portrayed in a videotaped reenactment less sympathetically (Linz et al., 1988), and less favorable reactions to the same rape victim on a more global measure (Krafka, 1985)). But, it is important to note that even these effects, while somewhat consistent across studies, are sparse. In all three of these studies, a large number of dependent measures showed no differences between groups, regardless of the type of film exposure. For example, Krafka (1985) found that women exposed to approximately eight hours of sexually explicit degrading materials over a four-day period did not engage in more sex role stereotyping, experience lower self-esteem, less satisfaction with body image, more negative beliefs about rape, or show greater acceptance of violence against women compared to control subjects who did not view films. Similarly, Donnerstein (1984) and Linz et al. (1988) obtained significant differences on only a few dependent variables after exposure to either sexually violent or nonviolent sexually explicit material (see Table 2).

We would have to conclude that the data, *overall,* do not support the contention that exposure to nonviolent pornography has significant adverse effects on attitudes toward rape as a crime or more general evaluations of rape victims. Most consistently, in long-term and short-term studies, negative effects (e.g., lessened sensitivity toward rape victims, greater acceptance of force in sexual encounters) emerge when subjects are exposed to portrayals of overt violence against women or when sex is fused with aggression. This is particularly the case with the so-called "slasher" films. Every study that has included a "slasher" condition has found antisocial attitudinal effects resulting from exposure to these films. However, this has certainly not been the case for nonviolent pornography.

Pornography and Antisocial Behavior

It is important to reiterate that the research suggests that any anti-social effects arise either from exposure to *violent* pornography or from materials that are sexually violent but not sexually explicit. Research has demonstrated that a wide range of mass media images involving violence against women may foster anti-social attitudes about rape and rape victims.

Pornography and Rape Rates

Several recent studies have examined the relationship between the prevalence of pornography and rape rates in the United States. Studies by Baron and Straus (1984, 1985, 1986) compared the state-by-state differences in rape rates with state-by-state differences in pornography consumption as indexed by sales (subscription and newsstand) of eight "male sophisticate" magazines: *Chic, Club, Forum, Gallery, Genesis, Hustler, Oui,* and *Playboy.* Results indicated a positive correlation between rape rates and sex-oriented magazine consumption (.63 in 1979; .55 in 1980; .64 in 1980–1982). However, when the Violence Approval Index, a measure of what Baron and Straus call "hypermasculinity," was introduced into the analysis, the relationship between magazine circulation and rape rate disappeared.

Scott and Schwalm (forthcoming) also found a positive correlation between male sophisticate magazine consumption and rape rates in 1982. However, they found that an even higher correlation existed between the ratio of single males in a state and rape rates, again suggesting a spurious relationship between magazine sales and rape rates.

Another study by Scott and Schwalm (1988) examined the relationship between high and low adult theater rates and high and low rape rates by state. No statistically significant relationship could be found between adult theater rates and rape rates. However, other factors were found to be more related to rape rates than adult theaters, including readership of "outdoor-type" magazines, such as *Field and Stream, Guns and Ammo,* and *The American Hunter.*

The findings of these studies, as their authors suggest, may be explained by an aspect of culture which emphasizes a "hypermasculine" sexual and sex-role orientation. This underlying "macho" ethic may be a third variable which accounts for both consumption of pornography and rape rates in a particular region of the United States.

Interaction of Pornography, Individual Differences and Sexual Aggression

Malamuth and his colleagues have examined the questions of who is most likely to be attracted to sexual aggression, and which attitudes are associated with self-reports of sexual aggression. Malamuth and Check (1983), for example, highlighted the importance of the interaction between individual differences among men and various kinds of sexual depictions in affecting sexual arousal to rape portrayals. Personality variables, sexual motivations, sexual experience, and self-reported "likelihood of raping" were assessed for male subjects who were then exposed to an audiotaped depiction of a sexual interaction between a man and a woman. The content of the depictions portrayed women as either consenting or non-consenting, as in pain or not in pain, and as aroused or disgusted by the interaction, and subjects' sexual arousal was measured by penile tumescence and self-reports. Results indicated that when the woman was portrayed as experiencing disgust, both men low and high in "likelihood of raping" were less aroused by nonconsenting as compared with consenting depictions. When the woman was depicted as being sexually aroused, however, men low in likelihood of raping were equally aroused by the consenting and non-consenting portrayals, while the men high in likelihood of raping were significantly more sexually aroused by the non-consenting scenes. It was also found that self-reported arousal to rape was associated with psychoticism and power motivation, other measures reflecting aggressive tendencies in men.

Using several of the individual difference measures related to aggression, Malamuth (1983) attempted to predict laboratory aggression against women and later (Malamuth, 1986) attempted to predict self-reports of actual acts of sexually aggressive behavior. In the laboratory, he found that men with beliefs and attitudes more supportive of aggression, and with higher levels of sexual arousal to rape, were more aggressive (delivered more noxious noise) to a woman confederate and reported wanting to hurt the woman to a greater extent. With the addition of several other personality and attitude measures, Malamuth (1986) found that sexual arousal in response to aggression, dominance as a motive for sexual acts, hostility toward women, attitudes accepting of violence against women, and sexual experience were all significantly related to self-reports of sexual aggression. These factors, however, were most effective in predicting this naturalistic aggression when analyzed *interactively.* Malamuth (1986) concludes that the presence of any predictor alone is unlikely to result in high levels of sexual aggression. He argues, for example, that while sexual arousal in response to aggression has been used in the diagnosis and treatment of rapists (Quinsey, in press), this arousal pattern has been found within a substantial portion of the general male population (e.g., Malamuth, Check, & Briere, 1986). Malamuth concludes that sexual arousal in response to aggression is one factor which may contribute to aggression against women, but other factors must be present before such arousal will lead to aggressive behavior.

Use of Pornography by Those Engaging in Sexually Coercive Behaviors

In a survey of college students, Demare, Briere, and Lips (1988) assessed the amount of exposure to violent and nonviolent sexually explicit materials, attitudes supporting violence against women, likelihood of raping, and likelihood of using sexual force (if assured of not being caught). There were no significant associations between amount of exposure to either violent or nonviolent pornography and attitudes supporting violence against women. A significant association was found, however, between amount of exposure to *violent* sexually explicit media and likelihood of raping and likelihood of using sexual force. The authors suggest that it is "the unique combination of support for sex *and* aggression in some pornographic stimuli and certain attitudes that produces a proclivity toward sexual violence, a tendency which may interact with other relevant variables" (p. 150). However, one must be cautious about accepting the interpretation that exposure (whether or not in combination with anti-social attitudes) causes such a proclivity. It is equally likely that those with a proclivity toward sexual aggression are more likely to seek out sexually violent materials. In addition, the reported correlations may be due to some third variable which causes both consumption of sexually violent media and a proclivity toward sexual aggression, such as the "hypermasculinity" ethic discussed earlier.

One study which surveyed actual sex offenders was conducted by Marshall (Chapter 6) to assess the use of sexually explicit materials by outpatient rapists and child molesters. Rapists and child molesters reported significantly greater use of sexually explicit materials overall than either incest offenders or nonoffender controls. Perhaps more importantly, rapists and child molesters reported frequent use of these materials while preparing themselves to commit an offense. However, it is impossible with this data alone to determine whether exposure to sexually explicit materials contributes to sexually deviant behavior, or whether the fact that these offenders seek out this material is just another manifestation of their basic deviant interests. Furthermore, the data for this study derive from retrospective recall and therefore carry with them a host of interpretation problems.

The Indirect Effects of Pornography on Anti-Social Behavior

If any connection exists in the research between pornography and criminal behavior, it is this: Exposure to sexually violent materials may foster certain attitudes about women and rape, such as the myth that women unconsciously desire to be raped or enjoy being raped. Attitudes similar to this, such as hostility toward women and acceptance of violence against women, in combination with sexual arousal in response to sexual aggression, were found by Malamuth and his colleagues to be predictors of both self-reported likelihood of raping (if assured of not being caught) and self-reported actual acts of sexual aggression. Regrettably, it is difficult to determine how well a subject's likelihood of raping if assured of not being caught leads to that subject's actual commission of a rape. It is also difficult to assess the accuracy of self-reported acts of aggression, due to subjects' tendency to provide social desirable responses, exaggerate their sexual prowess, or differ in their perception of what constitutes aggression.

Researchers are hesitant to assert any *direct* relationship between pornography and sexual aggression. A large number of cultural and individual factors appear to mediate the effects of violent pornography on attitudes and behaviors. Malamuth and Briere (1986) posit one such indirect effects model:

> Individual conditions and the broader social climate are postulated as the originating environmental influences on the individual. The mass media are considered one of the *many* social forces that may, in interaction with a variety of many other cultural and individual factors, affect the development of intermediate attributes, such as thought patterns, sexual arousal patterns, motivations, and personality characteristics. These intermediate variables, in complex interactions with each other and with situational circumstances, such as alcohol consumption or acute arousal, may precipitate behaviors ranging from passive support to actual aggression.

It is important to note that even indirect media influences need not produce immediate violence in order to have seriously harmful effects. Sexually violent depictions may affect not only potential sex offenders but the attitudes and subsequent decisions of those who may have to judge them or support or oppose legislation aimed at them.

Policy Implications

First, the research suggests that there are several variables that distinguish nonrapists from potential rapists. Malamuth (1989a) introduced the "Attraction to Sexual Aggression" (ASA) scale to help identify men who are at risk for future sexual coercion. High scores on this scale are associated with attitudes supporting aggression against women, affective reactions to portrayals of rape, physiological and self-reported arousal, hostility towards women, dominance motives, and antisocial personality characteristics; many of these factors having been previously identified as predictors of self-reported sexual aggression (Malamuth, 1983). Once men at risk for future sexual coercion have been identified, it may be useful to encourage them to become involved in intervention programs that attempt to educate them about images of rape in the mass media. However, a great deal of caution must be used to guard against the misuse of such a scale in the identification of high "risk" groups, since there is always the potential for "false positives" (Malamuth, 1989b). Those men who report low levels of actual sexual aggression but score high on ASA may be attracted to sexual aggression, but they may never cross the threshold necessary for actually committing sexual crimes.

A second avenue for criminal justice policy concerns the development of clinical interventions for the treatment of sex offenders (or potential sex offenders seeking therapy) who use pornography to incite rape fantasies. Although the studies conducted with sex offenders have not established a causal relationship between pornography and sexual crimes, they do suggest that some rapists and child molesters use sexually explicit materials in preparation for a criminal act (Marshall, Chapter 6). Treatment programs should take the use of these materials into consideration for these men. Therapists may wish to discourage clients from using sexually explicit materials, if these materials are instrumental for the client's criminal preparation.

Finally, longitudinal studies are needed which follow the men identified as "at risk" and who have been exposed to sexual violence to see if they actually run afoul of the law. Ageton (1983) conducted one study, in which attitudes about general aggression, together with beliefs about sexual stereotypes and rape myths, were used to identify "potential offenders," who were asked some years later to report actual sexual aggression (although involvement with delinquent peers at a young age turned out to be the best predictor of later aggression). However, this study did not assess acceptance of sexual aggression or attitudes regarding violence against women, which Malamuth (1989b) has argued are the best predictors of sexual aggression.

REFERENCES

Ageton, S. S. (1983). On behaving in accordance with one's attitudes. In M. Zanna, E. T. Higgins, & C. P. Herman (Eds.), *Consistency in Social Behavior: The Ontario Symposium* (Vol. 2). Hillsdale, NJ: Erlbaum.

Attorney General's Commission on Pornography. (1986). Final Report. U.S. Department of Justice, Government Printing Office, Washington, DC.

Baron, L., & Straus, M. A. (1984). Sexual stratification, pornography, and rape in the United States. In N. M. Malamuth & E. Donnerstein (Eds.), *Pornography and sexual aggression* (pp. 185–209). Orlando, FL: Academic Press.

Baron, L., & Straus, M. A. (1985). *Legitimate violence, pornography, and sexual inequality as explanations for state and regional differences in rape.* Unpublished manuscript, Yale University, New Haven, CT.

Baron, L., & Straus, M. A. (1986). *Rape and its relation to social disorganization, pornography, and sexual inequality in the United States.* Unpublished manuscript, Yale University, New Haven, CT.

Berkowitz, L. (1984). Some effects of thoughts on anti- and pro-social influences of media events: A cognitive-neoassociation analysis. *Psychological Bulletin, 95,* 410–427.

Check, J. V. P. (1985). The effects of violent and nonviolent pornography. Report to the Department of Justice, Ottawa, Canada: Department of Justice, Department of Supply and Services contract 05SV. (1920) 0-3-0899.

Demare, D., Briere, J., & Lips, H. M. (1988). Violent pornography and self-reported likelihood of sexual aggression. *Journal of Research in Personality, 22,* 140–153.

Donnerstein, E. (1984, February). *Proceedings of the Symposium on Media Violence and Pornography.* Toronto: Media Action Group.

Intons-Peterson, M. J., Roskos-Ewoldsen, B., Thomas, L., Shirley, M., & Blut, D. (1987). *Will educational materials offset negative effects of violent pornography?* Unpublished manuscript, Indiana University.

Krafka, C. L. (1985). *Sexually explicit, sexually violent, and violent media: Effects of multiple naturalistic exposures and debriefing on female viewers.* Unpublished doctoral dissertation, University of Wisconsin-Madison.

Linz, D., Donnerstein, E., & Penrod, S. (1988). The effects of long-term exposure to violent and sexually degrading depictions of women. *Journal of Personality and Social Psychology, 55,*

Malamuth, N. M. (1983). Factors associated with rape as predictors of laboratory aggression against women. *Journal of Personality and Social Psychology, 45,* 432–442.

Malamuth, N. M. (1986). Predictors of naturalistic sexual aggression. *Journal of Personality and Social Psychology, 50,* 953–962.

Malamuth, N. M. (1989a). The attraction to sexual aggression scale: Part one. *The Journal of Sex Research, 26,* 26–49.

Malamuth, N. M. (1989b). The attraction to sexual aggression scale: Part two. *The Journal of Sex Research, 26,* 324–354.

Malamuth, N. M. & Briere, J. (1986). Sexual violence in the media: Indirect effects on aggression against women. *Journal of Social Issues, 42,* 75–92.

Malamuth, N. M. & Ceniti, J. (1986). Repeated exposure to violent and nonviolent pornography: Likelihood of raping ratings and laboratory aggression against women. *Aggressive Behavior, 12,* 129–137.

Malamuth, N. M., & Check, J. V. P. (1983). Sexual arousal to rape depictions: Individual differences. *Journal of Abnormal Psychology, 92,* 55–67.

Malamuth, N. M., & Check, J. V. P. (1985). The effects of aggressive pornography on beliefs of rape myths: Individual differences. *Journal of Research in Personality, 19,* 299–320.

Malamuth, N. M., Check, J. V. P., & Briere, J. (1986). Sexual arousal in response to aggression: Ideological, aggressive, and sexual correlates. *Journal of Personality and Social Psychology, 14,* 399–408.

Malamuth, N., Haber, S., & Feshbach, S. (1980). Testing hypotheses regarding rape: Exposure to sexual violence, sex differences, and the "normality" of rapists. *Journal of Research in Personality, 14,* 121–137.

Malamuth, N., Reisin, I., & Spinner, B. (1979, September). *Exposure to pornography and reactions to rape.* Paper presented at the 87th annual convention of the American Psychological Association, New York.

Mohr, D. & Zanna, M. (in press). Treating women as sexual objects: Look to the (gender schematic) male who has viewed pornography. *Personality and Social Psychology Bulletin.*

Padgett, V. R., & Brislin-Slütz, J. A. (1987). *Pornography, erotica and negative attitudes towards women: The effects of repeated exposure.* Unpublished manuscript, Marshall University, Huntington, West Virginia.

Penrod, S., & Linz, D. (1984). Using psychological research on violent pornography to inform legal change. In N. M. Malamuth & E. Donnerstein (Eds.), *Pornography and sexual aggression.* Orlando, FL: Academic Press.

Quinsey, V. L. (in press). Sexual aggression: Studies of offenders against women. *International Yearbook on Law and Mental Health.*

Scott, J. E., & Schwalm, L. A. (1988). Pornography and rape: An examination of adult theater rapes and rape rates by state. In J. E. Scott & T. Hirschi (Eds.), *Controversial Issues in Crime and Justice,* Beverly Hills, CA: Sage.

Scott, J. E., & Schwalm, L. A. (forthcoming). Rape rates and the circulation rates of adult magazines. *Journal of Sex Research.*

Tversky, A., & Kahneman, D. (1973). Availability: A heuristic for judging frequency and probability. *Cognitive Psychology, 5,* 207–232.

Weaver, J. B. (1987). *Effects of portrayals of female sexuality and violence against women on perceptions of women.* Unpublished doctoral dissertation, University of Indiana, Bloomington.

Zillmann, D., & Bryant, J. (1982). Pornography, sexual callousness, and the trivialization of rape. *Journal of Communication, 32,* 10–21.

Zillmann, D., & Bryant, J. (1984). Effects of massive exposure to pornography. In N. Malamuth & E. Donnerstein (Eds.), *Pornography and sexual aggression.* New York: Academic Press.

SYSTEM EFFECTS— POLICY FORMATION, IMPLEMENTATION AND AGENDA SETTING

S ection II, "Policy Formation, Implementation and Agenda Setting" contains six chapters of the media's influence on policy-forming activities in criminal justice. This section differs from the first section, in that behaviors here are not those that the criminal justice system must deal with (crime and violence) but are the behavioral responses of the system to those behaviors (individual policy-related decision making). The research in this area has focused upon the effects of news coverage, and the composition of the chapters reflect this. However, it should be noted that a number of authors believe that the content of entertainment media can also affect criminal justice policy and the system's agenda. (For a review, see Bortner, 1984.)

A basic underlying concern in these chapters is the fear that the media is directing the actions of the criminal justice system independent of any reality of crime. The study of the production of crime news has shown that an initial adoption of a crime theme by one news organization is frequently imitated and comes to dominate crime news selection for a regional news industry for significant periods of time. This news focus on a particular crime is independent of changes in actual crime levels but can be intense enough to influence criminal justice agency activities (cf. Fishman, 1978). A crime thus becomes a "serious type of crime" on the basis of what is going on inside newsrooms, not outside them.

With this potential in mind, the section opens with Chapter 9 by Doppelt and Manikas which introduces and reviews the relevant mass media and criminal justice decision-making literature. Defining the issues and reviewing the conceptual foundation of agenda setting, the authors point out the varying media effects that have been forwarded. These effects range from adding issues to the criminal justice agenda, to causing issues to disappear from the agenda, to impeding an issue's emergence and blocking its addition to the agenda. The current perspective is that the media's influence on criminal justice policy decisions exists and operates within policy "ecologies." These ecologies involve networks of actors (journalists, criminal justice personnel, legislators and community leaders) and their social/political environments that transport multidirectional media effects. The media can thus influence criminal justice policy in both immediate and lagged, direct and indirect ways. The challenge for researchers is to determine if generalizable patterns exist in the media criminal justice policy area.

Reflecting this challenge, Chapters 10 and 11 provide examples of ecological-based research. In Chapter 10 Pritchard looks at the relationship between newspaper coverage and prosecutors' willingness to plea bargain in homicide cases. Pritchard reports that newspapers help set the plea bargaining agenda of Milwaukee prosecutors in homicide cases. In Chapter 11, Leff, Protess and Brooks follow with a study of the impact of investigative coverage on the attitudes of the general public and policy leaders. They also report clear attitude and agenda effects for investigative reporting. The effects vary, however, between groups and issues, in that the less information the general public has about an issue, the more likely it is to be influenced by media reports. There also is some suggestive evidence of a general effect upon policymakers regardless of their direct exposure to the media content, apparently in response to their perceiving changes in the general public's attitudes.

A policy issue of continuing controversy involves the desire of criminal justice personnel to obtain information held by news reporters. In Chapter 12, Kirtley reviews the current state and effectiveness of shield laws as a result of this clash. The use of subpoenas against news reporters has resulted in a number of Supreme Court cases and the passage of shield legislation in many states. Both of these developments reflect the news media desire to protect their information sources from law enforcement investigations Kirtley reports. In practice, the effect of shield laws has depended upon their interpretation by state courts. Thus, there exists great variety in terms of how much subpoena protection a reporter can expect depending upon the jurisdiction he is reporting from. Surette, in Chapter 13, explores the concept of "media trials" and their potential for influencing the dispositions of similar, but non-publicized, criminal cases. Working from a typology of "Abuse of Power," "Sinful Rich," and "Evil Strangers," Surette argues that media trials are reported within entertainment programming themes and have significant far-reaching effects throughout the criminal justice system. There major effect is found in their potential to influence the processing of non-publicized cases. Lastly, in Chapter 14, Nienstedt reports on an Arizona case study of a state DWI (Driving Under the Influence) law and the media's influence on its development and impact. Utilizing a time series analysis, she reports that the publicity regarding the law is actually more influential than the implementation of the law. She points out that in many instances symbolic legislation may be more costly and less effective than media-based deterrence efforts.

As a group these chapters show that the media is significantly affecting decision making and the formation of the criminal justice agenda. The nature of this relationship is not fully comprehended, however, and its further specification needs to be empirically explored.

REFERENCES

Bortner, M.A. (1984). "Media Images and Public Attitudes toward Crime and Justice" in *Justice and The Media.* (ed.) R. Surette, Charles C Thomas.
Fishman, M. (1978). "Crime Waves as Ideology" *Social Problems,* 25:531–543.

Chapter 9

MASS MEDIA AND
CRIMINAL JUSTICE DECISION MAKING

Jack C. Doppelt and Peter M. Manikas

They're gonna place you under arrest. It's outrageous. They should take whatever they got before a grand jury and get an indictment and then see about an arraignment. Bernie knows that, but Weiss's gotta have a quick arrest to get the press off his back.

We could go to trial in two months or six months. It's hard to say in a case that's gotten as much publicity as this one has. When the media go crazy over something, it complicates things.

That dialogue from Tom Wolfe's 1987 best-seller, *Bonfire of the Vanities*, reflects what we all know, or at least assume, about the pervasive influence of the media. When the media talk, policymakers listen, or so goes the conventional wisdom. Yet, if that is a self-evident truth, why are scholars reluctant to embrace the wisdom? Why is it so difficult to empirically confirm what we casually observe and sense to be true?

To understand the complexities of mass media effects, the obvious must be separated from the not so obvious and potentially misleading. Although it may be apparent that media coverage attracts (or distracts) the attention of policymakers, that coverage does not necessarily spur them into action. Despite the clamor that a news story may bring, the policymaking agenda may remain unaltered, changed neither in priority nor pace, by the media's attention.

It is well established that media coverage can affect the public's attitudes toward policies and events. It is less clear, however, that these attitudinal shifts affect deeply felt beliefs or that they are long lasting. Public opinion can, at least sometimes, turn a deaf ear to the most sensational media events. Moreover, the link between a news story, public opinion and policy change is difficult to establish; often it is merely assumed.

129

Even the media coverage depicted in Wolfe's novel may have effects on the system that are difficult to document other than anecdotally. Research efforts to analyze media effects on policymaking, in criminal justice and other policy arenas, are marked with definitional and methodological complications.

Recurring Problems: Defining the Concepts for Media Criminal Justice Policy Research

Who are the policymakers? Government policy can be effectuated in many ways by a broad range of policy elites. Moreover, these policy elites are situated at various levels within each branch of government.

Regarding capital punishment, for instance, policy can be made at the top executive level. The governor can veto death penalty legislation, issue executive orders, appoint commissions and stay executions. Agency heads in the executive branch can promulgate rules on the method of execution and on prison conditions for death row inmates and can decide against whom to seek the death penalty. Subordinates, including prosecutors and bureaucrats, make daily policy decisions on how to apply laws, rules and procedures. Legislators pass and amend death penalty statutes and, with their aides and staff, decide what hearings to hold and which bills get priority. Judges set court rules and, in their role as arbiters in individual cases, make decisions on a case-by-case basis. And peculiar to the criminal justice system, jurors and grand jurors are thrust into policymaking roles because they too have government-sanctioned decision-making power. Each can be influenced in their decision-making capacity by the mass media.

What actions constitute policymaking? The activities of policymakers range from purely symbolic to decisive. In an attempt to gauge influences on policy, researchers might focus not only upon the most visible aspects of the policymaking process. They could also examine incremental shifts in the policymaking agenda. Media coverage, for instance, might affect the passage of legislation. However, to determine how legislators respond to the media, their preliminary actions—such as the actions they take in committee—should be examined as well as their votes on final passage of a bill.

Media attention may prompt activities, such as holding a news conference, writing an intra-agency memo, holding a series of meetings or hearings, shifting agency priorities or accelerating other policy responses. Or media stories might only lead to attitudinal changes among certain policy elites, with no discernible policy outcome.

What constitutes a "policy"? Is public policy in the criminal justice arena solely the province of policy elites, or does "policy" also emerge from the routine practices of police officers and other criminal justice personnel, or from individual case decisions by judges, juries and prosecutors? When police officers routinely confront groups of youths congregating on a street corner and search them for marijuana, is it the "policy" of the police department, even if the practice is abjured by higher-ranking officials? Do the daily accommodations between judges, prosecutors and defense lawyers on matters such as plea bargaining constitute "policy" even when actual practices conflict with the formal rules?

Which media should be included? Historically, scholars studying mass media effects concentrated principally upon newspaper coverage. Radio and television were virtually ignored. It was believed that audio and video images were ephemeral, that the medium provoked only passive responses and that its content was largely duplicative of print journalism. This newspaper orientation was disrupted by the powerful, enduring images television cast on the civil rights movement and the Vietnam War.

By the time scholars had liberated their research designs from the strictures of convention, the prevailing wisdom had changed. Video images were what really mattered to policymakers, advertisers and the public. Indeed, the general public spent so much more time watching television than reading newspapers that it seemed sheer folly to study mass media effects by focusing solely on print journalism. Moreover, research attention expanded to include not only news programming. It began to incorporate entertainment programming, features, documentaries, advertising, public relations and the specialized trade press as well.

As the scope of mass media research widens, the empirical task becomes even more complicated. Though the term "mass media" subsumes more than newspapers and television, the concept becomes analytically useless if it is not distinguished from interpersonal communications. Separating the effects of the media from that of face-to-face contacts, however, is not an easy task. In terms of policy influence, lobbying, coalition-building and word of mouth play primary roles. Yet they seldom occur independent of the mass media. The roots can become hopelessly entangled in an arena as image-sensitive as the criminal justice system. Fundamental images of crime and criminals are derived from numerous sources (Bortner,

1984), not only from the mass media, but from interpersonal contacts and personal experience as well (Stinchcombe et al., 1980).

The Conceptual Foundation: Agenda-Setting

The conceptual framework for research on mass media effects has evolved from a research interest in agenda-setting (McCombs & Shaw, 1972). Agenda-setting is a concept that derives from the theoretical work of political scientists who explored how and why certain issues emerged from the interplay of group politics (McConnell, 1967; Schattschneider, 1960). These interest group theorists see the political system as biased, favoring the issues promoted by well-organized business and professional groups. In this view, public opinion and the public interest can be thwarted by groups with the necessary resources and expertise who have a well-defined economic stake in government policy (Page & Shapiro, 1983).

The term "agenda-setting" has come to mean the inquiry into how issues receive serious attention by authoritative decision makers (Cook and Skogan, forthcoming). Paradoxically, most agenda-setting research does not inquire directly into the effects the mass media has on policy-making. Instead, much of the research has concentrated on the media's effects on public opinion, ostensibly in the belief that issues which receive governmental attention are chosen from among those issues that have become part of the public discourse.

Typically, this type of research measures news content (for example, in terms of the number, placement and type of crime stories that appear) and then proceeds to determine whether a change in the public's attitudes has occurred as a result of those stories (Stinchcombe et al., 1980). A similar research strategy has contrasted the news media's depiction of particular crimes, criminals and law enforcement with the facts contained in official statistical reports (Gordon and Riger, 1989; Reiner, 1985). In those cases in which the public's attitudes have more closely approximated the media coverage than the statistical reality, researchers have concluded that those attitudes derived from the less accurate media portrayal.

The agenda-setting conceptual framework allows researchers to determine when specific issues depicted by the media become more salient to the public or to particular segments of the public. However, it documents the media's effect on policymaking only if it is assumed that issue salience among the public necessarily triggers policy action. Recently, scholars have begun to challenge that premise (Graber, 1989, 1984; Swanson, 1988; Protess et al., 1985; Cook et al., 1983). One researcher has even commented that the ironic inadequacy of the agenda-setting framework is that media impact on the public may be of less consequence than media impact on policymaking, in that the average individual politically is "fairly unimportant" (Graber, 1989:19).

Despite its limitations, the agenda-setting approach was instrumental in rethinking the "minimal effects" view of the 1940s, 1950s and 1960s. The minimal effects view holds that the dominant influence of the media both on the public and on policymaking is reinforcement of the status quo (Noelle-Neumann, 1983; Roberts & Bachen, 1981). If the media only reinforce the status quo, the argument goes, research time is better spent studying forces other than the media that actually influence public attitudes and policy change.

With the television era and the visual mark it made on the civil rights movement and the Vietnam War, the "minimal effects" view fell into disfavor. Instead, scholarly research focused on identifying specific conditions that might affect the probability of the public agenda being influenced by the media. As a result, theories, such as the "uses and gratifications" approach, the "need for orientation" response and the "ambiguity-recurrence" model, emerged. The "uses and gratifications" theory contends that people tend to ignore personally irrelevant messages and pay attention to information they need and find gratifying (Swanson, 1979; Blumler & Katz, 1974). The "need for orientation" theory suggests that the more people need to be oriented to a topic, the more likely they are to change their agendas once oriented by the media. Those studies have found that where segments of the public have an inherent curiosity about the topic, the media agenda has had the more palpable impact (Weaver, 1980; McCombs & Weaver, 1973). The "ambiguity-recurrence" theory argues that the more ambiguous the message and the more recurring the theme, the less likely the public's agenda will be influenced by the media message. Or at the other end of the continuum, the clearer the villains and victims and the more novel the theme, the more likely that the media will have influence on the public's agenda (Protess, 1987; Protess et al., 1987). The cumulative effect of these theoretical thrusts was to firmly discredit the view of minimal media effects and invigorate the search for significant special case media effects. Though most of the agenda-setting literature analyzes media effects in the political and electoral arenas, it is thought to be equally applicable to the criminal justice system (Graber, 1989; Gordon & Riger, 1989; Pritchard, 1986).

The Ecological View: Agenda-Building

At about the time that some scholars were beginning to note the dearth of research linking public agenda-setting responses to actual policy impact (Leff et al., 1986; McGuire, 1986; Graber, 1984; Gandy, 1982), others were beginning to question the assumptions of the agenda-setting framework itself (Ettema, 1989; Swanson, 1988; Molotch, 1987; Linsky, 1986; Ball-Rokeach, 1985; Nelson, 1984; Lang & Lang, 1983). A key assumption, for example, is that the media influence policy through a linear process: a news story appears, the public becomes alarmed, interest groups are mobilized and policymakers respond. However, the assumption of linearity, based largely on a muckraking model of the media influencing the public agenda, fails to capture the range of actions that can be set in motion by news coverage (Molotch, 1987).

For example, research into the effects of investigative reporting found that the most consistent factor that determined policy impact was the relationship that formed between the media and the policymakers who reacted to the coverage (Protess et al., 1987; Leff et al., 1986; Cook et al., 1983). The bystanding, largely passive public could be circumvented (Lang & Lang, 1983). Consequently, the term "agenda-building" evolved to connote a collective process of interacting and often reciprocal influences between media and policymakers that helps create a climate that determines the likely composition of the public agenda (Graber, 1989; Lang & Lang, 1983). The model is depicted as an evolving ecology—a trisected chamber of reverberating effects among the media, the public and policymakers. Effects are multidirectional, prompted by the media and impacting on the media, by the public and on the public, and by manipulating policymakers as well as on responsive policymakers (Ettema, 1989; Molotch, 1987; Lang & Lang, 1983).

The ecological view, with its refracted media messages, makes empirical research more complex, untidy and perhaps chaotic enough to render firm conclusions on causality inappropriate, if not impossible. However, by reconceptualizing the role of the media in the policymaking process, the diverse nature of the news media's role in shaping the public agenda is being more fully explored.

The ecological view has only recently been applied to research on the effects of the mass media on the criminal justice system. Consequently, it is too early to tell whether its promise will be fulfilled. As with other agenda-setting research, firm conclusions are sparse and anecdotes fill the void.

Divergent Trends: Research on Media Policy Effects in Criminal Justice

In the criminal justice area, media effects research has evolved in two strands. One strand focuses on the media's effect on policymaking and on shaping public opinion on criminal justice issues. Its source lies in the agenda-setting (pre-ecological) model described earlier. The second strand examines the impact of the media on the adversarial process. Its origins can be found in the fair trial-free press debate. The strains are conceptually different, in that the former is studied principally to document the extent, if any, of the media's *contribution* to the policymaking process; the latter is studied to determine the extent, if any, of the media *taint* on the adversarial process. It is generally believed that while criminal justice policymakers ought to be receptive to external forces such as the media, criminal justice decision makers—such as judges, prosecutors and juries— should be insulated from potentially prejudicial forces, including the media.

One study which combines both approaches focused on the impact news coverage had on prosecutorial decision making in homicide cases (Pritchard, Chapter 10). Pritchard found that prosecutors in Milwaukee County, Wisconsin were less likely to engage in plea bargaining in those homicide cases which received extensive news coverage. The study recognizes the policymaking implications inherent in the adversarial part of the criminal justice system. It addressed empirically what Wolfe treated anecdotally: that the media can *directly* affect what actors in the criminal justice system do. The public's attitudes and agendas need not be affected first.

Pritchard's study also avoided one of the pitfalls of much of the agenda-setting research. It did not rely on self-reported data. By using court records, the study was not bound by self-assessments of impact, a measuring device that is even more unreliable in relation to policymakers than to the public because of the interests policymakers may have in making the media seem either more or less influential than they really are.

Paradoxically, while the agenda-setting literature has moved away from a "minimal effects" orientation, the fair trial-free press strain may be rekindling it, but from a different perspective. The research on pre-trial publicity continuously raises the question: does pre-trial publicity, no matter how pervasive, really influence juror decision making? (Surette, forthcoming). Mock jury studies predominate in the absence of real world data (as in Pritchard's study) which would examine the relationship between actual news coverage and jury decision making. Media effects on juror decision making are counteracted by the justice system's various devices (e.g., jury selection and sequestration) to thwart influence. Consequently, it might be expected that these effects would be minimal compared to the media's impact on criminal justice policymaking. It is all the more surprising, then, that many lawyers and judges cling to the dissonant belief that media influence is more of a threat to the impartiality of the adversary system than it is a contributing factor to criminal justice policymaking. The same scrutiny that has been brought to bear on media influence of the jury process needs to be applied to media impact on the criminal justice policy agenda.

The advantage of Pritchard's work and of most mock jury studies is that they examine direct media impact on a process. Other mediating factors are kept to a minimum. Causes and effects are more pronounced. The limitation of these studies is that they fail to account for indirect effects, which are arguably the more pervasive influence the media have on decision making (Jacob & Lineberry, 1982). The media can create social perceptions, such as crime waves, that may be "things of the mind" but that have real consequences (Fishman, 1978). Media messages can reverberate throughout a system and have an echo effect on unintended policies or unrelated decisions (Surette, forthcoming; Greene & Wade, 1987). This is particularly plausible in the criminal justice system where daily coverage of unrelated crimes can have a cumulative effect, not only on public attitudes (Einsiedel, 1984), but on later criminal cases or on comprehensive policies and where news coverage may mirror the distorted images projected by the media's entertainment programming (Surette, forthcoming; Reiner, 1985).

Much has been written about the disparity between crime reporting and crime statistics (Gordon & Riger, 1989; Hughes, 1987; Reiner, 1985; Garofalo, 1981; Stinchcombe et al., 1980) and whether the distortions are likely to result in more punitive or more lenient treatment by the criminal justice system (Surette, forthcoming; Greene & Wade, 1987; Kaplan & Skolnick, 1982; Graber, 1980). Here too the literature is more apt to examine the attitudinal impressions left on the public by those distortions than the policy consequences resulting from the distorted messages and images.

In their study on rape, for example, Gordon and Riger (1989) document that crime is dramatically underreported in contrast to murder and misreported in favor of sensationalized rapes by strangers. Reiner (1985) discusses the overdramatized, heroic professionalism of police that is cast both by the news and entertainment media. And Hughes (1987) concludes that reporting of child abuse cases in Britain misleads the public into believing that sentences are more lenient than they are.

This body of literature assumes that media-fed distortions necessarily set the policymaking and decision-making agendas by limiting policy alternatives. Hughes writes of a judge who "has rated the press highly as a source of public opinion, which he finds helpful when sentencing: 'First of all I am an avid reader of newspapers, secondly I am an avid watcher of television chat programmes—one picks up a great deal from the press and television.' " And he concludes, "The sentencers are put under pressure by the papers, they must be seen to be responsive to public opinion as the criminal justice system needs to command the respect of the public" (Hughes, 1987:47).

In his study on the influence of television crime dramas on the criminal justice system, Carlson (1985:195) concludes: "The messages transmitted by crime shows may have important implications for the operation of the criminal justice system. Because of increased fear of victimization there may be an increase in demand for police protection. Since television police are portrayed as being particularly effective, the public may develop unrealistic expectations concerning police performance. The combination of increased demand for protection and the perceived 'inability' of police to deal with the problem of crime may lead to a deterioration of police-community relations." Accordingly, the public, inured to misperceptions of violent crime, police professionalism or lenient sentencing, will not tolerate policies or court decisions that undermine their preconditioned attitudes.

That hypothesis needs refinement. Do policy elites respond, if at all, to public pressure because, as Hughes suggests, they fear cognitive dissonance among the public (indirect media effects), or because they too have adopted the misperceptions (direct media effects)? If policymakers become cognizant of the misperceptions, will they acquiesce to them, act in the face of them, or avoid the conflict, if possible, by turning their attention to the myriad of other policy arenas on their agenda?

One theory, to borrow from the fair trial-free press literature, suggests that policymakers might reject the distorted messages and images as a threat to their autonomy. This "theory of reactance" has been used to explain why juries, in perceiving negative media coverage about a defendant as a threat to their decision-making role, might not allow prejudicial publicity to color their impartiality (Davis, 1986). Another theory, dating back to the early days of agenda-setting research, suggests that media effects on policymaking might depend more on the characteristics of the decision makers than on the content of the message (Noelle-Neumann, 1983). In fact, if one applies the "need for orientation" theory to policymakers rather than the public, it might be hypothesized that because policy elites have a more limited need than the general public for the media-based orientation, the media's effect on the agendas of policymakers may be relatively limited.

Converging Implications

Several recent studies have shifted focus from media effects on attitudes to effects on policy outcomes. The research of Lineberry, Jacob and their colleagues in the early 1980s set the stage for much of the research that followed. In their Government Responses to Crime project, they examined the newspaper attention crime received in nine cities between 1948 and 1978. The researchers concluded that "trends in front-page reports of crime contributed to and reinforced the growing salience of crime on the urban (and national) political agenda during the 1960s and 1970s" (Jacob & Lineberry, 1982:112).

Their findings were later refined in a more methodologically sophisticated study. Using a randomized experimental design with pre-test and post-test measurements, a group from Northwestern University's Center for Urban Affairs and Policy Research found that viewing a television program on fraud in a federal home health care program influenced the attitudes of the governmental decision makers who viewed the investigative report. However, it did not affect how officials ranked the issue's priority relative to other issues (Cook, Tyler et al., 1983).

More recently, the researchers have envisioned the media not only as a message carrier but as a direct actor in pressure group politics. In this view, the media help shape criminal justice policy by establishing relationships with policy initiators, including government officials (Protess et al., 1985). This conceptual framework is what we earlier referred to as the "ecological view," in which media effects on policy "come from the capacity of journalists to play a role . . . in this larger ecology of individual and institutional practices" (Molotch, 1987:46). Investigative reporters sometimes collaborate with officials to "build official reaction *into* their stories" (1987: 39). Moreover, not only do reporters sometimes "leap over" the public by directly dealing with officials, policymakers sometimes respond to media investigations that are ultimately killed by editors and never reach the public. The media also sometimes work cooperatively with citizens' groups to expose wrongdoing. In other cases, though, an expose is broadcast, the public is outraged and galvanized, yet no significant policy response follows.

The ecological view has perhaps been most effective in challenging the notion that the media's role is largely confined to disseminating information. Journalists are part of a network; they are actors embedded in a policy web in which they and other actors form shifting alliances. All of these actors both initiate and respond to policy change.

In applying the ecological view, Nelson (1984) gauged media coverage of child abuse through content analysis of newspapers and magazines, academic attention through scholarly publications and government action through funding allocations and legislation. She also asked why certain stories found their way onto the media's agenda.

In concluding that the media both created and responded to the issue of child abuse, she highlighted the media imperative of topic differentiation. "Topic differentiation" refers to the tendency of the media to divide general policy areas into more narrowly defined topics. These more narrow categories both capture the moment (of a child abuse incident) and reinforce newsworthiness by their recurrence (a child abuse crisis).

By definition, the case-by-case nature of the criminal justice system guarantees some degree of topic differentiation (Fishman, 1978). As Nelson puts it, "the crime-and-victims approach to covering child abuse cases always assured a minimum of coverage for the issue" (1983:66). Whereas "minimal effects" theorists find comfort in the incongruity between the media with its short attention span and public policy which is often painfully plodding, the disparity may be narrowed significantly in the criminal justice system through such topic differentiation. Not only might a differentiating media have dramatic effect on the system over time, but the system through its judges, prosecutors and juries is open to media influence on a case-by-case basis. Both the long-term policy effects and the short-range decisional case effects are possible and worth study.

The ecological view stresses the media's role in placing issues on the criminal justice (and other policy) agendas. But can the media also perform a role in taking an issue off the policy agenda? Cook and Skogan have found that in the criminal justice area, the issue of criminal victimization of the elderly disappeared from the congressional agenda because academic researchers were able to dispel the widespread belief that the elderly were disproportionately affected by crime (Cook & Skogan, 1990). If that role can be performed by scholars and bureaucrats acting as "divergent voices" (that is, by disagreeing with the prevailing view), might not the media also perform that role on other issues? There appears to be little research available on if, and under what conditions, the media might impede the emergence of a policy. However, non-decision making as well as decision making leads to policy of a sort. And the media role in the non-emergence or suppression of policy might well be explored.

That competing and untested hypotheses have left scholars near where they began—trying to empirically challenge the notion of "minimal effects" (McGuire, 1986)—suggests the need for continuing to study the media's effects on the criminal justice agenda. Advances in agenda-setting research have paradoxically toughened the challenge by reformulating the model as one of reverberating effects in an evolving ecosystem. Coming full circle, scholars are now raising questions about the initial role of criminal justice policymakers in setting the media's agenda (Pritchard, 1986; Protess et al., 1985; Gandy, 1982) and about the disappearance of particular criminal justice issues from the policy agenda (Cook & Skogan, 1990). The task of taming the methodological wilderness is itself foreboding. But paths are now marked where only anecdotal morsels existed five years ago.

REFERENCES

Ball-Rokeach, S.J., "The Origins of Individual Media-Source Dependency: A Sociological Framework," *Communication Research,* 12:485–510 (1985).

Blumler, Jay and Katz, Elihu, *The Uses of Mass Communications: Current Perspectives on Gratifications Research,* Beverly Hills: Sage (1974).

Bortner, M.A., "Media Images and Public Attitudes Toward Crime and Justice," in Ray Surette (ed.), Springfield: Charles C Thomas (1984).

Carlson, James M., *Prime Time Law Enforcement: Crime Show Viewing and Attitudes Toward the Criminal Justice System,* NY: Praeger (1985).

Cook, F.L. and Skogan, W.G., "Agenda setting: convergent and divergent voice models of the rise and fall of policy issues," *Journal of Politics* (forthcoming).

Cook, F.L., Tyler, T.R., Goetz, E.G., Gordon, M.T., Protess, D. and Molotch, H.L., "Media and agenda setting: Effects on the public, interest group leaders, policy makers, and policy," *Public Opinion Quarterly,* 47:16–35 (1983).

Davis, Roger W., "Pretrial Publicity, the Timing of the Trial, and Mock Jurors' Decision Processes," *Journal of Applied Social Psychology,* 16:590–607 (1986).

Einsiedel, Edna F., Salomone, Kandice L., and Schneider, Frederick P., "Crime: Effects of Media Exposure and Personal Experience on Issue Salience," *Journalism Quarterly,* 61:131–136 (1984).

Ettema, James S., Protess, David L., Leff, Donna R., Miller, Peter V., Doppelt, Jack C., and Cook, Fay L., "Agenda-setting as Politics: A Case Study of the Press-Public-Policy Connection at the Post-Modern Moment," presented at the Association for Education in Journalism and Mass Communication convention, Wash., D.C. (1989).

Fishman, Mark, "Crime Waves as Ideology," *Social Problems,* 29:531–543 (1978).

Gandy, Oscar, *Beyond Agenda-Setting: Information subsidies and public policy,* Norwood, N.J.: Ablex (1982).

Garofalo, James, "Crime and the Mass Media: A Selective Review of Research," *Journal of Research in Crime and Delinquency, ?:* 319–350 (1981).

Gordon, Margaret T. and Riger, Stephanie, *The Female Fear,* NY: The Free Press (1989).

Graber, Doris A., *Crime News and the Public,* NY: Praeger (1980).

Graber, Doris A., *Mass Media and American Politics,* Wash., D.C.: CQ Press (1980, 1984, 1989).

Greene, E. and Wade, W., "Of private talk and public print: General pre-trial publicity and juror decision-making," *Applied Cognitive Psychology,* 1:1–13 (1987).

Hughes, Sian, "The Reporting of Crime in the Press: A Study of Newspaper Reports in 1985," *Cambrian Law Review,* 18:35–51 (1987).

Jacob, Herbert and Lineberry, Robert, *Governmental Responses to Crime: Crime and Governmental Responses in American Cities,* Wash., D.C.: National Institute of Justice (1982).

Kaplan, John and Skolnick, Jerome H., *Criminal Justice,* Westbury, NY: The Foundation Press (1982).

Lang, Gladys E. and Lang, Kurt, *The Battle for Public Opinion,* NY: Columbia University Press (1983).

Leff, Donna R., Protess, David L. and Brooks, Stephen, "Crusading Journalism: Changing Public Attitudes and Policy-Making Agendas," *Public Opinion Quarterly,* 50:300–314 (1986).

Linsky, Martin, *Impact: How the Press Affects Federal Policymaking,* NY: W.W. Norton & Co. (1986).

McCombs, Maxwell E. and Shaw, Donald L., "The agenda-setting function of mass media," *Public Opinion Quarterly,* 36:176–187 (1972).

McCombs, M.E. and Weaver, D.H., "Voters' need for orientation and use of mass communication," presented at the International Communication Association annual meeting, Montreal (1973).

McConnell, Grant, *Private Power and American Democracy,* NY: Alfred A. Knopf (1967).

McGuire, William J., "The Myth of Massive Media Impact: Savagings and Salvagings," *Public Communication and Behavior, vol. I,* Academic Press, Inc. (1986).

Molotch, Harvey L., Protess, David L., and Gordon, Margaret T., "The Media-Policy Connection: Ecologies of News," in Paletz, D.L. (ed.), *Political Communication Research,* Norwood, NJ: Ablex (1987).

Nelson, Barbara J., *Making an Issue of Child Abuse: Political Agenda Setting for Social Problems,* Chicago: University of Chicago Press (1984).

Noelle-Neumann, Elisabeth, "The Effect of Media on Media Effects Research," *Journal of Communication,* 33:157–165 (1983).

Page, Benjamin I. and Shapiro, Robert Y., "Effects of Public Opinion on Policy," *American Political Science Review,* 77: 175–190 (1983).

Pritchard, David, "Homicide and Bargained Justice: The Agenda-Setting Effect of Crime News on Prosecutors," *Public Opinion Quarterly,* 50:143–159 (1986).

Protess, David L., *Muckraking Matters: The Societal Impact of Investigative Reporting,* Institute for Modern Communications monograph series, Evanston, Il.: Northwestern University (1987).

Protess, David L., Cook, Fay L., Curtin, Thomas R., Gordon, Margaret T., Leff, Donna L., McCombs, Maxwell E., and Miller, Peter, "The Impact of Investigative Reporting on Public Opinion and Policymaking: Targeting Toxic Waste," *Public Opinion Quarterly,* 51:166–185 (1987).

Protess, David L., Leff, Donna R., Brooks, Stephen C., and Gordon, Margaret T., "Uncovering Rape: The Watchdog Press and the Limits of Agenda Setting," *Public Opinion Quarterly,* 49:19–37 (1985).

Reiner, Robert, *The Politics of the Police,* NY: St. Martin's Press (1985).

Roberts, Donald F. and Bachen, Christine M., "Mass Communication Effects," *Annual Review of Psychology,* 32:307–356 (1981).

Schattschneider, E.E., *The Semi-Sovereign People,* Hinsdale, Il.: Dryden Press (1960).

Stinchcombe, Arthur L., Adams, Rebecca and Heimer, Carol A., *Crime and Punishment: Changing Attitudes in America,* San Francisco: Jossey-Bass Publishers (1980).

Surette, Ray, "Media Trials and Echo Effects," *Journal of Criminal Justice* (forthcoming)

Swanson, David L., "Feeling the Elephant: Some Observations on Agenda-Setting Research," *Communication Yearbook* 11:603–619 (1988).

Swanson, David L., "Political Communication Research and the Uses and Gratifications Model: A Critique," *Communication Research,* 6:37–53 (1979).

Weaver, D.H., "Audience need for orientation and media effects," *Communication Research,* 7:361–376 (1980).

Wolfe, Tom, *Bonfire of the Vanities,* NY: Farrar, Straus & Giroux (1987).

Chapter 10

HOMICIDE AND BARGAINED JUSTICE

DAVID PRITCHARD

G enerally overlooked in the fair trial/free press debate is the fact that as many as 90 percent of all criminal convictions in the United States are the result of plea bargaining rather than full-blown adversary trials (Heusmann, 1978; Brosi, 1979). The defendant admits guilt in return for some implicit or explicit concession from the prosecution. Because there is no jury, there is no chance that press coverage will prejudice the jury. Nonetheless, it is possible that press coverage will taint the *process.* This study addresses that issue by examining the relationship between newspaper coverage on individual cases and whether prosecutors engage in plea bargaining in those cases.

Previous Work

Prosecutors are avid readers of newspaper stories about their cases, and most say that the news media are good indicators of the public image of the criminal justice system (Drechsel, 1983). So it is not entirely surprising that some prosecutors acknowledge that they take press coverage of a case into consideration in deciding whether to engage in plea negotiations.

Why might publicity make a prosecutor unwilling to plea bargain a case? Alschuler (1968) studied prosecutors in a dozen large American cities and found that they were motivated more by what they perceived to be their self-interest than by considerations of justice or fairness for the defendant. In other words, prosecution is a political process, and prosecutors have a political stake in how their actions are perceived. Maintaining a public image as a crimefighter is important to the prosecutor, perhaps to the extent of stressing adversary dispositions in publicized

Reprinted by permission from the University of Chicago Press from *Public Opinion Quarterly,* Vol. 50 (1986).

cases, regardless of the strength of evidence against the defendant. In some cases, however, prosecutorial self-interest can lead to negotiations. This is most likely to happen when the prosecutor feels a need to get a conviction—any kind of conviction—despite weak evidence against the defendant. Alschuler writes: "Political considerations may, on occasion, make it important for a prosecutor to secure a conviction for a particular crime, and plea negotiations may provide the only practical means of achieving this objective" (Alschuler, 1968:109). However, prosecutors' most common reaction to publicity, the existing research makes clear, is a desire to avoid being perceived as soft on criminals.

The Context of the Study

This study focuses on prosecutors in the district attorney's office in Milwaukee County, Wisconsin. The basic business of prosecutorial organizations is prosecuting criminal cases. Although in theory defendants decide whether to plead guilty or to exercise their constitutional right to a jury trial, in practice the prosecutor generally controls whether a case is plea bargained (Blumberg, 1967; Alschuler, 1968; Casper, 1972; Alschuler, 1975; Heumann, 1978; Gifford, 1981, 1983). On the one hand, limited resources compel prosecutors to use plea bargaining as the normal mode of settling criminal cases. On the other hand, the public's anger about crime suggests that the electorate may not respond warmly to a prosecutor who plea bargains a visible case. Clearly, then, not all cases can go to full-blown adversarial trial (resource constraints), but some trials are necessary (the influence of public opinion).

This study hypothesizes that newspaper coverage of a criminal case influences whether prosecutors engage in plea bargaining in a given case, and that the more extensive the newspaper coverage of a case, the less likely the district attorney's office is to negotiate in the case.

DATA

Data to test this study's hypothesis were extracted from police and court records and from news stories. Information was obtained on every nonvehicular homicide case presented to the district attorney's office for possible prosecution during the 18-month period between January 1, 1981 and June 30, 1982. The study focuses on homicides because lesser crimes seldom receive press coverage in a major metropolitan community like Milwaukee. In all, the cases of 90 homicide defendants were included in this study.

To find out how the cases were processed, every publicly available document on each case was scrutinized. Included were the inmate registration log at the Milwaukee County Jail; case files at the office of the Milwaukee County Clerk of Courts, Felony Division, which contained copies of criminal complaints, autopsy reports and other pieces of documentary evidence, summaries (and sometimes transcripts) of hearings, and memos from the prosecution and defense; and all news items about the cases published by Milwaukee's daily newspapers, both owned by the Journal Company, which granted full access to its files of clippings.

Measures

The independent variable in this study is the level of newspaper interest in the defendant's case. The dependent variable is the behavior of the prosecutor's office with respect to the case.

Level of Newspaper Interest in a Case. Conceptually, this variable is a function of the resources the newspaper organization is willing to devote to a case. Although newspapers have at their disposal several kinds of resources, the two that are most visible to outsiders like prosecutors are space in the paper and staff effort. This study divides total number of paragraphs by total number of stories to come up with a measure of the level of newspaper interest in the case: the average length of news items about the case. Both Milwaukee newspapers covered homicides similarly (Pritchard, 1985). For that reason, this study combines the newspapers' coverage to form a single variable: the average length of the stories the Milwaukee newspapers published about a defendant's case. Separate analyses were conducted for each newspaper's coverage, with results virtually identical to the result produced by the combined coverage variable. The newspapers published no stories at all about 5 of the 90 homicide prosecutions in this study. Those cases are coded as having an average story length of 0.

The amount of newspaper staff effort devoted to a given case was measured by analyzing newspaper content. The typical piece of crime news comes directly from routine law enforcement or judicial sources, often documentary sources such as police blotters, jail logs, and criminal complaints (Stanga, 1971; Cohen, 1975; Sherizen, 1978; Drechsel et al., 1980).

On some cases, however, reporters do more. They may use nonroutine sources such as witnesses to the crime, friends and relatives of the suspect and/or victim; or not-for-attribution comments from law enforcement officials. Editorials and staff-written columns of opinion also represent nonroutine kinds of coverage. Accordingly, stories about homicide cases can be categorized either as "routine" (if only routine sources were used) or "nonroutine" (if at least one nonroutine source was used). Of the 744 news items in this study, 13.4 percent were nonroutine by this definition. The variable created using the routine/nonroutine dichotomy is the proportion of nonroutine stories in the newspapers' coverage of a case.

This study did not attempt to determine whether predisposition coverage of individual cases was fair or accurate, however those terms might be defined. The independent variables attempt only to operationalize the level of press interest in a case, measured by the amount of organizational resources newspapers devoted to covering the case.

Prosecutor's Plea-Bargaining Behavior. Plea bargaining in this study is measured not by whether a case was settled consensually but by whether the prosecutor actually engaged in plea negotiations. This "negotiated/did-not-negotiate" variable measures the prosecutor's actual behavior, not whether that behavior led to a consensual outcome. In theory, the negotiated/did-not-negotiate variable is untainted by the behavior of other actors in the criminal justice system. For example, although negotiations cannot succeed without the participation of the prosecutor, a willing prosecutor can be stymied by a defense lawyer or defendant unwilling to accept the prosecutor's terms. Such cases would be disposed of adversarially, but not because the prosecutor failed to negotiate.

Court records and/or news items contained explicit evidence that prosecutors engaged in negotiations in 45 of the 90 cases in this study. In 35 of the cases in which prosecutors negotiated, the result was a consensual settlement, in which the prosecutor and the defense agreed on the appropriate disposition of the case. In the remaining 10 cases, defendants refused plea bargains offered by prosecutors. Those cases either went to jury trial or were dismissed over the objection of the prosecution.

Control Variables. This study uses an extensive set of control variables. Much of the variation in crime seriousness, a factor that could influence both newspaper interest and prosecutors' plea-bargaining behavior, is implicitly controlled by this study's exclusive focus on homicides.

Homicides themselves can vary in a number of ways, however, so additional control variables are used. They include personal attributes (race, age, and sex) of the homicide suspect and victim; whether the suspect and the victim knew each other; the suspect's prior record; the initial charge against the defendant (first-degree murder or a lesser homicide charge, such as manslaughter); whether the defendant was charged with crimes beyond the first homicide count; and the number of suspects alleged to have been involved in the homicide.

Some factors, such as the prominence of the homicide suspect and victim or the bizarreness of the incident, are difficult to quantify. In most cases, however, court records and news stories contain enough details of the incident and of the people involved in it to permit a qualitative evaluation of such aspects of the case.

Results

Discriminant analysis supported the hypothesis: press behavior — specifically, the average length of stories about a case — was the strongest predictor of whether prosecutors engaged in negotiations. The proportion of stories about a case that relied partly or entirely on nonroutine sources, however, was not a significant predictor of negotiations.

Table 1. Results of Discriminant Analysis, with Whether the Prosecution Negotiated as the Dependent Variable

Canonical correlation squared	.238
Improvement in ability to predict	53.3%
Relative contribution of significant discriminating variables:	
Average story length	34.8%
Suspect knew victim	26.9%
Prior record	19.5%
Initial charge	12.4%
Multiple charges	6.5%

Table 1 shows the results of the analysis. Of all the variables, five proved to be statistically significant (at $p = .05$) predictors: average story length (the shorter the average story, the more likely the prosecutor would negotiate); whether the defendant and the victim knew each other (negotiations were more likely if the defendant and victim had been acquainted); the defendant's prior record (negotiations were more likely if the defendant had no prior record); the seriousness of the initial charge (negotiations were more likely when charges were less serious); and whether the defendant faced multiple charges stemming from the incident (negotiations were more likely when there was only one charge).

incident (negotiations were more likely when there was only one charge).

The canonical correlation for the discriminant function is .4883, which means that the variables in the function account for 23.8 percent of the total variance in whether the prosecution engaged in plea negotiations. Average story length is the strongest predictor of prosecutorial behavior, contributing more than a third of the variance accounted for by the function, 34.8 percent, which is 8.3 percent of the entire variance. Easier to understand, perhaps, is the fact that the discriminant function correctly predicts the prosecutor's negotiating behavior in 69 of the 90 cases (76.6 percent). Without the information contributed by the variables in the function, successful predictions could be made only half of the time. In other words, knowing the values of the variables in the function provides a 53.3 percent improvement in predictive ability over chance guessing. The function is statistically significant at the .0003 level.

Despite the statistically significant results of the quantitative analysis, the cases in which the discriminant function makes an incorrect prediction merit some attention. In 5 of those 21 cases, the discriminant function computes a case's probability of membership in a given category (negotiated or not negotiated) at more than 80 percent.

There was no explicit evidence of negotiations in two of these extreme outlier cases (*Wisconsin v. Reynosa, Wisconsin v. Shelton*), despite circumstances in both—minimal press attention, previous relationship with victim, nor prior criminal record, etc.—that strongly predict bargaining. Both cases went to trial, and both defendants were convicted. The striking fact about the cases, however, is that both defendants may sincerely have believed they were innocent.[2] If so, it is not surprising they would be unlikely to be receptive to negotiations that would lead to guilty pleas and prison terms, as almost always is the case when a homicide case is plea bargained.

In the other three extreme cases (*Wisconsin v. Fraser, Wisconsin v. Crosley, and Wisconsin v. Murray*), prosecutors engaged in negotiations despite

---

2. Virginia Reynosa, for example, did not actually stab the person whose death led to her first-degree murder conviction; she merely urged her son on as he wielded the knife. In addition, there was some evidence of provocation on the part of the victim. The son was convicted of murder for the stabbing; the mother was convicted under a portion of Wisconsin law that makes parties to a crime as guilty as the actual perpetrators. Jessie Shelton said that she had been the victim of domestic violence and shot her husband in self-defense. The prosecutor who took her to trial for manslaughter and the jury that convicted her may have been skeptical of that claim; Jessie Shelton weighed 290 pounds and her husband was blind. The judge, however, was more sympathetic. Saying he found an element of self-defense in the shooting, he placed Shelton on five years' probation rather than sending her to prison.

circumstances—intense press attention, extensive prior criminal record, multiple charges stemming from the incident, etc.—that strongly predict no negotiations. All three homicides were fairly routine. The press attention to the cases resulted from chance occurrences unrelated to the nature of the people involved in it.[3]

Discussion

This study's findings suggest that newspapers help set the plea bargaining agendas of Milwaukee prosecutors, at least in homicide cases. The amount of space newspapers were willing to devote to the typical story about a case was a stronger predictor than any other variable in this study of whether the prosecutor would negotiate. This research found

---

3. The Fraser and Crosley cases were fairly typical inner-city homicides; both began with holdups at all-night gas stations and ended with the shooting of the gas-station attendants. In each case, the prosecution bargained with the defendant because it needed his testimony against an accomplice.

Those evidence-related considerations apparently outweighed the influence of extensive press coverage in the cases. But the press focused on the cases for reasons having little to do with the crimes themselves. Fraser's lawyer, for example, asked the judge to bar the press and public from the courtroom. In short, Fraser's crime was fairly routine; the coverage of it was not. It is a case that may have been plea bargained only because prosecutors had evidence problems that forced them to seek Fraser's agreement to testify against his accomplice.

The prosecution offered a similar bargain to Sylvania Crosley, charged with first-degree murder and armed robbery in connection with a crime similar to Fraser's. Crosley's crime took place in 1976, but no arrests were made until 1981, when an informant told police who had done it. By that time Crosley was in prison on unrelated charges; without his testimony, his alleged accomplice would go free. Crosley initially agreed to the deal. But when it was time for him to testify, he refused and charges against his alleged accomplice in the gas-station holdup had to be dismissed. Crosley's crime, like Fraser's, was fairly routine. The press coverage was routine, too, until allegations were made that money had been paid to Crosley's lawyer to buy Crosley's silence. The possibility of corruption sparked a 50-paragraph *Sentinel* story, "Probe of Payment to Lawyer Urged," and a 15-paragraph story a week later noting that authorities were probing ("Allegations on Payment of Lawyer's Fees Probed"). No other stories about the case were as many as 10 paragraphs long. The final case that was negotiated despite intense press coverage stemmed from a tavern shooting that was routine in all but one respect—a group of Milwaukee *Sentinel* staffers was at the bar when the shooting started. Two of the journalists were seriously injured by stray bullets. Because of weak and contradictory evidence, no arrests were made for more than a year after the shooting. Before any arrests were made, the *Sentinel* gave the case extensive publicity, including two lengthy first-person stories by one of the journalists who had been wounded. Other unusual stories during that period included a 63-paragraph story detailing victims and witnesses, disappointment with the police department's failure to make arrests in the case and a 33-paragraph feature about the widow of the man who was killed in the shooting.

Fifteen months after the homicide, two suspects were arrested. The evidence was so weak that charges against one were dismissed outright. The other defendant, Reagan Murray, faced first-degree murder and four non-homicide charges but agreed to plead guilty to reduced charges. Why were the charges reduced when publicity had been so extensive? The available evidence gives no definite answer to that question, but it appears likely that the prosecution realized that the shaky evidence made conviction at trial problematic. The public pressure from the *Sentinel* made some kind of conviction imperative: thus the negotiations (Alschuler, 1968).

evidence suggesting an agenda-setting effect of ordinary crime news, the kind produced day in and day out by beat reporters. Recent studies from Northwestern University's Center for Urban Affairs and Policy Research, on the other hand, have examined possible agenda-setting effects only of investigative news reports (Cook et al., 1983; Protess et al., 1985).

The examination of the five "outlier" cases revealed that the strength of evidence against a defendant (or a defendant's accomplice) could influence whether the prosecution negotiated a case. Evidence strength was not included as a quantitative variable in this study because it is extremely difficult to measure in any systematic way (Eisenstein and Jacobs, 1977:182–183). In addition, evidence strength may well be socially defined construct greatly dependent upon attributes of the relationships between the prosecutor and the defense lawyer, and between the defense lawyer and the defendant.

Finally, it is difficult to predict what effect a strength-of-evidence variable would have on plea bargaining. If evidence is weak, the prosecutor has an incentive not only to negotiate but to offer a good deal. If the evidence is strong, however, the defendant has an incentive to plead guilty even if not offered a good deal to avoid the so-called trial penalty (Uhlman and Walker, 1980: Shane-DuBow et al., 1981; Brereton and Casper, 1982; Pruitt and Wilson, 1983). Guilty pleas in cases where there is no evidence of negotiations often are implicit plea bargains (Heumann, 1978).

Related to the issue of evidence strength are questions involving the content of negotiations. Do prosecutors offer the same bargains to all similarly situated defendants, or does the defendant's race, how his or her case was covered, or other factors influence the content of the actual negotiations? This study did not have access to information about the offers and counter-offers that are a normal part of negotiations, but researchers should attempt to gain access to such information (see, e.g., Maynard, 1984).

REFERENCES

Alschuler, A.
   1968 "The prosecutor's role in plea bargaining." University of Chicago Law Review 36:50–112.
   1975 "The defense attorney's role in plea bargaining." Yale Law Journal 84:1179–1314.

Blumberg, A.
  1967 Criminal Justice. Chicago: Quadrangle Books.
Brereton, D. and J. D. Casper
  1982 "Does it pay to plead guilty? Differential sentencing and functioning of criminal courts." Law & Society Review 16:45–70.
Brosi, K. B.
  1979 A Cross-City Comparison of Felony Case Processing. Washington, D.C.: U.S. Department of Justice.
Casper, J.
  1972 American Criminal Justice: The Defendant's Perspective. Englewood Cliffs, N.J.: Prentice-Hall.
Cohen, S.
  1975 "A comparison of crime coverage in Detroit and Atlanta newspapers." Journalism Quarterly 52:726–730.
Cook, F. L. et al.
  1983 "Media and agenda setting: effects on the public, interest group leaders, policy makers and policy." Public Opinion Quarterly 47:16–35.
Drechsel, R. E., K. Netteburg, and B. Aborisade
  1980 "Community size and newspaper reporting of local courts." Journalism Quarterly 57:71–78.
Eisenstein, J., and H. Jacob
  1977 Felony Justice: An Organizational Analysis of Criminal Courts. Boston: Little, Brown.
Gifford, D. G.
  1981 "Equal protection and the prosecutor's charging decision: enforcing an ideal." George Washington Law Review 49:659–719.
  1983 "Meaningful reform of plea bargaining: control of prosecutorial discretion." University of Illinois Law Review 1983-37–98.
Heumann, M.
  1978 Plea Bargaining: The Experiences of Prosecutors, Judges, and Defense Attorneys. Chicago: University of Chicago Press.
Maynard, D. W.
  1984 "The structure of discourse in misdemeanor plea bargaining," Law & Society Review 18:75–104.
Pritchard, D.
  1985 "Race, homicide and newspapers," Journalism Quarterly 62:500–7.
Protess, D. L., D. R. Leff, S. C. Brooks, and M. T. Gordon
  1985 "Uncovering rape: the watchdog press and the limits of agenda setting." Public Opinion Quarterly 49:19–37.
Pruitt, C. R., and J. Q. Wilson
  1983 "A longitudinal study of the effect of race on sentencing." Law & Society Review 17:613–635.
Shane-DuBow, S. et al.
  1981 Wisconsin Felony Sentencing Guidelines: Phase I of Research and Development. Madison: Wisconsin Center for Public Policy.

Sherizen, S.

  1978 "Social creation of crime news: all the news fitted to print." In C. Winick, ed., Deviance and Mass Media. Beverly Hills, Calif.: Sage.

Stanga, J. E.

  1971 "The press and the criminal defendant: newsmen and criminal justice in three Wisconsin cities." Unpublished Ph.D. dissertation, University of Wisconsin.

Uhlman, T. M., and N. D. Walker

  1980 "He takes some of my time, I take some of his: an analysis of sentencing patterns in jury cases." Law & Society Review 14:323–341.

Chapter 11

CRUSADING JOURNALISM

DONNA R. LEFF, DAVID L. PROTESS, AND STEPHEN C. BROOKS

Investigative reporting is a costly and trendy enterprise used by publishers and broadcasters to build their audiences. Researchers studying mass media influence on the salience of issues before the public—their
"agenda-setting" function—seldom have studied this controversial form
of reporting. Nonetheless, agenda-setting research is growing, and with
it the question of the strength of the causal relationship between media
content and public opinion. The methodologies and the findings vary
from study to study, with the agenda-setting effects demonstrated both in
broadcast and print media. (See literature review by Roberts and Bachen,
1981.)

Researchers also have done little to assess the influence of the media
on the policy agendas of decision makers (Downs, 1972; Molotch and
Lester, 1974; Blanchard, 1974). Studies specifying the connections between
the media, public opinion, and policy information tend to be theoretical
(Molotch et al., 1982), normative (Paletz and Entman, 1981; Regier,
1930), or anecdotal (Bernstein and Woodward, 1974; Crouse, 1973;
Salisbury, 1980).

The current study, and analysis of the agenda-setting effects of a
five-part television investigative series about repeatedly brutal Chicago
police officers, found that the reports had a significant impact on the
general public who viewed or heard about them. Response of policymaking
"elites" surveyed was less conclusive. Significant changes could be detected
in the elites' view of public opinion about police brutality, but they did
not increase their own concern about police brutality as a social problem.
The series did, however, have an educational impact on exposed elites
according to their responses to questions about specific information in
the televised reports. The police brutality series resulted also in major

Reprinted by permission from the University of Chicago Press from *Public Opinion Quarterly*, vol. 50
(1986).

policy changes within the Chicago Police Department, in contrast to the largely symbolic gestures that followed the home health care and rape reports.

Research Design

The pretest, posttest experimental design is highly appropriate but not traditionally utilized in research involving nonlaboratory studies of media agenda setting. One significant obstacle to its application is inherent in the definition of news. Even media personnel are unaware of specific stories they will cover in the future, making pretesting and experimental or quasi-experimental manipulation difficult or impossible.

In this study, however, two factors made it possible for researchers to apply a quasi-experimental research design. The local NBC affiliate, WMAQ–TV (Channel 5), spent six months investigating allegations of police brutality. While the high drama in the broadcast of the allegations may have made the stories seem immediate, in fact the lengthy preparation gave researchers ample time to obtain preseries measurement of public attitudes toward this problem. Further, the policy relevance of most investigative reporting, such as the police brutality series, makes such stories particularly appropriate for studying their effects on both citizen and policymaking agendas.

The second factor in this study was the close cooperation between Channel 5 reporters and our researchers. In the months before the series aired, researchers were informed continually of the developing investigative findings. Questions could be tailored carefully to the content of the television reports, and issues unrelated to its subject matter could be explored as controls.

The series, "Beating Justice," was broadcast on five successive nights beginning on February 7, 1983—a ratings sweepstakes period coinciding with Chicago's mayoral primary election campaign. The reports included dramatic footage of police wagons used as weapons to bounce handcuffed victims during harrowing rides to jail and interviews with victims maimed by police. Reporters reviewed all lawsuits filed against police in federal courts in Chicago in the previous five years and found 107 officers named more than once. Despite procedures developed by the department in response to earlier investigative reports, officers found by the department to have used excessive force were given only minor discipline and no psychiatric counselling. The series included a statistical review of brutality cases against police describing how the department systematically whitewashed brutality charges. Reporters revealed that millions of taxpayer dollars were being spent to compensate victims of police brutality who successfully sued the department. The cameras graphically depicted—although reporters never explicitly stated—that most police brutality victims were nonwhite. Finally, reporters conducted a live interview with the superintendent of police, who by the conclusion of the series had become an issue in the city's mayoral primary that would be held February 22.

Respondents surveyed about offending police officers and the department's tax handling of complaints against them included a random sample of the general public and a purposive sample of policymakers. The methods used in drawing the sample and analyzing data are described below.

General Public. The sample was stratified according to television viewing habits into watchers of Channel 5 (253 respondents) and watchers of other evening newscasts or nonwatchers of any television news (171). One week after the series was broadcast, researchers recontacted the entire sample. 279 persons agreed to be reinterviewed, and they comprise the public sample in this study. Those respondents reflected attitudes on the pretest about police brutality that were similar to those on the pretest of persons not reinterviewed, although minorities and the less well-educated were less represented in the reinterviewed group.

At the conclusion of the posttest interview, respondents were asked whether they had "seen, read or heard anything about news media investigations of police brutality in Chicago?" This screening question was used to include in the exposed group persons who may not have seen the series under study but who heard about it in some other way, such as in reports picked up by other media, in conversations with friends, or in advertisements promoting the Channel 5 series. This question also corrected for persons who said they were regular viewers of Channel 5 news but who did not see the series on police brutality. Those responding "yes" to the question were considered "treatment" and those who answered "no" were considered "control" group members. It is important to emphasize that respondents in both analyses are from the overall sample. It is only the quasi-experimental definition of "treatment" and "control" that changes.

In the pre- and posttest interviews, respondents were asked about a variety of topics including police brutality. We hypothesized that change would occur in the "treatment" group on questions about police brutality, while responses to other questions would remain consistent from pre to posttest. We expected the "control" group responses to remain consistent on all questions.

We asked respondents to rate the importance of brutality as a problem and to assess the quality of the Chicago Police Department. Further, respondents were asked to agree or disagree with statements about police brutality occurring more frequently against nonwhites, about the police department's lax discipline of brutal officers, and about the need for adequate compensation of victims of police brutality. These questions addressed specific points made in the television report. The subject areas of questions could be divided into four categories: (1) measurement of attitudes and agendas, (2) measurement of knowledge (specific facts learned from the reports), (3) measurement of emotions, and (4) measurement of changes in behavior. Thus, we hypothesized that in posttest interviews, treatment group members would consider police brutality a more important issue, would increase their knowledge of police brutality to incorporate facts revealed in the series, and would change their attitudes, feelings and actions about the problem.

Policymakers. A purposive sample of "policy elites" was selected for its interest and potential influence on law enforcement policymakers. The 35 persons surveyed included several suburban police chiefs, state legislators, members of the Chicago city council, and members of a citizens advisory police group. Interviews were conducted by telephone and all 35 were reinterviewed after the police brutality series. In previous studies, researchers made no attempt to establish an elite group of non-exposed ("control") respondents. We expected that persons with a great deal of interest in the topic of investigative reports almost certainly would hear of them, even if they failed to read or view the specific stories. In this study, however, about a third of respondents could be grouped as "controls" who were unaware of the Channel 5 reports. Separate analyses were conducted for the exposed and unexposed groups of elites.

The policymakers were asked a series of pretest and posttest questions that were identical to those in the survey of the general public. Additionally, however, they were asked to estimate the public's views on the issues in question. They also were asked a set of questions about their policymaking activity related to police brutality. After the series, researchers tracked policy changes that might be attributable to the

Channel 5 series by interviewing policymakers and by content-analyzing local media.

Findings

General Public. In examining public attitudes before and after the policy brutality series, we wanted to learn whether attitudes toward police brutality changed significantly among persons who watched or heard about the reports. We attempted to measure agenda-setting changes using the two different definitions of "treatment" groups as discussed above.

Table 1 shows the mean responses of the general public to questions that measured attitude changes and knowledge about specific facts contained in the television reports. The data indicate that persons in the two treatment groups significantly increased their views of the importance of police brutality after being exposed to the reports, although they did not change their ranking of brutality relative to other urban problems. In contrast, persons in the two control groups did not change their opinion of police brutality. However, the strength of these findings was weakened by unexplained significant changes on the importance of welfare fraud (see Table 1), which was the only topic on which control group responses changed.

A second attitude question asked persons about the importance of police brutality and four other law enforcement problems not related to material in the series. Again, persons in the two exposed groups showed significant changes in attitude toward police brutality in the post-test survey. Persons in the two nonaware groups showed no changes on any of the issues, as expected.

On factual questions related to the specific content of the police brutality series, change in the exposed groups was weaker. Following the series both treatment groups increased their agreement with a statement that the city compensated victims of police brutality, while persons aware of the series increased their agreement with a statement about the lack of police discipline. Neither of the "control" groups changed their views about any of the content issues relevant to the series, although, as discussed above, both treatment and control groups changed their views significantly on the ability of the government to identify perpetrators of welfare fraud. Neither treatment nor control groups changed their opinions about the veracity of a statement that police brutality victims were

Table 1

Mean Responses for General Public[a]

| | Channel 5 Watchers/Nonwatchers | | | | Series Aware/Not Aware | | | |
| | Watchers (Treatment) (N = 171) | | Nonwatchers (Control) (N = 108) | | Aware (Treatment) (N = 163) | | Not Aware (Control) (N = 114) | |
	Pre	Post	Pre	Post	Pre	Post	Pre	Post
Importance of problem								
Police brutality	3.09	3.34*	3.42	3.28	3.18	3.36*	3.28	3.27
Violent crime	3.83	3.81	3.82	3.85	3.80	3.80	3.88	3.87
Welfare fraud	3.50	3.53	3.54	3.35*	3.48	3.38*	3.56	3.56
Unemployment	3.91	3.93	3.88	3.87	3.91	3.93	3.89	3.89
Govt. corruption	3.55	3.54	3.65	3.60	3.58	3.56	3.60	3.57
Importance of law enforcement problem								
Police brutality	3.15	3.38*	3.34	3.29	3.22	3.41*	3.23	3.28
Traffic safety laws	3.02	3.10	3.01	3.10	2.95	3.06*	3.09	3.13
Discrimination in department	2.96	3.05	3.14	2.98	3.02	3.07	3.01	3.01
Underreporting of crime	3.59	3.61	3.51	3.51	3.57	3.65	3.55	3.46
Police bribery	3.60	3.59	3.60	3.51	3.59	3.54	3.65	3.63
Fact statements								
Brutality more likely to nonwhites	2.95	2.88	3.07	3.00	3.02	3.01	2.92	2.81
Lack of police discipline	3.59	3.61	2.75	2.93	2.82	3.11*	2.82	2.68
Brutality victims get money	2.03	2.34*	2.09	2.09	2.05	2.28*	2.10	2.20
Able to identify welfare fraud	2.44	2.65*	2.51	2.79	2.49	2.65*	2.46	2.80*
Punishment for govt. corruption	2.15	2.20	2.08	2.09	1.96	2.09	2.27	2.24
Quality of service								
Police department	3.06	2.98	2.09	2.99	3.00	2.96	2.99	3.02
Garbage collection	3.28	3.35	3.15	3.07	3.25	3.29	3.16	3.18
Fire department	3.66	3.66	3.57	3.53	3.63	3.60	3.58	3.63
Street repair	1.83	2.09*	1.85	1.87	1.86	1.98	1.81	2.00
Parks and recreation	2.82	2.79	2.79	2.72	2.71	2.77	2.91	2.76

[a] Higher numbers indicate more positive responses: (4 equals "very important," "agree strongly," and "very adequate").

* p .05 (asterisks indicate significant change from pre- to posttest using a dependent t-test).

more likely to be nonwhite, which was only implied and never directly stated in Channel 5 series.

Finally, on the question of the quality of the Chicago Police Department's services in general, no similar agenda-setting effect could be detected in any group, although one might have expected a change after the repeated brutality emphasized in the television reports.

To summarize the findings for the general public survey, then, we found significant attitude changes among those exposed to the series. Seven of the 12 tests for related items changed significantly in the hypothesized direction. Such changes were strongest on the general issue questions and weaker on statements of fact. Lack of expected change occurred in respondents' evaluation of police services in general. Tests run on items in which no change was hypothesized showed that 61 of 68 failed to change significantly.

Policymakers. Table 2 reports the mean responses of policymakers to the pre- and posttest surveys. Responses are divided according to aware and unaware groups, as divided above. Responses are given for policymakers' as well as for their perceptions of the public view. These results have limited implications due to sample size and nonrandom selection.

Researchers expected less significant changes in elite opinions in all groups because policymakers already are familiar with the issue (and were selected for this sample because of their interest in it). Thus, neither group showed a statistically significant change on the question of police brutality as a general urban problem or as a law enforcement problem. Policymakers who said they had not seen or heard about the Channel 5 reports nonetheless demonstrated a statistically significant change in their opinion on the posttest of the importance of police brutality as a law enforcement problem. (Both aware and nonaware groups in the posttest also increased their views of the importance of discrimination in the police department as a law enforcement problem, which we address in the analysis below.)

The series had its most significant impact for elites on their views of fact statements based on the content of the reports and on their opinions of the public's view of police brutality. Aware elites show statistically significant changes on two of the three fact questions about police brutality. The nonaware groups showed significant changes in their responses to the question of how important the public deems the problem of police brutality. They did not change their views of the more specific question about the public's view of brutality as a law enforcement problem.

Policymaking. Policymakers were questioned in the pre- and posttest about their perceptions of the amount of time they are, will be, and should be spending on problems related to police brutality. We hypothesized that after viewing the series, they would increase their time commitment to related issues. While both elite aware and nonaware indicated a limited increase in time commitment, their responses do not allow us to draw any conclusions about their time committed to the problem of police brutality.

We also measured policymaking changes by interviewing public officials after the series and by monitoring the media to learn of changes in

Table 2
Mean Response for Policy Elite[a]

	Aware (N = 24)		Not Aware (N = 11)	
	Pre	Post	Pre	Post
Personal View				
Importance of problem				
Police brutality	3.00	3.17	2.73	3.09
Violent crime	3.67	3.54	3.91	3.91
Welfare fraud	2.41	2.29	2.63	2.91
Unemployment	3.96	3.92	4.00	3.91
Govt. corruption	3.25	3.00	3.36	3.36
Importance of law enforcement problem				
Police brutality	3.04	3.25	2.73	3.18*
Traffic safety laws	1.78	1.91	1.91	2.09
Discrimination in department	2.82	2.45*	2.56	3.11*
Underreporting of crime	3.18	3.27	3.64	3.72
Police bribery	3.16	3.21	3.64	3.72
Fact statements				
Brutality more likely to nonwhites	2.96	3.26*	3.00	3.63*
Lack of police discipline	2.45	2.95*	2.55	2.91
Brutality victims get money	1.65	2.00	1.80	1.70
Able to identify welfare fraud	2.62	2.19	2.64	2.09
Punishment for govt. corruption	2.50	2.33	2.55	2.73
Public View				
Importance of problem				
Policy brutality	2.64	3.36*	2.63	3.37*
Violent crime	4.00	4.00	3.74	3.87
Welfare fraud	3.09	3.27	2.65	2.74
Unemployment	4.00	4.00	3.96	3.96
Govt. corruption	3.27	3.45	2.78	3.09
Importance of law enforcement problem				
Police brutality	2.81	3.00	2.68	3.00
Traffic safety laws	2.09	2.00	1.86	1.90
Discrimination in department	2.70	3.10	2.70	2.80
Underreporting of crime	3.36	3.55	2.52	3.00*
Police bribery	3.36	3.45	2.86	2.86

[a] Higher numbers indicate more positive response (4 equals "very important" and "agree strongly."
* p .05 (asterisks indicate significant change from pre- to posttest using a dependent t-test).

policy that might be attributable to the Channel 5 report. The most significant change was a general order, issued by the superintendent of police on March 8, 1983, one month after "Beating Justice" was broadcast. The order established an extensive program for identifying and treating police officers exhibiting "patterns of behavior which would warrant concern," including those against whom complaints of excessive force had been filed. Two new management positions were created to implement the new program.

Discussion of Findings

This study found clearly discernible effects in the posttest survey of persons exposed to the investigative reports. This is consistent with the growing support for the notion that the impact of television is greater than newspapers when the subject is dramatic and the event short-term (McClure and Patterson, 1976; Graber, 1980). "Beating Justice," with its interviews with brutalized victims and disguised voice, shadow-faced former police officers, certainly was powerful drama. It also was high-quality journalism, as evidenced by the recognition it received, winning the 1983 Chicago "Emmy" for outstanding investigative reporting and the Robert F. Kennedy Foundation award for social justice in media reporting, the first television report so honored. Thus, while the difference in medium may not be the only explanation for the difference in impact, it probably is at least a partial factor and worth exploring in future studies.

The issue itself may also be an important explanatory variable in distinguishing the effects of various investigative reports. It appears that the less information and sensitivity the public has to an issue prior to its treatment in the media, the more likely it is to be influenced by subsequent media reports. Pretests on home health care showed the public to be poorly informed and not concerned about alternatives to institutionalizing the elderly. Similarly, the public surveyed had little concern about police brutality either as a general urban problem or as a law enforcement problem. This lack of prior interest correlated to significant changes in the posttest survey responses in aware groups. In contrast, the public already demonstrated much knowledge and concern about violent crime, including rape, at the pretest stage in study two. It is possible that rape as a social problem already had reached a saturation level on the public's agenda.

Additionally, we need to understand responses to investigative reporting as functions of the media's presentation of an issue. The home health care expose focused on a limited number of unscrupulous operators who already were targets of official investigations. The rape series was largely informational in nature, including statistics on the incidence of rape, victim and perpetrator profiles, and geographic data comparing the city to the suburbs. The police brutality stories, however, practically cried out for reform. Villains and victims were portrayed in unambiguous terms. The evidence presented in the series appeared to be irrefutable.

In sum, the stylistic form of an investigative report—equivocal or unequivocal—may affect profoundly its degree of impact. As we study additional investigative reports, we will continue to try to understand the link between the form of the media messages, the nature of the issues exposed, and the opinion and policy responses to them.

REFERENCES

Bernstein, C., and B. Woodward
    1974 All the President's Men. New York: Warner Books.
Blanchard, R. O. (comp.)
    1974 Congress and the News Media. New York: Hastings House.
Crouse, T.
    1973 The Boys on the Bus. New York: Ballentine.
Downs, A.
    1972 "Up and down with ecology: the issue attention cycle." Public Interest 28:38–50.
Graber, D.
    1980 Mass Media and American Politics. Washington, D.C.: Congressional Quarterly Press.
McClure, R., and T. Patterson
    1976 "Print vs. network news." Journal of Communication 26:23–28.
Molotch, H., and M. Lester
    1974 "News as purposive behavior: on the strategic use of routing events, accidents and scandals." American Sociological Review 39:101–12.
Molotch, H. D. Protess, and M. T. Gordon
    1982 "The media-policy connection." Working Paper Series. Evanston, IL. Northwestern University Center for Urban Affairs and Policy Research.
Paletz, D., and R. Entman
    1981 Media Power Politics. New York: Free Press
Regier, C. C.
    1930 Era of the Muckrakers. Chapel Hill: University of North Carolina Press.
Roberts, D. F., and C. M. Bachen
    1931 "Mass communication effects." Annual Review of Psychology 32:307–56.
Salisbury, H. E.
    1980 Without Fear or Favor. New York: Time Books.

Chapter 12

SHIELD LAWS AND REPORTER'S PRIVILEGE: A NATIONAL ASSESSMENT

JANE E. KIRTLEY

Introduction

The Justice Department's attempt in August 1985 to force the television networks, wire services and news magazines to turn over outtakes and photographs of the hijacking of TWA flight 847 to Beirut focused public attention on an issue that has troubled the news media since the early 1970s: the use of subpoenas to compel production of the names of news sources and unpublished information.

This highly publicized incident, which evoked editorial comment and protests from the news media,[1] was by no means an isolated occurrence. Both prosecutors and criminal defendants frequently subpoena journalists in attempts to obtain information they believe may assist them in presenting their cases.

Under traditional common law analysis, journalists enjoyed no testimonial privileges similar to the doctor-patient or attorney-client privileges. But the tension between the Sixth Amendment right to a fair trial and the First Amendment guarantees of freedom of the press posed hard problems for judges and legislatures alike. Also troublesome was the desire of investigators and prosecutors to compel reporters to present evidence on behalf of the state or before a grand jury, often jeopardizing the independence of the press.

The last situation culminated in a trilogy of cases decided by the U.S. Supreme Court in 1972. *Branzburg v. Hayes*[2] involved subpoenas seeking testimony about confidential sources from a Kentucky reporter who had written stories on illegal drug manufacture and from two reporters who had "infiltrated" the Black Panthers Party.

In an opinion by Justice Byron White, four members of the high court ruled that reporters are not privileged under the U.S. Constitution to

163

refuse to testify before grand juries as to criminal activities they have observed. Justice Powell concurred but noted that no harassment of reporters would be tolerated and that journalists would be free to file motions to quash if they could show that they had been subpoenaed without legitimate need.

Justice Stewart, joined by Justices Brennan and Marshall, dissented.[3] He articulated a three-part test which the government must meet before it can compel a journalist to reveal confidential sources: there must be probable cause to believe that the information is clearly relevant to a specific probable violation of law; that the information cannot be obtained by alternative means; and that there is a compelling and overriding interest in the information. Justice Powell's concurring opinion has generally been interpreted by courts as providing the basis for the so-called "qualified privilege" for journalists, which can be divested only if the three-part test is met.

With the exception of a handful of in-chambers decisions, the Supreme Court has not addressed the question of reporter's privilege in a criminal justice context since *Bransburg.* However, in addition to the qualified constitutional privilege, journalists also enjoy statutory and state constitutional or common law protection in most states.

Although there is no federal shield law,[4] twenty-six states have enacted legislation to protect reporters from compelled disclosure of confidential or unpublished information. As shown in Table 1, the laws vary widely in scope. Some, such as New Jersey's, offer virtually absolute protection from testimony, even about information that was published or broadcast by the news media.[5] Others are more limited. Some protect only confidential sources and information,[6] some do not protect broadcast journalists' "outtakes," and others are subject to divestiture in certain types of proceedings,[7] if the three-part test is met,[8] or if the reporter has somehow waived the privilege.

For example, the Arizona statute[9] does not apply before a grand jury or magistrate during an investigative proceeding; the Delaware statute does not apply before a grand jury.[10] The Maryland statute, the oldest in the country, was amended in 1988 to add a qualified privilege for unpublished information; it had previously offered an absolute privilege for confidential sources only.[11] Montana's shield law is waived if a reporter testifies voluntarily.[12]

More flexible is the court-created common law privilege, recognized in some form in virtually every state and in most federal circuits.[13] Many

Table 1
Status of Shield Laws by State

State	Who	Sources	Information	Confidentiality	Comments
Alabama	Person connected with or employed by a newspaper, radio or television station "while engaging in a news-gathering activity".	Absolute.	Not specified.	Not specified.	Publication or broadcast of material required for privilege to attach.
Alaska	Newspaper, television, radio, periodical, motion picture or press association "reporter" acting in the course of his duties. Person must have been a reporter at the time of communication.	Qualified; privilege may be divested if withholding material would result in miscarriage of justice, denial of fair trial, or be contrary to the public interest.	Not specified.	Not specified.	
Arizona	Person "connected with or employed by a newspaper, radio or TV station."	Absolute (in any legal proceeding).	May subpoena evidence if "relevant and material to the affiant's cause of action or defense" and the affiant "has attempted to obtain each item of information from all other available sources."	Not specified.	Does not apply before a grand jury or magistrate during an investigative criminal proceeding.
Arkansas	Publisher, editor, reporter or writer for newspaper, periodical and radio station manager or owner.	Qualified; divested if article is written "in bad faith with malice and not in the interest of the public welfare."	Not specified.	Not specified.	Privilege attaches when material is "written, published or broadcast."
California	Publisher, editor, reporter or other person "connected with" a newspaper, magazine, radio or television station, or press association.	Absolute.	Absolute for unpublished information obtained "for communication to the public."	Case law states nonconfidential information covered.	Bars contempt sanctions only.
Delaware	"Reporter" employed at least 20 hours a week or an assistant thereto.	Absolute in non-adjudicative proceedings [i.e., legislative proceedings]; qualified in adjudicative proceedings; no privilege before a grand jury.	Same.	Not specified.	Court may order disclosure (1) of material in the "public interest" [i.e., look to relevance, availability of alternate sources, likely effect disclosure would have on future flow of information to the public, an the circumstances under which the reporter obtained the information] or (2) if reporter's sworn statement of need for non-disclosure is proven false by a preponderance of the evidence.

State	Who	Sources	Information	Confidentiality	Comments
Illinois	Person regularly engaged in work for "news medium" [i.e., newspaper, news service, radio, television, cable system news reels, and motion pictures].	Qualified; divestiture may occur where all "other available sources have been exhausted" and the material is essential to the interest in protection of a public interest.	Not specified.	Case law states non-confidential information covered.	In libel actions, privilege may be divested if all other available sources have been exhausted and plaintiff's needs for disclosure outweighs the public interest in protecting the reporter's confidentiality. Privilege continues while appeal is pending.
Indiana	Owners and paid "editorial or reportorial" employees of a newspaper, television or radio station or press association.	Absolute.	Not specified.	Case law interpretations in conflict.	
Kentucky	People "connected with" newspapers, radio or TV broadcasting station.	Absolute.	Not specified.	Not specified.	Material must be published for privilege to attach.
Louisiana	People regularly engaged in editorial activities of the "news media" [i.e., newspapers, press associations, wire services, radio, television and motion pictures.]	Qualified; privilege divested if disclosure is "essential to the public interest.	Not specified.	Not specified.	In defamation cases, the burden is on the reporter to prove that the material was obtained from a confidential source. Separate statute governs procedural requirements for subpoenaing media. Elaborate rules govern procedures for subpoenaing the news media.
Maryland	Person "connected with" a newspaper, magazine, journal, radio or television station, wire service, press association or news agency.	Absolute.	Qualified.	Case law states non-confidential information covered.	Case law states privilege can be waived.
Michigan	"Person who is involved in the gathering or preparation of news for broadcast or publication."	Qualified; for crimes punishable by life imprisonment, reporters may be compelled to turn over material if the affiant demonstrates that the material is essential to the proceeding and is not available from another source.	Same.	Not specified.	Statute applies to unpublished information.
Minnesota	Person "directly engaged in the gathering, procuring, compiling, editing or publishing of information for dissemination or publication to the public.	Qualified; privilege may be divested if material is (1) clearly relevant to specific violation of law, (2) cannot be obtained by alternative means, (3) needed to prevent injustice.	Same, limited to unpublished information.	Unpublished information from non-confidential sources protected under case law.	In defamation actions, privilege may be overcome if (1) source will lead to relevant evidence on the issue of actual malice or (2) the material sought is clearly relevant to the issue of defamation and cannot be obtained by less destructive alternative means.

State	Who	Sources	Information	Confidentiality	Comments
Montana	Any person "connected with" a newspaper, magazine, press association, news agency, news service, radio station, television station, cable station "for the purpose of gathering, writing, editing or disseminating news."	Absolute.	Absolute.	Not specified.	Applies to published and unpublished material. Precludes contempt sanction only. Privilege waived if newsperson volunteers to produce source or information.
Nebraska	Person "engaged in procuring, gathering, writing, editing or disseminating news or other information." Includes, but is not limited to, newspapers, magazines, periodicals, books, pamphlets, news agencies, news services, wire services, news syndicates, broadcast stations or networks and cable systems.	Absolute.	Absolute.	Not specified.	Privilege applies to material whether or not published or broadcast.
Nevada	Any reporter, former reporter or editorial employee of a newspaper, periodical, press association or employee of a radio or television station.	Absolute, if obtained in such person's "professional capacity."	Same.	Not specified.	Privilege applies to published and unpublished material.
New Jersey	Person "connected with" the news media [i.e., newspapers, magazines, press associations, news agencies, wire services, radio and television].	Absolute.	Absolute.	Not specified.	Privilege applies whether or not material is published. Special recordkeeping requirements for broadcasters. Waiver possible by voluntary disclosure.
New Mexico	Person employed by news media [i.e., newspapers, magazines, press associations, news agencies, wire services, radio and television.	Qualified; privilege may be divested if material is relevant and crucial to the case of the party seeking disclosure, and if alternative means of discovering the material have been reasonably exhausted and the interest in disclosure "clearly outweighs" the public interest in protecting the reporter's confidentiality.	Same.	Rule applies only to confidential sources and information [i.e., communication "not intended to be disclosed to third persons"].	Special record-keeping requirements for radio stations.

State	Who	Sources	Information	Confidentiality	Comments
New York	Professional journalist or newscaster "associated with" a newspaper, magazine, news agency, press association, wire service, radio or television station, network, book, free-lancers, and still and moving picture photographers.	Absolute.	Absolute.	Case law construes statute as requiring confidentiality.	Protects published and unpublished material.
North Dakota	Any person "employed by or acting for" any organization engaged in publishing or broadcasting news.	Qualified; divested if court determines that failure to disclose would cause a "miscarriage of justice."	Same.	Case law states non-confidential information covered.	
Ohio	Person "connected with" newspapers, press associations, radio or television stations, or networks.	Absolute.	Not specified.	Not specified.	Case law states privilege may be overcome in criminal cases. Radio and television stations have special recordkeeping requirements.
Oklahoma	Person regularly engaged in "preparing news" for medium of communication [i.e., newspaper, magazine, periodical, book, pamphlets, news service, wire service, news syndicate, broadcast station or network or cable system.]	Qualified; may be divested if material sought is relevant and not otherwise available "with due diligence."	Same.	Not specified.	Protects published and unpublished information. Privilege does not apply in defamation actions "where defendant asserts a defense based on the content or source of such information."
Oregon	Person "connected with" a medium of communication [i.e., includes but is not limited to newspapers, magazines, periodicals, books, pamphlets, news services, wire services, news syndicates, broadcast stations or networks and cable systems].	Absolute; published and unpublished material.	Absolute; unpublished material only.	Not specified.	Statute precludes searches of papers, effects or work premises of person connected with a medium of communication (unless there is probable cause to believe the person has committed, is committing or will commit a crime). Statute does not apply to defamation actions "where the defendant asserts a defense based on the content or source of such information."
Pennsylvania	Person "connected with" a newspaper, press association, radio or television station or magazine.	Absolute.	Case law states qualifiedly privileged.	Case law states non-confidential information is qualifiedly priviliged.	Radio and television stations have special record-keeping requirements.

State	Who	Sources	Information	Confidentiality	Comments
Rhode Island	"Person directly engaged in the gathering or presentation of news for any accredited newspaper, periodical, press association, newspaper syndicate, wire service or radio or TV station."	Qualified; privilege may be divested where material is necessary in a criminal case or where there is a threat to human life and the material is not available from other prospective witnesses.	Same.	Privilege applies only to confidential sources and information.	Privilege does not apply to the source of any allegedly defamatory information.
Tennessee	Persons "connected with" the news media or press.	Qualified; privilege may be divested if there is "clear and convincing evidence" that (1) the material sought is clearly relevant to a probable violation of law, (2) the material sought cannot reasonably be obtained by alternative means and (3) there is a compelling and overriding public interest in the material.	Same.	Case law states non-confidential information covered.	The source privilege does not apply in defamation actions "where the defendant asserts a defense based on the source of such information."

states have adopted the three-part test or some variation on it. Some courts have blurred the distinction between relevance and materiality; others impose a fourth element—that the party seeking disclosure show that the underlying claim is not frivolous.[14]

A handful of states have recognized at least a qualified privilege based on the state's constitution.[15] One, California, has even incorporated shield provisions into the state constitution.[16]

In addition to the doctrine of federal common law privilege recognized by most federal courts, the state interests articulated in shield laws are frequently considered by federal courts; some courts have even assumed that Federal Rule of Evidence 501 requires the application of the shield law from the forum state.[17] In the criminal justice context, the threshold requirements of admissibility, relevance and specificity of Rule 17(c) of the Federal Rules of Criminal Procedure have been construed to protect journalists from fishing expeditions by defense or prosecution.[18]

In addition, in 1973 the Attorney General issued guidelines governing the issuance of subpoenas to the media by the Department of Justice.[19] Recognizing what is, in effect, a qualified privilege, the guidelines are intended to protect journalists from "compulsory process . . . which might impair the news-gathering function." They require the government to make all reasonable attempts to obtain the information from non-media sources and to negotiate with the journalists before serving a subpoena.

If a subpoena is contemplated, it is to be narrowly drawn and should not be used to obtain peripheral information but only information "essential to a successful investigation—particularly with reference to directly establishing guilt or innocence." In most cases, the subpoena should be limited to the verification of published material. Approval of the attorney general is required in most instances and particularly in cases involving the arrest or indictment of a journalist for an offense arising out of the coverage or investigation of a news story. Failure to obtain prior approval may result in administrative sanctions against the government employee.

Application of the Reporter's Privilege in Specific Contexts

Grand juries. A reporter who has witnessed a crime may be compelled to testify before a grand jury in many cases. As noted above, some shield laws either specifically exempt or have been interpreted to exempt grand jury testimony.[20] Many states have followed the guidance of the Supreme Court in *Branzburg*, ruling, as did a Florida appellate court in 1988, that the common law privilege has "utterly no application to information learned by a journalist as a result of being an eyewitness."[21] But there are exceptions. For example, in 1984 the Illinois Supreme Court held that the statutory privilege could not be divested from the journalist without a showing that the investigatory had exhausted all other sources. Mere inconvenience would not be sufficient, the court said.[22] Also in 1984, the New York Court of Appeals, the state's highest court, held that the New York shield law protects journalists from forced disclosure of sources of information even when revealing that information—in this case, a grand jury report—was itself a crime.[23]

In cases where a journalist has not actually witnessed criminal activity but has other information, the results are even more mixed. Interviews with suspects or other potential defendants frequently result in subpoenas, but in such cases, the state is usually required to demonstrate both exhaustion and a compelling need sufficient to override press freedom.[24]

Grand jury subpoenas are usually vigorously resisted by the press. Since such proceedings are secret, most journalists regard them as presenting the greatest threat to their credibility with sources, because there will be no way for the source to know whether the journalist revealed the source during the closed proceeding. As a practical matter, lengthy delays in the appellate process often result in a finding of mootness, because by the time the appeal reaches the state's highest court, the grand jury will have been dismissed.[25]

Pre-Trial and Trial Subpoenas by Prosecution. Probably the most common type of subpoena issued by the prosecution during trial seeks information from "jailhouse interviews" with the defendant. Often, the prosecution merely wants to confirm that statements in a published or broadcast piece were in fact made by the defendant; in other cases, the prosecution seeks unpublished confessions or other impeaching statements. Unless there is a clear showing of confidentiality, courts are often reluctant to recognize a privilege if any part of the interview has been publicized.[26] But even if the interview was not confidential, some courts still quash the subpoenas if the government cannot demonstrate that the information is necessary to the prosecution of the case.[27] The court may elect to review the material *in camera* prior to ordering disclosure.[28]

Subpoenas by Criminal Defendants. The inevitable collision between the Sixth Amendment right to compulsory process and the First Amendment right to press freedom has resulted in a number of courtroom confrontations between criminal defendants and the news media. Generally, defendants subpoena journalists to obtain exculpatory evidence, to impeach a witness, or to demonstrate misconduct on the part of intestigators or prosecutors. Several courts have ruled that there is no First Amendment privilege protecting journalists from such subpoenas,[29] but others attempt to balance the interests, frequently by conducting *in camera* inspections prior to compelling public disclosure of the material sought.

One celebrated case, *In re Farber*,[30] involved an investigative reporter who wrote a series of articles which led to a murder indictment. The defendant subpoenaed most of the material relating to the articles. When the reporter refused to comply with a court ruling ordering *in camera* inspection, he was jailed and the newspaper ordered to pay substantial fines until the subpoena was obeyed, with the court holding that the First Amendment should not be balanced against the Sixth Amendment rights. On appeal, the New Jersey Supreme Court ruled that a court must make a preliminary determination as to materiality, relevance, necessity and alternative sources before compelling *in camera* disclosure. This test was later codified in an amendment to the New Jersey shield law.[31]

Similarly, the Wisconsin Supreme Court, recognizing a qualified, constitutionally based privilege, ruled in 1983 that before *in camera* inspection can be compelled, the defendant must show by a preponderance of the evidence that the testimony sought will be competent, relevant, material, and favorable to the defense, and that the defendant investigated other sources for the information.[32] Overly broad subpoenas may be quashed if they encompass irrelevant or inadmissible information. For example, the Vermont Supreme Court requires defendants to demonstrate relevance of the subpoenaed material or testimony to the issue of guilt or innocence, in addition to exhaustion of other sources.[33]

Criminal defendants sometimes seek reporter's testimony regarding evidence of prosecutorial misconduct. They are seldom successful. Alternative sources—the law enforcement agents involved—are generally available. And, the mere fact that disclosures have been made to the press is usually not sufficient to justify dismissal of an indictment.[34]

Violations of Grand Jury Secrecy. When reporters are subpoenaed to testify as to the source of grand jury leaks, courts are required to balance the interest in maintaining the secrecy of government operations against the public's right to know. Generally, the balance is struck in favor of the latter.[35] However, there have been some instances in which the courts have ruled that protecting the integrity of grand jury proceedings is a superior interest.[36]

Newsroom Searches

In 1978, following the search of the offices of a campus paper by California police, the U.S. Supreme Court ruled in *Zurcher v. Stanford Daily*[37] that news organizations are not exempt from the general rule that law enforcement officials may search the premises of a person not suspected of a crime. Investigators must comply with the Fourth Amendment requirements of probable cause to believe that evidence of a crime will be found on the premises, that the search is reasonable, and that the items to be seized are specified.

In response to *Zurcher,* Congress enacted the Privacy Protection Act of 1980.[38] The statute applies to both federal and state searches and makes it unlawful for officials to search for or seize either "work product" or "documentary materials" from those involved in producing or disseminating newspapers, books or broadcasts to the public, except in very limited circumstances.

"Work product" includes written drafts, edited tape, and film footage. They may only be seized if officials can show probable cause to believe that the person possessing them has committed or is committing a crime relating to the materials, or if seizure is necessary to prevent death or serious bodily harm.

"Contraband" or "fruits of a crime" are not protected. However, if the crime consists of receipt or possession of information, these materials still may not be seized unless they are classified or relate to national security.

"Documentary materials," which include unedited audio or videotapes, notes and photographs, may be seized for the above-listed reasons, or if there is reason to believe that the materials would be destroyed if a subpoena were served, if a court has ordered production and all appeals have been exhausted, or if officials represent that delay would threaten the interests of justice. Even in that case, the person possessing the materials must be allowed to contest the officials' representation prior to seizure.

A journalist whose office is searched or whose materials are seized may sue the governmental unit that conducted the search. If the reporter prevails, the statute provides for a minimum award of $1,000 in damages, plus any actual damages sustained and attorneys' fees incurred.

Even though the Privacy Protection Act applies to state searches as well as those conducted by federal authorities, nine states[39] have laws providing similar or greater protection. For example, Oregon's law prohibits the serach or seizure, with or without a warrant, or the work premises, or of any documents of a person connected with the media, unless there is probable cause to believe that the person is committing, or about to commit, a crime.[40]

Prospects for the Future

Why do journalists resist subpoenas? Many are fiercely protective of the editorial and news-gathering process and resent any intrusion on these activities. They fear that if they are forced to reveal confidential sources, their sources will dry up, diminishing the flow of news to the public.

Journalists also strive to maintain their independence, both in fact and appearance. They do not wish to be "hired guns" for either side in a criminal case and are particularly loathe to be labeled an investigatory arm of the government.

Nevertheless, it is often difficult for the public, as well as members of both the criminal defense and prosecution bars, to understand the motivations behind a news organization's determined fight to quash subpoenas. Particularly during the investigation or prosecution of sensational crimes, journalists who refuse to cooperate are labeled as "obstructionist," "un-American," or worse.

Small wonder, then, that although there are occasional attempts to enact shield laws in those states that do not have them, most of the legislative activity dealing with reporter's privilege concerns attempts to alter existing legislation. With few exceptions, most are generated by some particularly egregious case, such as the jailing of a broadcast reporter in Michigan in 1986 after he refused to turn over to a grand jury outtakes from interviews with juvenile gang members.[41] Had the reporter worked for the print media, he would have been protected. But at that time, the Michigan shield law covered only reporters working for "newspapers or other publications," not broadcasters.

In the wake of that case, the Michigan legislature amended the shield law to include broadcasters. But it also changed the law to permit compelled production of confidential information in criminal cases where the crime is punishable by life imprisonment, provided that the party demonstrates that the information is essential and unavailable from other sources.[42]

This example underscores two essential problems with statutory protections generally. The first is that even the best shield law may be inartfully drafted and may be misinterpreted by a court. Second, shield laws are, and always will be, subject to amendment by legislatures. They do not and cannot provide the same protection to journalists as federal and state constitutions.

Many journalists believe that, absent an absolute privilege, application of balancing tests to accommodate the sometimes conflicting constitutional guarantees of a free press and fair trial is best left to the courts. In the words of Justice Stewart, "the interests protected by the First Amendment are not antagonistic to the administration of justice. Rather, they can, in the long run, only be complementary, and for that reason must be given great 'breathing space.' "[43]

ENDNOTES

1. *See, e.g.,* Wicker, "The Usual Suspects," N.Y. Times, July 26, 1985, p. A27; "Reporters Committee writes to Meese," *Editor & Publisher*, Aug. 10, 1985, p. 20.
   2. 408 U.S. 665 (1972).

3. Justice Douglas also dissented, arguing in favor of an absolute constitutionally based privilege.

4. Repeated attempts to enact a shield law on a federal level have failed due to lack of consensus among lawyers, scholars, and journalists. Carter et al., *The First Amendment and the Fourth Estate* 411 (3d Ed. 1985).

5. N.J. Stat. Ann. §2A:84A-21 to 21.9, 2A:84-29 (West 1976 & Supp. 1987).

6. For example, R.I. Gen. Laws §9–19.1-1 to 9–19.1-3 (1987 & Supp. 1988).

7. For example, in defamation suits, the Minnesota, Ohio and Oregon shield laws limit the application of the privilege.

8. *See, e.g.,* the Tennessee shield law, Tenn. Code Ann. §24-1-208 (1980 & Supp. 1988), which permits divestiture if there is clear and convincing evidence that the material sought is clearly relevant to a probable violation of the law, the material cannot reasonably be obtained by alternative means, and there is a compelling and overriding public interest in the material.

9. Ariz. Rev. Stat. Ann. §12-2237 (1982); Ariz. Stat. Ann. §12-2214 (1981 and Supp. 1988).

10. Del. Code Ann. tit. 10, §§ 4320-26 (1975 & Supp. 1988).

11. Md. Cts. & Jud. Proc. Code Ann. §9-112 (1984 & Supp. 1986), *as amended* 1988 Md. Laws ch. 113, eff. July 1, 1989.

12. Mont. Code Ann. §26-1-901, 902 & 903 (1985 & Supp. 1987).

13. Hawaii, Maine, South Carolina, South Dakota, Utah and Wyoming have no reported decisions recognizing a reporter's privilege. The Sixth and Ninth Circuits have not recognized a privilege.

14. *See, e.g., Mitchell v. Superior Court,* 37 Ca. 3d 268 (1984).

15. Idaho, New Hampshire, New York, North Carolina and Wisconsin.

16. California Constitution Art. 1, § 2.

17. *See, e.g., Riley v. Chester,* 612 F.2d 708 (3d Cir. 1979).

18. *See, e.g., U.S. v. Cuthbertson,* 630 F.2d 139 (3d Cir. 1980), *cert. denied* 449 U.S. 1126 (1981).

19. 28 C.F.R. § 50.10.

20. For example, Rhode Island and Michigan.

21. *Miami Herald v. Gross,* 15 Med. L. Rep. 1834 (Fla. Ct. App. 1988).

22. *In re Special Grand Jury Investigation,* 104 Ill.2d 419 (1984).

23. *Beach v. Shanley,* 62 N.Y.2d 241 (1984).

24. *See, e.g., Tennessee v. Curriden,* 739 S.W.2d 192 (1987).

25. *See, e.g., Corsetti v. Commonwealth,* No. 80-724 (Sup. Ct. Middlesex Co. March 20, 1980).

26. *See, e.g., Maine v. Hohler,* 543 A.2d 364 (Me. 1988).

27. *U.S. v. Blanton,* 534 F.Supp. 295 (S.D. Fla. 1982).

28. *New York v. Korkala,* 472 N.Y.S.2d 310 (1st Dep't 1984).

29. *See, e.g., Hurst v. Georgia,* 8 Med. L. Rep. 2374 (Ga. Ct. App. 1982).

30. *In re Farber — State of New Jersey v. Jascalevich,* 78 N.J. 259, *cert. denied* 439 U.S. 997 (1978).

31. P.L. 1979, Chapter 479, approved Feb. 27, 1980.

32. *Wisconsin ex rel. Green Bay Newspaper Co. v. Circuit Court,* 9 Med. L. Rep. 1889 (Wis. 1983).

33. *State v. St. Peter,* 132 Vt. 226 (1974).

34. *U.S. v. Lane, 5 Med. L. Rep. 2306 (N.D. Ga. 1979).*

35. *See, e.g., Morgan v. State,* 337 So. 2d 951 (Fla. 1976).

36. *See, e.g., In re Grand Jury January 1969,* 315 F. Supp. 662 (D. Md. 1970).

37. 436 U.S. 547 (1978).

38. 42 U.S.C. §§ 2000aa-2000aa-12 (1976 & Supp. 1980).

39. California, Connecticut, Illinois, Nebraska, New Jersey, Oregon, Texas, Washington and Wisconsin.

40. Or. Rev. Stat. §44.510 to 44.540 (1987).

41. *In re Grand Jury Proceedings, Storer Broadcasting v. Michigan,* 13 Med. L. Rep. 1901 (Mich. Ct. App. 1986).

42. Mich. Stat. Ann. § 28.945(1) (Callaghan 1985 & Supp. 1988); Mich Comp. Laws § 767.5a (1982) (as amended Dec. 1986).

43. *Branzburg v. Hayes,* 408 U.S. 665, at 746 (1972).

Chapter 13

MEDIA TRIALS AND ECHO EFFECTS

RAY SURETTE

That publicity can influence the outcome of [criminal] cases is an argument that does not rest on firm empirical support. Rather, the argument is based on a vague commonsense notion (Rollings and Blascovich, 1977:59). Unfortunately, this decade-old observation still holds true. Despite the fact that there has been much speculation and judicial concern about the relationship between media news coverage and the processing of criminal cases, the issue has yet to be fully and adequately addressed. Research has narrowly focused upon the possible effects of media coverage within trials, usually on jurors and infamous cases. Ideas about more general full systematic effect of news coverage on criminal cases is predominantly deduced from a set of anecdotal references, isolated single case studies, or more frequently, mock jury research.[1]

---

1. As an example of the single case study approach, Brady (1983), focusing upon "political trials," reviewed the 1976 press coverage and trial of guerrilla-bombers in Portland, Maine. From this single episode and without reference to other specified trials, he concluded that the Portland case exemplified an historical trend toward biased trials for political defendants resulting from the effects of sustained and hostile media coverage (Brady, 1983:241; see also Becker, 1971; Sullivan, 1967; Treuhaft, 1957). The mock jury studies are either laboratory or field studies using variously formed "juries." In the laboratory studies, subjects were drawn from actual jury pools, community members, voting lists, high school students, undergraduate college psychology students, and law school students. These subjects reviewed the transcripts or heard tapes of cases with and without accompanying media accounts and decided guilt or recommended sentences (see Hoiberg and Stires, 1973; Greene and Loftus, 1984; Greene and Wade, 1987; Kline and Jess, 1966; Simon, 1977; Sohn, 1976; Sue et al., 1974; and Wilcox and McCombs, 1970). The laboratory studies have several weaknesses which limit the generalization of their findings. These include the artificiality of the publicity presented and the lack of variance in the types of media used (all involved printed material); short unrealistic time lags between publicity and verdicts; and the questionable match between subjects and actual jurors (Rollings and Blascovich, 1977:60; Simon, 1977:520–21). Field studies have consisted of surveys of communities involving real cases. Tans and Chaffee (1966) and Riley (1973) reported a prejudicial relationship between publicity and juror opinions. Robinson (1974), however, found that televised publicity did not result in increased feelings among the general public that President Nixon was guilty. Rollings and Blascovich (1977:65) also report that media publicity did not significantly influence public opinion as concerned the Patty Hearst case. Simon and Eimermann (1971) found high level of recognition and knowledge about a case among registered voters and sentiments favoring the

More significant than the mixed results and the difficulty of generalizing the findings from this body of research, the focus of this anecdotal case study and mock jury research runs counter to the operational reality of the criminal justice system in which trials are the exception rather than the norm.

To examine only for a possible media effect on juries and the infamous trial, while important, ignores possible effects on the great bulk of criminal cases. As Lofton (1966:139) notes, "since only about 8 percent of criminal cases are ultimately disposed of by jury trials, the impact of the press on those involved in the non-jury law enforcement process is extremely important." However, an extensive review of the literature reveals few quantitative studies of a general media coverage effect. The best is that by Pritchard (see Chapter 10), who examines the relationship between news coverage and plea bargaining by prosecutors in Milwaukee. Other studies tend to focus on massively covered cases and fair trial issues. The actual empirical effect, if any, of the media on the bulk of crime has not been adequately investigated and is currently unknown (Blumstein et al., 1983:268; Carroll et al., 1986).[2] The focus on trials and infamous cases is, however, not felt to be entirely wrongheaded, just wrongly focused. Trials are felt to be an important beginning point of study, but the research must extend beyond them. Therefore, in order to begin to study a systematic effect of media coverage on the criminal justice system, two related concepts need to be developed. They are "media trials" and "echo effects." The concept of "media trials" is basic to comprehending the media's systematic effects, but effects cannot be understood by looking at the dispositions of media trials, but instead their "echos" must be examined. Media trials receive the coverage; non-media trials receive the bulk of the coverage effects. It is the tangential influences of media trials that are forwarded as the most significant effect of media coverage.

---

prosecution but note that most respondents stated an ability to serve as a juror with an open mind and be receptive to new evidence. This positive citizen self-appraisal is supported by the fact that in the actual trial the defendant was found not guilty by jury.

2. The two studies that are cited in the literature that attempt to relate publicity with verdicts involved samples of 32 (Hough, 1970) and 20 (Reuben, 1974). Neither study was revealing and both suffered severe methodological deficiencies (cf. Carroll et al., 1986:191). The only extensive content analysis study in this area was conducted in 1968 as a dissertation by William Dulaney. Dulaney, however, did not examine coverage and case handling but investigated factors that were related with whether a newspaper did or did not publish prejudicial material.

Media Trials. In the twentieth century, trials are often media events. Twentieth century demographic and technological developments have encouraged the mass media to coop the criminal justice system by reporting and broadcasting mini-series style docu-dramas involving real crimes, people and trials.[3] One of the primary factors in the development of media trials is that due to competition over ratings between news, organizations caused the news to be increasingly structured along entertainment lines. The news came to be presented within themes, formats, and explanations originally found solely in entertainment programs (Comstock, 1980). Eventually, dramatic, fast-paced, superficial presentations and simplistic explanations became the norm (cf. Fishman, 1978; Snow, 1984; Comstock, 1980; Cohen and Young, 1981). As this trend developed, some criminal trials came to be covered more intensely and coverage was expanded from "hard" to "soft" news to emphasize extra-legal and human-interest elements in order to maximize viewers and readers. The cumulation of this process is the total merging of news and entertain-

---

3. The reason media trials did not develop until this century is that they could not develop until there was a rise in the literacy levels of the general population in the United States, thereby providing a market for a printed mass media. Additionally, the mass media had to be easily, inexpensively, and simultaneously accessible to large segments of the population. The development of inexpensive papers, the "penny press," in the 1830s and the general diffusion of inexpensive printing techniques and rapid communication systems in the nineteenth century fulfilled these conditions. With the creation of the public radio and the film industry in the early twentieth century, the electronic and visual components of the modern mass media matrix were in place (cf. Lofton, 1966).

ment in the "media trial."[4] Analogous to the recurring themes of criminality found in entertainment programming, recurring categories have
dominated the portraits of crime found within media trials (cf. Gerbner,
1980). These media trial themes are categorized as "Abuse of Power and
Trust," "Sinful Rich," and "Evil Strangers." These three media trial
categories provide thematic explanations of the style and content of the
news media trial coverage.

Media trials that fall within the "Abuse of Power and Trust" category
include those cases in which the defendant occupies a position of trust,
prestige, or authority.[5] "Sinful Rich" media trials include cases in
which socially prominent defendants are involved in a bizarre or sexually related crime.[6] The category of "Evil Strangers" can be considered
as composed of two subgroups: "Non-Americans" and "Psychotic Killers."
"Non-American Evil Stranger" media trials denote, depending upon the
political climate, immigrants, Blacks, Jews, socialists, union and labor
leaders, anarchists, the poor, counterculture members, fringe religion
members, political activists, crusaders, or advocates of various unpopu-
lar causes. "Psychotic Killers" media trials usually focus upon bizarre

---

4. Media trials are a specific subset of the cases that would be found in the "celebrity layer of cases"
referred to by Samuel Walker (1985; citing Friedman and Percival, 1981; and Gottfredson and Gottfredson,
1981 in *Sense and Non-Sense About Crime*). Media trials, however, make up only a small portion of Walker's
"celebrity cases" which include all cases that make the news and those cases that become newsworthy
following their trial due to subsequent appeals or court rulings. The latter are referred to landmark cases
and include such cases as Miranda and Escobedo (Walker, 1985:17). Media trials involve only those cases
that attract intense coverage either immediately at the time of discovery or at the time of arrest. All of the
covered "celebrity" cases provide a pool of potential candidate "media trials" that can be subsequently
tapped.

5. The general rule is "The higher the rank the more media interest in the case." The crimes normally
involve the malfeasance of a position for personal gain and a moral fall from grace and often involve the
corruption of publicly elected or appointed officials and the general corruption of government. Police
corruption cases and criminal justice system personnel in general are especially attractive to the media as
these defendants represent law and order in society and allow the presentation of the paradox of the law
enforcers as lawbreakers.

6. These trials have a voyeuristic appeal and are covered in such a way as to infer to the public that they
are being given a rare glimpse into the world of the upper class. Love triangles and inheritance-motivated
killings among the jet set are primary examples. The message is that the world of the rich and famous is an
immoral, depraved place occupied by asocial, often murderous, people. Recent examples of this category
include the Pulitzer divorce and child custody trial in Palm Beach, Florida, The Saint Petersburg Benson
Car Bombing murder, and the New York Claus von Bulow murder trial. The image and message of these
trials are similar to the theme in F. Scott Fitzgerald's novel, *The Great Gatsby:* equating success with
deviance and stating that the rich, famous and successful are fundamentally different and basically
untrustworthy.

murder cases in which the defendants are portrayed as outwardly normal appearing persons but who in reality are maddened, dangerous killers.[7]

Within media trials coverage of all aspects of a case are reported and extra-legal facts are often highlighted. Extensive coverage is directed toward judges, lawyers, police, witnesses, jurors, and particularly defendants, who are interviewed, photographed, and often raised to a celebrity status. Personalities, personal relationships, physical appearances, and idiosyncrasies are commented upon regardless of legal relevancy. Coverage is live whenever possible, pictures are preferred over text, and text is characterized by conjecture and sensationalism (cf. Barber, 1987:112–114). In addition, within media trials, direct and simple explanations of crime are forwarded such as lust, greed, immorality, jealousy, revenge, or insanity. As with the entertainment media, causes of crime rooted in individual failings rather than social ills dominate the images.

An example of dramatized coverage within an entertainment format is provided by the following headline and paragraph from the front page of the *Miami Herald.*

BENSON IS HOTTEST SHOW IN TOWN
(Byline by S. Freedberg and T. Holzman)
Monday, August 4, 1986

Ladies and gentlemen, welcome to the wild side of the Benson pipe-bomb murder trial. Step right up and see the contortionist. See the country-boy prosecutors who rock their swivel chairs in sync, and see the defendant the jailers call "Boom Boom." Sometime within the next few days, a jury will begin deliberations in what is a humdinger of a courtroom spectacle underlying a terrible tragedy.

And again, regarding the coverage of the von Bulow trial in Rhode Island, Barber (1980:113) notes:

The von Bulow trial took on the proportions of an international television drama, with participants who resembled characters in a soap opera. WPRI–TV produced a 30-minute special called "The Von Bulows of Newport" and aired this documentary at the close of the trial. During the trial itself, there was live coverage by Cable News Network. Thames Television from London covered the trial for about 4 weeks,

---

7. Recent examples in this category include Albert DeSalvo (alias the Boston Strangler), Richard Speck, and the Theodore Bundy Florida sorority murders trial.

and also aired a half-hour special on American "aristocracy" based on the von Bulows of Newport.

Media trials represent the final step in a long process of merging the news and entertainment components of the mass media. That the source of media trials is the judicial system eases this process, for media trials allow the news industry to attract and entertain a large general audience while allowing it to maintain its preferred image as an objective and neutral reporter of news (cf. Terry, 1984). In addition, the courts have been described as already not so much in the business of producing decisions as they are of giving a performance (Ball, 1981:62).[8] The judicial system therefore sometimes assists in its co-optation. The end result is that in media trials, news as entertainment is fully achieved (cf. Comstock, 1980; Gerbner, 1980). The three categories of media trials (Abuse of Power, Sinful Rich, and Evil Stranger) provide the news media with entertainment style themes to direct and develop their coverage, and at the same time simplify the task of reporting, interpretating and explaining a trial. In this way they serve a function analogous to the crime news themes developed by Fishman (1978).[9] The media trial categories provide the news media with stereotypical perspectives to fit, choose, and sometimes mold the various parts and aspects of a trial that will be reported or highlighted.

In order to argue that media trials define judicial coverage, media trials should dominate and be the most prominent component of judicial system news coverage. A test of this hypothesis is offered using a content analysis of the front pages of the *London Times, Miami Herald, Miami News,* and the *Washington Post* (see also Surette, forthcoming). The front pages for May, June and July of 1987 were analyzed and a total sample of 364 front pages and 149 individual front-page items covering 102 distinct

---

8. Ball (1975, 1981) describes courtroom action as a distinct type of theater, "judicial theater" comparing the courtroom to a stage, legal arguments to script, and a trial to a performance, while the trial itself is in the theatrical format of protagonist and antagonist. According to Ball judicial theater serves various functions for society, the primary one being the definition and legitimization of law. See also Simonett, "The Trial as One of the Arts, 552 A.B.A.J.:1145 (1966).

9. In an examination of news coverage of crimes against the elderly in New York City, Fishman determined that individual crimes are chosen and molded by news people to fit within general crime themes. Thus, crimes that may have no linkage in reality are reported as if part of a trend such as "crimes against the elderly." These themes are changed by the news media as the newsworthiness of the current dominant theme declines.

crime and justice stories were reviewed.[10] Employing an operational definition of a media trial as a case that receives front-page coverage at least twice during the 3-month time span, 17 media trials are derived. Of the 17 media trials, 13 (76%) fit clearly into an "Abuse of Power," "Sinful Rich," or "Evil Stranger" category.

Addressing the question of coverage emphasis on media trials, a breakdown of the 149 crime and justice front-page items shows that media trials absorb the bulk of the coverage devoted to crime and justice. Of the 149 separate items, 63 (42%) refer to media trials, while 49 (33%) refer to media trials fitting the typology. Hence, one-third of all coverage items of crime and justice in the four papers are columns covering typology media trials. Media trials were found to comprise a significant portion of all crime and justice front-page news, and more significantly, trials fitting within the typology make up the bulk of trial coverage.[11] It was further conjectured that these trials would receive the most prominent coverage. Two features of newspaper coverage are examined: story length and picture usage.

Concerning story length, for typology media trials, individual items average 103.5 centimeters across 49 items, while for non-typology trials they average 85.4 centimeters across 14 items. For these sample sizes the average item length difference of 18.1 centimeters is not statistically great enough to conclude that typology media trials average greater coverage than non-typology media trials (T = 1.55, df = 39, sig. < .10 1 tail test). However, regarding picture usage, typology media trials average nearly twice the number of accompanying pictures, 1.45 versus .74 per item (t = 2.19, df = 58, Sig. < .025 1 tail test). Thus, while typology media trials may not receive significantly longer column space per item, they do receive significantly more pictorial coverage, receiving more than twice the number of accompanying pictures.

In sum, the analysis supports the contention that media trials falling within the three themes of the typology dominate crime and justice coverage. No paper had no media trials and each individual paper had a

10. Besides the date and newspaper in which the story was reported and the story classification as either a typology story or an anomaly, information was collected regarding story length in centimeters, the number of accompanying pictures and diagrams, the characteristics of the crime, the victim and the defendant as described, and the factors highlighted or represented as particularly newsworthy. A single day's coverage is termed an "item." Total case coverage is termed a "story."

11. On a per story comparison, media trials classified as fitting within the typology averaged a slightly, though not statistically significant, greater number of items per story (mean of 3.76 items per story) than those classified as not filling the typology (mean of 3.5 items per story).

majority of its media trials classified within the typology. The typology does classify and predict media trial coverage and suggests an explanation for this coverage; that trials are chosen that match the pre-established themes and images of crime and justice found in the entertainment media.

Echo Effects. In order to fully understand and appreciate the significance and impact of media trials it is necessary to look beyond them. For although the coverage focuses upon them, the effect of the coverage is felt to reverberate throughout the justice system. Specifically, it is hypothesized that the influence of media coverage remains after a case is initially reported and that this coverage subsequently affects other similarly charged cases. This is termed an "echo effect."

This effect is described first by Lofton (1966:138):

> But while the impact of the press is most direct on specific cases covered, there is a good reason to believe that [their] sway extends considerably beyond the cases actually appearing.... From the cases that are covered, officials become conditioned to expect demands for stern treatment from the press, and in the unpublicized cases they probably act accordingly.

And again by Kaplan and Skolnick (1982:467–468):

> This unwillingness [to plea bargain] appears to occur relatively infrequently. It is most likely to occur when there is strong pressure upon the prosecution to obtain maximum sentences for a particular class of crime: for example, after a notorious case of child rape, the prosecutor may refuse to bargain, for a time, with those charged with sex offenses involving children; after a series of highly publicized drug arrests allegedly involving dealers or pushers, the prosecution may be unwilling, for a time, to engage in reduction of charges from sales to possession.

Since Mark Fishman's seminal work "Crime Waves as Ideology" in 1978, it has been accepted that the mass media has effects that can be generalized throughout the system. Coverage can create the perception of "crime waves" by emphasizing and reporting particular types of crime (Fishman, 1978; see also Cohen and Young, 1981; Hall et al., 1981). Media coverage has also been credited with creating social panics and directing public crusades against classes of individuals (Cohen and Young, 1983:432–434; Fishman, 1978; Hall et al., 1981; Frankel, 1976; Ross, 1965; Treuhaft, 1957). It has been further credited with affecting enforcement, prosecution, and disposition policies regarding those crimes (cf. Brummett,

1980; Fishman, 1978; Hall et al., 1980). An associated belief is that the mass media can also influence the general dispositions of criminal cases.[12]

An echo effect therefore portends that the influence of media trials extends beyond a single instant case to affect the dispositions of a large number of subsequent cases, including those that receive no coverage. As such, it is offered as the most important potential mechanism of media influence upon the judicial system, but the actual extent or direction of the effect is undetermined. Despite the fact that a common perception of a media influence exists, a general model of the effect of publicity is not agreed upon. How common an echo effect is, its strength, its importance, or whether its effects are generally punitive or lenient are not known.[13]

Discussion

The mass media has developed during this century to be an important socializing agent, which socializes by projecting repeated images and portrayals of society (Althiede and Snow, 1979; Comstock, 1980). The mass media not only selectively reflects aspects of society but over time actively shapes society (Jowett and Linton, 1980:108–109; Cohen and Young, 1981). Crime-related media has been forwarded as playing an eminent role in this process (cf. Cohen and Young, 1981, Gerbner et al., 1978, 1979, 1980; Surette, 1984). Media trials, as indicated by this research,

---

12. A number of academic works have referred to such relationships. See Antunes and Hurley, 1977; Brady, 1983; Becker, 1971; Brummett, 1980; Dreton and Duffy, 1983; Dulaney, 1968; Friendly and Goldfarb, 1968; Lofton, 1966; Meyer, 1969; Rollings and Blascovich, 1977; Roshier, 1973; Sue et al., 1974; Sullivan, 1967. In one of the few relevant empirical studies, Greene and Wade (1987) examine for the effects of what they term "general pre-trial publicity" upon mock jurors, defining general pre-trial publicity as trial-related information that is prominently in the news, and that affects jurors in wholly unrelated cases.

13. A lenient echo effect argues that media coverage results in more lenient than normal treatment by the criminal justice system. This position states that publicity results in more lenient dispositions due to the effect of publicity on justice system personnel, the coverage ensuring that all appearances of fairness are maintained and that suspects are not singled out for punishment (Frankel, 1976; Graber, 1980; Greene and Wade, 1987; Simon, 1977:528; see also Greene and Loftus, 1984). In essence, because of media scrutiny, criminal justice system personnel are more conscious of adhering to formal rules and procedures and of appearing fair and impartial. The result is that a close attention to due process protections in media-covered cases is felt to result in more lenient dispositions. A lenient echo effect would be particularly likely following a highly publicized case in which the defendant is portrayed as a sympathetic character, as being unfairly or arbitrarily treated by the criminal justice system, or the victim of official corruption, malfeasance, or vendetta.

A punitive echo effect holds that a media focus and publicity increases both the likelihood of punishment and its degree of severity. Paradoxically, here also media attention is also seen as forcing the criminal justice system to adhere to its formal procedures. But the effects are seen as punitive because the coverage is seen as discouraging the usual practice of plea bargaining (Blumberg, 1967; Friendly and Goldfarb, 1968; Kaplan and Skolnick, 1982; Lofton, 1966:156). The result is an increased likelihood of a trial and a more severe sentence.

their consistent popularity, and the resources that the media is willing to expend to cover them not only are a prominent component of crime-related media but have become the single most dramatic, dominant and significant piece. Their importance is not because of a media influence on the processing of individual media trials but is due to the coverage influencing an unknown number of unpublicized but similar cases.

Part of the explanation of media trial's importance is because their content, themes, and messages of media trials mirror the distorted images found in the mass media entertainment programming.[14] The social acoustics for "media trial echos" to develop have been long established and the public has been attuned to their images through similar images in the entertainment media. The repeated news and entertainment media message is that crime is largely the result of predatory individuals who are basically different from the rest of us and that criminality is the result of individual problems and freely committed by criminals.

This pervasive entertainment and news image has been associated with specific viewer attitudes and perceptions, a "mean world view," and subsequent attitudes of fear, isolation and suspicion (Gerbner et al., 1978, 1979, 1980). Additionally, recent research suggests that media-generated views regarding crime and justice influence the amount of criminality deemed acceptable by viewers; expectations and public perceptions of the effectiveness of the criminal justice system; and the level of public support for various competing criminal justice policies (see Surette, 1985; Barrile, 1984; Hennigan et al., 1982). To the extent that they are the most prominent component of crime news, media trials significantly extend these effects previously associated with entertainment and daily news programming. Lastly, media trials further the mystification of the judicial process by presenting justice as a high-stakes complicated contest within the highly credible and authoritative framework of news and

---

14. Crime in entertainment media is the result of either twisted vengeance or unexplained random acts of violence committed by psychopaths or corrupt authority figures (Lichter and Lichter, 1983). The predominant image is that of a dangerous and crime-ridden world where violent murderous attacks are numerous and unpredictable (Surette, 1986:29; cf. Estep and Mcdonald, 1984; Dominick, 1978; Garofalo, 1982; Lichter and Lichter, 1983). Common plot lines involve criminals motivated by greed or irrationality, occupying positions of authority, and committing dramatic violent crimes. This portrayal has not radically altered over the 80-year history of the mass entertainment media. This image of crime and justice forwarded in the entertainment media corresponds on many points with the image of criminality portrayed in the common daily news, also a distorted world of violent, individual, interpersonal crimes.

courtrooms. And by emphasizing crimes that appear to be due to greed or irrationality, media trials forward individual explanations for crime and downplay broader structural, social, and economic explanations.[15] All of these images reiterate images found within the broader mass media.

Media trials therefore are an additional highly visible and credible component of the total media image of the justice system that serves to perpetuate and extend the distorted images forwarded in the entertainment and general news portions. Their selection of unique and often bizarre cases only further misleads and incorrectly instructs the public about the nature of the judicial system and criminality (Gerbner, 1980). Because they are "real" trials it is likely that media trials add significantly to the media's total impact on attitudes and criminal justice policy support while surreptitiously influencing through their echos the processing of an unknown number of unpublicized cases.

This suggests that a close examination of the impact of these trials is in order. Learning about the criminal justice system from media trials is analogous to learning geology solely from volcano eruptions. You will surely be impressed, but the display will not be very informative about the more common daily criminal justice system process. The media trial reality of high-stakes trials, confrontations, oratory, and detailed deliberations versus the criminal justice system daily reality of plea bargains, compromises, and assembly-line justice are in stark opposition (Snow, 1984). Given the nature of most trials covered to date, it would appear that such coverage provides greater appeal to voyeuristic instincts than it serves any educational service (Barber, 1987:113; Gerbner, 1980). What is most needed at this time is research that will detail the possible echo effects of media trials and their effects upon the perceptions and actions

---

15. The common elements of the Abuse of Power and Trust trials are the malfeasance and resultant fall from grace of previously prominent people of authority and influence. The image these cases project is that of pervasive corruption within government and the subliminal message is that the authorities should not be trusted, an image and message that matches the common entertainment portrayal of businessmen and high government officials (see Bortner, 1984; Lichter and Lichter, 1983). The trials are presented as morality plays in which the defendants have succumbed to greed or moral weaknesses. As such, the latent message of both media trials and the entertainment media is to taint all people in positions of authority. Success is presented as synonymous with corruption (Bortner, 1984; Lichter and Lichter, 1983). Similarly, both non-American and evil stranger trials tend to foster attitudes of mistrust and isolation and to encourage the polarization of society (Bortner, 1984). For in these trials the public receives a message that states that not only people who look or act different are untrustworthy, but that even the pleasant-appearing stranger should not be trusted, for a murderous psychosis may lurk just below. By adding to the portrayal of outsiders and strangers as potential criminals and the rich and powerful as immoral and motivated by lesser values, these trials provide additional imagery supportive of a "mean world view."

of decision makers within the criminal justice system (cf. Pritchard, Chapter 10). Within the system, the dynamics of lenient and punitive echo effects and the importance of coverage amounts and content need to be understood.

These trials are, of course, of public interest and newsworthy and therefore should be covered. The issue is are they being covered to the exclusion of other equally important and noteworthy trials and are they covered in a sensational, distorting entertainment style format? Initial research indicates that this is the case.[16] The recent experiments with the live televising of entire criminal trials in Florida and nationally on CNN harbingers the creation of future national media trial echos. The continued growth of this phenomena highlights the crucial need for more serious examination of the nature of media trials and their echos.

REFERENCES

Althiede, D. and Snow, R. (1979). *Media Logic.* Sage.

Antunes, G. and Hurley, P. (1977). "The representation of criminal events in Houston's two daily newspapers. *Jour. Quart.* 54:756–768.

Ball, M. (1975). "The play's the thing: An unscientific reflection on courts under the rubric of theater" *Stanford Law Review.* 28:81–115.

Ball, M. (1981). *The Promise of American Law.* Chapter 4 Judicial Theater, Univ. of Georgia Press.

Barber, S. (1987). *News Cameras in the Courtroom.* Ablex Publishing.

Barrile, L. (1984). "Television and attitudes about crime: Do heavy viewers distort criminality and support retributive justice?" in *Justice and The Media.* (ed) R. Surette, Charles C Thomas.

Becker, T. (1971). *Political Trials.* Bobbs-Merrill.

Blumstein, A. et al. (1983). *Research on Sentencing: The Search For Reform.* vol. I, National Academy Press.

Blumberg, A. (1967). *Criminal Justice.* Quadrangle Books.

Bortner, M.A. (1984). "Media images and public attitudes toward crime and justice" in *Justice and The Media.* (ed) R. Surette, Charles C Thomas.

Box, G. and Jenkins, G. (1976). *Time Series Analysis: Forecasting and Control.* Holden-Day.

Brady, J. (1983). "Fair and impartial railroad: The jury, the media and political trials," *J. of Crim. Just.* 11:241–263.

Brummett, B. (1980). "Symbolic form, Burkean scapegoating, and rhetorical exigency in Alioto's response to the "Zebra" murders," *Western J. of Speech Communication,* 44:64–73.

---

16. A number of authors have stated that the types of crimes and criminal cases that are ignored by the media is as significant and damaging as what is actually shown. Thus, corporate crime is seldom reported as crime news (cf. Evans, and Lundman, 1983; Coleman, 1974; Quinney, 1979; Molotch and Lester, 1975).

Carney, T. (1972). *Content Analysis.* Univ. of Manitoba Press.

Carroll, J. et al. (1986). "Free press and fair trial: The role of Behavioral research" *Law and Human Behavior,* 10:187–201.

Campbell, D. and Stanley, J. (1966). *Experimental and Quasi-Experimental Designs for Research.* Rand McNally.

Campbell, D. (1969). "Reforms as experiments" *Am. Psychologist.* 24:409–429.

Cohen, S. and Young, J. (1983). *The Manufacture of News.* Sage.

Coleman, J. (1974). *Power and the Structure of Society.* Norton.

Comstock, G. (1980). *Television in America.* Sage.

Cook, T. and Campbell, D. (1979). Quasi-Experimentation: Design and Analysis Issues for Field Settings. Houghton Mifflin.

Danielson, W. (1963). "Content analysis in communication research" in Nafziger and White (eds) *Introduction to Mass Communications Research.* Louisiana State Univ. Press.

Dominick, J. (1976). "Crime and law enforcement on prime-time television" *Public Opinion Quart.* 37:241–250.

Drechsel, R. (1985). "Judges' perceptions of fair trial-free press issue" *Journalism Quarterly* 62:388–390.

Dreton, J. and Duffy, J. (1983). "Bias in the newspaper reporting of crime news" *B. J. of Crim.* 13: 157–170.

Dulaney, W. (1968). *An Assessment of Some Assertions Made Relative to the Fair Trial and Free Press Controversy.* Dist. Northwestern Univ.

Estep, R. and Mcdonald, P. (1984). "How prime-time crime evolved on tv, 1976 to 1983" in *Justice and The Media.* (ed) R. Surette, Charles C Thomas.

Evans, S. and Lundman, R. (1983). "Newspaper Coverage of Corporate Price-fixing" *Criminology.* 21:529–541.

Fishman, M. (1978). "Crime waves as ideology" *Social Problems.* 25: 531–543.

Frankel, M. (1976). U.S. District Court, S.D.N.Y. 416 F. Supp. 496 cited in J. Kaplan and J. Skolnick *Criminal Justice.* Foundation Press, 1982.

Frayn, M. (1983). "Unit headline language" in Cohen and Young (eds) *The Manufacture of News.* Sage.

Freedberg, S. and Holzman, T. (1984). "Benson is hottest show in town" *The Miami Herald,* Monday, Aug. 4: 1A,5A.

Friedman L. and Percival, R. (1981). *The Roots of Justice: Crime and Punishment in Alameda County, California, 1870-1910.* Univ. of N. Carolina Press.

Friendly, A. and Goldfarb, R. (1968). *Crime and Publicity.* Vintage.

Garofalo, J. (1982). "Crime and the mass media" *Journal of Research in Crime and Delinquency* 11:319–350.

Gerbner, G. (1980). "Trial by television: are we at the point of no return?" *Judicature,* 63(9):416–426.

Gerbner, G. et al. (1978). "Cultural indicators: Violence profile no. 9" *J. of Comm.* 29:176–207.

Gerbner, G. et al. (1979). "The demonstration of power: Violence profile no. 10" *J. of Comm.* 29:177–196.

Gerbner, G. et al. (1980). "The mainstreaming of America: Violence profile no 11" *J. of Comm.* 30:10–29.

Glass, G., Wilson, V. and Gottman, J. (1975). *Design and Analysis of Time-Series Experiments.* Colorado Associated University Press.

Goldfarb, R. (1974). "Politics and the justice department," in *Conspiracy.* ed. J. Raines, Harper and Row.

Gottfredson, M. and Gottfredson, D. (1980). *Decision Making in Criminal Justice.* Ballinger.

Graber, D. (1980). *Crime News and the Public.* Praeger.

Greene, E. and Loftus, E. (1984). "What's new in the News? The influence of well-publicized news events on psychological research and courtroom trials" *Basic and Applied Soc. Psych.* 5:211–221.

Greene, E. and Wade, W. (1987). "Of private talk and public print: General pre-trial publicity and juror decision-making" *Applied Cognitive Psych.* 1:1–13.

Hall, S. (1983). "The determination of news photographs" in *The Manufacture of News.* (eds) S. Cohen and J. Young. Sage.

Hall, S. et al. (1983). "The social production of news: Mugging in the media" in *The Manufacture of News.* (eds) S. Cohen and J. Young, pps. 335–367, Sage.

Harper, T. (1984). "When your case hits the front page" *Am. Bar. Assoc. J.* 70:78–82.

Hennigan, K, et al. (1982). "Impact of the introduction of television on crime in the United States: Empirical findings and theoretical implications" *J. of Personality and Social Psychology* 42:88–106.

Hoiberg, B. and Stires, L. (1973). "The effect of several types of pretrial publicity on the guilty attributions of simulated jurors" *J. of App. Soc. Psych.* 3:267–275.

Hough, G. (1970). "Felonies, jury trials and news reports" in C.R. Bush (ed) *Free Press and Fair Trial.* Univ. of Georgia Press.

Jowett, G. and Linton, J. (1980). *Movies as Mass Communication.* Sage.

Kaplan, J. and Skolnick J. (1982). *Criminal Justice.* Foundation Press.

Kline, F. and Jess, P. (1966). "Prejudicial publicity: Its effects on law school mock juries: *J. Quart.* 43:113–116.

Lichter, L. and Lichter, R. (1983). *Prime Time Crime.* Media Institute.

Lofton, J. (1966). *Justice and the Press.* Beacon Press.

Marcus, P. (1982). "The media in the courtroom: Attending, reporting, televising criminal cases" *Indiana L. J.* Spring:235–287.

Meyer, B. (1969). "The trial judge's guide to news reporting and fair trial" *J. of Crim. Law, Crim, and Pol. Sci.* 60:287–298.

Molotch, H. and Lester, R. (1975). "Accidental news: the great oil spill as local occurrence and national event" *Amer. J. of Sociology.* 81:235–260.

Patterson, O. (1982). *The Vietnam Veteran and the Media: A Comparative Content Analysis of Media Coverage of the War and the Veteran 1968-1973.* Dist. Univ. of Tennessee.

Pember, D. (1984). *Mass Media Law.* Wm. C. Brown.

Pritchard, D. (1986). "Homicide and bargained justice: The agenda-setting effect of crime news on prosecutors" *Pub. Opinion Q.* 50:143–159.

Quinney, R. (1979). *Criminology.* Little, Brown.

Radin, Edward (1964). *The Innocents.* Morrow.

Reiman, J. (1984). *The Rich Get Richer and the Poor Get Prison.* Wiley.

Reuben, D. (1974). Confidential study discussed in "The men at the bar meeting debate Gannett v. DePasquale" *The Quill,* 1980, 68:8.

Riecken, H., et al. (1974). *Social Experimentation: A method for Planning and Evaluating Social Innovations.* Academic Press.

Riley, S. (1973). "Pretrial publicity: A field study" *J. Quart.* 50:17–23.

Robinson, J. (1976). "Interpersonal influence in election campaigns: Two step-flow hypotheses" *Public Opinion Q.* 40:304–319.

Robinson, M. (1974). "The impact of the televised Watergate hearings" *J. of Comm.* 24:17–30.

Rollings, H. and Blascovich, J. (1977). "The case of Patricia Hearst: Pretrial publicity and opinion" *J. of Comm.* Spring:58–65.

Roshier, B. (1983). "The selection of crime news by the press" in Cohen and Young (eds) *The Manufacture of News.* Sage.

Ross, I. (1965). "Trial by newspaper" *The Atlantic* 2:63–68.

Salas, R. (1984). "The press and the criminal justice system" in *Justice and the Media* (ed) R. Surette, Charles C Thomas.

Schlesinger, P. (1977). "Newsmen and their time-machine" *Brit. J. of Soc.* 28:336–350.

Seidman, M. (1977). "The trial and execution of Bruno Richard Hauptmann: Still another case that "will not die," *Geo. L. J.* 66:6–16.

Siebert, F. (1970). *Free Press and Fair Trial.* Univ. of Georgia Press.

Simon, R. (1977). "Does the court's decision in Nebraska Press Association fit the research evidence on the impact on jurors of news coverage" *Sanford Law Re.* 29:515–528.

Simon R. and Eimermann, T. (1971). "The jury finds not guilty: Another look at media influence on the jury" *J. Quart.* 48:343.

Snow, R. (1984). "Crime and justice in prime-time news: The John Hinckley, Jr. Case" in *Justice and The Media.* (ed) R. Surette, Charles C Thomas.

Sohn, A. (1976). "Determining guilty or innocence of accused from pretrial news stories" *J. Quart.* 53:100–105.

Sue, S. Smith R. and Gilbert, R. (1974). "Biasing effects of pretrial publicity on judicial decisions" *J. of Crim. Just.* 2:163–171.

Sullivan, H. (1967). *Trial by Newspaper.* Patriot Press.

Surette, R. (1984). *Justice and The Media.* Charles C Thomas.

Surette, R. (1985). "Television and punitive criminal justice policy support" *Journalism Quart.* Summer:373–377,450.

Surette, R. (1986). "The mass media and criminal investigations: Crime stoppers in Dade County, Florida" *J. of Justice Issues* 1:21–38.

Surette, R. (forthcoming). "Media Trials" *J. of Criminal Justice.*

Tans, M. and Chaffee, S. (1966). "Pretrial publicity and juror prejudice" *J. Quart.* 43:647–54.

Terry, C. (1984). "Crime and the news: Gatekeeping and Beyond" pgs. 31–50 in R. Surette (ed) *Justice and the Media.* Charles C Thomas.

Treuhaft, D. (1957). "Trial by Headline" *The Nation.* October:279–282.

Walker, S. (1985). *Sense and Nonsense about Crime.* Brooks Cole.
Wilcox, W. and McCombs, M. (1970). "Crime story elements and fair trial/free press" in Chilton R. Bush (ed) *Free Press and Fair Trial: Some Dimensions of the Problem.* Univ. of Georgia Press.

Chapter 14

THE POLICY EFFECTS OF A
DWI LAW AND A PUBLICITY CAMPAIGN

B. Nienstedt

INTRODUCTION

On July twenty-fourth, 1982, the state of Arizona implemented a strict drinking-and-driving law which was hailed as a major policy weapon in the war against the drunk driver. Diversion and plea bargaining under this new drinking-and-driving law were prohibited and there were provisions for mandatory sentences to jail and prison. The medical and therapeutic rehabilitation of alcoholics was viewed as subordinate to the main goals of punishment of offenders and protection of the public. The entire concept of the drinking driver changed from a person in need of treatment into an image of the "killer drunk" (Gusfield, 1981). This paper will discuss the effect of the punitive new DWI law and the role that publicity played in its evolution and impact.

Certain national trends such as the growth and popularity of organized activism against driving-while-intoxicated (DWI) motorists and the availability of large amounts of federal funding provided fertile ground for emotional and political events in Arizona. An analysis of driving-while-intoxicated (DWI) newspaper coverage and media campaigns in Phoenix and Tucson demonstrated that the *timing* of publicity in Arizona was distinctly different from that of other areas. Dramatic changes in the numbers of articles preceded the law by seven months. Extensive multi-media campaigns in the two largest cities in Arizona began in March 1982, five months before implementation of the law. This media blitz was atypical, in that it occurred considerably before the law was passed. Other DWI publicity usually accompanied new legislation or preceded it by only a short time. As a result, the effect of this advance publicity, rather than the later implementation of the law, produced the primary impact on alcohol-related accidents. The present research uses a triangulation of research methods, including a quantatitive time series quasi-experimental design, and qualitative methods, such as content analysis of newspapers and a process evaluation, to assess one state's experience in deterring drinking drivers.

QUALITITATIVE ANALYSIS OF THE DWI LAW

Legislative activity against the drinking driver has been almost frantic in the United States since 1980. In Arizona, politicians of both parties worked together to get a tougher drunk-driving law passed during the 1982 legislation session. The concerted bipartisan effort was seen by some cynics as being inspired by an election year. Others attribute the crackdown on the drinking driver to the sentiment aroused by the media when a legislator and her companion (both Catholic nuns) were killed by a young, alcohol-impaired driver in the fall of 1981. Reports of several other deaths prompted public outrage and legislative action. Three Boy Scouts and their leader were struck down by a drinking driver while standing by their disabled vehicle. Another fatal accident caused by a drinking driver led to the death of a popular young owner of a local sports team. A bill to "get tough" with drunk drivers passed quickly and without a single dissenting vote. It would have been political suicide to appear "soft" on any drunk-driver legislation. The new law was to become effective July 24, 1982.

Arizona's experience with passage of this DWI legislation follows a typical pattern. As seen in other cases, publicity plays a major role in the passage of legislation aimed at deterring offending behaviors. While the highlighted events may change from one location to the other, the effect appears to be similar. A pattern is identified by the media, the movement gathers momentum, lobbying follows and legislation results.

A second important role played by publicity is its accompaniment to the theoretical deterrence components of severity, certainty and celerity. Publicity is sometimes acknowledged as a fourth component which aids in the deterrence of drinking and driving behavior. It "advertises" the law and usually serves an educational function which tends to have an impact on auto accidents. The effect usually lasts only as long as the publicity is generated, however. Once the publicity dies down, the law's impact on accidents tends to diminish (Ross, 1982). With these important roles in mind, Arizona publicity needed to be examined in detail for an understanding of its role in the state's experience with DWI deterrence.

Publicity

To investigate the impact of newspaper publicity and to look for changes in the volume or emphasis of articles over the years, the content analysis of Arizona newspapers began in 1975 and continued through December 1985. The rehabilitation model of alcoholism was popular at the start of the time frame and current movements to get tough with drunks had not yet begun. Figure 1 illustrates the growth in publicity during those years. Note the dramatic surge in the number of articles which *preceded* passage of the DWI law. There was also a distinct change over the years in the attitudes of news reporting. A metamorphasis occurred and the image of the drinking driver as a person with a problem who needed help gradually gave way to a perception of the socially irresponsible "killer drunk." Changes in the tone of the articles were reflected in headlines such as "PACT [rehabilitation] Program Aids Drivers" (*Phoenix Gazette,* 1975) and "Punish Drunk Drivers in Way That Will Hurt Most" (*Phoenix Gazette,* 1981).

Multi-Media Campaigns in Phoenix and Tucson

A press conference at the Phoenix City Council Chambers on February 22, 1982 announced the beginning of a multi-media public information and education campaign to be conducted during the month of March to address the problem of drinking drivers. The campaign was designed to tie in with the launching of a federally funded special enforcement motorcycle squad on March 1, 1982. It would let the motoring public know that there would be additional specially trained motorcycle officers who would be seeking out problem drivers and getting them off the streets. The electronic media responded with gusto. The local television station aired announcements several times per day during the latter part of February, all of March and part of April. Major network affiliates also devoted considerable television time during March to public service announcements and editorials.

Publicity spots were distributed to radio stations which aired them during the latter part of February and all of March. Personalized letters to 176 news announcers and disk jockeys resulted in hundreds of requests for a DWI brochure as well as generating more editorials and interviews on talk shows. The print media included full-page ads in the March, April and May issues of a local Phoenix magazine. The two major newspapers in the state, *Arizona Republic* and the *Phoenix Gazette,* carried

FIGURE 1.

NEWSPAPER ARTICLES OF DRINKING AND DRIVING
January 1976–December 1985

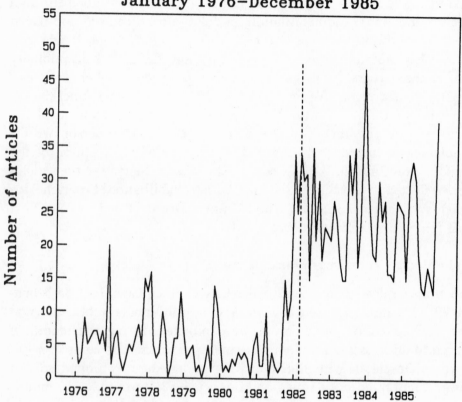

Dotted line represents March, 1982 publicity campaign

advertisements several days in March. Posters were displayed in all police stations, city offices and at conventions; billboards and bumper stickers were affixed to all city-owned cars and then given to civic organizations for wider distribution; city paychecks and all city mail contained advertisements; and one-hundred thousand brochures were printed and requested by the public (Traffic Safety Coordination Office Report, 1982). People were reminded everywhere they turned of the campaign theme "Drunk Drivers Should be Barred."

After the content analysis was completed, the process evaluation of the impact of the DWI law uncovered a surprising and almost humorous state of affairs. The motorcycle squad was not funded for DWI enforcement at all—it was funded by the federal government to deal with other, more site-specific, traffic problem areas. The DWI campaign, however, capitalized on the squad in its advertisements, giving the impression that the squad and the funds were targeted for DWI offenders. The police department cooperated by lending credibility to the impression. Ten ominous-looking motorcycle officers in a flying-wedge formation were shown riding in an aggressively threatening manner over the crest of a road with the caption "A Sobering Message for Drunk Drivers."

Another article showed two officers (again, federally funded for other traffic problems) standing before a new motorcycle and pointing a radar gun. The information under the picture stated "Phoenix Patrolman . . . demonstrates the use of a motorcycle-mounted radar gun to be used in a crackdown on drunken driving. . . . " While it is clear that radar does indeed help detect speeding, it is less obvious that it is able to separate drinking from nondrinking drivers.

The Tucson campaign consisted of similar numbers of television, radio, outdoor billboards, newspaper, posters and direct-mail inserts. A different theme was used, but like Phoenix, materials were also designed to generate a response from the public aimed at the deterrence of drinking drivers, along with pressure on elected officials to do something. The theme ("How Do You Spell Relief—J–A–I–L") was based on a well-known stomach antacid commercial of the time. It is estimated that over $150,000 worth of production and publicity was obtained for only $12,000. The large donations of media coverage attested to the popularity of the deterrence approach over others in dealing with drinking drivers. A selective alcohol enforcement squad was also funded through a federal grant and became operational earlier than the law's passage. Between the two media blitzes in Phoenix and Tucson, the majority of the state's population was exposed to intensive advertising during the month of March (Governor's Office on Highway Safety Report, 1982).

QUANTITATIVE ANALYSIS OF THE DWI LAW

To attribute a decrease in traffic accidents solely to the deterrent effect of a DWI law, quasi-experimental logic suggests that we should find impacts due to the law in the appropriate indicators of alcohol-involved accidents but also that we will *not* find them in nonalcohol-related indicators.[1] Deterrence theory, then, leads us to believe that an optimally effective DWI law will have large impacts on some indicators of traffic but little or no effects on other indicators. Moreover, in the present research we have reason to suspect that there may be an additional consideration. Results of the process evaluation indicated that the publicity campaigns which preceded the law had to be factored into the timing of the DWI intervention. Therefore, two hypotheses are proposed. The first is termed the "law implementation" hypothesis, since it is assumed that the intervention took place solely because of the law and that the impact was felt shortly after the law was implemented. The law implementation hypothesis is the typical theoretical expectation in tests of the impact of DWI laws. The second hypothesis calls for testing for an impact in March 1982—five months prior to implementation of the law—because of the multi-media blitzes in Arizona's two largest cities. Further, because newspaper articles increased dramatically starting in January 1982, the accumulation of these articles with the added "punch" of multi-media blitzes justified a different intervention date. The second hypothesis, then, states that the deterrent effect actually took place in March, not as a result of the DWI law, but as a result of earlier media publicity campaigns against DWI.

Data

Since previous research has established relationships between drinking and certain types of traffic accidents, it is possible to consider particular traffic time series as more indicative of the presence of alcohol than others. Consequently, they are considered experimental series. Their counterparts are the control series which have not been found to be predominantly alcohol related.

Because there is likely to be some crossover between these series, however, testing several different pairs of experimental and control indicators for impacts adds to the robustness of the findings.

Traffic series which prior research has found a predominant presence of alcohol involvement are: Single-vehicle accidents, nighttime accidents, severe (i.e., fatal) accidents, and those accidents in which police officers judge that drinking is involved. Their respective nondrinking control

---

1. Hilton (1983:1) notes "the idea of a deterrent effect that is caused by a drinking-driving countermeasure involves something more than merely the existence of some *general* (italics added) reduction in accident rates. It postulates that the reduction should be an alcohol-specific one."

series are: multiple-vehicle accidents, daytime accidents, injury-producing accidents and those which police officers report as not involving alcohol (Jones and Joscelyn, 1978; Filkins et al., 1970; Ross, 1982; Ross and McCleary, 1983). Comparisons are therefore made between experimental and control time series indicators of level of severity (injury vs. fatal), subjective assessment of alcohol involvement by police (alcohol-involved vs. nonalcohol-involved), time of day (daytime vs. nighttime) and number of vehicles (single vs. multiple) in accidents.

Data for both experimental and control series were collected by the Arizona Department of Public Safety, Statistical Analysis Center, and covered the years from 1968 through 1983.

Results of the Time Series Analysis

Four contrasting sets of time series are used to test the impact of the 1982 DWI law. In addition, a time series for gasoline sales acts as a surrogate indicator of traffic volume. Each contrasting set contains an experimental and a control series which is analyzed for an impact based on the law implementation hypothesis of August 1982 and the alternative media publicity campaign of March 1982. AutoRegressive Integrated Moving Average (ARIMA) time series analyses begin with specification of the impact model for gasoline sales (Box and Jenkins, 1976). Table 1 shows t-values for the impact of both interventions on gasoline sales as an indicator of overall driving and the specific experimental and control series.

Summary and Discussion of the Quantitative Analysis

The purpose of this research is to examine contrasts between traffic data which are indicative of drinking and those which are not. Results indicate that there was no significant increase in miles driven (as represented by gasoline sales) at the time of either intervention. Therefore, any impact could not be attributed to an increase or decrease in driving. The law did not impact either experimental alcohol series or control nonalcohol series except in two cases. These exceptions are found in Single-Vehicle Accidents (an experimental series) and Daytime Accidents (a control series). The experimental series, however, proved significant only in the bivariate model which uses the law implementation intervention. Once the publicity intervention is added to the model as a control, the significant impact which is attributable to the law vanishes and only the publicity effect is significant.

TABLE 1

IMPACT ANALYSES FOR LEGAL IMPLEMENTATION AND PUBLICITY INTERVENTION

	t-values	
Data Indicator	Legal	Publicity
	August, 1982	March,1982
Gasoline Sales	- .44	- .63
Experimental--Fatal Accidents	- .54	2.00*
Control--Injury Accidents	- .39	- .07
Experimental--Nighttime Accidents	- .38	-2.42*
Control--Daytime Accidents	-2.20*	-2.47*
Experimental--Alcohol-involved Accidents	-1.42	-3.08*
Control--Nonalcohol-involved Accidents	- .25	- .62
Experimental--Single-vehicle Accidents	-2.98*	-4.46*
Control--Multi-vehicle Accidents	- .55	-1.17

* Significant at the p=.05 level

The media publicity intervention had significant impacts on all the experimental series, along with the other exception, the control series Daytime Accidents. Prior research has shown that this exception of Daytime Accidents is not particularly surprising. Hilton (1983) also found a significant reduction in daytime fatal accidents in a time series analysis of California data. He was unable to separate the impact of publicity from the impact of the law, however, and he offers the supposition that publicity campaigns conducted at the time of passage of the law may have caused *all* drivers to be more cautious. The significant effect on Daytime Accidents in Arizona also supports Hilton's suggestion that publicity impacts daytime drivers. Judged by the criteria of effectiveness for an alcohol countermeasure, then, publicity has had a significant impact on the desired target audience (the drinking drivers) while having little effect on nonalcoholic drivers.

To summarize, it may be said that the March 1982 publicity campaigns work better than the August 1982 DWI law in deterring accidents due to drinking drivers. Additionally, it has a "spillover" effect to daytime drivers, a group which is generally assumed to be nondrinking. A major contribution of this research has been the consideration of the timing of publicity campaigns in addition to the timing of the law's implementation. Through the occurrence of this natural experiment in which publicity campaigns preceded the law, the research was able to separate the two and test for statistical significance of both interventions. Although previous research has acknowledged the concomitant presence of publicity in deterrence through laws, it has been unable to separate the impact of the law from the impact of publicity. The results clearly indicate that future research can no longer ignore empirical investigation into the extent and timing of publicity in deterrence research.

POLICY IMPACTS OF THE DWI LAW AND PUBLICITY

Findings of the analysis which separated the law from publicity then comes to bear upon the policy implications of the research. Factoring the high costs and consequences of the law's implementation, it becomes clear that policymakers must resort to less costly alternatives to getting the drunk driver out of the car. There are certain crimes for which publicity may be encouraged as a less costly and more effective alternative to largely symbolic mandatory sentences.

Policymakers need to consider not only whether a drinking-and-driving law significantly impacts accidents but also the social and financial costs resulting from enforcement of the law. It has been the case in many states (Arizona being no exception) that the unintended consequences of a law swamp and subvert the law's intended consequences. Court backlogs have shortcutted the mandatory sentencing provisions of the law. Moreover, the law's ban on plea bargaining is ignored and DWI offenses are routinely pled down to loitering. DWI prosecuting attorneys are leaving public service for the more lucrative private defense of drinking drivers. Consequently, comparisons need to be made with alternative methods (such as publicity) of achieving the same impact without incurring the large social and economic costs to governments and society.

The effectiveness of using publicity to diminish alcohol-related traffic accidents instead of taking a legal approach which purports to (but, in reality, does not) deal harshly with DWI offenders has been demonstrated with the present research. While the cost of multi-media publicity campaigns is not inconsiderable, it is nowhere near the costs of using legislation as a deterrent approach to drinking and driving. Furthermore, much of the publicity costs were offset as public service donations by private companies.

There is a question connected to this use of publicity, however. We must ask if there is a long-term ability of publicity to sustain decreases in DWI until people's attitudes about drinking and driving change to the point of being incorporated into their value systems. The fact that most people's attitudes toward drinking and driving have changed dramatically since the early 1980s is hardly able to be disputed. But is it enough? And, will it last?

A problematic consideration of using publicity results because the type of publicity that appears to be the most effective is that which is threatening—specifically, the threat of new legislation and increased punishments. How effective the threat will be when perceptions are not consistent with the reality of shortcuts and plea bargaining in the criminal justice system remains to be seen. DWI enforcement through arrests actually decreased at the time of the law and have not increased markedly from January 1984 through December 1987 (27,460 to 29,540), but this is not to be taken as an indication of police sloth. Despite the threat of punishment, the symbolic law has not really prescribed drastic changes in police methods of operation. They continue to arrest DWI offenders as readily as they have in the past. It is the prosecution of offenders that is problematic due to court backlogs and the need for court administrative efficiency. The threat of arrest is the same, but the threat of imprisonment is more imagined than real for the majority of drinking drivers.

CONCLUSIONS: FUTURE DIRECTIONS FOR CRIMINAL JUSTICE POLICY

Since the beginning of the 1980s, we have witnessed major changes in public attitudes and ways of dealing with DWI offenders. The fervent, almost religious, devotion to eradicating the problem through enactment of severe penalties in criminal law serves a symbolic purpose in addition to protecting the public.

Publicity campaigns as seen in this research have caused drinking-and-driving accidents to decrease. Despite this more effective short-term method of impacting alcohol-related accidents and long-term method of changing people's attitudes, the political reality remains that it is popular and politically expedient to mandate action through laws which are largely symbolic (Nienstedt, 1986). Legislators find it appealing to appease powerful automotive and liquor industries at the same time they are courting voters by being "tough" on drinking drivers. The task of evaluation research into this area is to educate the public about the costs and the consequences of symbolic legislation in comparison to the potential of using publicity to achieve desired effects.

REFERENCES

Box, G., & Jenkins, G. (1976). *Time-Series Analysis: Forecasting and Control.* San Francisco: Holden Day.

Filkins, L.D., Clark, C.D., Rosenblatt, C.A., Carlson, W.L., Kerlan, M.W. & Manson, H. (1970). *Alcohol abuse and traffic safety: A study of fatalities, DWI offenders, alcoholics, and court-related treatment approaches.* Washington, D.C.: National Technical Information Service.

Governor's Office on Highway Safety. (1982). *Final Report: DWI Publicity Campaigns.* Tucson, Arizona.

Gusfield, J. (1981). *The Culture of Public Problems: Drunk Driving and the Symbolic Order.* Chicago: University of Chicago Press.

Hilton, M. (1983). *The effectiveness of recent changes in California law as drinking-driving countermeasures: An interrupted time series analysis.* Berkeley: Alcohol Research Group.

Jones, R., & Joscelyn, K. (1978). *Alcohol and highway safety: A review of the state of knowledge.* Washington, D.C.: U.S. Department of Transportation.

Phoenix Gazette. (1975). PACT program aids drivers. May 16: B11.

Phoenix Gazette. (1981). Punish drunk drivers in way that will hurt most. September 21: A7.

Nienstedt, B.C. (1986). The use of mandatory sentencing legislation as symbolic statements. *Policy Studies Review, 6*(1):36–43.

Ross, H.L. (1982). *Deterring the Drinking Driver: Legal Policy and Social Control.* Lexington, Massachusetts: D.C. Heath.

Ross, H.L. & McCleary, R. (1983). Methods for studying the impact of drunk driving laws. *Accident Analysis and Prevention, 15,* 415–428.

Traffic Safety Coordination Office. (1982). *Report on DWI Publicity Campaign.* Phoenix, Arizona.

Section III

SYSTEM APPLICATIONS OF MEDIA TECHNOLOGY

Section III examines a new media justice policy phenomena, that of the criminal justice system embracing media technology. This criminal justice system adoption of the equipment and capabilities of the mass media is a reversal of the traditional adversarial relationship that usually exists between the media and the criminal justice system and is related to a number of trends. It ties in one sense into the general public reaction to the perceived failure of the criminal justice system to deter and punish crime adequately. Under the general rubric of target hardening via technology it is hoped that media-based technology can aid in a number of anti-crime efforts (Dinitz, 1987:5). Simultaneously, it is hoped that the technology can aid in reforming the criminal justice system, increasing its effectiveness, and better meeting crime control model standards.

The importance of examining programs in this area revolves around several issues. The most obvious issue is the effectiveness of these programs: do they result in a reduction in crime? A second issue is the trade-off of privacy versus security. In response to crime, the criminal justice system, often prodded by the public, has begun to increasingly turn to media technology for more innovative countermeasures against crime. However, because of their nature, such programs inevitably result in a reduction in citizen privacy. A basic question is how these programs' social costs compare against their benefits.

The technology's reception within the criminal justice system seems to lie in whether it is felt that a crucial element of justice is lost when media is transmitted. For preliminary and short procedural steps, most participants, including defendants, appear to feel that the integrity of the process is unaffected. For longer, more significant, and more symbolic steps such as trials, concerns and resistance rise. However, while initially promising, effects of this technology upon participants, upon the atmosphere and decorum of the judicial system, upon the perception of the legitimacy of the entire system, and thereby ultimately on justice in our society have not been fully answered. There is a danger in their rapid adoption, in that their administrative benefits are clear and tend to emerge quickly while their costs are less clear and tend to emerge over the long term.

The chapters in this sections report on various projects in operation around the country that incorporate the media into the efforts and goals of the criminal justice system. The first two chapters in this section review projects that utilize the existing mass media distribution system to either impart anti-crime information to the general public or tap the public for investigative information regarding crimes. In Chapter 15, O'Keefe and Reid discuss the McGruff "Take a Bite Out of Crime" public information campaign. They report that well-developed and conceptualized media campaigns can be successful vehicles for imparting crime prevention information to the general public. In Chapter 16, Lavarkas, Rosenbaum, and Lugiogio review the development of Crime Stoppers programs in the United States and the symbiotic relationships that often develop between the Crime Stoppers programs, local law enforcement and local news media. Such cooperative relationships are of course opposite to the more common neutral or adversarial relations found between news media and law enforcement. A concern of both of these projects is the long-term erosion of the media's ability to serve as criminal justice system watchdogs while simultaneously being involved in anti-crime efforts. In the short term, however, both projects display evidence of successful utilization of the mass media in distributing crime prevention information and gathering crime-related tips.

The direct application of media technology in the criminal justice system is covered for the courts in Chapter 17 and for law enforcement in Chapters 18, 19 and 20. All of the projects described report positive administrative applications of the technology. In Chapter 17, Surette and Terry evaluate a video arraignment system for a misdemeanor court. They report that nearly all participants, except for public defenders but including defendants, favored the use of video for processing their arraignments. In Chapter 18, Sechrest, Liquori and Perry review the use of video equipment in police patrol cars. They also favorably evaluate the technology's incorporation into the system. In another application in law enforcement, Grant in Chapter 19 describes the videotaping of police interrogations in Ontario, Canada. As with the other projects the use of the technology is positively evaluated in direct terms of efficiency, reliability, and administrative goals. What is left unanswered in all of these evaluative chapters are long-term policy concerns such as increased depersonalization, work-group disruption, and degraded public images and legitimization of the justice system. Partly in response, Surette in Chapter 20 reviews the growing use of the technology for surveillance by law enforcement agencies. Surveillance applications have been the only justice system use of media technology that has come under sharp criticism, reflecting the specter of *1984* scenarios.

Closing this section, Jeffery presents an engaging overview of the history of media technology in crime control and the implications inherent in its use in Chapter 21. Jeffery essentially argues that all of these programs may or may not be administratively effective. But that is besides the point, in that none have been shown to actually reduce crime in society. As crime control (i.e., management) projects, they are policy mistakes that divert resources from crime prevention research and projects while undermining individual freedom and forwarding punishment-dominated public policies. While not rejecting the use of technology, Jeffery clearly rejects its usefulness as applied in Section III.

REFERENCES

Dinitz, S. (1987). "Coping with Deviant Behavior through Technology." *Criminal Justice Research Bulletin*, Vol. 3, No. 2.

Chapter 15

MEDIA PUBLIC INFORMATION CAMPAIGNS AND CRIMINAL JUSTICE POLICY— BEYOND "MCGRUFF"

GARRETT J. O'KEEFE AND KATHALEEN REID

The use of mass media to promote more active citizen involvement in reducing crime has emerged as a major component of criminal justice policy over the past 20 years (cf. Heinzelmann, 1987; O'Keefe, 1986; Sacco & Silverman, 1984a). Countless state and community-wide publicity campaigns have been inaugurated, as have such coordinated national efforts as "Take a Bite Out of Crime" and Crime Stoppers. This trend has followed the implementation of a wide range of public information campaigns and other promotional efforts in recent years dealing with various social welfare and health-related topics (cf. Rice & Atkin, in press; Salmon, 1989).

Campaigns in general: (1) intend "to generate specific outcomes or effects, (2) in a relatively large number of individuals, (3) usually within a specified period of time and (4) through an organized set of communication activities" (Rogers & Storey, 1987, p. 821). While public information campaigns share common interests in informing and influencing the citizenry, they often go about the job in widely varying ways depending upon the type of problem or issue being addressed and the specific campaign objectives. Other factors affecting campaign strategies include the characteristics of their target audiences and the time and money available for the effort. Most such projects attempt to combine public information or media publicity campaigns with community participation and training activities. Media tend to be more effective at building citizen awareness of an issue, while complex attitudinal or behavioral changes are apt to be accelerated by more direct forms of citizen contact and intervention.

The studies reported were sponsored in part under grants from the National Institute of Justice.

209

The development of successful informational and promotional programs in crime prevention and other issue areas remains part art, part science. Even the more well-wrought efforts depend upon diverse and often scattershot approaches for reaching their audiences. Equally important, the programs are typically difficult to evaluate in terms of having achieved their goals. The criteria for success or failure of these campaigns are often vague. While more formal evaluations are increasing, they tend to be of low order scientific validity. Tight experimental controls are seldom used, largely because of the cost and complexity of implementing them in "naturalistic" field situations. Even when statistically significant findings are obtained under reasonably controlled conditions, questions often arise concerning how generalizable the results are to larger populations and whether the program was cost and/or effort efficient.

Crime prevention campaigns pose special problems in their own right. Crime prevention fits under the umbrella of what Weinstein (1987) calls self-protective behavior. This construct also encompasses anticipatory reactions to many health risks, as well as natural and occupational hazards. Weinstein identifies the key variables in precautionary behaviors as including beliefs about the probability and severity of the harm; the efficacy of a precautionary action; and the cost-taking action. Persuading people to increase such actions can be difficult, in part because of complex interactions among the above factors. Also, as Rogers and Storey (1987) note, programs advocating the adoption of behaviors to help "prevent" a possible unpleasant occurrence in the future tend to be less successful than those offering more timely and obvious rewards.

Adding to the problem is that the salience of crime and perceived efficacy of preventive behavior varies considerably across social class, geographic locale and other demographic boundaries (Greenberg, 1987; O'Keefe & Reid-Nash, 1987a; Bureau of Justice Statistics, 1985; Sacco & Silverman, 1984a; Skogan & Maxfield, 1980). (Such variations can be claimed for health issues, traffic safety and other societal concerns as well, but for crime the differentiations are typically more visible to the average citizen, as well as readily documented in crime rate figures.) This heterogeneity across citizen groups calls for more careful—and more effortful—targeting of messages to specific subgroups for greater effect.

Crime reduction programs in general have been particularly marked by lack of formal evaluation. For example, in 1986 the authors surveyed 149 crime prevention programs aimed at elderly citizens in urban areas across the U.S. We found only six with any empirical evaluative component, and none including control group comparisons or even probability sample survey methodology. However, in recent years the effects of a small number of media-based crime prevention programs have been more closely measured, and some generalizations about what can make such campaigns more effective are emerging.

This chapter will primarily review significant research on the most wide-ranging, as well as the most evaluated, crime prevention campaign, the "Take a Bite Out of Crime" or "McGruff" endeavor. It will update previously reported findings and tie those to results of other recent media campaign studies. Recommendations will follow for the design of more productive prevention campaigns and for the role of such programs in the criminal justice system.

The McGruff Campaign

The National Crime Prevention Campaign, with its "Take a Bite Out of Crime" theme, was initiated in 1979. It is managed by the National Crime Prevention Coalition and relies on public service announcements produced by the Advertising Council to generate an overall national image and publicity. The media campaign was originally produced under voluntary agreement by the advertising agency of Dancer Fitzgerald Sample (now DFS Dorland), which continues in that role. Equally important are a wide range of supplemental campaign activities promoted at local levels across the country by law enforcement agencies, community groups, and businesses. These include speaker's bureaus, workshops, school programs, and non-media strategies to involve the public. The campaign's trenchcoated "spokesdog," McGruff, over the years perhaps has become as familiar as Smokey the Bear to most children and adults alike.

McGruff's Early Impact

"Take a Bite Out of Crime" also appears to have been the first national PSA campaign to undergo a large-scale formal survey evaluation of its impact (O'Keefe, 1985, 1986). A dual approach was used incorporating both a national probability sample survey of 1,200 adults two years into the campaign, and a quasi-experimental panel survey of 426 adults in three representative cities interviewed just prior to the campaign and again two years later. Campaign effects were assessed following a model of citizen crime prevention competence, or the extent to which exposure to McGruff was related to: (1) awareness of appropriate prevention techniques; (2) positive attitudes toward citizen prevention actions; (3) feeling personally efficacious about preventing crime; (4) personal concern about crime; and (5) taking various crime prevention actions.

The findings indicated that McGruff had a sizable impact during its first two years. Over half of the samples studied recalled seeing at least one of the PSAs, typically via television, and the spots were regarded as well-liked and effective. Nearly a quarter of those exposed in the national sample said they had learned something new, and about half said they had been reminded of things they'd forgotten about crime prevention. Almost half reported more positive attitudes toward citizen involvement in crime prevention, although general concern about crime and sense of personal responsibility were less affected. The taking of specific preventive actions was reported by about a quarter of those exposed. The panel study results confirmed significantly greater action-taking by exposed citizens for behaviors advocated by the campaign, with no change for non-advocated behaviors. These effects were unaltered when such competing variables as exposure to other crime-related media content and direct victimization experience were controlled for.

The findings also supported a view that effects of campaigns do not always follow a traditional persuasion-model hierarchy beginning with learning, working through attitude change and motivation, and concluding in behavioral change. Rather, it was quite clear in this case that for some persons behavioral change took place independently of cognitive or attitudinal changes. And, cognitive changes did not always appear to precede attitudinal ones. A possible explanation is that predispositions toward victimization risk, direct opportunity for taking action, and issue involvement were partial determinants of the kinds of effects McGruff had on any one group of individuals.

The Continuing Campaign

Most durable advertising themes go through successions of incarnations using fresh individual messages and contexts. McGruff is no exception, with the campaign having evolved through over a half-dozen phases including home security, neighborhood watch, child abduction and drug abuse. A critical ingredient in the campaign's longevity has been the tie-ins with community crime prevention-related organizations. Local practitioners have been able to capitalize on the familiarity of

McGruff and use the more general campaign themes as umbrellas for their own more interpersonally based efforts.

While studies updating the direct impact of McGruff on the general public have unfortunately not been carried out, some smaller-scale research suggests if nothing else a continuing presence of the campaign in the public eye. DFS Dorland has continued focus group and copy-testing research on potential audience groups, including children, prior to new topic phases of the campaign. Mall-intercept surveys indicate increasing recognition of McGruff as a crime prevention symbol, as well as high credibility ascribed to him (National Crime Prevention Council, 1987). Perhaps a more revealing insight into the effectiveness of McGruff comes from two recent studies of intermediaries between the campaign and the public: professional crime prevention practitioners and television station public service managers responsible for choosing which PSAs are aired (DFSD Research, 1987).

An early 1987 national survey of 759 crime prevention practitioners (a 39 percent response rate), typically law enforcement officers, found widespread support for McGruff as a crime-fighting symbol in community prevention programs. Three-fourths of the respondents reported that booklets and pamphlets tied to McGruff circulated throughout their communities, and about half said costumed McGruff characters made personal appearances at shopping malls, parades, and schools. Half also cited McGruff-based advertising appearing in their communities. At the time of the interviews McGruff's tenure in most local programs had been about three to five years, and the longer he had been used, the more positive the perceptions of him.

The vast majority of practitioners said McGruff was an effective spokesperson for all age groups. Most attributed his effectiveness largely to his high recognizability and mass appeal, which they tied to his backing by a national media campaign. The advertising also made their local programs more credible and noteworthy, many said. Most respondents believed McGruff to be particularly effective among children, to whom he appeared as a symbol of trust and security. Many said that McGruff helped children learn crime prevention steps and safety tips. Almost 90 percent agreed that the PSAs and other McGruff materials aided them in their work, and most called for more publicity and coverage using McGruff. His main perceived weakness was in reaching teens and adults more effectively, but that was cited by only 16 percent of the sample.

Concurrent with the above study, 53 television station public service managers were interviewed (a 33 percent response rate) about their receptivity to the continuing McGruff PSAs. Nearly all regarded McGruff as an effective crime prevention symbol, and most cited his mass appeal and status as a public figure as reasons. DFS Dorland researchers indicated that they believed the McGruff PSAs continued to receive adequate placement by stations because the spots were of high quality, with state-of-the-art technology, and the subject matter was of ongoing community concern, encouraging people to become involved. The McGruff messages were also seen as easily targeted, as in the case of children's programs, and simplified placement decisions. The spots were also part of an ongoing campaign at the national and local levels, and the Advertising Council sponsorship gave them additional credibility (DFSD Research, 1987).

Again, while not necessarily indicative of continued public response to the McGruff-based efforts, the above results do suggest that the program has after several years gained a strong identity and presence in both crime prevention and mass media circles.

McGruff's initial and apparent continuing impact can be traced with reasonable speculation to a number of other factors than those mentioned above. For one, at the time of the campaign's early 1980s inception phase, crime was often mentioned as the most important issue on the public agenda. McGruff thus did not have to create issue salience but rather build on it and offer solutions. This is contrasted to, for example, the failure of a 1978 crime prevention campaign in Alberta which Sacco and Silverman (1984b) attribute in part to the low salience of crime at the time among the province's citizenry.

Another factor to consider is the role of pre-campaign formative research in the development of the McGruff character and basic messages and themes. The early studies found audiences to regard McGruff as nonthreatening and humorous, yet authoritative. McGruff also was seen as avoiding the more menacing or fear-arousing symbols equated with previous (as well as many present) anti-crime messages. Moreover, McGruff offered positive, and in most cases simple, suggestions that people could readily act on without a great deal of thought or effort.

It is also important to note that McGruff's "handlers" have carefully restricted his usage to crime-related issues, resisting temptations to diffuse his image by relating it to other social problems. Use of the campaign logos, or McGruff himself by doll and toy manufacturers and the like, is rather stringently controlled, leading to a more effective centrality of message.

Directions for Crime Prevention Media Campaigns

Several attributes of media campaigns found in McGruff and in other recent, largely successful efforts can be recommended for consideration in future designs. These include: (1) the above-noted use of formative research; (2) incorporation of appropriate theoretical models into campaign planning; (3) tying media campaigns to interpersonal and community-based programs; (4) using innovative programs with specialized objectives; and (5) being more attentive to the role of news media.

Use of Formative Research in Design and Planning

Campaign effectiveness is apt to be enhanced if greater use is made of basic advertising and marketing research planning principles in their design and execution. This includes using such formative research methods as copy testing and focus group analysis to pretest campaign materials, as has been done for successive stages of McGruff. It also should involve carefully identifying and segmenting audience groups for various message and channel combinations. This concern with responding to audience dispositions is a central tenet of "social marketing" approaches to information campaigns (Solomon, 1981) and can greatly enhance the efficiency of campaign execution (O'Keefe & Reid, in press; Rogers & Storey, 1987).

The crime issue poses special problems in this regard because of its complex nature and the variations in citizen response to it, as noted earlier. For example, in part because the early research on McGruff found the elderly less impacted by the campaign, a recent large-scale formative research effort has focused on that audience. The National Institute of Justice-sponsored project attempted to describe not only crime-related needs and concerns of elderly persons but their communication behaviors as well (O'Keefe & Reid-Nash, 1987a). The goal was to use the findings, drawn from a national sample survey of elderly persons, to recommend specific campaign strategies for reaching that group with crime prevention information.

The research uncovered some fairly complex relationships among the aged with respect to their perceptions, and fear, of crime and what they thought they could do about it. Among the findings with especially high

relevance for campaign design was that while realistically seeing themselves less at risk—as victimization statistics suggest—the concerns of the
elderly are greater and they feel less knowledgeable about and responsible for crime prevention than do younger adults.

Recommendations included directing information at the elderly that
would try to build their knowledge as well as, importantly, their sense of
responsibility and actual involvement in prevention activity. Lower income
and less educated elderly were deemed a particularly important audience for certain kinds of messages and media mixes, and elderly women
across all socioeconomic levels warranted messages tailored and dissemi-
nated particularly for them. The study in sum uncovered reasons why
the needs of elderly persons were being less attended to by McGruff and
likely other prevention campaigns, and showed possible directions to
take to address those shortcomings. Such precampaign research could
well benefit design and planning for a number of other audiences and
topics as well.

Utilizing the above strategic recommendations in the design of successful campaigns also requires application of basic communication planning principles. A wealth of previous research on source, message, and
channel factors in influencing audiences provides a substantial resource
for campaign planners intent upon matching messages to particular
audiences (cf. Percy & Rossiter, 1980; Bogart, 1986; Rice & Atkin, in
press). Elements such as source credibility, fear appeals, use of humor,
elements of message design, and channel information capacities have all
been the subject of considerable research, and many of the findings have
implications for media message design. More audience-directed formative research can also present profiles of the mass and interpersonal
communication patterns of specific target groups, as well as address their
motives for communicating and the kinds of gratifications they seek
from doing so (cf. Rosengren, Wenner, & Palmgreen, 1985).

Use of Appropriate Theoretical Models

Campaigns on crime prevention and as other topics appear to stand a
better chance of success if they make use of theoretical models of communication or persuasion in their design. At the least, this brings a broader
base of knowledge to bear on the specific problem; moreover, it can
provide a guiding structure to better organize the sometimes disparate
components of large-scale media-related campaigns (O'Keefe & Reid, in
press). The application, for example, of Bandura's (1977) social learning

theory in the multifaceted Stanford Heart Disease Prevention Program (Flora, Maccoby & Farquhar, in press) served to refine the campaign's objectives of reducing heart disease risk by emphasizing modeling behavior and the need for interpersonal reinforcement.

The competence paradigm used to evaluate McGruff, while not incorporated into the campaign's initial design, has allowed a more appropriate delineation of the levels of effects that are possible with subsequent stages of the campaign. Campaign strategists would do well to specify the precise objectives being sought, including such potential outcomes as awareness, information gain, attitude change, motivation and behavior change. These objectives also need to be translated into campaign message components that can be realistically evaluated as the program progresses. Sacco and Silverman (1984b) trace at least part of the failure of the Alberta campaign to a lack of such process specification.

Citizen involvement with an issue may influence the kinds of effects a campaign is able to have. Recognition of this has led to a rethinking of the traditional hierarchical view of persuasion processes (Petty & Cacioppo, 1986). It may be that the "rational" model of persuasion, in which cognitive change leads to attitudinal change, which then leads to behavioral change, is appropriate only in cases where issue involvement is relatively high (Chaffee & Roser, 1986). In instances of low involvement, behavioral change may occur more simply without a great deal of rationalization or thought, as may have been the case for some audiences of the early McGruff campaign. (For example, getting into the habit of locking a door may for some people not require deliberation as much as just being reminded.)

Combined with communication models should be the use of more definitive theories of how publics regard crime and their own roles in reducing it (cf. Skogan & Maxfield, 1980; Tyler & Lavrakas, 1986). As Heinzelmann (1987) has suggested, it may be appropriate to in some instances borrow from some of the more extensively developed preventive behavior conceptualizations in health-related areas. For example, the health belief model (cf. Janz & Becker, 1984) hypothesizes that individuals are motivated to carry out actions they see as efficacious in lowering the risk of events that they see as having potentially severe consequences. According to the model, the greater the perceived risk and the more serious the threat, the more likely people are to take necessary precautions if they perceive themselves as capable of doing so. Thus, the potential for communication program influence increases when the perceived benefits of taking the suggested action outweigh the costs, i.e., when the sense of efficacy or prevention competence overshadows the doubts.

Media, Interpersonal, and Community Interventions

As Yin (1986) has noted, the most successful crime reduction programs are those involving not just one or two specific actions but a wide array of complementary and supplementary activities. The findings also make a strong case for the integration of local neighborhood groups with more generalized media campaigns. Small neighborhood self-help groups not only prompt social interaction but also build the kinds of self-confidence that lead to control over one's environment, thereby setting the stage for learning and practicing new behaviors. As our findings suggest, group participation may have particular benefits for the elderly in fighting crime.

In addition, Heinzelmann (1987) has pointed out that citizen involvement in program planning is more likely to occur if done in the context of an existing community network or organizations of citizens who had a history of joint decision making. Lavrakas (1985) emphasizes that the initiation and subsequent reinforcement of community groups is accelerated by local governmental and police support. Such community authorities at least appear to recognize the value of citizen group action. A 1983 study of criminal justice experts found that such group activity was the most often mentioned program type believed to actually reduce crime (following opportunity reduction). Significantly, public information programs were the fourth most often mentioned (Research & Forecasts, 1983).

A critical dimension here may be a need for campaign planners to project citizens' likely involvement in a combination of communication and action programs. People are unlikely to risk involvement in a public communication campaign and the actions it advocates without some perceived chance of success. As noted above, likely audience involvement in preventing crime can be seen as functions of their beliefs and the likelihood that the advocated actions will reduce or eliminate the vulnerability.

Use of Innovative, Specialized Programs

Apart from full-fledged information campaigns, it is possible for more specialized—as well as innovative—media-based preventive efforts to sometimes bear fruit. Media-based programs to more directly involve citizens in at least one form of crime reduction—tipstering by anonymous witnesses—appear to have had measured success (Surette, 1984; Rosenbaum, Lurigio & Lavrakas, 1986). Over the past decade hundreds of communities have organized such "Crime Stopper" programs in which police and news media cooperate to publicize selected unsolved crimes. Witnesses are urged to contact police, under a guarantee of anonymity and with the promise of a cash reward should their information lead to an arrest.

Rosenbaum et al. found law enforcement agencies as well as news executives to be quite enthusiastic about the programs as a cost-effective means of solving troublesome cases, and citizen interest and participation in them seem to warrant their continuation at least for now. They may have the added benefit of giving citizens at large at least a vicarious sense of participation in the process of crime solution. Risks here include the potential for civil liberties violations, and the sometimes unseemly aura of having to pay for what some might see as civic duty. Moreover, the programs are still fresh enough so that it is difficult to predict their long-term viability and impact.

Another innovative experiment has involved local police departments sending newsletters to their constituents. Lavrakas (1986) found citizens positively disposed to receiving the bulk-mailed newsletters, especially if such new information as crime statistics was included. However, exposure rates to the newsletters varied considerably across the communities studied, suggesting that such factors as mailing formats, educational level, and community cohesion can strongly affect the success of such efforts. While immediate effects of the newsletters on reader anti-crime dispositions appeared slight, there was no evidence that the materials increased fear of crime. Such findings reinforce views of Greenberg (1987), Heinzelmann (1987) and others that existing community structure is a critical variable in prevention program design.

The Role of News Media

In many if not most of the communities with Crime Stopper programs, they are presented as legitimate news items or features either in newspapers or on television. Most public information campaigns attempt at least in part to involve the news media in the dissemination process. Print or televised news stories can lend greater credibility than most other forms of publicity to a campaign's goals. However, the role of news media in campaigns has been at best minimally evaluated.

With respect to crime reporting per se, however, there is evidence that news content exaggerates the quantity and nature of incidents, focusing on the more violent and/or bizarre (Graber, 1980; Gordon and Heath, 1981; Sheley and Ashkins, 1984). However, evidence is mixed as to whether such portrayals have any meaningful impact on perceptions of crime by media audiences. Using national sample data, O'Keefe (1984) found that greater attention to televised crime news correlated with more worry and concern about victimization, particularly when news credibility was high. However, exposure to crime news in newspapers was unrelated to fear or concern, going against previous findings (Gordon & Heath, 1981; Jaehnig, Weaver & Fico, 1981). A subsequent over-time lagged regression analysis suggested it was more likely that increased attention to televised crime news resulted in greater fear rather than the reverse hypothesis (O'Keefe & Reid-Nash, 1987).

Such differences may stem from variation in the way in which crime-related content is handled journalistically in each medium (an under-explored issue in its own right). Another possible explanation is that televised crime stories are more difficult to selectively avoid or tune out than are newspaper accounts and thus are capable of increasing the salience of crime to persons perhaps initially less interested or concerned. Notably, knowledge about and the carrying out of certain preventive activities associated positively with attention to crime stories in newspapers but not to televised ones. These findings suggest if nothing else a strong interplay between news coverage of crime and public perceptions of it. It may be productive for campaigns to make more effort to incorporate news related to crime prevention into the daily agenda of reported events.

Conclusions

Media-based public information campaigns have become a staple of contemporary crime prevention efforts. Promoting crime prevention among the public poses special problems associated with both the advocating of self-protective behaviors in general and of crime-related ones in particular. While formal research on such campaigns has been limited, some important lessons may be learned from evaluation of the national McGruff program and the few other documented campaigns.

McGruff seems to have had some success in promoting various aspects of crime prevention competence among a fairly wide range of citizens. Moreover, the campaign has served as a centerpiece for a host of allied preventive efforts at local, statewide and national levels. McGruff's effectiveness may be tied in part to use of formative research in its design and to the integration of interpersonal and community-level support with the media components. In addition to these factors, subsequent campaigns would do well to pay more attention to the use of theoretical models of communication and persuasion in their design. A more detailed examination of characteristics of audiences should be included in campaign design. Such innovative programs as Crime Stoppers need a more careful look to determine why they've had the impact they've appeared to. News media can play a critical role in campaign dissemination, and that relationship needs closer study.

Given the ubiquity of crime prevention information campaigns, we need to know more about their direct impact on the public, particularly at the local level. Given the great expense and effort that go into their production and dissemination, the lack of continuing, systematic evaluation may lead to distortion of their impact and perhaps inefficiency in the communication process. More importantly, the research gap clearly hinders our understanding of why some techniques work while others don't, from the point of view of both information campaigns and citizen-based crime prevention per se.

REFERENCES

Bandura, A. (1977). *Social learning theory.* Englewood Cliffs, NJ: Prentice-Hall.

Bogart, L. (1986). *Strategy in advertising.* Lincolnwood, IL: NTC.

Bureau of Justice Statistics. (March, 1986). *Crime prevention measures.* Washington, DC: U.S. Department of Justice.

Chaffee, S.H. & Roser, C. (1986). Involvement and the consistency of knowledge, attitudes and behaviors. *Communication research, 13,* 373–399.

Cohn, A. (1985). *The role of media campaigns in preventing child abuse.* National Committee for Preventing Child Abuse, Chicago.

DFSD Research. (1987). *An assessment of the McGruff effort among crime prevention professionals and public service station managers.* New York: DFS Dorland.

Ettema, J., Brown, J. & Luepker, R. (1983). Knowledge gap effects in a health information campaign. *Public opinion quarterly, 47,* 516–527.

Research and Forecasts, Inc. (1983). *The Figgie Report Part IV: Reducing crime in America — successful community efforts.* Willoughby, OH: Figgie International.

Flora, J., Maccoby, N. & Farquhar, J.W. (in press). Communication campaigns to prevent cardiovascular disease: The Stanford studies. In R.E. Rice and C.K. Atkin (Eds.), *Public communication campaigns* (2nd ed.). Newbury Park, CA: Sage.

Gordon, M. & Heath, L. (1981). The news business, crime and fear. In D. Lewis (Ed.), *Reactions to crime* (pp. 227–250). Newbury Park, CA: Sage.

Graber, D.B. (1980). *Crime news and the public.* New York: Praeger.

Greenberg, S.W. (1987). Why people take precautions against crime: a review of the literature on individual and collective responses to crime. In N.D. Weinstein (Ed.), *Taking care: Understanding and encouraging self-protective behavior* (pp. 231–253). Cambridge, MA: Cambridge University Press.

Heinzelmann, F. (1987). Promoting citizen involvement in crime prevention and control. In N.D. Weinstein (Ed.), *Taking care: Understanding and encouraging self-protective behavior* (pp. 254–279). Cambridge, MA: Cambridge University Press.

Jaehnig, W., Weaver, D., & Fico, F. (1981) Reporting and fearing crime in three communities. *Journal of communications, 31,* 88–96.

Janz, N.K. & Becker, M.H. (1984). The health belief model: A decade later. *Health education quarterly, 11,* 1–47.

Lavrakas, P.J. (1985). Citizen self-help and neighborhood crime prevention. In L. Curtis (Ed.), *American Violence and Public Policy.* New Haven, CT: Yale University Press.

Lavrakas, P.J. (1986). Evaluating police-community anti-crime newsletters: The Evanston, Houston and Newark field studies. In D.P. Rosenbaum (Ed.), *Community crime prevention: Does it work?* Newbury Park, CA: Sage.

McGuire, W.J. (1981). Theoretical foundations of campaigns. In R.E. Rice & W.J. Paisley (Eds.), *Public communication campaigns* (pp. 41–70). Beverly Hills, CA: Sage.

McQuail, D. (1987). *Mass communication theory* (2nd ed.). Newbury Park, CA: Sage.

National Crime Prevention Council. (1987). *An attitude and awareness study of McGruff the Crime Dog.* Washington, D.C.: NCPC.

O'Keefe, G.J. (1984). Public views on crime: Television exposure and media credibility. In R.N. Bostrum (Ed.), *Communication yearbook 8.* Beverly Hills, CA: Sage.

O'Keefe, G.J. (1985). "Taking a bite out of crime": The impact of a public information campaign. *Communication research, 12,* 147–178.

O'Keefe, G.J. (1986). The "McGruff" national media campaign: Its public impact and future implications. In D. Rosenbaum (Ed.), *Community crime prevention: Does it work?* (pp. 252–268). Beverly Hills, CA: Sage.

O'Keefe, G.J., & Reid-Nash, K. (1987). Crime news and real-world blues: The effects of the media on social reality. *Communication research, 14,* 147–163.

O'Keefe, G.J., & Reid-Nash, K. (1987a). *Promoting Crime Prevention Competence Among the Elderly.* Washington, DC: National Institute of Justice.

O'Keefe, G.J. & Reid, K. (in press). The uses and effects of public service advertising. In J.E. Grunig and L.A. Grunig (Eds.), *Public Relations Research Annual.* Hillsdale, NJ: Erlbaum.

Percy, L. & Rossiter, J. (1980). *Advertising Strategy: A Communication Theory Approach.* New York: Praeger.

Petty, R.E. & Cacioppo, J.T. (1986). *Communication and persuasion: Central and peripheral routes to attitude change.* New York: Springer-Verlag.

Rice, R.E. & Atkin, C.K. (in press). *Public communication campaigns* (2nd ed.). Newbury Park, CA: Sage.

Roberts, D.F. & Maccoby, N. (1985). Effects of mass communication. In G. Lindzey & E. Aronson (Eds.) *The handbook of social psychology* (3rd ed., vol. 2). New York: Random House.

Rogers, E.M. & Storey, J.D. (1987). Communication campaigns. In C.R. Berger and S.H. Chaffee (Eds.), *Handbook of communication science.* Newbury Park, CA: Sage.

Rosenbaum, D.P., Lurigio, A.J., & Lavrakas, P.J. (1986). *Crime Stoppers—a national evaluation.* Washington, DC: National Institute of Justice.

Rosengren, K.E., Wenner, L.A., & Palmgreen, P. (1985). *Media gratifications research: Current Perspectives.* Newbury Park, CA: Sage.

Sacco, V.F. & Silverman, R.A. (1984). Crime prevention through mass media: Prospects and problems. In R. Surette (Ed.), *Justice and the Media: Issues and research.* Springfield, IL: Charles C Thomas.

Sacco, V.F. & Silverman, R.A. (1984a). Selling crime prevention: The evaluation of a mass media campaign. In R. Surette (Ed.), *Justice and the Media: Issues and research.* Springfield, IL: Charles C Thomas.

Sheley, J.F. & Ashkins, C.D. (1981). Crime, crime news and crime views. *Public opinion quarterly, 45,* 492–506.

Skogan, W.G. & Maxfield, M.G. (1980). *Coping with crime.* Beverly Hills: Sage.

Surette, R. (1984). Two media-based crime-control programs: Crimestoppers and video street patrol. In R. Surette (Ed.), *Justice and the Media: Issues and research.* Springfield, IL: Charles C Thomas.

Solomon, D.S. (1981). Social marketing & health promotion. In R. Rice & W. Paisley (Eds.), *Public communication campaigns* (pp. 281–292). Beverly Hills, CA: Sage.

Tyler, T., & Lavrakas, P.J. (1985). Mass media effects: Distinguishing the importance of personal and societal level effects. In S. Kraus & R. Perloff (Eds.), *Mass media and political thought: An information-processing approach.* Beverly Hills, CA: Sage.

Weinstein, N.D. (1987). Cross-hazard consistencies: Conclusions about self-protective behavior. In N.D. Weinstein (Ed.), *Taking care: Understanding and encouraging self-protective behavior.* Cambridge, MA: Cambridge University Press.

Yin, R.K. (1986). Community crime prevention: A synthesis of eleven evaluations. In R.P. Rosenbaum (Ed.), *Community crime prevention: Does it work?* Newbury Park, CA: Sage.

Chapter 16

MEDIA COOPERATION WITH POLICE: THE CASE OF CRIME STOPPERS

Paul J. Lavrakas, Dennis P. Rosenbaum, and Arthur J. Lurigio

There are many inherent sources of conflict between the media and the police in a free society. In their expressed role as "watchdog," the media have a history of exposing wrongdoings on the part of the police, including poor quality of service, corruption, brutality, falsification of information, and other problems. At the same time, the media are dependent upon the police for facts about specific crimes and about crime in general. The police, for their part, believe they have many valid reasons for not releasing information about crime to the media, because they often view the media as interfering with their own investigations of particular crimes (cf. Lavrakas, Rosenbaum and Kaminski, 1983). There are also times when the police feel the media betray their confidence by unfairly blaming them for circumstances beyond their control.

In the past 12 years, however, a cooperative relationship between many local media and local police has developed under the Crime Stoppers concept. Also known as Crime Alert, Silent Witness, or Crime Line, these self-sustaining programs represent a new and growing effort to address the problem of crime. Compared to other anti-crime approaches, Crime Stoppers is unique in that it features the cooperation of the local media, local police, and local business community in an attempt to enhance the quantity and quality of information about serious crime, which is made available to the police from the citizenry. Based on the premise that many citizens are unwilling to provide information to the

The research reported in this paper was conducted with the support of the Medill School of Journalism, Northwestern University, and under Cooperative Agreement #NIJ-83-IJ-CX-K050 between the National Institute of Justice and the Center for Urban Affairs and Policy Research, Northwestern University. The authors would like to thank Jennifer Friedman, Cheryl Whittenmore and Gaye Haugh for their assistance in gathering and preparing the data reported in this manuscript.

police about criminal activity either because of apathy and/or fear of retaliation (MacAleese and Tilly, 1983), Crime Stoppers offers monetary incentives (typically ranging from $100 to $1000) and the protection of anonymity to persons who come forth with details that lead to the arrest, indictment and/or conviction of suspected criminals.

Recognizing the critical role played by private citizens in solving crimes, Greg MacAleese, a police officer in Albuquerque (NM), started the first Crime Stoppers program in 1976. Although similar to other programs in the early 1970s that had employed monetary rewards and anonymity as incentives (cf. Bickman and Lavrakas, 1977), Crime Stoppers was the first to feature *the media* in a central role. Since 1976, Crime Stoppers has spread across the United States, with more than 700 programs operational in 1988. The program has also emerged in Canada, and its adoption is being considered in some European countries.

Media participation in Crime Stoppers serves an educational/publicity function. The media disseminate basic facts about the program's objectives, operations, and achievements. Moreover, they regularly publicize the details of unsolved offenses, typically by presenting a reenactment (broadcast) or descriptive narrative (print) of a selected "Crime of the Week." In some communities, Crime Stoppers programs have the participation of several different media organizations, including both print and broadcast. In others, an "exclusivity" arrangement has developed whereby one media outlet (most typically a television station) has negotiated an understanding with the local Crime Stoppers program to be the sole media participant.

Although Crime Stoppers appears to be effective in solving certain crimes and in recovering stolen property, the program has been criticized on a number of "philosophical" grounds. Rosenbaum and Lurigio (1985) identified four types of arguments that have been raised against Crime Stoppers. First, some assert that a free society should not pay citizens to do something (i.e., report knowledge of crimes to law enforcement authorities) that is their inherent civic duty. Second, the argument has been made that large sums of money and anonymity may encourage false accusations, violations of civil rights and mutual distrust among the citizenry, which may lead to harassment of innocent persons. Third, some hypothesize that the practice of encouraging "informants," which has been likened to Crime Stoppers" use of rewards, engenders a police-state mentality and fosters an unhealthy dependence on criminal justice agencies to try to resolve social problems. Finally, some fear that intensive media involvement in Crime Stoppers may compromise the media's objectivity in their general coverage of their local police and other crime-related topics.

In 1983, the National Institute of Justice, interested in the advantages and disadvantages of Crime Stoppers, sponsored a national evaluation of these programs. This paper presents select findings of the evaluation research, focusing on what was learned about media participation/nonparticipation in Crime Stoppers. The findings are primarily descriptive, as this was the first empirical effort at the national level to assess the media's involvement in Crime Stoppers. Given the rather uncritical publicity the Crime Stoppers concept has received from the national media (e.g., ABC's "20-20"), media scholars and practitioners need to look more closely at whether this type of cooperation merits active support and encouragement, or whether this is a type of activism that might be better avoided by the media in a free society.

Methodology

Two different mail surveys provided the data. In the first survey, 203 questionnaires were completed by the police coordinators of local Crime Stoppers programs. In the second survey, 237 questionnaires were completed by media executives.

Police Coordinators Survey

The first stage of the research was conducted in early 1984 and involved a telephone screening interview of all known Crime Stoppers programs. Police coordinators at each of these programs were then mailed a detailed questionnaire, which included several items regarding the nature and extent of media participation with their program. Two hundred and three questionnaires, or 46 percent of those mailed, were returned. The questionnaire included open-ended and closed-ended items measuring aspects of the local media's participation with Crime Stoppers, both at the inception of their own program and at the time of data collection in 1984. These aspects included ratings on media cooperation, operational parameters (e.g., Crime of the Week), program difficulties, and perceptions of media motives for participation.

Media Executives Surveys

In addition to gathering information from police coordinators about the media, a mail survey was conducted of two separate samples of media executives regarding their organization's participation/nonparticipation in Crime Stoppers. In the aforementioned screening interview of police coordinators, names and addresses of participating media had been gathered from operational Crime Stoppers programs. A random sample of 514 media organizations was drawn from this listing and a questionnaire was mailed to the organization's chief executive (e.g., publisher or general manager). This sample comprised executives at 203 newspapers, 180 radio stations, and 131 television stations. Completed questionnaires were received from about one in four of each type of media identified as participating in Crime Stoppers.

A second sample of media executives was drawn randomly from industry yearbooks (e.g., *Editor and Publisher Annual*). It was assumed that most of these organizations would not be participating in a Crime Stoppers program and thus would provide a contrast with the information gathered from executives at media organizations that were sampled from the Crime Stoppers program files. This sample included executives at 248 daily newspapers, 180 radio stations and 115 television stations (UHF and VHF). Completed questionnaires from the random sample were received from about one in four newspapers, compared to 14 percent of the television stations and 12 percent of the radio stations. A likely explanation for the lower response rate of broadcast executives in this second sample is the fact that many of the television and radio stations that were randomly chosen from the industry yearbook did not have their own news departments; thus the questionnaire was not germane to their organization.[1] The questionnaire that was completed by the 235 media executives include open-ended and closed-ended items measuring aspects of the local media's evaluation of and participation with Crime Stoppers. These aspects included the executives' awareness of the program, the nature of their participation or nonparticipation in the program, perceptions of the success of the program and value of the program to society.[2]

---

1. Several broadcast executives cited this reason in mailing back a blank questionnaire.

2. Although the final samples were not "random" in the strictest sense of the term, they are quite heterogeneous and we believe they are fairly representative of the populations of interest. For example,

Results

Police Coordinators Survey

Start-Up Phase. A number of questions were asked about the role of the media in starting a Crime Stoppers program and about problems that may be encountered during the start-up phase.

Coordinators reported that in about one-fourth of the cases (24%), their community became aware of the Crime Stoppers concept through the local media; and in a few instances, it was a local media organization that approached and convinced the police to start Crime Stoppers.

In contrast to those cases where the media were instrumental in starting the local program, another quarter of the program coordinators (28%) reported that enlisting media participation had been a major problem in becoming operational. This problem was associated with the size of the community: Half of the programs serving populations greater than 50,000 reported that initial media cooperation was the first or second greatest obstacle their program had to overcome, whereas only a third of the programs serving smaller population areas reported this problem. Overall, a majority of programs stated that they had no major problem getting initial cooperation from local media. One consistently mentioned difficulty of those that did have start-up problems with their local media was that of "exclusivity," i.e., one media organization wanting a monopoly on Crime Stoppers coverage.

Police coordinators were asked a series of questions about five types of media organizations that might be participating with their program: daily newspapers, weekly newspapers, radio stations, UHF and VHF

comparing the demographic characteristics of the programs that responded to the police coordinators sample showed a very close match to the population demographics as identified in the national screening interview. For the media samples, no national standards were available. However, a comparison of the two media executive samples (from the Crime Stoppers listing and the industry yearbooks) showed that responding organizations did not differ significantly in terms of executives' ratings of the crime rate and fear of crime in their organization's market. Furthermore, there were no significant differences between the two samples in executives' ratings of the accuracy of the local citizenry's perception of crime, the citizenry's involvement in crime prevention, the citizenry's interest in crime news, or the organization's satisfaction with the quality of local police service. The two samples did not differ in the extent to which they felt cooperation with local police on an anti-crime program would compromise their objectivity in covering police/crime news. Finally, there was no difference in self-ratings of their organization's editorial stances on a conservative/liberal dimension. In sum, we believe these survey results provide a useful first look at the nature of the relationship between the media and the police in this relatively new anti-crime program.

television stations, and cable television companies.[3] The results indicate that local programs have the greatest access to radio stations (86%), followed by daily newspapers (77%), weekly newspapers (60%), UHF/VHF television (60%), and cable companies (36%).

Regarding ratings of the cooperativeness of different types of local media at the start-up of Crime Stoppers, coordinators rated radio stations, weekly newspapers and cable companies as more cooperative than UHF and VHF television stations and daily newspapers. However, as shown in Table 1, the majority of all five types of media, including daily newspapers and television stations, were rated as cooperative. The size of the community served (in terms of population) was negatively correlated with ratings of the cooperation of print media during the program's start-up phase ($p < .05$), but was uncorrelated with the cooperativeness of broadcast media. That is, newspapers (dailies and weeklies) in smaller population areas were judged by coordinators as significantly more cooperative than those serving larger areas. For television and radio, no correlation was found between cooperation and size of area served.

Subsequent Program Operations. In general, there were no differences in the ratings given by police coordinators regarding the degree of cooperation their program received from local media at the time of the survey (1984), compared to the level of cooperation they had received at the start of their program. Once again, it was found that daily newspapers and UHF/VHF television stations were rated as significantly less cooperative than weekly newspapers, radio stations, and cable companies (see Table 1).

Despite this overall pattern, there was a good deal of variation across programs in the *number* of media that participated at individual program sites. As would be expected, the larger the population area served, the greater the average number of media that participated (see Table 2). This correlation also held for the likelihood that an individual program had the participation of even *one* media of each type. This was especially true for television: whereas only one in six programs serving small population areas reported having a participating television station, nine out of ten programs serving areas of 250,000 or more population reported the participation of at least one television station.

---

3. Not all Crime Stoppers programs operate in areas that are served by each type of media organization.

Table 1
Program Coordinator's Perception of Cooperation of Local Media

| Media Type | At Program Start-up | | | At Present Time | | |
| | Percentage of Ratings[1] | | | Percentage of Ratings[1] | | |
	Cooperative	Neutral	Uncooperative	Cooperative	Neutral	Uncooperative
Daily Newspapers	66.4	20.3	13.3	68.3	22.7	9.0
Weekly Newspapers	79.3	15.3	5.4	85.8	11.5	2.7
Radio Stations	83.1	11.9	5.0	81.8	10.9	7.3
VHF/UHF TV Stations	68.8	20.2	11.0	73.5	15.0	11.5
Cable TV Companies	80.3	10.6	9.1	78.1	12.3	9.6

[1]Ratings of cooperation were made on a 0–10 scale. For the purposes of this table, ratings of 0–3 were grouped as "Uncooperative", 4–6 were grouped as "Neutral" and 7–10 were grouped as "Cooperative."

Table 2
Size of Population Served and Media Participation Rates in 1984

Market Size	Daily Newspaper		Weekly Newspaper		Radio		VHF/UHF Television		Cable Television	
	% With	Ave. #	% With	Ave. #	% With	Ave. #	% With	Ave. #	% With	Ave. #
Small (< 50,000)	51	.75	59	1.25	73	1.83	15	.22	35	.41
Medium (50,000–99,999)	73	1.11	59	1.52	75	3.48	52	.86	23	.39
Medium Large (100,000–249,999)	86	1.44	58	1.50	86	4.75	69	1.19	36	.44
Large (≥ 250,000)	75	3.34	61	3.18	80	7.50	89	2.68	36	.55

Crime of the Week. Most coordinators reported that at least one of their participating media runs a "Crime of the Week" feature (84%), with another 8 percent indicating that their local media run "Crime of the Month". In about half of the participating daily newspapers (53%) the feature always gets front-page coverage, with another 23 percent usually giving it front-page coverage. With weeklies, about one-fourth always cover it on the front page, whereas another 30 percent usually do. In short, when newspapers cover the Crime of the Week it typically receives high visibility.

There is not consistent pattern of coverage of the Crime of the Week given by radio stations, i.e., they appear to run these spots at all time of the day and night. For television, though, the 6:00 P.M. to 12:00 A.M. time slot was the most common placement of the Crime of the Week, most typically run on an evening local news program.

About three-fourths of the programs with participating daily newspapers, weekly newspapers, and/or radio stations indicated that Crime Stoppers program personnel regularly prepare the news copy for the Crime of the Week feature. In contrast, only one-third of those Crime Stoppers programs with participating television stations prepare their own copy: instead, most prepare it in cooperation with the stations' staff. However, almost all coordinators indicated that participating media *did not* have direct editorial control over the choice of the unsolved crime that served as the Crime of the Week.

Perceptions of Media Motives for Participation. When asked *why* the media cooperated with Crime Stoppers, police coordinators mentioned two basic reasons: (1) to fulfill their public service requirements and (2) to increase their "rating" (i.e., readership or viewership). The latter reason was mentioned more frequently by program coordinators from larger population areas. Open-ended responses indicated that coordinators objected to media participation solely for the purposes of furthering viewership or readership.

Other findings. In general, the relationships that have developed between local media and local Crime Stoppers programs appear to be quite satisfactory to both. Only 20 percent of the coordinators reported that they had received complaints from participating media, with missed deadlines being the most common complaint.

When asked what was the most successful type of media for creating public interest in Crime Stoppers, about six in ten programs in smaller population areas indicated newspapers, whereas seven in ten programs from larger population areas reported it was television. Yet, answers to other open-ended questions suggested that despite this difference of opinion there is not overwhelming preference for any particular type of media. Instead, coordinators were most pleased with whichever media they perceived as reaching the largest local audience.

Media Executives Surveys

Awareness of and Participation in Crime Stoppers. In an open-ended item at the start of the questionnaire, media executives were asked if their news organization "encouraged citizen involvement in crime prevention activities/programs," and if so, what type? Nearly all (94%) of the Crime Stoppers sample replied affirmatively, as did 70 percent of the random sample (72 percent of newspapers and television stations, and 62 percent of radio stations).[4] Eighty-two percent of the executives from the Crime Stoppers sample reported that their organization was currently participating in a Crime Stoppers program, compared to only 24 percent of those from the random sample. (As a comparison, about one-fifth of the Crime Stoppers sample reported that their organization has encouraged

---

4. Nearly 60 percent of the media in the random sample were located in communities with no local Crime Stoppers program. An additional 13 percent of the media from the random sample were located in communities with a Crime Stoppers program, but did not participate. Finally, 28 percent of the media from the random sample participated in Crime Stoppers. In contrast, only 2 percent of the media from the Crime Stoppers sample indicated that there was no Crime Stoppers program in their community. Another 5 percent reported that their organization did not participate in their local program. It is likely that some of the Crime Stoppers programs that were initially identified in the screening interview as operational had become inactive by the time of the media executives sampling. This would account for why a small number of media executives from the Crime Stoppers sample reported there was no program in their community. Furthermore, some media organizations that were participating at the time of the initial screening might have stopped their participation by the time of the sampling of media executives.

citizens' participation in local "Neighborhood Watch" type programs, as have one-fourth of the media in the random sample.)

The questionnaire also included a more detailed sequence of close-ended items to examine whether the organization was aware of and presently participated in Crime Stoppers. This questioning determined that 93 percent of the Crime Stoppers sample presently participated with a local Crime Stoppers Program, compared to 28 percent of the random sample.[5] As might be expected, all executives in the Crime Stoppers sample were aware of the existence of an anti-crime program called "Crime Stoppers," even those whose organizations were not participating in a local Crime Stoppers program at the time of the survey. More significantly, and as a more representative measure of national media "awareness" of Crime Stoppers, only 10 percent of those in the random sample had *never* heard of Crime Stoppers.

Of all the media organizations that currently participated with Crime Stoppers, slightly over half (54%) of the executives from the Crime Stoppers sample, and three-fourths of those reached via the random sample, indicated that their organization helped start Crime Stoppers in their community. None of the three media types were any more likely than the other two types to have helped start their local Crime Stoppers program.

When asked "why" their organization participated in Crime Stoppers, the most frequent reason (given by 50 percent) was that their organization felt that Crime Stoppers was helping in the fight against crime. A similar proportion of executives (46%) indicated that participation was part of their public service responsibility as a media organization. About one in five (17%) also noted that participation had helped their image (i.e., ratings) with the public. As mentioned earlier, these latter two reasons were the ones most frequently noted by Crime Stoppers' coordinators in explaining their own perceptions of the motives of the local media for participating in the program.

When asked to explain what their organization did as part of their participation in Crime Stoppers, a majority of executives (52%) indicated that they gave daily and/or weekly coverage to Crime Stoppers, but not necessarily by running a "Crime of the Week" feature. Nearly three in 10

---

5. This increase in reported participation, as measured by the close-ended sequence compared with the aforementioned open-ended question, is a standard finding in surveys that measure participation in anti-crime programs (Lavrakas and Jason, 1979).

(28%), though, did indicate that their organization ran "Crime of the Week." And about one-fourth noted that they publicized Crime Stoppers' successes as part of their regular news coverage. Finally, about one-tenth indicated that their organization was represented on the local Crime Stoppers Board of Directors, helped with raising funds for rewards, provided free advertising for the program, and/or helped produce re-enactments for broadcasting (in the case of television and radio).

Less than one in 10 of the executives (7%) stated that their organization had an "exclusivity arrangement" with Crime Stoppers, in which they were the only media that participated in the local program. This arrangement differed significantly by media type, with only 2 percent of radio stations and 8 percent of newspapers indicating they had exclusivity. In contrast, 29 percent of the participating television stations had an exclusive relationship with their local Crime Stoppers program. When asked if their organization would continue to participate in Crime Stoppers if they could not maintain the exclusivity, nearly nine in 10 (86%) of those currently operating with exclusivity indicated that it was at least "somewhat likely" that they *would continue* to participate.

Another sequence of items dealt specifically with "Crime of the Week" (or "Crime of the Month," in some cases). Eighty percent of the media executives indicated that their local Crime Stoppers program had a Crime of the Week feature, but as reported above only about one in three stated their organization participated in it. Three-quarters of the executives with knowledge of Crime of the Week said that each week's publicized crime was chosen by the police or by the Crime Stoppers program, with the rest stating that it was chosen by a committee that included media input. There was no pattern reported concerning the type of crime regularly chosen, but in general, the executives were "quite satisfied" with the specific crimes chosen to be featured.

For those executives who had not heard of Crime Stoppers, the questionnaire provided a basic explanation of Crime Stoppers' operations and philosophy. All executives located in communities *without* a Crime Stoppers program (59 percent of the random sample) were then asked if such a program were to exist in their community how likely would it be that their organization would participate. Nearly two-thirds (64%) said it would be *very likely* that their organization would participate in a local Crime Stoppers program if one were available. Comparing these responses by different types of media, it was found that eight in 10 radio stations, half the newspapers and one-fourth the television stations said it would be very likely that they would participate. In contrast to the two-thirds that indicated it was "very likely" their organization would participate, about one-fourth (22%) said it would be *very unlikely* that their organization would participate.

Reasons for Nonparticipation. All executives in the random sample that did not have a local Crime Stoppers program and did not indicate that their organization would be "very likely" to participate if one were available, were asked "why might your organization not want to participate in such a program?" The most frequent reason given had to do with "operational problems" that presumably might keep the media organization from being able to coordinate its activities with those of a Crime Stoppers program (e.g., meeting production deadlines). Several other reasons were mentioned, most of which centered around a belief that it was beyond the proper role of the media to be participating in such a program. There were no consistent patterns across media types in the reasons given for possible non-participation.

Finally, executives located in communities with a Crime Stoppers program, but whose organizations did note participate (n = 20), were asked the reasons for their organizations's non-participation. Each of the following was mentioned by two or more of the non-participants: (1) another media has an exclusive arrangement with the program that preempt our participation; (2) our organization has never been asked to participate; (3) participation on our part might interfere with our efforts to provide objective coverage of police and crime news; (4) Crime Stoppers is beyond the scope of what a news organization should be doing; (5) we have a basic disagreement with the philosophy that underlies Crime Stoppers; (6) there are administrative problems in coordinating our participation; and (7) we do not believe it would be an effective anti-crime program in our community.

Perceptions of Crime Stoppers' Success. All executives with a Crime Stoppers program in their community were asked to rate the success of the local program and to rate their perception of local public opinion towards the program. Overall, the average rating given to the local program was that it was "quite successful" (2.92 on a four-point scale ranging from 1, "not at all successful," to 4, "very successful"). The average rating by executives of local public opinion towards the program was "positive" (6.04 on a seven-point scale ranging from 1, "very negative," to 7, "very positive"). Newspaper executives, on the average, rated the success of their local program as significantly lower ($p < .05$) than did executives from radio and television stations.

Furthermore, executives whose organizations did not participate in the existing local Crime Stoppers program were significantly less positive in their assessment of the program ($p < .05$). For example, executives from media that participated with Crime Stoppers rated their local program as "quite successful" (mean of 2.96), whereas the non-participating media rated their local program as "somewhat successful" (mean of 2.36). In addition, compared to the participating media's rating of local public opinion towards Crime Stoppers as "positive" (mean of 6.09), the non-participants rated public opinion as only "somewhat positive" (mean of 5.22).

A final issue regarding the media's overall assessment of the Crime Stoppers concept concerns the question of whether, in the long run, anti-crime programs such as Crime Stoppers might cause an erosion of citizen initiative to participate in the criminal justice process without special inducements. A majority of executives from both the Crime Stoppers sample (77%) and the random sample (62%) believed that Crime Stoppers would not, in the long run, undermine the public's intrinsic motivation to come forth voluntarily with information useful to law enforcement agencies. However, executives reached via the random sample were significantly less likely to feel this way ($p < .05$). Furthermore, Table 3 shows that regardless of how they were sampled, three-fourths of the executives at participating media organizations saw no potential for undermining citizen initiative. On the other hand, those at non-participating organizations were significantly more concerned ($p < .05$) about this potential problem.

Table 3

Media Executive's Perceived Effect of Crime Stoppers on Citizen Initiative by Type of Relationship to Crime Stoppers

	Percentage by Sample Type		
Perceived Effect	No Local Crime Stoppers Program	Local Crime Stoppers, but Don't Participate	Participate in Local Crime Stoppers
Think It Will Undermine	9	21	5
Don't Think It Will Undermine	60	58	77
Uncertain	31	21	19

Validation of Ratings of Success

Fifty-seven (57) of the executives responding to the media surveys were located in cities for which independent data were also available from police coordinators and archival sources, thereby providing a validity check on each groups' perceptions about the success of these Crime Stoppers projects. As shown in Table 4, two ratings of local program success made by media executives correlated significantly ($p < .05$) with coordinators' ratings of local program success.

Furthermore, the executives' ratings of public opinion towards the local Crime Stoppers programs was significantly related to four of the five measures of program success. These included higher crime reporting by the local citizenry, higher clearance rates and arrest rates by the local police department, and higher sustained motivation on the part of the local coordinator. While none of the media's own ratings of program success correlated significantly with these statistical measures, all but one were in the direction (i.e., a positive correlation) that would be expected for validation.

In sum, the opportunity to compare independent ratings of program success indicated a fair degree of validation of the various measures. This, of course, does not demonstrate conclusively that these independent measures are accurate, but it does strengthen our confidence in them.

Discussion

The research reported in this chapter showed that, overall, there is a very high level of media awareness of Crime Stoppers. Media participation is especially high in those communities where a Crime Stoppers program exists. In fact, one-fourth of the program coordinators reported that local media played a direct role in *starting* their program.

Our research also found that there is a fair amount of variation across different types of media in the media's reactions to Crime Stoppers. In general, the print media (daily and weekly newspapers) were not as positive towards Crime Stoppers as the broadcast media (radio and television). In particular, daily newspapers were (1) the least likely type of media to participate in a local Crime Stoppers program, (2) were perceived as being the least cooperative when they did decide to participate, and (3) were least favorable in their assessment of local Crime Stoppers

Table 4
Correlation of Media Executives' Ratings of Crime Stopper Success
and Independent Measures of Success

Independent Measure	*Media Rating of Program Success*	*Rating of Public Opinion Toward Crime Stoppers*
Coordinators's Success Ratings	.243**	.196*
Calls Received Per 1,000 Reported Crimes	.149	.202*
Calls Received Per 100,000 Population	.090	.052
Crimes Cleared Per 1,000 Crimes Reported	.158	.251**
Suspects Arrested Per 1,000 Crimes Reported	.118	.255**
Rewards Paid Per 100,000 Population	.019	.136
Rewards Unspent Per 100,000 Population	-.108	-.044
Avoiding Burnout	-.025	.173*

* $p < .10$
** $p < .05$

programs and the overall Crime Stoppers concept.

These observed differences among media types could be due to many factors. First, it is reasonable to assume that the "Crime of the Week" feature has greater audience appeal when it is presented via live reenactment, especially in both the audio and visual form that is available via television. In contrast, a factual written description of the crime is likely to be less "grabbing" when presented in a newspaper. Therefore, participation with Crime Stoppers seems to offer the broadcast media, particularly television, greater payoffs in terms of generating greater audience interest and satisfactions. In addition, to the extent that participating in Crime Stoppers increases viewership for those television stations that have negotiated an exclusivity agreement, participating in Crime Stoppers may become a profitable business decision.

Second, the print media might not be as positively disposed toward cooperating with a police-based program such as Crime Stoppers because of the long-standing "watchdog" role that daily newspapers have embraced.

On the surface, it may appear inherently contradictory to many newspaper editors and reporters to get involved with an anti-crime program run by the police, when these same editors and reporters often have been the ones that relish the ferreting-out of police inadequacies and wrongdoings. In contrast, local broadcast news departments traditionally have not had the reputation of hard-hitting investigative reporting. As such, broadcast journalists may perceive themselves in less adversarial roles with the police than do some print journalists.

Conclusion. The purpose of this research was not to determine whether media cooperation with Crime Stoppers is good or bad. Rather, we have tried to document the extent and nature of this cooperation. It awaits future research to assess whether such ventures ultimately benefit the media, the police, or society as a whole. We find it interesting to note, though, that this changing relationship between the media and the police has occurred within the changing social and political environment of the past decade. In contrast to the extreme antagonism that was prevalent in the late 1960s between many journalists and their local law enforcement agencies, Crime Stoppers is an example of the public/private sector cooperation that was touted by the Reagan administration.

Ultimately, it remains the responsibility of the media to decide whether they can serve the public interest in aiding the fight against crime via cooperation in anti-crime efforts such as Crime Stoppers *and* simultaneously serve the public interest in their capacity as government "watchdog." If the two goals are judged to be incompatible, we believe our society has more to lose from the media relaxing the standards of accountability to which they hold our public institutions, than from the media declining to cooperate with programs such as Crime Stoppers, even though non-cooperation may result in some crimes going unsolved.

REFERENCES

Bickman, Leonard B. and Lavrakas, Paul J. (1977). *Citizen crime reporting projects: national evaluation summary report.* Washington, DC: US GPO.

Lavrakas, Paul J. and Jason, Gary. (1979). "Methodological study II: Evanston recall survey." Evanston, IL: Center for Urban Affairs and Policy Research. (working Paper CP-4F).

Lavrakas, Paul J., Rosenbaum, Dennis, P., and Kaminski, Frank. (1983). "Transmitting information about crime and crime prevention to citizens." *Journal of Police Science and Administration*, 13(5), 392–405.

MacAleese, Greg and Tilly, H. Coleman. (1983). *Crime Stoppers Manual: How to Start and Operate a Program.* Albuquerque, NM: Crime Stoppers USA.

Rosenbaum, Dennis P. (1982). "Police responses: Conventional and new approaches to local crime problems." Symposium: crime's impact, more than a mere tally of reported crimes. *American Psychological Association,* Washington, DC.

Rosenbaum, Dennis P. and Lurigio, Arthur J. (1985). "Crime Stoppers: Paying the Price." *Psychology Today,* June, 56–61.

Skogan, Wesley G. and Antunes, George. (1979). "Information, apprehension, and deterrence: exploring the limits of police productivity." *Journal of Criminal Justice,* Fall, 217–242.

Chapter 17

MEDIA TECHNOLOGY AND THE COURTS: THE CASE OF CLOSED CIRCUIT VIDEO ARRAIGNMENTS IN MIAMI, FLORIDA

RAY SURETTE AND W. CLINTON TERRY

Abstract. *The normative and policy implications of introducing video technologies into the courtroom are analyzed in this work. Examining video misdemeanor arraignments conducted in Miami's Eleventh Judicial Circuit, reveals a disruption of normative expectations within the courtroom, especially on the part of public defenders. Such latent consequences suggest that some defendants may not be getting the full benefit of constitutionally guaranteed due process protections. They also suggest an increased depersonalization of court-room interactions and the possibility of negatively altered perceptions upon the part of courtroom actors and public onlookers. Because these perceptions affect the legitimacy with which courtroom procedures are held, the policy implications of introducing video technologies, along the lines of this study's findings, require careful consideration.*

Introduction. With the rapid development of telecommunications, especially within the areas of television and videotape, it was inevitable that video technology would find its way into courtroom use. Trials and other court proceedings may be videotaped as a means of creating a visual and audio record of the trial proceedings, thus replacing the stenographic notes of the court reporter. Videotapes may also be used during many facets of pretrial preparation. Of particular importance is its use as a substitute for the "live" testimony of witnesses. Similarly, videotape may be used to record physical evidence prior to its presentation in the courtroom. It may be used in lineups, confessions (particularly where the voluntary nature of the confession is questioned [cf. Benowitz, 1974, p. 86]), drunken-driving tests, (Greenwood, Skupsky, Tollar, Jeske, & Veremko, 1978, p. 27), Miranda warnings, shoplifting cases, police

---

Portions of this chapter were originally published in *Criminal Justice Review*, Vol 11, No. 2, (1986).

surveillance of narcotics transactions (Salvan, 1975, p. 226), and the booking of suspects.

Videotape may also be used to produce Prerecorded Videotaped Trials (PRVTTs). Unlike the in-court use of video equipment for purposes of creating a taped transcript of trial proceedings, PRVTTs prepare an entire videotaped trial prior to being shown to the jury.[1]

It is evident from these uses of media technology in preparing and presenting case materials that the general policy of incorporating the media and its equipment into the courtroom has great promise and has in fact, already experienced considerable experimental use. The controversies surrounding this policy initiative suggest that deep changes in the normative structure of the courtroom itself are a concern. This is perhaps nowhere more clearly the case than in the area of media-conducted misdemeanor arraignments.

Court Changes and the Use of Video. The critics of courtroom videotaping, in observing that its use, especially the use of prerecorded trials, disrupts and even dislocates the normative expectations and social relationships among court personnel, make a point worthy of reflection. As Brakel (1975) notes:

> The trial process itself will be altered as will the relationships between and among lawyers, parties, witnesses, and judges. From a drama directed and to various extents controlled by a professional and "impartial" judge, the trial will be transformed to a far more "partisan" event, directed and controlled by a larger variety of participants— lawyers in all their variety of competence, personality, and partisanship: cameramen of varying degrees of neutrality and proficiency: and witnesses who will be less readily surprised or otherwise made to lose their poise (p. 957)

Applied to the use of videotaped first appearances, these observations raise a number of questions. What effect does the introduction of video

---

1. According to proponents, prerecorded video trials have been very successful in reducing crowded court dockets and have cut the amount of time needed to complete the hearing of a case (see McCrystal, 1976; McCrystal, 1978; Miller & Fontes, 1979; Murray, 1978).

Critics of PRVTTs (Benowitz, 1974; Brakel, 1975; Burt, 1978; Hartman, 1978; Kosky, 1975), many of whom are also critical of the creation of trial records through the use of videotape (Benowitz, 1974; Burt, 1978; Kosky, 1975) frequently mention the effect of videotape upon juries and jury deliberations (Boster, Miller, & Fontes, 1978; Hocking, Miller, & Fontes, 1978; Juhne et al., 1978; Kaminsky, Fontes & Miller, 1978; Miller & Fontes, 1979), as well as the resultant changed social relationships between courtroom actors (Brakel, 1975). As Kosky (1975) notes in citing Doret (1974), "Many authors embraced videotape as a panacea for all the infirmities of the judicial process. The literature of enthusiasm, however, has been excessively concerned with the advantages of the technique, but not concerned enough with its practical and normative difficulties (p, 321)."

equipment into the arraignment process have upon the relationships between judges, attorneys, and other court personnel? What effect does it have upon the ability of defendants to interact with their attorneys, judges, members of their family, and friends who have come to court to offer them support or to take them into custody? How do defendants feel about the use of videotaped arraignments? Are they indifferent to their use? Do they favor it? Or, do they resent it? Do these sentiments result from the use of television within the courtroom or are they affected by past experiences with the court, the number of prior arraignments experienced? Or, are they affected by the outcome of present arraignment, by whether they are released from jail and the type of sentence they receive?

In order to better understand the manifest and latent effects of video systems upon the perceptions and normative expectations of participants during misdemeanor arraignments, and thus to better understand the effects of this policy implementation upon the sentiments of courtroom personnel, over 350 Miami defendants as well as all available judges, prosecutors, and public defenders were questioned concerning the Eleventh Circuit Court's use of closed circuit television. Manifest effects include the accomplishment of such goals as increasing the efficiency and lowering the cost of processed cases, which are traditional organizational goals that are attuned to the desires and interests of court administrators. Ideal like manifest goals, which are consciously sought, latent effects or goals involve unanticipated changes, which are always unwanted, but which nevertheless accompany the pursuance of the manifest objectives. Such latent effects often appear as changed attitudes. In this case it is felt that a possible critical latent effect would involve changes in perception of fair play or "justice" within the courtroom.

User Reactions: The Miami Case

As with efforts to employ video technology during the arraignment of misdemeanor defendants, Miami's manifest goals included reducing the number of court and correctional personnel involved in first appearances, thus reducing the cost of processing individuals through the court system, increasing levels of courtroom security by eliminating the need to transport individuals from jail to court, alleviating courtroom crowding that occurred when prisoners were brought over from the jail, and speeding up the process of handling cases.

Defendants are brought to the country jail from any of the 27 munici-
palities within Dade County served by the Eleventh Judicial Court,
where they are booked. The paperwork generated, including a criminal
background and outstanding warrants investigation, is sent to the court
clerk's office. Copies of these files are made available to the presiding
judge, the state's attorney, the public defender, all of whom have offices
in the courthouse adjacent to the jail. Generally speaking, counsel sees
these files for the first time the day of the arraignment in court, or at the
jail in the case of the public defender.

Utilizing video equipment, prisoners no longer have to be brought to
court from the jail. They are now brought as a group to the chapel of the
jail, which contains the closed circuit television equipment on the jail's
side of the system, thus relieving the crowding that has frequently
occurred in the court's holding cells. Several correctional officers guard
the prisoners and operate the jail's video equipment. Assistant public
defenders are present at the jail. The judge, court clerk, prosecuting
attorney, onlookers, and friends and family of the accused, if present, are
situated in the courtroom. There is no longer a court reporter because
the videotape of these proceedings serves as the sole court record.

When arraigned, defendants are called to a podium in the chapel,
where they are informed by the judge via closed circuit television of the
charges against them and in most cases asked how they would like to
plead. If they plead guilty, which is frequent, they are often sentenced,
usually to credit time served. If they plead not guilty, bail is set or the
person is released on their own recognizance and the time of another
court appearance is set. Persons who are denied or who are unable to
post bail, or persons who are given additional time to serve, are returned
to their cells. By 1985, some 38,000 defendants had been arraigned by
video.

Judges. Eleventh Circuit Court judges clearly favor the system. The
four judges using the video agreed that it is an improvement over
previous means of conducting arraignments and that there is less general disruption during video arraignments. They also reported that the
use of video either increases or has little effect upon their ability to
maintain control, to evaluate a defendant's demeanor, or to communicate
with defendants. They all felt the video either increases or has little
effect upon the speed of the arraignments, the effectiveness of the
defendant's legal representation, or the humanization of the arraignment

process. Finally, they felt that the use of video did not increase the likelihood of defendants pleading guilty.

Judges' complaints focused upon the technical quality of the video picture and sound system, especially feedback and echo problems. They also expressed a desire to be able to see all of the defendants waiting to be arraigned, which would entail the addition of more cameras and monitors. In other words, all of the judges felt that the system should be expanded. None felt that it should be restricted.

Prosecuting Attorneys. The four state prosecutors questioned viewed the video arraignment of defendants favorable but to a lesser degree than did the judges. Two felt that the video was an improvement over prior arraignment methods. Two did not. One state's attorney was uncertain whether the video arraignment of defendants was more or less disruptive than previous methods used. Nevertheless, they all felt that the use of video detracted nothing from the overall quality of legal representation received.

In criticism of the system, several prosecutors felt that the video system made it difficult for defendants to communicate with the judge, their counsel, the prosecutor, and their family. Nevertheless, all four prosecutors concluded that video arraignment is a good idea. In fact, several of them thought that more cameras should be added to the system and that it should be expanded to include DUI cases. None felt that the system should be restricted.

Public Defenders. All seven public defenders felt that the video arraignment of misdemeanor defendants decreased the judge's ability to control the courtroom. Six felt that there was more general disruption during video arraignment than during traditional arraignment hearings. They felt that judges were less able to evaluate a defendant's demeanor and that it was more difficult for the judge, prosecutor, public defender, defendant, and defendant's family to communicate with one another. Six out of seven public defenders felt that the quality and effectiveness of legal representation were negatively affected. They felt that video arraignments were more impersonal (i.e., bureaucratic) and less humane than more traditional arraignment proceedings. They believed that their defendants were nervous, intimidated, more likely to plead guilty, and generally disliked the video arraignment. In sum, none of the public defenders felt that video arraignment was a good idea, nor that it represented an improvement over previous arraignment methods.

Public defenders frequently criticized video arraignments for ruining the aura of judicial hearings and for destroying the adversarial character of these judicial proceedings, as the following comments indicate:

> "The video system presents only an image of the accused. The personal confrontation which is essential is effectively removed." "No Courtroom atmosphere—the prison chapel with a TV screen on the altar beneath the crucifix—totally lacks any courtroom atmosphere." "By having the arraignment in the chapel, judges can "turn us off. The state attorney, however, is five feet from the judge. It makes our positions very unequal." It puts the judge and prosecutor on the same side and the public defender and the defendants on the other—the goods guys versus the bad guys."

Other comments focus upon not knowing who the state prosecutor is, coercion of defendants and processing paperwork. The thrust of the comments, as above citations indicate, focused upon the normative environment of the courtroom. Public defenders now have to carry on their duties within the confines of the jail's chapel, They are thus located in a nonjudicial location; whereas their counterparts, the judge and prosecutor, remain in the more familiar surroundings of the courthouse. Consequently, they felt that the traditional courtroom atmosphere had been lost and their ability to act as an effective advocate for the defendant had been diminished.

Defendants. Contrary to what public defenders think, defendants are largely supportive of their video arraignments. Based upon a survey of 352 video-arraigned defendants, the majority felt that their ability to argue their case remained unhindered (64.3%), as was their ability to ask questions (78.4%). More than three-quarters of these defendants (79.1%) felt they acted and spoke as they would have, had they been in a "regular" courtroom. They did not feel unduly nervous (70.2%), nor was there any feeling that their rights had been violated (79.5%). Eighty-five-point-five (85.5) percent felt that their plea was the same as it would have been had they pled in "regular" court. In short, 72.1% felt that using video for misdemeanor appearances was a good idea; 78.5% were happy with their court appearances; and, 84.4% thought that the video made their case go faster. Table 1 summarizes these findings.

To state these findings differently, some 22 to 28% of the defendants interviewed were dissatisfied with their video arraignments. Further analysis of these findings reveals that these negative perceptions are related to the arraignment outcomes. In other words, whether defendants are released or returned to jail shapes their attitude towards video

Defendant's Attitudes Toward the Use of Video in Court

Survey Item	(N)	Percent		
		Yes	No	Unsure
I think that using video limited my ability to argue my case.	345	31.6	64.3	4.1
There were questions I wanted to ask but didn't because I was on T.V.	338	20.1	78.4	1.5
I acted or spoke differently because I was on T.V.	339	18.9	79.1	2.1
The use of T.V. made me nervous	342	29.2	70.2	.6
I feel that the use of T.V. violated my legal rights.	342	15.2	79.5	5.3
If I wasn't on T.V. I would have pled differently	338	10.7	85.5	3.8
I think that using T.V. for court appearances is a good idea.	348	72.1	20.4	7.5
I was happy with my televised court appearance.	344	78.5	19.5	2.0
I feel that the use of video made my case go faster.	340	84.4	12.1	3.5

arraignment. When compared to non-video group of defendants, these findings remain the same, thus indicating that such sentiments are basically unrelated to the use of these video technologies.

Discussion and Policy Implications

From the comments of judges and prosecuting attorneys, as well as the more critical comments of public defenders, it is apparent that the installation and operation of a closed video system between the courthouse and jail for purposes of conducting misdemeanor first appearances has achieved its manifest objectives, namely, easing the mechanics and cost of processing misdemeanor defendants. In the process, however, its operation has lead to the development of at least on latent (i.e., unintended) consequence; to wit, a disruption of the "traditional" courthouse culture. Such disturbance raises several questions that have both policy and research implications regarding due process, increased courtroom depersonalization, and the public image of the judicial system. The public image of the courts is particularly significant as it has much to do with how people view the legitimacy of the entire criminal justice system.

Due Process. Public defender comments indicate that the normative system of courtroom expectations has been upset, not so much by the introduction of video equipment into the process of misdemeanor first appearance, but by the removal of public defenders from the courtroom. Aside from interpreting these comments as reflecting their ire at being removed from the courtroom, the concerns of public defenders focuses attention upon the due process implications of the use of video within the courtroom. Despite its cost effectiveness, does such use of video technologies abridge a person's constitutional rights to due process and fair trial? Even if this is not unconstitutional, do attorneys deliver equivalent representation if they feel legally and organizationally disadvantaged in video-conducted hearings? Does their morale and subsequent effort suffer? An examination of case outcomes in Miami reveals no significant differences between video and non-video cases. The possibility remains, however, that such an effect develops only after a large number of cases have had a chance to impact upon the slower development of attitudinal and behavioral responses.

Nevertheless, critics have argued that rights of public trial, confrontation, and basic procedural fairness are compromised by the interjection of video equipment between the defendant and other participants, particularly between the defendant and the judge (Brakel, 1975; Doret, 1974; Shutkin, 1973). Video images are not felt to be adequate substitutes for live interactions. However, appeals based upon the loss of due process protections, and the inherent inability of a video proceeding to be fair, have been unsuccessful (see Rypinski, 1982). An important feature of this approval is that defendants have the option to have a traditional courtroom appearance if they desire. As stated earlier, defendants have been largely supportive of the new procedure and have not expressed feelings that they had been denied their rights or treated unfairly.

Increased Depersonalization. Although the current use of video technologies in the Eleventh Judicial Circuit of Miami aids the processing and management of cases and is thus cost effective, expansions of the current system, which are now being planned, will perhaps lead to the increased depersonalization of criminal justice processes.[2] Adjudication within the criminal justice system, for example, is based upon the principle of face-to-face interaction. The accused are entitled to face their accusers. With the extended use of video technologies, however, there would be a decline in face-to-face encounters, thereby seriously altering the current normative and communicative structure of the courtroom. This process will most likely be hastened by equipment advances that make it more economic and less obtrusive.

---

2. The future of video usage in Miami is for its expansion to include other facets of processing individuals through the court system, such as bond hearings and proceedings where motions are heard, and for the upgrading and expansion of the current system to include other jail locations. In particular, current plans include adding six other correctional facilities, including the City of Miami jail, the jail at the women's detention center, and the youth hall, thus eliminating the need to transport defendants to the county jail. There are also desires to expand the use of the system to include the hearing of motions.

Here again, the overall effects of these changes may become apparent only after such practices have been in place for a longer period of time. The realignment of communication channels and changes in behavior and attitudes seldom occur simultaneously (Lipetz, 1980). Possible changes in the socialization process and the relative status and perception of work group roles are crucial (see Sudnow, 1965). For example, if these systems ultimately result in the significant loss of prestige or credibility of public defenders within the courtroom, either in the eyes of any of the several judicial work groups' participants found within the court or in the eyes of defendants, the social costs of such losses would probably outweigh any organizational benefits that might have accrued from them. Long-term studies are needed to address whether such policy-relevant effects are in fact developing.

Public Image. The justice system is a mechanism of adjudicating guilt and administering punishment. It is also a means of legitimating the overall social system it serves. As such, the courtroom and its players take on a symbolic value; their actions and courtroom decorum contain a "majesty" and "mysteriousness" pointing to the sanctity and well-being of the larger society. Loss of these qualities may diminish the aura of authority and legitimacy surrounding the judicial system, the laws of the land, and the social order which they represent. From this systematic perspective, how the system treats individuals is crucial (Casper, 1978). If people become alienated from the system or if they feel intimidated or dehumanized by it, all the monetary or efficiency gains made by the employment of video technologies within the courtroom may be worthless.

One possible unexamined consequence of video systems is their effect on courtroom visitors and the friends and family of defendants. These external observers also gather impressions of the criminal justice system— impressions which will affect how they view the legitimization of the entire system. It is reasonable to expect that defendants, who are immediately threatened by punitive sanctions, would be more concerned with "processing outcomes" than "processing mechanics." However, unthreatened observers may gain an image of the system that is unacceptable if they see the video as a degrading process in which the judge will not even allow the defendant into the courtroom. Inasmuch as these observers represent a larger body of individuals than the actual defendants, effects upon them cannot be ignored. There is considerable desire, especially upon the part of administrators, to make the court system more effective and efficient. Nevertheless, the system must remain a moral system in the eyes of its beholders if indeed it is to remain a legitimate and viable system of justice.

From the data gathered in the present study, there is little indication, apart from the concerns of public defenders, that courtroom personnel are dissatisfied with the current usage of video in the courtroom; nor does it appear that defendants are dissatisfied. In fact, defendant dissatisfaction with the court system is more likely wedded to the outcome of cases rather than to particular mechanisms whereby cases are processed (Surette & Terry, 1984). Nevertheless, note should be taken of the effects that a changed normative climate, an increased sense of depersonalization, and a possible loss of due process protections might have upon people's sentiment towards the criminal justice system. At this time current findings indicate that the use of video in the courtroom can be summarized as manifestly successful; albeit containing potentially latent problems.

REFERENCES

Benowitz, H. A. (1974). Legal applications of videotape. *Florida Bar Journal, 48*(2), 86–91.

Boster, F. J., Miller, G. R., & Fontes, N. E. (1978). Videotape in the courtroom. Effects in live trials. *Trial, 14*(6). 49–51, 59.

Brakel, S. J. (1975). Videotape in trial proceedings: A technological obsession? *American Bar Association Journal, 61,* 956–959.

Burt, L. W. (1978). The case against courtroom TV. *Trial, 12*(7), 62–63, 66.

Casper, J. (1978). *Criminal courts: The defendant's perspective.* Washington, DC: National Institute of Law Enforcement and Criminal Justice. Department of Justice.

Doret, D. M. (1974). Trial by videotape—can justice be seen to be done?" *Temple Law Quarterly, 47,* 228–268.

Greenwood, M. J., Skupsky, D., Tollar, J. R., Jeske, V. H., & Veremko, P. (1978), Audio/video: Technology and the courts. *State Court Journal, 2*(1), 26–28.

Hartman, M. J. (1978). Second thoughts on videotaped trials. *Judicature, 61*(6), 256–257.

Hocking, J. E., Miller, G. R., & Fontes, N. E. (1978). Videotape in the courtroom: Witness deception. *Trial, 14*(4), 52–53.

Juhnke, R., Vought, C., Pyszcynski, T. A., Dane, F. C., Kaminski, B. D., Edmund, P., Fontes, N. E., & Miller, G. R. (1978). Videotape in the courtroom: Responses in editing techniques. *Trial, 14*(5), 38–42, 64.

Kaminsky, E., Fontes, N., & Miller, G. (1978). Videotape in the courtroom. *Trial, 14*(4), 38–42, 64.

Kosky, I. (1975). Videotape in Ohio: Take 2. *Judicature, 59*(5), 229–238.

Lipez, M. (1980). Routine and deviations: The strength of the courtroom work group in the misdemeanor court. *International Journal of Sociology of the Law, 8,* 47–60.

McCrystal, J. L. (1976). The case for PRVTTs. *Trial 12*(7), 56–57.

McCrystal, J. L. (1978). Videotaped trials: A primer. *Judicature, 61*(6), 250–256.

Miller, G. R. & Fontes, N. E. (May, 1979). Trial by videotape. *Psychology Today,* 92, 95–96, 99–100, 112.

Murray, T. J. (1978). Videotaped depositions: The Ohio experience. *Judicature, 61*(6), 258–261.

Rypinski, I. (Winter, 1982). Videotaping depositions. *Hawaii Bar Journal,* 67–76.

Salvan, S. A. (1975). Videotape for the legal community. *Judicature, 59*(5), 222–229.

Shutkin, J. (1973). Videotaped trials: Legal and practical implications. *Columbia Journal of Law and Social Problems, 9,* 363–393.

Sudnow, D. (1965). Normal crimes. *Social Problems, 12,* 255–276.

Surette, R., & Terry W. C. III. (1984). Videotaped misdemeanor first appearances: Fairness from the defendant's perspective. In R. Surette (Ed.) *Justice and the media: Issues and research* (pp. 305–320). Springfield, IL, Charles C Thomas.

Chapter 18

USING VIDEO TECHNOLOGY IN POLICE PATROL

DALE K. SECHREST
WILLIAM LIQUORI
JIM PERRY

The development of technologies in support of law enforcement is very much entwined with its history and has in many instances pointed law enforcement in new directions. No clearer example of this is the coupling of police radios with patrol cars in 1929. As Rubenstein (1973: 20) points out, "The radio combined with the patrol car... transformed the relationships between the police and the public, and among policemen...."

New technologies are at work today that will continue to change the nature and scope of police work. One of these innovations is the use of video technology to film police contacts. Video technology presents both advantages and disadvantages. Any type of photograph or film may be incriminating evidence, but it may also misrepresent a situation. It can show that a police officer has made an improper infringement on individual rights or conversely, and hopefully, it can show that the officer is operating within constitutional guidelines in the performance of his or her duties.

There are two basic applications of new technologies in law enforcement. One involves the better management of internal police operations. Except in the sense that they may be inaccurate or untrustworthy, there are few arguments with devices that speed police response or assist them in analyzing evidence. It is in the area of public freedom or civil rights that these technologies will be most questioned in the future. For this reason, among others, they require careful study and evaluation.

Police Use of Video Equipment

Video equipment has a wide range of uses in law enforcement. Initially, video equipment was used primarily for education, training, and sur-

255

veillance. In patrol car use, it has recently found wide use for recording drunk-driver arrests and drug buys. These situations appear to have been comfortably embraced by law enforcement personnel, perhaps because they take place in more controlled settings. Also, filmed drug busts have become almost routine television fare in the war on drugs and, as such, have been good advertising as to the seriousness of that effort. The use of video technology in patrol cars is a more recent development. It appears to be viewed less enthusiastically by police, and its use is in the experimental stage in only a few jurisdictions. The purpose of this paper is to document progress in the general use of video equipment in patrol cars, focusing on exemplary efforts in Florida and Georgia, while presenting some problems and prospects for its future use.

The concept of using video cameras in patrol cars has proven itself through extensive testing in the Altamonte Springs, Florida, Police Department beginning in 1986 (Liquori & Perry, 1988). Research began as early as 1984 on the idea of a patrol car video system. In reviewing the Uniform Crime Reports data on assaults and fatal attacks, it appeared that four out of every five officers assaulted were on uniform vehicle patrol. There appeared to be a need for a video system to record assaults that could provide a record of the assailant and the vehicle description and could be utilized in court (Liquori and Perry, 1988: 35). By 1984, however, the technology had not advanced enough to make it affordable for law enforcement agencies due to a number of drawbacks, including the camera size, the availability and the quality of video recorders capable of 12-volt operation. Tube-type cameras were still the industry standard. For these reasons, the development of the concept was delayed until better equipment could be acquired and improved for rigorous mobile use.

By June 1986, technology had progressed to allow a prototype of the "video observer" to be developed. Unlike the tube-type cameras, this system uses a microchip low-light camera outfitted with a 16mm wide-angle lens, complete with filtration. The half-inch VHS format recorder, with time and date features, can record up to two hours. The recorder is designed to be securely encased and mounted in a vehicle trunk. A firm called 1070 Inc. solicited the Altamonte Springs Police Department to be the law enforcement test site for vehicle-mounted video equipment. This relationship led to the development of an operational vehicle-mounted video-camera system.

The use of the video camera in police patrol has several advantages.

Police administrators are often called upon to determine what really happened during a police encounter. The courts are equally interested in what happened, due to their need to decide any resulting litigation fairly and to determine any related liability claims. Testimony, written reports and other information must be relied upon to determine what actually occurred in a given situation. Video technology installed as permanent equipment now provides an alternate way of reporting what happened and, in doing so, has the potential for improving conviction rates. The use of the video camera can also help identify suspects and may both provide additional protection for the officer and serve as a deterrent to resisting arrest. At the flip of a switch an officer can activate both a video and audio recording system, using a microchip camera and a wireless microphone, to record what is occurring during a stop and during all subsequent activities. (Activation can be automatically tied to the blue lights, ignition, either, or done manually.)

Applications in Georgia and Florida

The Georgia State Patrol began to use "on-board video systems" in 1986 as part of the Drug Enforcement Administration "Operation Pipeline" effort to control drug trafficking along Federal Highways 75 and 95, which pass North to South through Georgia. Since the Georgia Department of Public Safety began to receive a share of seized assets and this money could only be used for improvements, such as video equipment and/or enforcement-related technology, the development of the video observer was expanded (Wilson, 1988: 1). This expansion was consistent with other anticipated needs such as recording accident scenes, high-speed pursuits, felony arrests, and contraband seizures. Benefits included a possible increased conviction rate, a record of events for "investigative purposes," training opportunities provided by the tapes, better performance evaluation and determination of related additional training needs, a record of seized contraband, and a record of accident scenes (Wilson, 1988: 2).

The most striking instance to date of the use of such equipment is provided by the Georgia State Patrol. Officer Benji Hodges had a video camera on when he shot a suspect who was reaching for a gun in the presence of another suspect. Officer Hodges made a daytime traffic stop of two individuals in a large rental car from Florida who later were found to be transporting illegal drugs. He turned on the video camera in his patrol car, which he was using for the first time. Hodges was alone, and after going over the car rental papers with the driver in the (videotaped) area between the cars he wrote a traffic warning. The passenger remained in his seat, and neither suspect knew they were on camera. During this period Hodges had made the decision to search and radioed for a backup. The men were told they were free to go, but Officer Hodges then asked to search the vehicle, which the suspects agreed to in writing, probably hoping for a short, cursory, search. They completed a standard consent form allowing permission to search. In the course of asking the passenger to exit the vehicle he produced a gun; Officer Hodges drew his gun and made—at actual (video) count—26 requests for the suspect to place the gun on the dashboard, whereupon he shot the passenger as he reached for the weapon. Minutes later (on tape) Hodges says that he said it 15 times. The suspect survived, and four kilos of cocaine were found in the vehicle. The film is excellent for training because it documents also some of the problems with the performance of the backup officer (Crandlemire, 1989).

Advantages: Anticipated and Realized

Georgia State Patrol videotapes document other successful uses of the video camera in drug interdiction and include a television news account of these efforts. The Patrol now has 54 patrol cars with cameras of a total of 645 vehicles. They are used in each traffic stop made by one of these vehicles. Based on their experience to date the eventual goal is to install "audio/video recording equipment . . . in every patrol vehicle operated by a Georgia State Trooper who is assigned to routine patrol duty, which appears to amount to about 50 percent of all vehicles (Wilson, 1988: 6).[1]

In Altamonte Springs, Florida, it is anticipated that most suppression hearings from DUI cases will be reduced based on the videotape evidence. Trial time could be shortened since the probable cause to stop a vehicle for suspected DUI, and any and all sobriety testing, would be audible as well as videotaped. Officers have used the video equipment in other applications as well. They are doing field interrogations and interviews in front of the patrol vehicle to capture statements and admissions right on the scene, saving time, and thus eliminating station-house interviews.

---

1. They have documented 24 requirements for the purchase and use of audio/video equipment for patrol use. These include solid-state electronics, VHS format for compatibility, automatic focus and light compensation features, no automatic rewind, a compact, shielded microphone with a built-in antennae capable of transmitting up to 300 yards, a good mounting, sufficient power from the 12-volt battery, and a "date/time" generator (Wilson, 1988: 2–5).

Figure 1. Patrol Car Video Camera Controls

The key to the system is the camera's ability to capture details of a given incident. The system is felt to add to the capabilities of law enforcement personnel and to support increased professionalism.

Video cameras mounted inside police vehicles may in some instances act as a deterrent to resisting arrest or acts of violence against police officers. For example, Altamonte Springs police officers pointed out to a potentially violent person that he was being videotaped and he quickly calmed down, perhaps because his behavior was being recorded. During many lawsuits much depends on the officer's word against the defendant's word. The camera is impartial and unbiased. It presents to the jury what happened, rather than what was perceived to have happened by either party.

Figure 2. Rear view of windshield mounted Patrol Car Video Camera

Legal Issues and Other Problems

When video equipment was first introduced in booking rooms of police agencies nationwide, many police officers were camera-shy and there was a reluctance to get in front of the camera. Many officers feel the same way about vehicle-mounted video equipment. When video cameras were used in one large Florida Sheriffs' Department five years ago they were discontinued for regular patrols, largely because officers were uncomfortable with having *their* actions recorded also (Freeman, 1989). There may be times when officers must take precautions in the interests of protecting themselves that might raise legal issues under closer scrutiny. On the other hand, there appear to be more instances when the reverse is true—where correct behavior protects the officer in court. Some observers feel that the officer almost always benefits from use of the videotape (McEver, 1989).

In addition to video systems appearing to be valuable in a wide range of field situations, they can solve a difficult problem for the courts. Video is useful in verifying the methods used to obtain permision to search. Judges, with some justification, sometimes have a difficult time believing that a suspect actually gave permission for a vehicle search, especially where illegal drugs or other fruits of a crime are found. Video documentation can provide an accurate record of voluntary consent to search absent any coercion (cf. Whitebread and Slobogin, 1986: 238–239; see especially *Lightford v. State*, 90 Nev. 136 520 P2d 955, 1974). In Altamonte Springs, the system consistently provides a very accurate record that has assisted officers in completing their assignments and gaining convictions (Liquori and Perry, 1988: 39).

Judge H. Greg Adams of the Walton County, Georgia, Probate Court, has indicated that the video of a DUI defendant presented to him by Georgia State Troopers not only made the defendant's guilt clear, it shortened and simplified what could have been a lengthy trial (Adams, 1987). A training memorandum by the Georgia Department of Public Safety acknowledges the acceptance of videotapes by the courts, and advises that the use of video cameras is a "relatively new concept" that requires good judgment in order to avoid abuse of individual rights (Pinyan, 1989). No opposition to the use of this equipment could be cited.

To date there appear to be no legal challenges to the use of the video camera in patrol stops. Related cases concern the practice of photographing field detainees without arrest. These situations generally involve some level of "reasonable belief" that a crime has been committed. The vehicle-mounted video camera is used prior to any level of suspicion arising. Is this legally permissible? The taking of photos is seen as an invasion of individual privacy by civil rights groups. The Supreme Court has indicated that "an invasion of privacy cannot result unless the area is one in which there is a constitutionally protected reasonable expectation of privacy" (*New York v. Class*, 1986: 960, 965). This appears to allow for the use of the video observer under almost all circumstances because there is no expectation of privacy in a traffic stop. Others argue further that these drug trafficking suspects match a "drug courier profile" that provides the degree of reasonable suspicion necessary to make the stop and, therefore, to use the video camera. As recently as April 1989 the Supreme Court has ruled that government agents may stop and question airline passengers who look and act like drug couriers. That is, several factors, or "articulable facts," taken together—the "totality of circumstances' '—may constitute "reasonable suspicion" that criminal activity may be occurring and allows a stop for investigative purposes (*U.S. v. Sokolow*, 109 S.Ct. 1581, 1989).

Praet (1988: 52) has formulated a model policy for the use of photographs that emphasizes the "totality of circumstances" coincident with their use. Considerations for the officer prior to photographing any field detainee include articulation of a reasonable suspicion of criminal activity, possible voluntary consent, the "legitimate police purpose" of the photo, and its level of intrusiveness with respect to verifying or dispelling the officer's reasonable suspicion of criminal activity (Praet, 1988: 52). Where photos are taken, Praet recommends that such photographs—in this case, videotapes—should be destroyed as soon as possible to avoid "false light defamation," i.e., casting someone in a criminal light when they are not. This caution should be observed when using such videotapes for training purposes.

Future Uses

The use of vehicle-mounted video cameras in drug interdiction is well documented and will continue along the lines of the Georgia experience. Video equipment has proven to be valuable in other areas as well. For example, Altamonte Springs officers have used the observer system when checking buildings by leaving the camera fixed on the back door and then continuing to the front, thus capturing any activity missed while at the other side of the building.

The video equipment is a valuable and stimulating aid in training for law enforcement. Training officials, using actual tapes of officers in action, can analyze methods and pinpoint strong and weak areas for additional training. At the same time, good police work on film can be used in training to highlight for officers the effective use of correct methods.

Future development of the observer system for Altamonte Springs includes the transmission of real-time video from police car to the police station, the use of voice recognition in controlling the operation of the camera, and the use of the observer during undercover operations.

Need for Research

Both technical research and field research should continue. Needs are for smaller cameras with greater image stabilization when used with moving vehicles. Lens control is critical for some situations, and sound equipment appears to require improvements that will reduce extraneous noise to a minimum. Field research is needed to determine when it is most appropriate to use video cameras and when its use might represent problems for the officer or the suspect. Terry and Surette (1986) note some of the manifest and latent consequences of using video cameras in court. Perceptions and normative expectations change when people know they are on camera. In the situation described above only the officer knew about the video camera. What would be the outcome if the suspect was told about the videotaping at the time of the stop? What if the suspect discovered the camera and refused to cooperate until it was turned off? How useful a tool is it in protecting the officer in making a stop? What if the camera inadvertently films individuals who are not suspects—are their rights violated? Research must be done regarding the best ways to present these videotapes. Will they be accepted as evidence in all circumstances (Blakey, 1975, p. 50)? What assurance does the average citizen have that tapes of him or her will be used only for their intended purposes? From a management perspective, in what percentage of cases do the tapes show improper procedure, and what is being done to correct these procedures? To what degree are these real-life videos effective as training tools? In looking at all these areas, a determination must be made as to the costs of this sophisticated equipment in relation to the benefits of its use in patrol cars, i.e., as a whole, are the benefits sufficient to justify the additional expense?

Research and evaluation can help to define the areas in which this promising technology can contribute to the future successes of law enforcement. The use of video cameras may legitimately extend into other areas of police investigation, and this should be explored from both technical and legal perspectives. Failures in the use of new technology do occur, and often they occur because the innovation is not used for its intended purpose, or its use is not well planned, or both. The time to do the research and develop better procedures is as the use of this technology expands. In discussing video telephone technology, Blakey (1975, p. 54) advises that there can be problems in the immediate acceptance of a new technology. He states, however, that the costs, legal issues, and other delays in implementation may be a blessing in disguise. They may allow time for an evaluation of the foreseen and unforeseen consequences of these technologies prior to their wide adoption.

REFERENCES

Adams, H.G. (1987, September). Probate Judge, Walton County, Georgia, letter to Col. Curtis Earp, Jr., Georgia Department of Public Safety.

Blakey, G.R. (1975). Application of the video telephone to the administration of criminal justice: a preliminary assessment. *J. of Police Science and Admin.*, 3(1), 44–54.

Crandlemire, M. (1989, January). Georgia Police Academy, personal communication.

Freeman, R. (1989, January). Division Commander, Telecommunications Division, Department of Organized Crime, Broward Sheriffs' Department, personal communication.

Liquori, W., & Perry, J. (1988, February). The video observer: A friend on the side of law enforcement. *The Florida Police Chief,* 35–41.

McEver, S. (1989, January). Institute of Police Technology and Management (IPTM), personal communication.

New York v. Class ____ U.S. ____, 106 S.Ct., 960, 965 (1986).

Pinyan, C.R. (1989, February). "LTD MEMORANDUM NUMBER 7-89," Department of Public Safety, Atlanta, Georgia.

Praet, B.D. (1988, November). Defending the practice of photographing field detainees, *The Police Chief,* 52–55.

Rubinstein, J. (1973). *City police.* New York: Farrar, Straus and Giroux.

Terry, W.C., & Surette, R. Media technology and the courts: The case of closed circuit video arraignments in Miami, Florida. *Criminal Justice Review,* 11(2), 31–36.

U.S. v. Sokolow, 109 S.Ct. 1581 (1989).

Whitebread, C.H., & Slobogin, C. (1986). *Criminal Procedure,* 2d ed. Mineola, NY: The Foundation Press, 1986.

Wilson, A.M. (1988, June). Limited evaluation of audio/video recording equipment. Georgia Department of Public Safety.

Chapter 19

THE VIDEOTAPING OF POLICE INTERROGATIONS IN CANADA

ALAN GRANT

Introduction

The inherently coercive nature of police interrogation has been long recognized in common law countries,[1] and, as a result, procedures have often been laid down either legislatively[2] or judicially[3] to regulate the circumstances under which the answers suspects and accused persons give to questions posed by police (or other persons in authority) may be admitted into evidence in a criminal trial.

Many of those procedures were drawn up before the widespread availability of technology which permits the inexpensive audiovisual reproduction of such interrogations. Now that such technology is available, it may be time to reconsider some or all of the rules attaching to voluntariness in common law jurisdictions.

The responses to the availability of videotaping might be threefold:

1) In a jurisdiction which would continue to rely on warnings on the privilege of silence and offers of the right to counsel; to record such procedures, where practicable, on videotape as an added safeguard to police and accused persons.

2) In a jurisdiction which may wish to reassess the use of highly formalized warnings; to record such procedures to ensure an adequate record of the whole interview in a manner which may leave the issue of voluntariness to be tested by a more general standard than slavish compliance with carefully worded warning formulae.

3) In a jurisdiction which may be contemplating abandoning the right to silence or other forms of police warnings; to provide an objective record of what transpired during the interview with the accused including how reasonable it was, in the circumstances, for the accused to say nothing.

At the present time it could be argued that Canada would appear to be a jurisdiction in category 1, the U.S.A. in category 2 and England in category 3.

Canada

Between 1985–87 this author conducted an experiment with the Halton Regional Police Force in Ontario, Canada whereby, over a period of 24 months, the Burlington police district videotaped police questioning of suspects and accused persons and Oakville district continued to record such transactions in the traditional written-statement format. Since the experiment was judged to be a success, each police station in the Halton Regional Police Force now has videotaping equipment installed and no attempt is made to obtain written statements from suspects or accused persons. Instead, police questioning is captured in its entirety on videotape and the tape is used in all subsequent negotiations or trials without resort to transcription facilities. This method was superimposed on existing Canadian legal procedures, and police, on tape, give suspects a warning that they are not obliged to say anything and that anything they say may be given in evidence. Police also inform accused persons of their right to counsel.[4] Several other Canadian police forces are experimenting with using videotape to record police questioning of suspects, i.e., Metropolitan Toronto Police, Durham Regional Police, York Regional Police (all in Ontario) and Vancouver Police Department in British Columbia. There appears to be no intention, at present, to change the law on voluntariness in Canada; the videotaping technology is simply being used as a better and less contentious method of recording the interrogation than the traditional police notebook and statement-form methodology.

U.S.A.

It should be remembered that the elaborate warning systems developed in the U.S.A. under the *Escobedo v. Illinois*[5] and *Miranda v. Arizona*[6] doctrines in the 1960s, occurred at an earlier stage in technological advance and were created *"in the absence of other effective measures"* to ensure fairness to the accused. Thus, in *Miranda* we read the following (at 478, 479):

> To summarize, we hold that when an individual is taken into custody or otherwise deprived of his freedom by the authorities in any significant way and is subjected to questioning, the privilege against self-incrimination is jeopardized. Procedural safeguards must be employed

to protect the privilege and *unless other fully effective means are adopted* (emphasis added) to notify the person of his right to silence and to assure that the exercise of the right will be scrupulously honored. . . .

The case then goes on to enumerate the need for the police to follow the now familiar litany:

1) Warning the suspect of the right to silence
2) Warning that anything that is said can be used against the suspect in a court of law
3) Offer of the right to presence of a lawyer
4) Offer of the provision of a lawyer in the case of an indigent accused
5) Only then can there be a knowing and intelligent waiver of rights which must be demonstrated by the prosecution.

Despite recent interpretations of *Miranda* in the U.S. Supreme Court which have held that the principles behind that case are not offended where the police failed to tell a murder suspect that a lawyer was attempting to contact him[7] or when the police obtained an inculpatory statement under *Miranda* procedures without first warning the suspect that an earlier confession obtained in violation of *Miranda* rules could not be used against him,[8] it is still true to say that the general edifice of *Miranda* remains intact in the U.S.A.

It is important, however, to recall that the *Miranda* ruling was made subject to *other fully effective means* being adopted to safeguard suspects' rights, and it is suggested here that effective videotaping of the whole interrogation which shows no threats, tricks, inducements or oppression might well pass muster as voluntary even if precise *Miranda* warnings did not occur. Compliance with the *Miranda* procedures is only necessary, it could be argued, when no adequate and objective record of the interview is available to show the total absence of a coercive or otherwise improper atmosphere during the entirety of the questioning.

England

Videotaping technology may also have timely lessons for part of the U.K. In October of 1988, Tom King, the Secretary of State for Northern Ireland, and Douglas Hurd, the Home Secretary, announced in written replies in the House of Commons that a suspect's right of silence without comment from either judge or prosecution is to be abolished in England, Wales and Northern Ireland. With the right to silence to be abrogated and the judge and the prosecutor given the right to comment on silence, it has already been pointed out in the literature in England that much will turn on the circumstances in deciding whether the refusal to speak was reasonable. It is suggested that a videotape of the interview will give the judge and jury the best view of exactly what transpired.[9] Otherwise, will the new allegation against the police be that they lied when they claimed, in evidence, that the accused remained silent, rather than the present complaint that the police lied when they claimed that the accused said something incriminating?

The following brief outline of some of the issues in the videotaping experiment should therefore be of interest to several jurisdictions whether the intention is to retain, modify or abolish the existing rules on the right to silence and the necessity to prove the "voluntariness" of statements made to persons in authority by suspects and accused persons.

The Experiment—Project T.I.P. (Taped Interviewing Procedures)

Over a period of two years 946 interrogations were videotaped at Burlington District resulting in 645 admissions or confessions (68%). There were 226 denials or other exculpatory responses (24%) and 30 suspects had nothing to say (3%). In all, 45 suspects/accused refused "on camera" to be videotaped at all (4.8%). Thus of the 901 people who did not refuse to be videotaped 71.6 percent made inculpatory responses on videotape.

The response from police, prosecutors and defence counsel was uniformly positive. Each group overwhelmingly supported the expansion of the project from experimental to operational status. Full details of the experiment have been reported elsewhere.[10]

An Evaluation of the Perceived Advantages of Videotaping Under Project T.I.P.

1. Police would be protected against unwarranted allegations of misconduct.[11]

Under traditional recording practices involving notebooks and written statements, allegations of misconduct on the part of the police often become a matter of dispute during a voir dire.[12] There being no objective record of the circumstances under which the interview occurred, counsel must often test conflicting accounts of an interview to ascertain the truth of the contradictory recollections of the principal witnesses.

Videotaping takes away this possible conflict. With a videotaped recording of the police interview an accurate and objective record is there for everyone to see. Although the argument can still be made that there is no equivalent evidence about pre-statement circumstances, the study has shown that videotaping does protect police against unwarranted allegations of misconduct. No cases of gross police misbehavior have appeared on any of the tapes. If anything, the tapes showed the police to be careful to avoid all possible suggestion of force, threats, inducements, or the creation of an atmosphere of oppression.

2. An element of publicity and accountability would be introduced into interrogation procedures.[13]

Prior to the advent of videotaping procedures a police interview was shrouded in mystery. No one who was outside the room where the interview took place could really know what happened inside. Videotape lifts the veil to this mystery. Now, not only is this area of police activity open to the scrutiny of the courts, but it is also opens to the public at large, either those present in court or those who may see excerpts of the videotape on television.

3. The danger of "verballing" and similar problems would be minimized.[14]

"Verballing" relates to the allegation that, on occasion, police claim that an accused made a verbal admission or confession to a crime which the defendant did not, in fact, make.

The Halton evaluation did not encounter an actual allegation of "verballing" during its study. As a rule it is a rare phenomenon in Halton courts. One can still conclude, however, that a videotape interview can reduce the likelihood of this occurring.

4. There would be a decrease in the number of voir dires.[15]

The evaluation showed that in the Halton region very few voir dires were held. However, while there were still some voir dires held in the Oakville court, the voir dire had virtually disappeared from the Burlington courtroom. Instead, it has been replaced by an out-of-court conference between Crown and the defense counsel, following a joint viewing of the videotape in the case.

5. There would be a reduction in disputes about who should testify at the voir dire[16]

Given that voir dires tend to disappear when video technology is used, this subsidiary problem disappears with it.

6. The court's ability to assess objectively the accuracy of testimony and the credibility of witnesses would be enhanced.[17]

What the Halton study has shown is that with videotaping, the court, in most cases, does not have to make this assessment. As noted previously the out-of-court conference between counsel usually results in tapes not being used in court at all, either because there is a plea of guilty (by far the most common result) or because neither counsel sees the tape as advancing the case they wish to make (the next most common category).

When the tapes are shown at trial, it is often for purposes other than to prove admissibility (for example, where it is used to show the state of mind of the accused) or at sentencing (for example, where the tape reveals a circumstance of aggravation or mitigation). In these cases the court's ability to assess objectively the accuracy of the testimony and the credibility of the witnesses would clearly be enhanced.

7. The admission into evidence of statements of accused persons would be facilitated.[18]

The police officers take great care to see that an accused is informed of his or her right to counsel and of the right to remain silent. Since this is on tape for everyone to see, it reduces much of what the defense counsel could do to undermine the introduction of the statement into evidence.

8. All doubt would be eliminated about the accuracy of the record and the contents of the statement.[19]

The traditional police notebook and written statement as ways of recording a statement has spawned a growing case law on "accuracy of the record." The use of videotape procedures would do away with this particular case-law issue. The Halton study has shown that it is common ground among police, Crown and defense counsel that the videotape is an accurate record of the interview as it occurred in the videotaping room.

9. There would be an increase in the number of guilty pleas.[20]

There are more guilty pleas in Burlington than in Oakville. However, this is true not only in "video" cases but also in cases where no police interviewing of any kind occurred. Therefore, it cannot be said that it was necessarily the use of videotape procedures that made the difference.

10. There would be an improvement in police interviewing techniques.[21]

There is certainly a heightened consciousness among police officers in the study about how they conduct their interviews, for now their taped interviews can be seen by everyone—their colleagues, judge, juries, lawyers and the public at large. This fact has made the Halton officers much more conscious of the need to be properly prepared before going into an interview. As they see it they only have one chance to get it right. Furthermore, they are also motivated by professional pride in being regarded as competent investigators by their colleagues.

11. There would be no need for additional officers to be present at the interview.[22]

Videotaping technology definitely helps to reduce the number of officers present at an interview. As was noted earlier in this summary, where two police officers were usually required for the traditional interview, now only one is needed to fulfil the same duties.

An Evaluation of the Perceived Disadvantages of Videotaping Under Project T.I.P.

1. Suspects would be inhibited by the camera and the general situation from making confessions or admissions otherwise made.[23]

The study did not support this perceived disadvantage. Just over two out of three of the people who accept the opportunity to have their statement to police videotaped make confessions or admissions useful to the Crown's case. Only a small minority refuse "on camera" to be videotaped (4.8%). Serious as well as minor offenses have been the subject of confessions, and on occasion previously unsolved crimes have been admitted to "on camera" when they were not even the original subject of the interview.

There is little evidence that the suspect or accused person pays much attention to the camera. The interviewing officer, relieved of the need for a typewriter, notebook and statement forms, can concentrate on the issues which are relevant to the investigation in progress. The suspect or accused is also relieved of extraneous objects upon which to concentrate his or her attention and tends to focus solely on the interviewer. It should also be noted that many more "video denials" of involvement in crime occur now than were ever recorded by police using traditional written procedures. In short, the videotaping procedures produce more recorded interviews of every type, be they confessions, admissions, denials or refusals to be interviewed.

2. There is the possibility of malfunctioning equipment whereby evidence may be lost and danger that the equipment could be tampered with to the detriment of the accused.[24]

No problems have arisen with malfunctioning equipment, although isolated cases of operator error have occurred, for example, failure to ensure that the recorder was in operation before commencing an interview whereby a confession was "lost." This problem has been solved by changing to a single-action "start-up" system; that is to say, one switch now controls lights, camera, and sound.

There have been no allegations, so far, that tapes have been tampered with in any way. In an experimental case, prior to this evaluation, there was a rigorous test of the taping process during a voir dire in a case of false pretenses. This interview had been taped by the investigating officer as part of the orientation process at Burlington. The videotaping procedures were upheld on the voir dire and the resulting interview was admitted in evidence.[25]

3. Implementation of these procedures would impose a significant capital burden upon law enforcement agencies.[26]

If a system can be validated which does not use multi-recording apparatus, universal transcription and professional camera crews, then one is dealing with a cost burden significantly lower than if these factors were included. The Halton scheme is a low-cost scheme which uses a video cassette as an electronic notebook, makes copy tapes available in lieu of transcription and employs no professional camera or lighting crews. As such, it is a "bare-bones," operation and over a two-year period, it has been shown to have produced accurate records of police interviews leading to the satisfactory resolution of criminal cases from the varying perspectives of the police, Crown and defense counsel.

Costs have to be looked at in the context of overall police budgeting allocations. It will cost Halton less than the price of a police car to extend the system to its two other districts. Since the force has over one hundred vehicles in its fleet, an expenditure of less than 1 percent of the vehicle budget will finance the expansion to a force-wide videotaping system.

4. Allegations of police misconduct would continue to be made about the period preceding taping.[27]

Although police officers were instructed that "dry-run" preparation before taping was contrary to force policy, some police officers at Burlington have, on occasion, run a "rehearsal" with the suspect or accused person of what should happen on tape before the videotaping occurred. Defense counsel raised this issue in court, where this conduct was admitted in cross-examination by the officers concerned, and the judge nevertheless allowed the tape to be entered into evidence because he found that the conduct did not raise a doubt about the voluntariness of the statement. However, it would seem unlikely that police officers would continue this conduct knowing the possibility of having the evidence not admitted into court.

  5. Suspects could be inhibited by the camera from giving useful information about offenses other than those under investigation.[28]

As mentioned earlier in this summary, the taping process does not appear to have had the effect, feared by some officers, of "drying up" the flow of such information. In fact, if anything, it appears that Burlington officers may receive more of such information than do Oakville officers.[29]

In short, almost all of the perceived advantages of videotaping tended to be confirmed while none of the perceived disadvantages appeared to emerge. The voir dire tended to disappear and be replaced by an out-of-court viewing of the tape by prosecutor and defense counsel followed by an agreement on the plea or on the use or non-use of the tape.

The major surprise was that the focus of the voir dire did not move to the period prior to the videotaped interview commencing. Apart from one or two allegations that "dry run" interviewing had occurred before the tape was switched on, this change of focus did not happen. Even in the "dry run" cases, the tapes were admitted into evidence, as no threats, inducements or other impropriety was alleged during the "rehearsal."

Implementation

Between 1987 and 1989 Halton Regional Police have extended videotaping to each police station in the region, and all interviews with suspects and accused persons are recorded on videotape.

No major changes have been noticed by either police, prosecutors or defense counsel in how the procedures are working now that it has become commonplace rather than experimental.

Police, prosecutors and defense counsel continue to be enthusiastic about the process, and it has not been found necessary to upgrade the "bare-bones" operation to a more technically advanced stage. The video cassette as electronic notebook, and the avoidance of professional camera crews and transcription services are continuing to work well, in practice, and there is no present intention to change the procedures in any significant way. The out-of-court viewing of tapes by opposing counsel usually disposes of all questions surrounding the police-suspect interview and the judges seldom see the tapes. When they do, it is often for a purpose other than voluntariness, e.g., drunkenness on the question of intent and remorse or the lack thereof for sentencing purposes.

Because of the very simple way in which the Halton tapes are recorded and used, expense has not been a negative factor in conducting the experiment or in expanding the procedures to operational status. General police research has shown that the most significant increase in effectiveness comes when one moves from no police presence to some police presence. Once a policing system is established, a law of diminishing returns tends to occur whereby similar increases in effectiveness can seldom be demonstrated by simply adding more police, i.e., by spending money on more of the same.[30]

In allocating scarce police resources, a major question must now be asked in police forces not using videotaping whether, for example, it is wise to add to the vehicle fleet rather than to retain the existing fleet and install videotaping equipment. If such choices are made, new budget allocation for installing videotaping may not even be necessary. If it is necessary, it should not, in the context of the overall policing budget, be prohibitive.

Conclusion

Whether a jurisdiction intends to continue with its existing approach to admissibility of accused's statements to police, to reconsider such rules or to abandon the so-called right to silence altogether, it would appear that the videotaping of the police-suspect interview will make a major contribution to resolving some of the more contentious aspects of this perennially challenging topic.

This experience with the use of videotaping during the interrogation function gives encouragement to an expansion of videotaping in other aspects of the criminal justice process. As courts become more familiar with the use of videotaped evidence, one can see it being used more freely, not only in the presentation of evidence, e.g., child-victim testimony, lineups and scene-of-crime reproductions, but also in recording court procedures themselves.

ENDNOTES

1. e.g. *Ibrahim v. The King* [1914] A.C. 599 (P.C.), *R v. Fitton* [1956] S.C.R. 958, *Escobedo v. Illinois* 378 U.S. 478 (1964).

2. *Police and Criminal Evidence Act* 1984 c.60 ss.76–78.

3. *Erven v. The Queen* [1979] 1 S.C.R. 926, *Miranda v. Arizona* 384 U.S. 436 (1966).

4. *Canadian Charter of Rights and Freedoms* s.10(b).

5. Note (1) *supra.*

6. Note (3) *supra.*

7. *Moran v. Burbine* 106 S.C. Rptr. 1135 (1986).

8. *Oregon v. Elstad* 470 U.S. 298 (1985).

9. Morton J. "Towards Video Recording" 4 *Policing* 256–263 (1988). See also Editorial [1989] Crim. L.R. 1 "By means of the *Criminal Evidence (Northern Ireland) Order* 1988, the government has brought about a major alteration in the evidential significance, in trials in Northern Ireland, of a defendant's silence during the criminal investigation and at court. The Home Secretary has indicated that similar changes are under consideration for England and Wales. The Northern Ireland Order permits a court to draw whatever inferences would be proper from a defendant's silence in any of four circumstances:

    (i) where D offered an explanation of his conduct for the first time at his trial, when he might reasonably have been expected to offer it when being questioned by the police;

    (ii) where the prosecution has satisfied the court that there is a case to answer, and D declines to give evidence;

    (iii) where D gave no explanation to the police about certain specific facts such as substances or marks on clothing; and

    (iv) where D gave no explanation to the police of his presence at a particular place."

10. Grant, A. "The Audio-Visual Taping of Police Interviews with Suspects and Accused Persons by Halton Regional Police Force, Ontario, Canada An Evaluation" Final Report prepared for the Law Reform Commission of Canada (1987). Details of interim reports can be found in (1986) 2 *Policing* 182 and [1987] Crim. L.R. 375. A summary of the evaluation is available from the Law Reform Commission of Canada, 130 Albert Street, Ottawa, Ontario, K1A 0L6.

11. See *"Questioning Suspects"* Working Paper 32 at 59 (1984); L.R.C.C. Report 23 at 19 (1984); P.H. Solomon, "The Law Reform Commission of Canada's Proposals for Reforms of Police Powers: An Assessment" (1984–85) 27 Crim. L.Q. 321 at 343.

12. In the Anglo-Canadian system a voir dire, or trial-within-a-trial, is held whenever it is necessary for a judge to rule on whether certain evidence may be adduced in the main trial. This function is performed in the U.S.A. by pretrial

motions to have the challenged evidence suppressed and the expression "voir dire" is only retained in the exercise of the jury selection process.

13. See Working Paper 32 at 60.

14. See *ibid.* at 59.

15. See *ibid.;* Report 23 at 18; M. Inman, "Royal Commission on Criminal Procedure—(4) The Admissibility of Confessions" [1981] Crim. L.R. 469 at 480; J. Vennard, "Disputes Within Trials Over the Admissibility and Accuracy of Incriminating Statements: Some Research Evidence" [1984] Crim. L.R. 15 at 24.

16. See Working Paper 32 at 59.

17. See *ibid.* at 61.

18. See *ibid.* at 61 and Report 23 at 18.

19. See report 23 at 18; E. Goldstein, "Using Videotape to Present Evidence in Criminal Proceedings" (1984–85) 27 Crim. L.Q. 369 at 377 and 383.

20. See Report 23 at 19.

21. See Editorial, "November 1985" [1985] Crim. L.R. 693; Editorial, 135 New Law Journal 877.

22. See C. Willis, "The Tape-Recording of Police Interviews with Suspects: An Interim Report" Home Office, Research Study 82 (London: H.M.S.O. 1984) at 26 and 32; D. Roberts, "Tape Recording the Questioning of Suspects—The Field Trials Guidelines [1984] Crim. L.R. at 543.

23. See Ontario, Office of the Public Complaints Commissioner, "Report on the Investigation of Allegations Made Against Some Members of the Metropolitan Toronto Police Hold-Up Squad" (March, 1984) at 109; C. Willis, *ibid.* at 21; G. Williams, "The Authentication of Statements to the Police" [1979] Crim. L.R. 6 at 21; McConville and Morel, "Recording the Interrogation: Have the Police Got It Taped?" [1983] Crim. L.R. 158; Editorial, "November 1985," *supra*, note 41.

24. See Working Paper 32 at 59 and 61; Report 23 at 19; C. Willis, *supra*, note 42, at 30.

25. See Heathcote (1985) 25-6-85, unreported, Robinson Prov. Ct. J., and see E. Goldstein, *Goldstein on Video-tape and Photographic Evidence* (Vancouver: Western Legal Publications, 1986) at 12-206.

26. See Working Paper 32 at 60; Report 23 at 19; M. Inman, *supra*, note 35, at 480; G. Williams, *supra*, note 43, at 15 and 17.

27. See Report 23 at 19; Ontario, Office of the Public Complaints Commissioner, *supra*, note 43, at 106; G. Williams, *supra*, note 43 at 10.

28. An experienced detective in the Halton Regional Police Force mentioned this concern to me during informal discussions prior to the project.

29. These findings have been extracted from the Summary of my Evaluation prepared for the Law Reform Commission of Canada by Joyce Miller.

30. Clarke R.V.G. and Heal K.H. "Police Effectiveness in Dealing with Crime: Some Current British Research" in Workshop on Police Productivity and Performance (1978), Solicitor General of Canada, 68–97.

Chapter 20

LAW ENFORCEMENT SURVEILLANCE PROJECTS EMPLOYING MEDIA TECHNOLOGY

RAY SURETTE

Introduction. Surveillance utilizing media technology involves the electronic deterrence and visual detection of crime. Specific small site uses such as bank, subway, and department store surveillance cameras have been in use for a number of years. But these prior uses differ from newer applications, in that the areas surveyed are small, there is a voluntary nature to the surveillance, and areas of public domain are not involved. In contrast, the new programs use media technology directly for general crime prevention and focus upon large public geographic areas. Encouraged by rapidly improving technology the new developing surveillance projects emerge in two basic forms: completely hidden systems that give potential offenders no indication that they are being observed or open systems that are clearly marked. Although the former is more geared as an evidence and apprehension mechanism, both types can take advantage of a "surveillance effect"—that is, the deterrence of crime through the psychological impact of creating the belief that one might be under surveillance.[1]

Interest in the use of surveillance is based upon the idea that a surveillance effect will increase the perceived risk of committing crime by potential offenders and thus deter a portion of them from offending (cf. Mayhew et al., 1979). Despite the increase in the number of these

---

1. For example, with a hidden system, deterrence is accomplished by having and publicizing a mobile system that can be set up and moved at will so that one cannot be sure when it is being employed. Such systems can easily be secreted in vans. The idea of increasing community surveillance to deter crime was theoretically forwarded and given prominence in the early 1970s by Newman whose concepts of defensible space employ the guiding premise that community and building design can minimize the opportunity and likelihood of crime by increasing the sense of community or by not providing favorable sites for crimes to occur (Newman, 1972; 1975; 1976; see also Jacobs, 1971).

projects, there is a distinct lack of information and discussion concerning community media surveillance programs.[2] Dated research based largely upon offender interviews does offer a limited number of propositions concerning the use of surveillance. First, it suggests that criminals take into account the perceived level of surveillance and likelihood of intervention when choosing to commit certain crimes (cf. Reppetto, 1974). Initial research also indicates that it is likely that efforts to increase surveillance efforts by the general public is probably the least effective approach for using surveillance in deterring crime, but that increasing the surveillance capability (or the perception of its increase) of law enforcement officers, neighborhood residents and employees does have promise (Mayhew et al., 1979). In addition, the impact of surveillance is related to the actual threat of intervention. An initial surveillance-induced crime reduction that is without real subsequent law enforcement interventions will soon wane (Mayhew et al., 1979). Surveillance—media-based and otherwise—has thus been recognized as a potential tool in crime reduction, and the utility of increasing its effectiveness through media and other technology is long-standing. Despite its promise, however, media technology based surveillance has undergone only limited evaluation and scrutiny.

Importance examination points in this area revolve around several issues. The most obvious issue is the effectiveness of these programs: do they result in a reduction in crime? A second issue is the trade-off of "privacy versus security." In response to crime, the criminal justice system, often prodded by the public, has begun to increasingly turn to media-based technology for more innovative countermeasures against crime (Surette, 1985; cf. Marx, 1985:23). A third set of issues involve the benefits and deficits associated with these projects. A long list of practical advantages have been forwarded regarding the use of media technology in surveillance efforts. These include the reduction of the number of officers needed for patrol, an increased ability to provide full 24-hour-a-day patrol capability, a reduction in citizen fear of crime, improved deterrence of street crime, an increased ability to apprehend and convict street criminals, increased response time, and an increased ability for supervisors to oversee and command line personnel and review field decisions. However, because of their nature, such programs inevitably

---

2. The majority of the available reports focus on other types of media anti-crime programs, the more common are of media anti-crime programs aimed at the abuse of drugs which rely upon media public service ad campaigns (see Swisher and Herman, 1978; Boldt, Reilly, and Haberman, 1976; Ostman, 1976).

result in a reduction in citizen privacy. A basic question is how these programs' social costs compare against their benefits (Surette, 1985:79). Surreptitious electronic surveillance invariably raises the issue of "1984" governmental abuses and the legitimacy and image of law enforcement. Irrespective of their pragmatic advantages, critics raise concerns that their use will be difficult to control (Marx, 1985:23):

> Yet there are also potential dangers in institutionalizing such systems. They may encourage paranoia and suspiciousness.... In a different political climate, [they] would lend themselves equally well to informing on those who are merely different or unpopular rather than criminal.

Even when actually ineffective, these systems and the associated surveillance effect have been criticized as psychologically too powerful and dangerous (Marx, 1985:21):

> ... [law enforcement] agents are clearly limited in the surveillance and coercion they can carry out, but they are free to create the impression of police omnipresence and omnipotence. What they cannot do by force or by the actual power of their technology, they may attempt to do by creating a "myth of surveillance."

The projects are also questioned regarding their costs and the effectiveness and reliability of the equipment, the community image that the deployment of such systems project, and the probability that their use will have merely a crime displacement rather than a crime reduction effect. Nearly a decade ago a prophetic assessment was offered on the difficulties of using surveillance-based programs in crime prevention (Mayhew et al., 1979:12):

> The use of surveillance to reduce crime shares some of the usual problems of methods which attempt to reduce opportunities of crime (cf. Mayhew et al., 1976; Clarke, 1977); they do not tackle underlying factors that may motivate offenders; they can appear negatively "defensive"; and they cannot guarantee that crime is not merely displaced in time, place or method.

The London Subway and Miami Beach Systems. Despite the belief in its advantages and associated concerns and the increasing use of media surveillance by law enforcement agencies,[3] there are no definitive

---

3. For example, the City of Indianapolis Police Department makes extensive use of video technology. In crime prevention efforts the department employs a mobile van to supply video surveillance as needed. It has been used to tape crowd and people movement in gay areas in an attempt to trace and solve gay-related murders, and is periodically used to tape in areas of high prostitution to deter both prostitutes and their customers (based upon interview with representative of the Indianapolis P.D. Public Information Office, 6/30/87). It is unknown how many police department have similar capabilities, but the number is most likely quite high.

studies of the actual impact that media-based surveillance systems have on crime. Only two open system projects have been even closely examined. The best documented effort involved the placement of closed circuit television cameras in the London subway system in the 1970s. This open system effort placed cameras in four London stations with transmissions sent to a central monitoring site. The cameras provided viewing of all principal station areas, were conspicuously mounted, and accompanied by notices stating the closed circuit television was in use. Monitor operators could either contact the station staff or nearest police station, make a public address announcement, or contact train drivers (Mayhew et al., 1979:25–26).

The evaluation shows that the cameras reduce the incidence of both theft and robbery, with some evidence of displacement of theft offenses to other non-camera stations. The evaluators caution, however, that the effectiveness of the system might result from its novelty and that in time offenders may discover that the system is less to be feared than they imagine. Analogous to the announcement effect noted for highly publicized crackdowns in traditional law enforcement efforts (cf. Ross et al, 1970; Campbell and Ross, 1968), they warn that only the installation of cameras without actual intervention strategies will not likely be effective for a very long period (Mayhew et al., 1979:28).

The single examined effort covering a large, out-of-doors, public area involves the placing of microwave television cameras atop traffic lights in a downtown shopping district in Miami Beach, Florida in the mid-1980s. As was the London subway system, this video "patrol" program was a known open system and was designed to give a small city police department a significantly greater presence in its prime retail shopping district without the addition of patrol personnel by blanketing the retail shopping district with television surveillance. The stated goals of the program were "to accomplish a reduction in elderly fear of street crime and to create anxiety and a sense of paranoia among the criminal element in that they [will] fear that their activities may be televised and recorded by the police" (Wooldridge, 1981:6). Thus, it was expected that the project would drastically lower the perceived fear of crime among the elderly and simultaneously deter and detect street crime from the city's shopping district. The specifics of the project include the strategic placing of 100 video camera housings along the two retail shopping avenues of the city. A prominent sign stating "Police Television" is mounted with each housing. Of the 100 video housings located in the target area, 21 actually contained a camera at any given time (see Figure 1).[4] The television cameras could be moved from one housing to another by the police department. Therefore, "at no time would a criminal be able to determine which of the 100 housings actually contain a camera" (Miami Beach Police Department, 1982:1). The focus of deterrence in Miami Beach was a specific class of crimes: strong-arm robberies, muggings, purse snatchings, and other street crime. Originally, the project planned for the installation of the televisions in a four-block area with 90-day movement of the cameras. Start-up was to be a one-day affair, with housings being mounted, cameras being activated, volunteers being assigned, and the news media being called to record and report the events simultaneously.

However, after implementation it was discovered that the microwave equipment was highly sensitive to wind and weather and suffered significant amounts of down time. The central pan/tilt camera was not operating 80 percent of the time and frequently as few as three of the traffic light cameras were working. Technical problems with the equipment impacted on the effectiveness of the project as a crime detection system. These equipment problems are cited as one reason for the reduction of political support for the program due to their delaying its operational start-up date, causing volunteer dissatisfaction, and denying the program early supportive statistics and tangible successes for dissemination to local government officials and the news media.

Related to this lack of support, a serious community perception problem developed with the news media. The distribution of information is necessary for the success of deterrence efforts. Project developers recognized therefore that media publicity was crucial to the program's success. To entice coverage, the project was described as a crime detection and apprehension project, not a crime deterrence one. Local media coverage, however, was sporadic and somewhat negative and the portrayal and reporting of the project became a sensitive political issue in the community. Reasons for this media stance are traceable to initial promises by

---

4. The entire assembled system consists of the following:

    1. A portable TV camera which is wireless and controllable from an isolated area. The unit had a self-contained power source and received images that are then transferred via microwave to a monitor.

    2. A portable transmitter was contained at the same location as the camera. It trasformed the images into a microwave and sent them to a receiver.

    3. A micro-video receiver captured the microwave, interpreted it, and transferred it as a TV picture to a monitoring screen located in a central command center.

    4. There was also one manually operated pan/tilt camera located at the main intersection which could move vertically and horizontally and had a telescopic lens.

FIGURE 1

STREET VIDEO PATROL SYSTEM

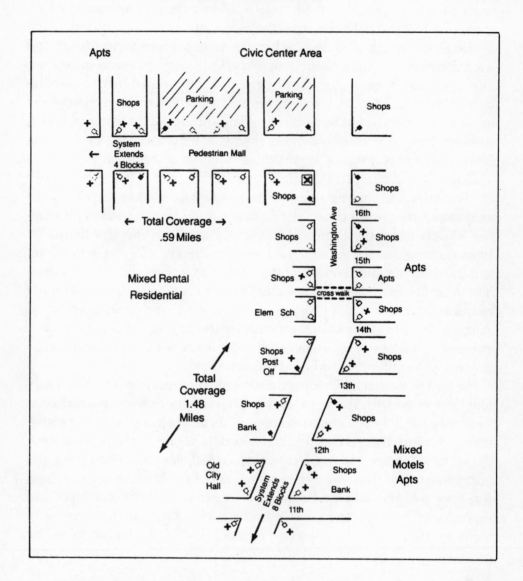

Key: ⊠ Pan Tilt Telescopic Camera Mounted on Building Roof
      □ Camera Housing
      ■ Camera Housing With Camera
      ✖ Police Camera Sign

the project's developers—that of providing action crime film and the immediate videotaped apprehension of suspects. Media disillusionment occurred when the project's start-up date was first delayed and when its impact was subsequently realized to be more crime deterrence than crime detection. This selling of the program to the media as an apprehension program which would provide good video "action footage" for newscasts is acknowledged as a basic mistake by developers. It was reasoned that a focus on its apprehension potential rather than its more realistic but unfilmable deterrent impact would attract more initial media attention and support. However, a failure to deliver, coupled with the media's resistance to an imposed timetable of coverage, eventually led to a souring of the media portrayal of the project.

Regarding the Miami Beach project's effect on crime, evidence is mixed. Its evaluation prepared by the city police department reports the results of a community survey of 305 target area merchants.[5] A total of 135 merchants reported that they had been crime victims since opening, and that 53 percent of these crimes had occurred since the video project had begun. Also, area merchants did not perceive a reduction in their victimization rate. While interpretation of these figures is hampered because the time spans in the area of the various merchants is not known (some had been there for years while others had only recently opened), the fact that more than half of the crimes reported by the merchants had occurred since the project's beginning cannot be interpreted as evidence of the program having a significant impact on general crime in the area. There is evidence however of a significant reduction in the number of targeted street crimes after the television system became operational. Police statistics did show a reduction in strong-arm robberies from a 4.83 per month average prior to the program to a 3.09 per month average (sig. @ .026) after program start-up (the mounting of the camera housings) (see Surette, 1985). Interpretation of these positive results must also be tempered, however, for analysis of other city area crime reports was not possible and thus it could not be to determined whether (1) the target area reduction was part of a general decline in crime in the city and thus not due to the television system[6] or (2) whether the cameras had a displacement effect, reducing crime in the target area while increasing it in adjacent areas.

---

5. The community survey was a one-day canvas of all retail merchants in the target area. The 305 merchants represent the total number of retail stores in the area.

6. Police department representatives did not feel the city had experienced a general decline in crime.

Irrespective of its impact on crime, the area merchants did report support for the project and hold positive attitudes toward its continuance. For example, only 3.9 percent felt that business had decreased due to the cameras, while 26.2 percent felt business had increased (67.2 percent felt the project made no difference). A total of 71.5 percent felt more secure since the system had been installed and 27.2 percent did not; 89.5 percent would have liked to see the project continue, while only 6.2 percent would not (Miami Beach Police Department, 1983).

Despite this evidence of support and an apparent positive effect on street crime, the project was dismantled by the city soon after the funding grant ended. Designed as an open, fully publicized deterrence system, the Miami Beach system nevertheless came to be faulted by the police department for not being a crime detection and apprehension system, even though at the end of its first year of operation the department credited it with aiding a 70 percent decrease in area crime (Security Today, 1983:13). By the end of two years the Miami Beach Police Chief was commenting that: "The system has failed totally. In the two years of operation, not one crime was recorded by the cameras" (Crime Control Digest, 1984:2 comment based upon interview with Miami Beach Police Chief Glassman). It is argued that this program suffered more from its political liabilities than its effect on crime,[7] and it is likely that such general public media-based surveillance systems are likely to be sensitive political issues whenever they are employed (cf. Surette, 1985).

Implications. To solve and deter crime more effectively sometimes requires that the government intervene in its citizens' lives in greater degrees. The media provides the technology to do so in new ways, ways that are felt to be both more efficient and less obtrusive. Based upon these two projects and other prior relevant research there is general agreement that media technology can oftentimes be useful in the criminal justice system. There is less agreement, however, about its suitability as a means of providing patrol and surveillance (cf. Surette, 1988). These concerns are traceable partly to technological feasibility questions but are even more rooted in social perceptions and value concerns. The use of the technology is in most cases efficient, and legal questions of

---

7. Between the time of its development and its initiation, the Miami Beach held municipal elections in which 5 of 7 city commissioners were replaced and the video project became identified with the prior administration. The project also developed problems with segments of the tourist industry who where concerned with the image of the city projected by such a system (Surette, 1985:81).

admissibility, privacy, and due process have been answered in support of the continued use of the technology in the United States. The technology's ultimate reception in the field, however, seems to lie in whether it is felt that a crucial element of justice is lost when media are transmitted. The more symbolically weighted the act or procedural step, the more concerns and resistance rise. Specifically, video patrol projects raise deep issues about the use of media technology in the daily policing of our society. Unresolved concerns include the perception of the legitimacy of the police to enforce laws, the depersonalization of the criminal justice process, and effects on established workgroups within the system.

Legitimacy. A prime unresolved issue is what is lost in legitimacy, symbolic impact, and public image of justice when media technology is employed? The justice system is a mechanism of adjudicating guilt and administering punishment. It is also a means of legitimizing the overall social system. As such, the police have a symbolic value. On the street, the presence of a live policeman or conversely the assurance of knowing when one is being observed support the values of voluntary consent and involvement, privacy, and public control of law enforcement. Loss of these symbolic qualities may diminish the aura of legitimacy supporting the entire system and, as was shown in Miami Beach, undermine an entire project. Surprisingly, concerns over "Big Brother" and "1984" were raised only by news media and external observers, and not by area residents who were quite ready to trade off a measure of personal privacy for a potential reduction in victimization and fear. Such a willingness encourages situations where these projects are subject to abuse. Another concern in the application of this technology is the prospect that it is successful only in displacing crime. Thus, one eventual result could be the isolation of crime, rather than its reduction, in poor neighborhoods that cannot afford such systems and the further polarization of society by crime rates.

Depersonalization. Planned expansions of these systems will lead to the increased depersonalization of criminal justice processes.[8] With the extended use of media technologies there would be a decline in face-to-face encounters between police and the public, attorneys and their clients,

---

8. The future experimentation with media technology in the courts seems assured with an extension of tests to additional procedural steps and the addition of new technology and capabilities. Other developing applications include the use of suitcase wireless video recorders and transmitter system, the mounting of video cameras on patrol cars to record driving behavior and vehicle stops (analogous to airline flight recorders) and multi-site full system networks linking jails, stockades, public defenders offices, state attorney's offices, courthouses, and police stations.

and judge's and defendants thereby seriously altering the current normative and communicative structure of the system. This process will be hastened by equipment advances that make this technology more economic and less obtrusive. The full overall effects of these changes may become apparent only after such practices have been in place for a long period of time.

Work Group Disruption. These systems also have the as yet largely unutilized potential to increase the supervision of line law enforcement officers by their superiors and thereby decrease line officer discretion. This could be accomplished either under live setups where supervisors could make actual field decisions or in lagged systems where actions and decisions are recorded for later review. Whether this capability would be a positive or negative change, what effect it might have on police morale or effectiveness, on street units' cohesion, or on the working relationships between officers are all unknown.

Conclusion. The basic problem presented by these projects is a balancing of intrusion and safety—how much safety is gained at what level of intrusion? The equation seems to clearly be that an increased fear of crime results in increased tolerance for intervention. Orwell's 1984 scenario is less feared than the local mugger, and law enforcement efforts to address crime via the media are strongly supported. The danger is that these crime control programs are driven by citizen fear and as such there exists a willingness to glibly surrender personal privacy for a measure of personal security. It is still an open question whether these programs provide enough crime reduction to warrant a reduction in privacy. They do provide, however, enough of a psychological reduction in the fear of crime to gain and maintain public support.

For example, the Miami Beach project, despite negative publicity and decreased political support, still sustained the support of local citizenry and merchants. The impact of these programs appears to be positive on citizen perceptions and support remains high even when effects on crime appear questionable. The study of these and other unanticipated changes in the socialization process and work group roles are crucial (cf. Casper, 1978; Sudnow, 1965). For if these systems ultimately result in the further isolation and separation of the police from the policed, the social costs of such losses would outweigh any organizational benefits that might accrue from them. As these systems are increasingly instituted, long-term studies are needed to address whether such policy-relevant effects are in fact developing.

REFERENCES

Boldt, R. et al. (1976). A survey and assessment of drug-related programs and policies in elementary and secondary school: In *Communication research and drug education* by R. E. Ostman, pp. 88–112. Beverly Hills: Sage.

Campbell, D. and Ross, L. (1968). "The Connecticut crackdown on speeding" *Law and Society Review* 3:33–53.

Casper, J. (1978). *Criminal Courts: The Defendants Perspective.* NIJ/LEAA Government Printing Office.

Clarke, R. (1977). "Psychology and Crime" *Bulletin of the British Psych. Soc.* 30:280–283.

Crime Control Digest, (1984) August 27:2–3.

Jacobs, J. (1971). *The Death and Life of Great American Cities.* Random House.

Marx, (1985). G. "The Surveillance Society" *The Futurist,* June:21–26.

Mayhew, P. et al. (1976). *Crime as Opportunity.* Home Office Research Study No. 34. London: HMSO.

Mayhew, P. et al. (1979). *Crime in Public View.* Home Office Research Study no. 49. Her Majesty's Stationery Office, London.

Miami Beach Police Department (1982). *Miami Beach news release.* Public Information Office. February.

Miami Beach Police Department (1983). *Micro-video project yearly report.* Miami, FL: Miami Beach P.D.

Newman, O. (1972). *Defensible Space: Crime Prevention Through Urban Design.* MacMillan.

Newman, O. (1975). "Community of interest—design for community control" in *Architecture, Planning and Urban Crime.* Report of NACRO Conference, 12/6/74, London.

Newman, O. (1976). *Design Guidelines for Creating Defensible Space,* NIJ/LEAA Government Printing Office.

Ostman, R. E. (1976). *Communication research and drug education.* Beverly Hills: Sage.

Reppetto, R. (1974). *Residential Crime.* Ballinger.

Ross, H., Campbell, D., and Glass, G. (1970). "The British breathalyser crackdown of 1967" *American Behavioral Scientist* 13:493–509.

Sudnow, D. (1965). "Normal Crimes" *Social Problems,* 12:255–276.

Security Today. (1983) September:13–14.

Surette, R. (1985). "Video Street Patrol: Media Technology and Street Crime" *The Journal of Police Science and Administration,* 13:78–85.

Surette, R. (1988). "Video Technology in Criminal Justice: Live Judicial Proceedings and Patrol and Surveillance" *The Proceedings of the 28th International Course on Criminology: New Technologies and Criminal Justice,* International Society of Criminology and The University of Montreal Centre on Criminology

Swisher, J., and Herman, R. (1964). *Evaluation of Temple University's Drug Abuse Prevention Program.* Philadelphia, PA. Temple Univ. Drug Ed. Activities Project.

Wooldridge, F. (1981). Micro video patrol. Grant application—Community Development Black Grant Program (HUD).

Chapter 21

MEDIA TECHNOLOGY IN CRIME CONTROL: HISTORY AND IMPLICATIONS

C. Ray Jeffery

General Theoretical Issues

Models of Behavior. Within the more narrow topic of "mass media and crime" two more basic and general issues are raised. The first issue involves the model of behavior that is used. Of three competing models of human behavior, most mass media studies use an "Environment → Mind → Behavior" model. That is, the environment impacts on the individual by creating mental states called self-concepts or attitudes. In social psychology this model is labeled the "social cognitive approach" or "symbolic interactionism" (Goldstein, 1980, p. 14 ff.; Gergen and Gergen, 1981, p. 18 ff.). Emphasis is given to attitude formation, social perception, an attribution of meaning, all of which are mentalistic processes of the mind. The Environment → Mind → Behavior model is derived from the Platonic philosophy of innate internal ideas which are totally independent of experience with the environment. It was further developed in western Europe into the rationalist philosophy of Kant and Descartes and labeled "Kantian psychology" due to its emphasis on the individual and their internal perceptual and thought processes (Rychlak, 1981; Schwartz, 1978; Jeffery, 1990).

In opposition to the Kantian view of human nature is the Lockian view derived from the empiricism of John Locke and the British empiricists. Locke held that all knowledge came from experience with the environment. "Lockean psychology" underlies the contemporary behaviorism of Watson and Skinner. The behaviorist's model of behavior is based on a stimulus-response model or an "Environment → Behavior" model in which the genetic and brain functioning of the individual are ignored and essentially conceptualized as an unobservable black box (Rychlak, 1981; Schwartz, 1978; Jeffery, 1990).

The third model is a bioenvironmental model as found in modern interdisciplinary theories of human behavior on genetics, the brain sciences, and learning theory. This model of behavior maintains that human behavior is a product of environment/organism interaction; with the biochemical organ, the brain, replacing the mentalistic concept of the mind. The model is represented as "Environment → Brain → Behavior" (Jeffery, 1990).

This third model emphasizes the physical nature of both man and his environment, whereas model I treats both as non-physical entities and model II ignores man's physical nature. Today, learning theorists regard learning as a product of genetics and the brain. Learning occurs in the brain where physical changes occur in the neurons and synapses. The neurotransmitters play a critical role in human behavior and are crucial to our understanding of mental illnesses, alcohol and drug addiction, sexual behaviors, and violent behaviors (Jeffery, 1990).

The model of behavior adopted by criminologists is critical to the success or failure of crime control programs, media based or otherwise, since all such programs aimed at controlling and/or changing human behavior. The general failure of the criminal justice system is very much related to the type of model of behavior used by the system. The most effective model for crime prevention is a bioenvironmental model wherein the physical organism interacts biochemically with a physical environment, the structure of which is important. The crime control model based upon an Environment → Brain → Behavior model is termed the "Crime Prevention Through Environmental Design" model (Jeffery, 1971, 1977, 1990) and is based on a potential crime target, a potential criminal, and an opportunity for a crime to occur.[1]

Deterrence and the Media. The second theoretical issue running throughout the media and crime literature is that of the concept of deterrence. Crime control policies are justified either in terms of revenge

---

1. *The Media and Human Behavior.* The impact of the media on human behavior is a basic issue in this book, and one addressed expressly in the first section, and although I am not going to review this section I will state that many of the problems found in testing the impact of media are related to the fact that either a mentalistic or a behavioral view of behavior is used. Questionnaires, interviews, and observation of behavior are used. All environmental experiences, including those involving the media, must be coded, stored, and used by the brain in order for behavior to occur. To my knowledge none has researched the impact of the media on the brain (Jeffery, 1990). From a bioenvironmental perspective individual differences are environmental stimuli in a different manner depending on past genetic history, learning experiences, and the state of the neurological system at that time. Studies of sex offenders who respond to violent sexual scenes differently than do normal subjects is illustrative of the point. The way in which we interpret such behavior depends on our theory of behavior.

and just retribution where a reduction in the crime rate is not expected, or in terms of deterrence where the assumption is made that criminals will be deterred from criminal acts if they or others are punished by the criminal justice system (Jeffery, 1990).

The media has been utilized primarily to deter criminal behavior through three target groups: (1) the potential criminals, (2) the potential victims, and/or (3) the general public (see Chapter 20 by Surette). In order for the media to impact on any of these groups the potential criminal also must be deterred. If we change the behavior of the potential victim or the general public effectively it must be in such a way that such behavior changes will result in the deterrence of potential criminals. Likewise, any programs aimed directly at the potential criminal must of course be capable of deterring the criminal. Deterrence of criminals ultimately relies on the ability of the criminal justice system to punish those criminals that are apprehended.

The problem is that punishment of criminals by the criminal justice system has never been shown to deter criminals or reduce crime rates. If criminals are not deterred by arrests, convictions, and prosecutions, how can we control the crime rate through the media, since such programs depend ultimately on the intervention and effective operation of the criminal justice system?

The History of Technology and Crime Prevention. Criminal activities are related to the technological advances of a culture. As technology changed we moved from horsethievry and cattle rustling to train robberies and auto theft and airplane skyjacking. The opportunity to commit crimes, i.e., the availability of targets is referred to in the literature as "opportunity theory or routine activities theory" by Gould, Cohen, Land and Felson (Gould, L. 1979; Cohen and Felson, 1979; Cohen, Felson and Land, 1980). The availability and distribution of targets is a major aspect of crime prevention through environmental design as developed by Jeffery and Brantingham.

Technology not only furnishes the targets for potential criminals, but it furnishes the means by which the police attempt to control crime. The police shifted from horses and foot patrols to heavily armored cars with radios in communication with central headquarters and with citizens by means of a 911 emergency number. At the same time the criminals started to use radios, telephones, and cars in the commission of crimes. As the police developed more powerful weaponry the criminals developed even more powerful weapons. The streets of American cities are today filled with gun battles between the police and drug dealers using military-type automatic weapons. The modern approach to drug control is a military offensive against drug dealers as is seen today in Colombia. The drug czar William Bennett recently commented that "there are many small Beiruts in most cities in the United States," and it might be added due to his antidrug policy. As better safes were developed, safecrackers developed better ways to crack them.

Surveillance technology has moved to such arenas as light amplifiers, satellite photography, video scanning, electronic monitoring, and electronic handcuffing. Some of the more controversial monitoring devises are internal, such as blood and urine tests and brain scans (Rubinstein, 1973; Geller, 1988; Marx, 1988a, 1988b). The legal and ethical implications of modern technology will be discussed below.

Crime Prevention Through the Media

Target Areas. As was stated above, target areas for crime prevention can be the potential criminal, the potential victim, or the general public. The projects discussed will be evaluated from the point of view of crime prevention, that is, actions taken before the of-view of crime prevention, that is, actions taken before the criminal act in order to reduce the chances of criminal behavior. By this definition most of the media projects discussed in this book are crime control efforts and not crime prevention efforts, that is, action taken after the crime has occurred. This point is central to my discussion of the media and crime.

Projects Aimed at the Potential Victim. The only project discussed in this section dealing with the potential victim is the "Taking a Bite out of Crime" project featuring McGruff (O'Keefe and Reid, Chapter 15; O'Keefe, 1986). This project is an educational program aimed at the general public with some basic crime prevention techniques and strategies which can be used to protect the average citizen from criminal acts. There has been no overall evaluation of the crime prevention strategies which are recommended for use, and the project has not been evaluated successfully (Chapter 15). The measurement of public response to McGruff has been primarily the response of community leaders and television stations to the program. I found no evaluation of the impact of McGruff on the intended audience, that is, the potential victim.

Programs such as "Taking a Bite out of Crime" suffer from the problems discussed above concerning changing human behavior through the media. We know that hundreds of individuals watched the program, all of them with different responses to the materials presented. Such a crime prevention effort depends on changing the behavior of the *potential victim*, and since each individual is different, each situation is different, and the controls over the behavior are questionable, the effectiveness of the program is limited by the psychology of human behavior.

Programs Aimed at the Potential Criminal. From the point of view of crime prevention, all of the programs are directly or indirectly aimed at the potential criminal. There is no potential victim or general public to involve in crime prevention except through an ultimate effect on the criminal. However, after the time the criminal act has occurred we are no longer involved in crime prevention but are instead involved in the reaction to crime via the criminal justice system.

The only program in Section III that is clearly identifiable as one aimed directly at the potential criminal is the video street project (Chapter 20, Surette). In this project, television cameras were placed in a retail shopping mall for surveillance purposes. The theory behind the program was that of deterrence through surveillance. Deterrence is a major assumption of the "defensible space" concept as put forth by Oscar Newman (1972, Jeffery, 1990). Newman's concept of defensible space has not been a success. Mayhew et al. (1979) and Jeffery (1990) found that the concept of surveillance as put forth by Newman was of limited value in crime control.

The video patrol project was judged by Surette to be of limited value in preventing crimes. The idea that human behavior can be controlled by a television camera is not consistent with modern psychology and biology. The presence of cameras in most banks has not stopped criminals from robbing banks. In fact, a source of films for Crime Stoppers programs is film taken from bank robberies in progress. These are used also as training films for police officers.

Programs Aimed at the General Public. There are a number of programs generally referred to as "Crime Stoppers" programs aimed at the identification and arrest of criminals after the crime has occurred. The Crime Stoppers program will portray on television or in a newspaper the re-enactment of a crime scene in the hope that a citizen will come forward with evidence concerning that crime. Rewards are often used as incentives for people calling in with information.

A National Institute of Justice study (Lavrakas, Rosenbaum, and Lurigio, Chapter 16) of Crime Stoppers concluded that public cooperation and acceptance was high, participation by the public and by media agencies was also high, and the programs were effective in terms of crimes solved: 92,000 felonies solved and $562,000,000 of stolen goods recovered. Even with these figures the authors concluded that Crime Stoppers will not substantially reduce the crime rate, and they recommended research to see if Crime Stoppers benefits society in general. There is also the fear that such programs may move us into a more authoritarian and "big brother" society, an issue discussed below.

Programs Aimed at the Criminal Justice System. Besides the target areas discussed above, media technology has been used by the criminal justice system. I already mentioned the use of cars and radios and telephones by police departments.

When video technology is used by the criminal justice system it is obviously not used to prevent crimes but as an after-the-fact effort to make the criminal justice system more effective. Computers are used to store the names and addresses of suspects and victims, to list license plate numbers, to keep track of those on bail, arraignments, and trial dates, among other matters. One of the major advances in court administration has been the use of computers to manage court calendars and judicial processes. This may help to expedite the judicial process, but it does not prevent crime or reduce the crime rate.

Two major examples of technology in the criminal justice system are cited. One deals with the use of video cameras in the courtroom. Terry and Surette (1985; Surette, 1988; Terry and Surette, Chapter 17) discuss the use of videotaping for arraignments in misdemeanor court. This allows for the defendant to appear before video cameras while in jail while judge and lawyers are in the courthouse. Such use of video technology expedites the logistical problems associated with legal procedures. Of course, the overcrowding of courts and prisons could better be handled if we prevented the crime in the first place. Terry and Surette (Chapter 17) found wide acceptance of videotaping, but they also cautioned about the issues raised concerning due process, the depersonalization of the judicial process, and the impact of such procedures on the public image of the judiciary.

The second use of video technology is found in the placement of video cameras in patrol cars to monitor and record police/citizen interaction. Records can be made of the arrest of drunk drivers, of assaults of citizens on police officers, and assaults by police officers on citizens (Sechrest, Lequori, and Perry, Chapter 18). In Canada, videotapes of police interrogations of suspects is also being employed (Grant, Chapter 19). Such videotaping raises issues concerning the legal rights of defendants and the right to use such tapes as evidence in court. At the same time, videotaping of such events can serve to protect suspects from less-than-desirable behavior on the part of the police, and it can preserve a record of what happened in contrast to the verbal exchanges between police and suspects that occur during the court trial.

The Dangers of the New Technologies. Mention has been made that these new technologies present dangers to human dignity and liberty. Surette (1988) questioned the use of video cameras as an intrusion into the privacy of individuals. Geller (1988) in a speech to the International Association of Chiefs of Police discussed the dangers of surveillance technologies. He highlighted democratic principles of freedom and liberty against the dangers of modern technology. He focused on the internal monitoring of individuals in terms of blood and urine samples and brain scans.

Marx (1988a, 1988b) has been a leading critic of the use of technology to control human behavior. He refers to the "maximum security society" as involved in testing, information gathering, and technological surveillance. Marx points to the dangers of some of these technologies, and rightly so, but there is a great deal more to the legal and ethical issues than a rejection of technology because it has been or can be used to punish and harm individuals. Technology is also used to control human suffering. All one has to do is walk into a modern hospital and observe the vast array of technology available for the treatment of disease.

The problem is one of not recognizing that the political state plays both a healing and a punishing role in our society. The state can educate, train, and furnish health and social services, or the state can execute and put into prisons people with medical disorders (Jeffery, 1990). Criminology is divided between legal criminology based on retribution and just deserts, and scientific criminology based on rehabilitation and prevention. Those like Marx (both Gary and Karl) who oppose state action do so on the basis of the police state, not the welfare state. Those condemning the use of technology to control human behavior do so on the basis of the argument that such controls interfere with the rights and freedoms of individuals. This same argument is not used when the state affords medical care or housing for the poor, or relief from racial and gender discrimination for blacks and females.

Criminology is certainly dominated by the punishment approach as emphasized in the criminal justice system. We build more prisons and declare a military-style war against drug addicts rather than create drug addiction treatment centers based on modern neurochemistry. However, this does not mean that a rehabilitation and prevention program cannot be utilized by society for its criminals. Such a model was outlined by Kittrie (1971) in his book *The Right to be Different* in which he concluded that the therapeutic state has an obligation to treat criminals even if such treatment is involuntary. Such treatment by the therapeutic state must be conducted within a network of legal protections. We now protect the criminal from cruel and unusual punishment, but we do not protect the criminal in terms of a treatment model. In our society we allow a needle to be stuck in the arm of a convict in order to execute him/her, but we are not allowed to take blood or urine or a brain scan in order to determine if the accused has a major brain disorder. We take hair and urine samples from individuals to determine if they are on drugs and thus can be fired and/or arrested, but we do not put such individuals in treatment centers. The development of medical technology has placed the issue of treatment versus punishment into a new and critical area. Today, scientists are able to determine defects in the brain which lead to addiction, violence, and mental illnesses (Jeffery, 1990). Violent people can be identified at an early age and treated before the violent behavior emerges as a major problem.

Lawyers in general oppose treatment and prevention strategies. They oppose mandatory treatment and interference with the liberties of individuals in the name of treatment, but they do not oppose mandatory punishment and the death penalty in the name of justice. Lawyers have opposed behavioral therapies, brain scans, brain surgery, and the use of psychotropic drugs for the mentally ill. Sociologists oppose social control measures and the "medicalization of deviance" (Cohen, 1985; Laing, 1971; Ssasz, 1961, 1963).

There are several legal arguments which can be used in support of the prevention and treatment model. The right to liberty doctrine was proposed by John S. Mill as one based on the doctrine of "harm to others," that is, my liberty extends to the right to behave as I wish insofar as such behavior does not harm someone else. Once my behavior is harmful to others I am no longer allowed to behave in this manner. The criminal law can criminalize those behaviors harmful to others but not behaviors which are not harmful to others. I may smoke but not in a place where my smoking may do harm to others. I may drink but not drive while drunk.

Other line or arguments have developed in support of a treatment and prevention model. There is the legal doctrine of the *right to treatment* under which criminals would have a legal right to be treated rather than punished. We have such a doctrine for the mentally ill but not for criminals. We also have a *right to medical treatment* doctrine which means medical services must be provided for those in our prisons and jails. Although we treat criminals with cancer and heart disease, we do not treat criminals for brain defects, hypoglycemia, PMS, violence, sex offenses, or drug addiction (Jeffery, 1990). It would be much more profitable for us to prevent crime as a disease than punish it as a moral wrong involving free will and moral responsibility.

We must establish crime prevention programs in place of more prisons. Such crime prevention efforts must involve both environmental design and biopsychological measures. The crime control measures discussed in this book which are aimed at the potential criminal or potential victim are of very limited success for the reasons mentioned. Those that identify criminals and are based on the concept of deterrence, such as video patrol and Crime Stoppers, or are used by the criminal justice system to record court procedures or police activities, do little if anything to reduce the crime rate.

More effort must be made to use modern technology and the media to prevent crimes. Training potential victims to prevent crimes must be done within a broad general framework of crime prevention and not as isolated projects. Most of the effort to prevent crime must be geared to the behavior of the potential criminal, primarily through the physical design of the community. There must be a major effort to study the relationship of crime to human ecology. Crimes occur in certain areas and on certain streets and not in other areas or streets. Computer mapping of crime sites wherein the geographical setting for crimes is analyzed is a high-priority research item. Police departments must learn to use computers for crime analysis rather than as a way of maintaining records and information. There must be an interdisciplinary effort by criminologists, urban planners, architects, and computer experts to study the interaction of criminals with the environment. At the same time efforts to understand the individual criminal must continue through similar interdisciplinary efforts involving geneticists, brain scientists, neurochemists, and psychopharmacologists. The concepts explored in this book as the interaction of the media and crime control can be expanded in many different ways.

REFERENCES

Cohen, L.E., and M. Felson (1979). "Social Change and Crime Rate Trends, A Routine Activity Approach." *American Sociological Review,* 44: 588–608.

Cohen, L.E., M. Felson, and K.C. Land (1980). "Property Crime Rates in the United States: A Macro-dynamic Analysis, 1947–1977." *American Journal of Sociology,* 1986: 90–118.

Cohen, S. (1985). *Visions of Social Control.* Cambridge: Polity Press.

Geller, W. (1988). "From Four-Star General of the Police Department to Community Leaders: The Police Executive's Responsibilities Concerning Twenty-First Century Surveillance and Control Technologies." Paper presented at the annual meeting of the International Association of Chiefs of Police, Portland, Or., 1988.

Gould, L. (1979). "The Changing Structure of Property Crime in an Affluent Society." *Social Forces,* 48: 50–59.

Jeffery, C. Ray. (1990). *Criminology: An Interdisciplinary Approach.* Englewood Cliffs: Prentice-Hall.

Jeffery, C. Ray. (1971, 1977). *Crime Prevention Through Environmental Design.* Beverly Hills: Sage.

Kittrie, N. (1971). *The Right to Be Different.* Baltimore: Johns Hopkins University Press.

Laing, R. D. (1971). *The Politics of Experience.* London: Penguin.

Marx, G.T. (1988a). "The Maximum Security Society" in *New Technologies and Criminal Justice,* ed. by M. Le Blanc et al., International Society of Criminology, University of Montreal.

Marx, G.T. (1988b). *Undercover Police Surveillance in America.* Berkley: University of California Press.

Newman, O. (1972). *Defensible Space.* New York: Macmillan.

O'Keefe, G.J. (1986). "The McGruff National Media Campaign: Its Public Impact and Future Implications." in *Community Crime Prevention,* ed. by D. P. Rosenbaum Beverly Hills: Sage.

Rychlak, J. (1981). *Personality and Psychotheraphy.* Boston: Houghton Mifflin.

Rubinstein, J. (1973). *City Police.* New York: Farrar, Straus, and Giroux.

Schwartz, B. (1978). *Psychology of Learning and Behavior.* New York: W. W. Norton

Ssasz, T. (1961). *The Myth of Mental Illness.* New York: Hoeber-Harper.

Ssasz, T. (1963). *Law, Liberty, and Psychiatry* New York: Macmillan.

Surette, R. (1986). "The Mass Media and Criminal Investigations: Crime Stoppers in Dade County, Florida." *Journal of Justice Issues,* Vol. 1, No. 1.

Surette, R. (1988). "Video Technology in Criminal Justice: Live Judicial Proceeding and Patrol Surveillance." in *New Technologies and Criminal Justice,* ed. by M. LeBlanc et al., International Society of Criminology, University of Montreal.

Terry, W. C. and R. Surette (1985). "Video in the Misdemeanor Court: The South Florida Experience." *Judicature,* Vol. 69, No. 1: 13–19.

Chapter 22

THE MEDIA AND CRIMINAL JUSTICE
PUBLIC POLICY—FUTURE PROSPECTS

RAY SURETTE

In 1984 in a companion volume, *Justice and the Media*, I wrote that sufficient knowledge about media effects was not available to recommend specific public policies. At this time that statement is only partially true and certain policies are now empically indicated and should be pursued. The premise explored and established in Chapter 1 that a media effect on crime and criminal justice policy is in operation led to a review in three areas: effects on individual behavior, effects within the criminal justice system, and effects from the utilization of media technology in crime control and case processing. The preceeding three sections provide a knowledge base from which media-criminal justice policy recommendations can be issued. Therefore, this concluding chapter will address the following questions: What do we currently know? What research is needed? What policies are indicated?

What Do We Currently Know?

Individual Level Behavior—Suicide, Sexual Offenses, and Copycat Crimes. The two debates regarding the effects of media violence and pornography upon the behavior of individuals involve competing interpretations of the research, more than conflicting research findings. There exists a rough agreement of the magnitude of the reported media-behavior relationships. Both proponents and opponents report similar findings: small, positive, sometimes statistically significant, sometimes not, correlations. However, how appropriate the research is for directing policy decisions is the crux of the polemics in Chapters 2 and 3. Does the research indicate effect levels that should be the focus of public policy, or are the effects marginal and at levels that can be safely ignored? Proponents argue that the findings are important, that these relationships, though small, are consistent and persistent. Opponents argue that the findings reflect weak, unimportant, inconsistent relationships. Representing the no significant effects position Howitt (1982:89, 120) argues that:

> The question is not whether the laboratory researchers have chosen methods which are too far removed from real life to be convincing, but whether we can use the findings in any way to ameliorate the social problem of violence in society. The theory is just not strong enough, nor is the empirical evidence. Policy recommendations do not flow freely from the evidence reviewed.

It is herein felt that the debate regarding effects becomes misfocused when the media's statistical significance and the magnitude of the research relationships are concentrated on. The media may be only marginally statistically significant for individual behaviors, but it is socially important. Rosenthal (Chapter 4) makes this point well by showing the cumulative effects on society from sources of small correlational relationships such as the media. On the positive side, it appears that our capability to mitigate the negative effects of media is also cumulatively significant. Therefore, as are the potential negative effects from ignoring this area, the benefits to be gained from good public policies in this area are also not trivial.

The general picture revealed by the research, particularly for violent media and suggestive for violent pornography, establishes the media as one of many significant factors in the generation of crime and violence in society. It must be given policy consideration. The fact that the correlations between media and behaviors are of a small size should not be given undo weight. The relationship between media content and individual behavior is as strong (or as weak) as the relationship found between social behavior and any other social factor (cf. Cook et al., 1983a). This is not a surprising finding, as individual violence and criminal behavior are the end result of many factors. Except in cases of specific biological causes, behavior is always the result of the interaction of multiple social and psychological variables. The media is revealed not to be a sole cause or even a primary cause in most instances, but neither is it a factor that can be safely ignored in policy development. And unlike other factors, the media is one source of effects that can be influenced through public policies (cf. Wilson, 1975; Wilson and Hennerstein, 1986).

The research shows that the media is particularly pernicious for specific "at-risk" groups. Differing groups appear to be "at risk" for differing media. For example, a role for pornography in sex offenses is indicated, but its primacy and causal role is yet to be established. A population identified herein as hypermasculine or "macho" (in other literature termed "angry males" (cf. Gray, 1982)) appears to be particularly prone to influence by pornography, especially aggressive violent pornography which links sex with violence toward women. What is not clear is what effect the removal of pornography would have in society. There is no evidence that the number of sexual offenders would be reduced, but the research suggests, while not clearly establishing, that the number of sex offenses would be reduced. That is, pornography is not established as a causative factor in the genesis of sex offenders, but it has been reported to be utilized in a preoffense role for established sex offenders (see Marshall, Chapter 6).

Regarding suicides, there is empirical evidence of a media-generating effect, especially for teenage females. Suicides increase as a result of either news media coverage or entertainment programming protrayals of them. Phillips and Carstensen (Chapter 5) describe media suicide coverage as "natural advertisements" and suggest that changes in the media treatment of suicide could reduce the media's suicide-inducing effect. In the area of copycat crime, initial research shows a media effect as significant, persistent, and predominant among pre-existing property criminals.

In sum, the current research indicates that "angry hypermasculine males" are at the greatest risk regarding aggressive violent pornogrphy, teenage females regarding suicide coverage, and pre-established property criminals regarding criminogenic, copycat media. It appears that the mass media should not be considered a monolithe, nor should its effects.

The media has individual level effects. What is not understood at this time is the mechanism through which the media exerts its influence on individual behaviors. As shown by the copycat model forwarded by Surette in Chapter 7, media effects at the individual level are complex and involve the content of the media, the immediate and cultural context of the viewing, and the characteristics of the viewer. Although they may watch it together, the same media content will have different effects on different viewers, and the same viewer will react variously at different times to the same media content. A specific media effect for any individual is therefore virtually unpredictable but has been consistently observed at the aggregate level.[1] This deficiency is a hindrance but is not crucial for assessing or developing public policy, however, which also deals with effects (desired effects at least) at the aggregate level.

With the research conducted to date, the mechanisms through which individual level media effects occur include a number of processes. All of these mechanisms are felt to operate on pre-existing pools of at-risk individuals, some portion of which will display the proper mix of characteristics to trigger the mechanisms and result in media-induced acts of aggression, copycat crime, or suicide. In terms of aggressive behavior mechanisms, the 1982 National Institute of Health report *Television and Behavior* (NIMH, 1982:38–39) forwards two processes through which violent media appears to encourage viewer aggressive behaviors: "observational learning" and "supportive attitude changes." In observational learning, which incorporates imitation, children learn aggression in the same way they learn other social skills: from watching parents, siblings, peers, teachers, and the media. Demonstrated in laboratory studies, children imitate aggressive behavior immediately after they have seen it on film or television. Field studies also provide support for this process occurring in natural settings. In addition, the more television children watch, the more supportive are their attitudes toward aggressive behavior. Looking at violent scenes for even a brief time makes young children more willing to accept the aggressive behavior of other children. This acceptance of aggression also makes it likely that the children will themselves be more aggressive through the disinhibition of internalized social restraints against aggression.[2]

Copycat crime has been most often credited to a simple and direct imitative mechanism (Livingstone, 1982; Bassiouni, 1981; Schmid and de Graaf, 1982; see also Gabriel Tarde, 1912). However, observational learn-

---

1. This is no different than attempting to predict or isolate the effects of other social factors on social behavior and underlies why the social sciences deal in probabalistic statements and rely heavily on aggregrate research.

2. Two other mechanisms are mentioned but are currently lacking supportive evidence: "Psychological Arousal Processes" — physiological arousal is thought to have three possible consequences: (1) desensitization to violence and thus less reaction to other's violence, (2) general arousal increase that boosts self-aggressiveness, or (3) the creation of desensitized persons who may act aggressively to raise their own levels of arousal. All these theoretical arousal mechanisms need empirical verification. "Justification" — people who are already aggressive like to look at violent media so they can then justify their own behavior. Watching violence is a result rather than a cause.

ing is not the only media influence to produce imitation. "Identification" and "priming" mechanisms have both been cited (cf. Berkowitz, 1984; see also Bandura, 1965, 1971, 1973). Thus, Berkowitz (1984) forwards priming as an additional, more general process through which the media can activate observed behavior. This "priming" effect results in media-portrayed behaviors activating a network of associated ideas and concepts within the viewer and increase the likelihood that similar but not necessarily identical behaviors will occur (Berkowitz, 1984:414).[3] The process of identification, in which the viewer sees himself as similar to the violent media actor, is associated with priming, in that priming is more likely to occur if identification also occurs.

The mechanism associated with pornography is thought to operate through the following process:

```
          "Hypermasculine"
   ┌─ (1)----At-Risk Males----(2)
   │                           │
   ↓  Sexually Violent Media ─↓> Anti-Social Attitudes* ---> Sexually Coercive Behavior**
      (R or X rated)
```

*Increased attitude support of aggression against women, increased belief in the rape myth (women secretly want to be raped), increased likelihood to blame rape victim, increased belief in general female promiscuity.

** Includes increased self reports of likelihood to rape.

The key unresolved issue in the pornography process is the placement of the "hypermasculine" at-risk males. If placed prior to violent media (position 1) rather than following it (position 2), then exposure to sexually violent media is not as causally significant for the development of anti-social attitudes, for pre-existing hypermasculine males would simply be seeking out sexually violent media which would be reinforcing rather than causing their anti-social attitudes. In addition, it is not clear whether the third variable, "sexually coercive behavior," actually develops or can be predicted as a result of the development of anti-social attitudes associated with exposure to sexually violent media. The sole link in the above process that has been empirically established is the "sexually violent media" → "attitude change" relationship, but the resultant behav-

---

3. This concept is analogous to the "cognitive maps" Graber (1980) forwards to explain the effects of crime news on viewers.

ior effects nor the causal order of the variables have yet to be established.

Systematic Effects—Criminal Justice Agendas and Policy Decision Makers.
The media can and does influence decisions and actions in the criminal
justice system. However, similar to individual level effects, it is difficult
to predict the direction and magnitude of influence in specific instances
or to specifiy the mechanism through which the media's influence is
being exerted. These difficulties arise because the most likely effects of
the media on criminal justice decision making are indirect rather than
direct (Doppelt and Manikas, Chapter 9). The case studies of Section II
reveal both general policy effects such as policy-influencing media crusades (Chapter 11), shield law legislation (Chapter 12) and criminal
legislation (Chapter 14), as well as influences upon individual decretionary
decisions within the system such as plea bargaining (Chapters 10) and
general case processing (Chapter 13). Indeed, media attention sometimes
emerges as more important and influencial than the resultant legislation
or policy initiative that results (cf. Nienstedt, Chapter 14). These effects
are however mediated through sets of agencies and decision makers so
that when direct effects are searched for, the media's influence appears
sparse.

Another reason there is not evidence of a stronger direct media influence on criminal justice policies and agenda may be due to the failure of
the media to provide in-depth treatment of the causes of crime, portraying
crime as an act rather than an issue, and leaving consumers to reach their
own understandings of the sources and likely solutions to the problem
(Stroman and Seltzer, 1985:345). Further complicating and masking the
relationship between the media and consumer crime and justice attitudes,
perceptions of crime and justice appear to be intertwined with other
social perceptions. Crime-related attitudes are not determined solely by
one's perception of the crime problem (Furstenberg, 1971; Garafalo and
Laub, 1978; Lotz, 1979; Sacco, 1982; Smith, 1984; Wilson, 1975). Therefore,
if perceptions of crime are intricately related to more general perceptions of the world, it is unrealistic to expect that they would covary solely
with media presentation levels or consumption. Instead, crime perceptions are also part of a larger conceptual picture of society and not a
unique separatable component (Sacco, 1982:490).

The bottom line is that the most important effects of the media appear
to be in terms of wider more general perceptions of social conditions—
are things getting better or worse overall. The likelihood is that these
broad media-influenced perceptions combine with pre-existing public

attitudes and experiences that in turn influence the public agenda regarding crime and translate into support for particular public policies (Bortner, 1984:21–22; Lichter, 1988). These broader effects are generally felt to be conservative status-quo supporting effects. What is finally media promoted is intolerance rather than tolerance and auto-heterodoxy—the desire to punish those who deviate from accepted mainstream norms (Carlson, 1985:190, 194).

At this time, reciprocal feedback models, in which causal influences are bi-directional, are the most plausible descriptive mechanisms for the relationship between the media and criminal justice public policy formation (see Garber, 1980:119–122); Sacco and Silverman, 1980; Smith, 1984; Cook et al., 1983b). For example, Fenigstein (1979) suggests that viewing violent media and viewer aggression have a bi-directional causal relationship, a pre-disposition toward aggression partly causing a preference for viewing media violence. And Huesman and Eron (1983) suggest a two-directional causal relationship in which an individual with higher inclination to be aggressive toward women may derive more gratification from images of violence against women and may be more susceptible to the influence of pornography. A similar causal relationship between a pre-disposition for punitive criminal justice policies and a preference for crime-related media is offered as the best hypothetical candidate in the area of media and criminal justice policy formation and decision making.

At the level of the individual criminal justice policy decision maker, the best model is analogous to the interactive models forwarded in Section I. The social/political "ecologies" in which the media exerts its policy effects represent a complicated, multi-directional social reality. The media's influence on the criminal justice system is determined by the interaction of the media's content, its timing of presentation, and the characteristics of the general public and policymakers at any particular time. In influence, the media can have both significant long-term policy effects and short-term case decision effects (Doppelt and Manikas, Chapter 9). In actual practice, policy decision makers can be influenced even by the potential of media coverage or conversely unaffected by massive coverage. In the final analysis the media must be viewed as both a messenger and an actor in the criminal justice policy arena. Journalists, programmers and editors are part of the policy-forming process they sometimes initiate and, in turn, they respond to criminal justice policy changes. Although it is clear that media effects occur, the study of these effects has not advanced to the point where the characteristics of decision makers likely to be sensitive to media attention (the "at-risk" criminal justice decision makers) or the instances where the criminal agenda may be influenced have been forwarded. Due to the highly ideosyncratic interactive nature of the media-criminal justice policy and decision-making process, here again the media cannot be ignored, but its effects cannot be predicted at the individual level.

Technological Effects—Pictures from Anywhere, Pictures to Everywhere. The above subtitle reflects the rapid development of the capabilities of the media and communication technology. Similar to computer technology, media-based technology has been steadily declining in cost while increasing in capacities. It is now technologically feasible for virtually any criminal justice system interaction to be videotaped and if desired to have a live visual and audio image transmitted to another location. Cost and equipment sensitivity currently make only the live transmission (but not the recording) of field patrol operations unweildy and beyond the resources of most jurisdictions. As Chapters 15 through 20 show, most other uses are feasible and have now been experimentally tested. What we know is that the technology works and in practice has achieved the majority of the administrative crime control goals set for it. The field record is one of once tried on an experimental basis, the technology has been nearly always permanently adopted. The prediction is for a future steady expansion and adoption of the technology throughout the criminal justice system. The issue of utilizing media technology in criminal justice is no longer can we do it but should we continue to do it.

The technology's capability is reflected in the positive evaluations of the systems covered in Section III. The media can be used to positively influence citizen attitudes and increase crime-related citizen information for the police. It can speed the processing of criminal cases. It can be used to videotape police patrols, vehicle stops, and interrogations. And it can be useful in the investigation, surveillance, and deterrence of crime. The administrative benefits associated with these projects emerge quickly and the projects have been consistently assessed as efficient and cost effective. However, there are concerns of potential social costs from the employment of this technology that do not emerge quickly and are difficult to quantify. The difficulty is that should evidence of negative social costs emerge, administrators will face entrenched programs and personnel. If eventually desirable, curtailment could very well be impossible.

These potential social costs include the increased depersonalization of the criminal justice system; the isolation of the police from the policed and associated increased citizen fear and suspicion of surveillance; and the polarization of society due to the creation of affluent media technology secured "garrison" communities. In addition, decreased citizen support for and legitimization of the criminal justice system are concerns. A final potential problem is tied to the media image of these projects. Projecting the idea that these efforts are effectively combatting overall crime rates and that such media-based programs are solutions to the general crime problem, the concern is that these technology-based efforts will drain resources from other ultimately more beneficial avenues of development (cf. Jeffery, Chapter 21).

Whether these costs are developing or will develop is not known. It must be stressed that there is no evidence of their existence at this time. However, the longitudinal research that would reveal such effects has not been undertaken and it follows that a basic concern in this area is that the necessary research will not be conducted.

What Research is Needed?

Media and criminal justice policy research needs can be subsumed in three areas. A first apparent research need are longitudinal studies to assess possible long-term negative developmental effects. Second, research into the verification and specification of the various media effects models is needed. Third, research that better describes and defines the at-risk populations that are most prone to media influences needs to be conducted.

Long-Term Media Effects. Research should be pursued into the long-term effects of the media-criminal justice relationship. In particular, the long-term effects of violent, criminogenic, and pornographic media needs to be examined. Within this research, qualities of the content and the medium should be considered and the media not simply perceived as a monolithic social influence. Prior research reveals important differences between print and electronic media that needs to be more fully explored (cf. Meyrowitz, 1985). The cumulative and interactive effects of television, print, and other types of media has yet to be explored. In addition, more attention to how viewers interact with and use the media should be paid. For example, concerning criminal justice policy support, does exposure to specific media-distributed crime and justice facts pre-date and thereby aid in determining public policy support, or does a preference or predisposition for particular policies form first and determine which crime and justice facts are culled and retained from the media?

Regarding media technology, a basic unanswered question is how these technology projects' social costs compare against their administrative benefits. All of these projects change the nature of the interactions between citizens and the criminal justice system, making it more indirect and more impersonal. By their pervasiveness, they also undermine the expectation of privacy in society, and the fear of surveillance can be as demoralizing and as damaging as the actuality of surveillance (cf. Marx, 1985). Due to these concerns, research into general social effects such as increased citizen alienation, polarization, and fear of victimization potentially associated with both media coverage of crime and justice and the use of media technology in anti-crime efforts must be explored.

Media Models. The empirical verification and specification of the underlying models for media and criminal justice agenda setting, decision making, copycat crime and echo effects is necessary in order to better comprehend the media's policy implications and effects. Although some effects are acknowledged for the media at both the individual and system level, the models and influence mechanisms that are in operation are not agreed upon. Research leading to such agreement would greatly enhance the ability to form and evaluate relevant policies. A primary media model question to be answered is the causal priority of the media. Does it cause changes in subjects, or do predisposed individuals selectively seek out and attend to specific supportive media? Is the relationship bi-directional and/or cumulative? These are crucial policy issues, for if the media is not causally important in the developemnt of attitudes and behaviors, then media-directed policies will not have any impact on the attitudes and behaviors whose reduction is socially desired.

At-Risk Populations. Lastly, associated with the long-term effects and media models research, the identification and description of media at-risk populations is needed. Their relative size and demographic composition is largely unknown. Furthermore, the ability to predict the degree of risk from media exposure for certain audience segments would aid in the assessment of media-related policies. In particular, policies concerning access to and the content of pornographic, criminogenic, and violent media and their distribution could be better assessed if the size and characteristics of the affected audiences are known. More detailed knowledge of the media-influenced consumer and the situations and media content that most influences them would allow more focused policies that are designed for and targetted at these consumers. However, because most of our knowledge is general, broad based and non-specific, the existing public policies are reflectively general, non-specific and aimed mostly at the general population rather than at specific at-risk groups.

What Policies are Indicated?

In suggesting policies it should be kept in mind that media has not been found to have negative behavioral effects on the vast majority of people. Small, at-risk sets of media consumers are the reciepents of media effects and thus should be the target of media-related policies. However, the absence of knowledge about specific individual level mechanisms and the identification of at-risk populations prevents the formulation of tightly targeted policies. A paradox results, effects are limited to small population segments, but due to limited information, policies must be general and aimed at the entire public.

This leads to the necessity of "minimum public policies" in this area, policies that intervene in the least degree possible. Therefore, serious curtailment of the media involving censorship or other Draconian restrictions are not indicated nor recommended, and most media critics recommend changes in style and emphasis rather than direct media restrictions. Heath (1984:275), for example, suggests a number of policy recommendations regarding crime news coverage. She suggests that the mix of local and nonlocal crime news should be made carefully because their relative proportions influences their impact on the public's fear of crime. In effect, wire news reports mollify the fear aroused by reports of local crimes, and nonlocal sensational crimes offset the frightening effects of local sensational crimes. Hence, the sensational aspects of local crimes should be presented with caution.

Phillips and Carstensen (Chapter 5) suggest a number of policy recommendations for reducing the effects of media-advertised anti-social behaviors. Although developed for suicide, their recommendations can be generalized and applied to criminogenic, copycat media also. The recommendations specify single or low in number stories, and these stories should that contain unobtrusive, non-sensational neutral coverage. Coverage should also mention (but as a rule does not) the negative aspects of mimicking the behavior such as pain, disfigurement and likely failure. Also, alternative actions (counseling, for example) should be specified whenever possible. In this way it is felt that the effects of the media can be greatly reduced by moderately changing the manner in which the anti-social behaviors are presented, without the necessity of ignoring them entirely. In a similar vein, aggressive pornography and R-rated media that links sex with violence should be eliminated, without necessarily eliminating all explicit sexual media. In fact, the wide access and popularity of R-rated slasher films makes them a medium of great concern at this time, more so than X-rated depictions of mutually consenting sex. In addition, explicit erotic media should contain elements that counteract the general stereotyping and objectification of women.

In terms of policy recommendations regarding the systematic effects of the media on the criminal justice system, at this time the research is at a stage similar to the individual level effects research of a decade ago. The research is in its preliminary stages and although effects have been detected the findings are ambiguous. Specific media-sensitive, at-risk sets of decision makers have not been identified, nor specific influencial media content or coverage delineated. Until the dynamics of the media criminal justice policy relationship are better studied and understood, the recommendations for practitioners that can be currently forwarded are admittedly inadequate admonitions to observe, take notes, and learn the history of the local media criminal justice system relationship. Intimate detailed knowledge of the actors and history of one's local media and justice system is the most useful information to currently possess, as there are available no generalizable media-criminal justice system propositions or research findings to refer to. We now have just some tantalizing research findings that establish that something significant is in operation without revealing precisely how or when it operates.

In the third area of media technology, the policy recommendations based on the positive evaluations are for continued and expanded experimentation. The technology's application appears to be more acceptable for earlier, shorter, low visibility steps of the criminal justice process (bookings, lineups, first appearances, arraignments). Resistance to the use of the technology increases as more symbolic steps such as trials are media processed. Applications should be expanded to explore the range of uses in which the technology can be positively applied. However, the increased application should not develop without accompanying evaluations and monitoring. Close scrutiny of developments in this area is needed in order that the potential development of longer-term negative effects can be guarded against and the abuse of the intrusive power of this technology does not arise.

The future is one of increased media, crime, and justice interactions. More of the processing of justice will be conducted through the media and its equipment. Broader based, better informed policies must be developed in this area to prevent administrative goals from being the sole determinants of whether these projects are instituted or not. It must also be recognized within the public, the media, and the criminal justice system that the media is a major actor in the formation of criminal justice policy. Failure to acknowledge and eventually to understand its role will allow a significant influence on our public policy to operate unawares and unaccountable.

REFERENCES

Bandura, A. (1965). "Influence of models' reinforcement contingencies on the acquisition of imitative responses" *J. of Person. and Soc Psych.*, 1:589–595.

Bandura, A. (1971). *Social Learning Theory.* N.Y., General Learning Press.

Bandura, A. (1973). *Aggression: A Social Learning Analysis.* Prentice-Hall.

Bassiouni, M. (1981). "Terrorism, law enforcement, and the mass media: Perspectives, problems, proposals," *J. of Crim. Law & Criminology*, 72: 1–51.

Berkowitz, L. (1984). "Some effects of thoughts on anti- and prosocial influences of media events: A cognitive-neoassociation analysis" *Psych. Bulletin*, 95:410–417.

Bortner, M. A. (1984). "Media Images and Public Attitudes toward Crime and Justice" in *Justice and The Media.* (ed) R. Surette, Charles C Thomas.

Carlson, J. (1985). *Prime Time Law Enforcement.* Praeger.

Cook, T. et al. (1983a). "The implicit assumptions of television research: An analysis of the 1982 NIMH report on television and behavior." *Public Opinion Quarterly*, 47:161–201.

Cook, T. et al. (1983b). "Media and agenda-setting: effects on the public, interest group leaders, policy makers, and policy" *Public Opinion Quarterly*, 47:16–35.

Fenigstein, A. (1979). "Does aggression cause a preference for viewing media violence?" *J. of Person. and Social Psych.*, 37: 2307–2317.

Furstenberg, F. (1971). "Public reactions to crime in the streets." *Amer. Scholar*, 40:601–610.

Garafalo, J. and Laub, J. (1978). "The fear of crime: broadening our perspective" *Victimology*, 3:242–253.

Graber, D. (1980). *Crime News and the Public.* Praeger.

Gray, S. (1982). "Exposure to Pornography and Aggression toward Women: The case of the Angry Male." *Social Problems*, 29:387–398.

Heath, L. (1984). "Impact of newspaper crime reports on fear of crime: Multimethodological investigation." *J. of personality and Social Psych.*, 47:263–276.

Howitt, D. (1982). *The Mass Media and Social Problems.* Pergamon.

Lichter, S. (1988). "Media power: The influence of media on politics and business." *Florida Policy Review,* 4:35–41.

Livingstone, N. (1982). *The War Against Terrorism.* D.C. Heath.

Lotz, R. (1979). "Public anxiety about crime." *Pacific Soc. Re.,* 22:241–254.

Marx, G. (1985). "The Surveillance Society." *The Futurist,* June:21–26.

Meyrowitz, J. (1985). *No Sense of Place.* Oxford Univ. Press.

NIMH [National Institute of Mental Health]. (1982). *Television and Behavior: Ten years of scientific progress and implications for the Eighties.* Vol. 1, Summary Report. Rockville, Med. Nat. Inst. of Mental Health.

Sacco, V. (1982). "The effects of mass media on perceptions of crime." *Pacific Soc. Re.,* 25:475–493.

Sacco V. and Silverman R. (1981). "Selling crime prevention: The evaluation of a mass media campaign." *Canadian J. of Criminology,* 23:191–201.

Schmid, A. and de Graaf, J. (1982). *Violence as Communication.* Sage.

Smith, S. (1984). "Crime in the news." *Brit. J. of Crim.,* 24:289–295.

Stroman, C. and Seltzer, R. (1985). "Media use and perceptions of crime." *Journalism Quarterly,* 62:340–345.

Surette, R. (1984). *Justice and the Media.* Charles C Thomas.

Tarde, G. (1912). *Penal Philosophy.* Boston, Little, Brown.

Wilson, J. Q. (1975). *Thinking About Crime.* Basic Books.

Wilson, J. Q. and R. Hennerstein. (1986). *Crime and Human Behavior.* Simon and Schuster.